# Asset Analytics

## Performance and Safety Management

The main aim of this book series is to provide a floor for researchers, industries, asset managers, government policy makers and infrastructure operators to cooperate and collaborate among themselves to improve the performance and safety of the assets with maximum return on assets and improved utilization for the benefit of society and the environment.

Assets can be defined as any resource that will create value to the business. Assets include physical (railway, road, buildings, industrial etc.), human, and intangible assets (software, data etc.). The scope of the book series will be but not limited to:

- Optimization, modelling and analysis of assets
- Application of RAMS to the system of systems
- Interdisciplinary and multidisciplinary research to deal with sustainability issues
- Application of advanced analytics for improvement of systems
- Application of computational intelligence, IT and software systems for decisions
- Interdisciplinary approach to performance management
- Integrated approach to system efficiency and effectiveness
- Life cycle management of the assets
- Integrated risk, hazard, vulnerability analysis and assurance management
- Adaptability of the systems to the usage and environment
- Integration of data-information-knowledge for decision support
- Production rate enhancement with best practices
- Optimization of renewable and non-renewable energy resources

More information about this series at http://www.springer.com/series/15776

Millie Pant · Tarun K. Sharma ·
Sebastián Basterrech · Chitresh Banerjee
Editors

# Computational Network Application Tools for Performance Management

Springer

*Editors*
Millie Pant
Department of Applied Science and Engineering
Indian Institute of Technology Roorkee
Roorkee, Uttarakhand, India

Tarun K. Sharma
Amity School of Engineering and Technology
Amity University Rajasthan
Jaipur, Rajasthan, India

Sebastián Basterrech
Department of Computer Science
Czech Technical University in Prague
Ostrava, Prague, Czech Republic

Chitresh Banerjee
Amity Institute of Information Technology
Amity University Rajasthan
Jaipur, Rajasthan, India

ISSN 2522-5162 ISSN 2522-5170 (electronic)
Asset Analytics
ISBN 978-981-32-9584-1 ISBN 978-981-32-9585-8 (eBook)
https://doi.org/10.1007/978-981-32-9585-8



This Springer imprint is published by the registered company Springer Nature Singapore Pte Ltd.
The registered company address is: 152 Beach Road, #21-01/04 Gateway East, Singapore 189721, Singapore

# Contents

# Editors and Contributors

## About the Editors

**Dr. Millie Pant** is Associate Professor at the Department of Applied Science & Engineering, IIT Roorkee, India. She has published over 180 research papers and has edited a number of conference proceedings volumes published by Springer. She is Associate Editor, Guest Editor and Reviewer for many Springer and Inderscience journals and IEEE Transactions. She has served as General Chair, Program Chair, Session and Track Chair at national & international conferences, and has delivered guest lectures at various leading national and international institutions. She has been involved in international collaboration with MIRS Lab, USA; Liverpool Hope University, UK; and Université Paris-EstCréteil Val-de-Marne, Paris, France.

**Dr. Tarun K. Sharma** is Associate Professor at Amity University Rajasthan, India. He holds a Ph.D. in Soft Computing from IIT Roorkee, and has published over 90 research papers. He has served as General Chair, Program Chair, Track Chair in the conference series—Soft Computing: Theories and Applications (SoCTA) and Soft Computing for Problem Solving (SoCPros). He has edited a number of conference proceedings volumes, published by Springer. He is Associate Editor, Guest Editor and Reviewer for many Springer and Inderscience journals and IEEE Transactions. He has delivered guest lectures at various leading national and international institutions. He is member of IET, IANEG, CSTA, and MIRS Lab.

**Dr. Sebastián Basterrech** is Associate Professor at the Department of CS, Faculty of Electrical Engineering, Czech Technical University, Prague, He has 70+ research publications to his credit. He is Associate Editor, Guest Editor and Reviewer Springer and Inderscience journals and IEEE Transactions. He has acted as Program Chair and Technical Chair at numerous national & international conferences, and has made valuable contributions in areas related to quasi-Newton optimization, random neural networks, reservoir computing, neural computation & soft-computing techniques.

**Dr. Chitresh Banerjee** is Assistant Professor at Amity University, Rajasthan, India. He has published over 60 research papers and has also worked as Executive Officer on the Board of Studies at The Institute of Chartered Accountants of India, New Delhi. He is member of 15 international societies and associations. Under the Institute-Industry linkage program, he delivers expert lectures on various themes related to IT. He has authored several books, and has acted as Editor, Associate Editor, Guest Editor and Reviewer for numerous national and international journals and conference proceedings.

## Contributors

**Shreyansh Agarwal** Institute of Infrastructure Technology Research and Management, Ahmedabad, Gujarat, India

**Kritika Agrawal** Department of Computer Science, Jaypee Institute of Information Technology, Noida, India

**Siddharth Agrawal** Institute of Infrastructure Technology Research and Management, Ahmedabad, Gujarat, India

**K. Anuradha** Gokaraju Rangaraju Institute of Engineering and Technology, Hyderabad, India

**Nidhi Verma Arya** Faculty of Science, Dayalbagh Educational Institute, Dayalbagh, Agra, India

**Palak Bansal** Department of Computer Science, Jaypee Institute of Information Technology, Noida, India

**S. Barkath Nisha** Sri Krishna College of Technology, Coimbatore, India

**Shahin Ara Begum** Department of Computer Science, Assam University, Silchar, Assam, India

**Paritosh Bhattacharya** National Institute of Technology, Agartala, Tripura, India

**Ankur Biswas** Tripura Institute of Technology, Narsingarh, Tripura, India

**Nabanita Choudhury** Department of Computer Science, Assam University, Silchar, Assam, India

**Ravins Dohare** Centre for Interdisciplinary Research in Basic Sciences, Jamia Millia Islamia, New Delhi, India

**M. Esther Hannah** St. Joseph's College of Engineering, Chennai, India

**Payal Garg** G L Bajaj Inst. of Engineering and Technology, Greater Noida, India

**K. Geetha** Hindusthan College of Engineering and Technology, Coimbatore, India

**Deepanshu Goyal** Institute of Infrastructure Technology Research and Management, Ahmedabad, Gujarat, India

**Ankita Gupta** Department of Computer Science, Jaypee Institute of Information Technology, Noida, India

**Sandeep Gupta** JECRC University, Jaipur, Rajasthan, India

**Sushma Jain** Thapar University, Patiala, India

**Tarun Jain** Manipal University Jaipur, Jaipur, India

**Rekh Ram Janghel** National Institute of Technology, Raipur, Chhatisgarh, India

**Mahesh Jangid** Manipal University Jaipur, Jaipur, India

**Damandeep Kaur** ECE Department, GNDEC, Ludhiana, India

**Ambreesh Kumar** EC Department, Mewar University, Rajasthan, India

**Jitendra Kumar** Department of Applied Mathematics, Madhav Institute of Technology & Science, Gwalior, MP, India

**Naresh Kumar** Department of Mathematics, Indian Institute of Technology Roorkee, Roorkee, India

**Pawan Kumar** Centre for Interdisciplinary Research in Basic Sciences, Jamia Millia Islamia, New Delhi, India

**Ginika Mahajan** Department of IT, Manipal Univeristy, Jaipur, India

**Santi P. Maity** Indian Institute of Engineering Science and Technology, Shibpur, Howrah, West Bengal, India

**Yogesh Meena** MNIT, Jaipur, India

**Anuranjan Mishra** Noida International University, Noida, U.P, India

**Divya Mishra** Noida International University, Noida, U.P, India

**Anilkumar V. Nandi** B.V. Bhoomaraddi College of Engineering and Technology, Hubli, India

**Prabha C. Nissimagoudar** B.V. Bhoomaraddi College of Engineering and Technology, Hubli, India

**Aamir Khan Nurkhani** JECRC University, Jaipur, Rajasthan, India

**L. Padma Sree** VNRVJ Institute of Engineering & Technology, Bachupally, India

**Girish Paliwal** Amity University Rajasthan, Jaipur, India

**Saroj Kumar Pandey** National Institute of Technology, Raipur, Chhatisgarh, India

**Lilly Raamesh** Department of I.T, St. Joseph's College of Engineering, Chennai, India

**T. Rajesh Kumar** Sri Krishna College of Technology, Coimbatore, India

**Sukhchandan Randhawa** Thapar University, Patiala, India

**G. Remmiya Devi** Sri Krishna College of Technology, Coimbatore, India

**Rajneesh Sharma** Division of Instrumentation and Control Engineering, NSIT, New Delhi, India

**Vikas Shinde** Department of Applied Mathematics, Madhav Institute of Technology & Science, Gwalior, MP, India

**Amit Kumar Singh** Institute of Infrastructure Technology Research and Management, Ahmedabad, Gujarat, India

**Preetvanti Singh** Faculty of Science, Dayalbagh Educational Institute, Dayalbagh, Agra, India

**Swapnesh Taterh** Amity University Rajasthan, Jaipur, India

**Vivek Kumar Verma** Manipal University Jaipur, Jaipur, India

**R. Vijaya Saraswathi** VNRVJ Institute of Engineering & Technology, Bachupally, India

**Gurjot Kaur Walia** ECE Department, GNDEC, Ludhiana, India

# Performance-Enhanced Hybrid Memetic Framework for Effective Coverage-Based Test Case Optimization

**Lilly Raamesh**

**Abstract** The rapid advancement of computer and database technologies has increased the importance of feature selection. The filter methods or wrapper methods may be used for feature selection. The filter method is computationally cheap but has a risk of selecting subsets of features that may not match the chosen induction algorithm, whereas the wrapper method engages the induction algorithm to evaluate the feature subsets and is computationally more intensive and has better prediction accuracy than filter method. Memetic algorithm, a family of metaheuristics coined by R. Dawkins from the term meme, denotes an equivalent to the gene to maintain a population pool comprising several solutions simultaneously for the problem. In this research work, the authors propose a hybrid wrapper–filter feature selection algorithm (WFFSA) using a memetic framework for effective coverage-based test case optimization. The test cases are optimized using a hybrid memetic framework method by combining the call stack and memetic algorithm. A call stack is a sequence of active calls associated with each thread in a stack-based architecture. Methods are pushed onto the stack when they are called and are popped when they return or when an exception is thrown. In this research, each of these solutions is termed individually, and an empirical experiment has also been conducted to demonstrate that the hybrid method improves the performance and results in reduction of the cost factor.

**Keywords** Test case optimization · Memetic algorithm · Feature selection · Call stack · Wrapper method · Filter method

## 1 Introduction

A call stack is a grouping of dynamic calls related to each string in a stack-based design. A call stack contains the method's return type, name, and parameters lists, including any package or namespace qualifiers. This system proposed the tools and

L. Raamesh (✉)
Department of I.T, St. Joseph's College of Engineering, Chennai, India
e-mail: lillyraamesh@yahoo.co.in



M. Pant et al. (eds.), *Computational Network Application Tools for Performance Management*, Asset Analytics,
https://doi.org/10.1007/978-981-32-9585-8_1

techniques that allow to dynamically collecting call stacks in multithreaded GUI applications.

This system proposed the test suite reduction tool to validate the GUI in an application. It reduces the number of test cases compared to the existing test case. It includes the entries from the libraries that GUI used. It empirically demonstrated the feasibility and effectiveness of using dynamically collected call stacks as a coverage criterion for GUI applications.

The event-driven GUI applications are adequately not quite the same as customary applications to require new coverage criteria. The fundamental instinct behind call stack-based reduction is that two test cases are "equivalent" in the event that they produce a similar arrangement of call stacks; thus, one of them could be eliminated to preserve the assets. It has a benefit of encapsulating valuable context information.

The rapid advances of computer and database technologies have increased the importance of feature selection. The filter methods or wrapper methods may be used for feature selection. The intrinsic characteristics of the data evaluated in filter method are computationally cheap since it does not engage the induction algorithm. It has a risk of selecting subsets of features that may not match the chosen induction algorithm.

Wrapper method, Zhu et al. [1], engages the induction algorithm to evaluate the feature subsets which are computationally more intensive and have better prediction accuracy than filter method.

The proposed wrapper–filter, Zhu et al. [2], feature selection algorithm (WFFSA) using a memetic framework is a combination of genetic algorithm (GA) and local search (LS). Memetic algorithms (MAs) are population-based metaheuristic search methods.

This hybrid method is practically an effective basis for performing test suite optimization, advancing the state of the art for coverage-based test suite reduction in combination with memetic framework-based optimization. Empirical evaluation indicated that hybrid-based test suite optimization produces better results for applications compared to traditional techniques.

## 2 Literature Review

Rui et al. [3] introduced an algorithm by applying particle swarm optimization into genetic algorithm. Singh and Gupta [4] proposed a new test case reduction hybrid technique based on genetic algorithms and ant colony optimization (ACO) to generate various paths; then output of these paths is provided to genetic algorithm to do selection, crossover, and mutation so as to get better result. In initial iteration, this hybrid technique gives better results. It provides positive feedback, and it can lead to better solutions in optimum time.

Various local search algorithms such as simulated annealing, Tabu search, iterated local search, and variable neighborhood search were used.

Arcuri and Briand [5] and Gendreau et al. [6] considered only the neighborhood of a candidate solution. Korel [7] used Korel's Alternating Variable Method (AVM) technique similar to hill climbing.

For more globally optimal solutions, global search algorithms were used by Harman et al. [8]. Memetic algorithms (MAs) have been used over a wide range of problem domains. Merz and Freisleben [9] used it for combinatorial optimization.

Vavak et al. [10] used it for optimization of non-stationary functions. Knowles and Corne [11] used it for multi-objective optimization. Krasnogor [12] used it for bioinformatics.

## 3 Test Suite Reduction

Test suite reduction is done using call stack, McMaster and Memon [13]. The number of redundant test cases is reduced. Techniques are used to dynamically collect call stacks in multithreaded GUI applications. It reduces the number of test cases compared to the existing test case. It includes the entries from the libraries that GUI used. It empirically demonstrated the feasibility and effectiveness of using dynamically collected call stacks as a coverage criterion for GUI applications.

Initially, the GUI application with multiple function calls is developed for event handling. This was given as an input to generate the test case.

Then the structured information like event handlers, invocation of declared methods, and declared values in event handlers are retrieved. The event handlers are analyzed. The declared events are searched to get the declared methods in that particular event. These methods are executed while performing the action on the particular button.

The test case was generated based on the event coverage for each event. This makes the redundancy while executing the same methods. By this, they take the same test case for the same events.

The stack-based approach is used to generate the test case. The event in which the user performed is maintained in a stack procedure. In the stack, the method was popped, and it is pushed when it returns the value or it throws the exception. So each and every event is handled and stored in stack procedure.

The full set of unique call stacks that an execution of the full suite can be expected to generate was calculated. The full set is computed by merging the unique call stacks observed by each test case in the suite. These values are stored in a main stack it consist of event handlers, which method called, parameters passed to that method are all stored.

The event and call stack coverage based on performance were compared. Call stack-reduced suites were substantially larger than suites reduced by other criteria. Thus, it seemed possible that the call stack coverage may have been preserving more fault detection solely on the basis of including more test cases.

## 4 Test Suite Optimization

Memetic algorithm (MA), a feature selection method [2, 5, 14] for gene selection, is used for test suite optimization. This feature selection method synergies filter and GA wrapper methods using a memetic framework and search the feature space efficiently and with high prediction accuracy.

The memetic algorithm [2, 5, 14] template provides the basic structure of an evolutionary algorithm and the places where hybridization could take place. Evolutionary algorithms in combination with local search form the memetic algorithm.

The pseudocode for memetic algorithm:

Create an initial population of test cases.

- Repeat (to get better test cases)
  - Create a mating pool by sampling the population with fitness proportional probability.
  - Crossover: Randomly pair test cases to produce two new offspring and add to the set.
  - Mutation: apply with low probability the mutation operator to the offspring set.
  - Replace the worst solutions in the population with the new offspring.
- Until the stopping condition execute the mutation parameter.

The output from test suite reduction forms the initial population. Crossover is a process of recombination that constructs new test cases composed of information taken from a number of selected test cases encapsulates the mutual cooperation among several test cases mostly two test cases sometimes more test cases. Crossover used is uniform crossover.

Mutation operator injects the new material into the population to modify the existing solution at a low rate and generates a new solution. A fitness function selects the test cases for reproduction by steadily improving the fitness values with each generation until a solution is found.

## 5 Experiments and Results

The hybrid system is tested with five different applications, and the detailed status is given for two applications. The coverage of test cases is mainly checked.

Test cases are executed to detect the fault detection capability of a test suite and to estimate the amount of code covered by test cases in a test suite at run-time, Basili and Selby [15]. A test case that has high coverage has a higher potential fault detection capability than the test case that has low coverage.

The amount of code statements exercised during the execution of a given test case t is CCov(t) according to Marchetto et al. [16] which is computed as

$$\sum_{s \in \text{statements}} \begin{cases} ns, \ s \in \text{code covered} \\ 0, \quad \text{else} \end{cases} \tag{1}$$

where statements is the set of source code statements, and code covered is the set of statements covered by the execution of the test case *t*, while s is a code statement of an application.

In the first application, there were 1782 test cases in the test suite. The executed versus unexecuted test cases are calculated. The status of the first application is shown in Fig. 1.

Out of 1782 test cases, 1689 are executed, 26 not executed, and 67 did not show any status as they do not belong to that particular application.

The function coverage is tested by using CCov(t). If all statements in the function are covered, then the function is classified under fully covered, and if only part of the statements is covered, then it is a partially covered function, otherwise uncovered function. In the first application, there were 34 total numbers of functions. The test suite covered 31 functions fully and 2 functions partially, and 1 was not covered as shown in Fig. 2. The partial coverage and uncovered functions were the reason for the unexecuted 67 test cases.

In the second application, there were 1936 test cases in the test suite. The executed versus unexecuted test cases are calculated. The status of the second application is shown in Fig. 3. Out of 1936 test cases, 1781 are executed, 31 not executed, and 56 did not show any status as they do not belong to that particular application.

The function coverage is tested for second application; there were 52 total numbers of functions. The test suite covered 48 functions fully and 3 functions partially, and

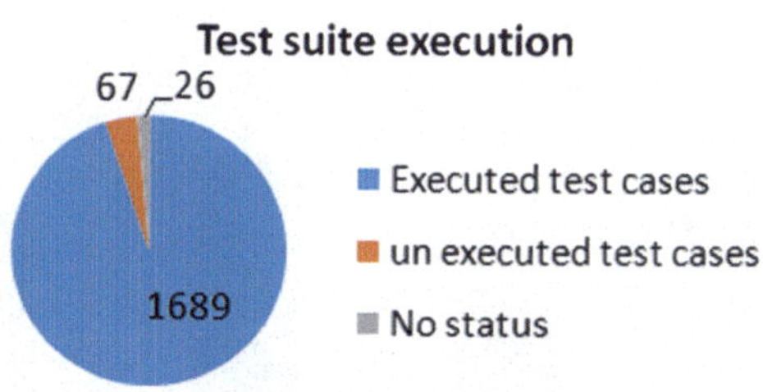


**Fig. 1** Test suite execution status of Application 1

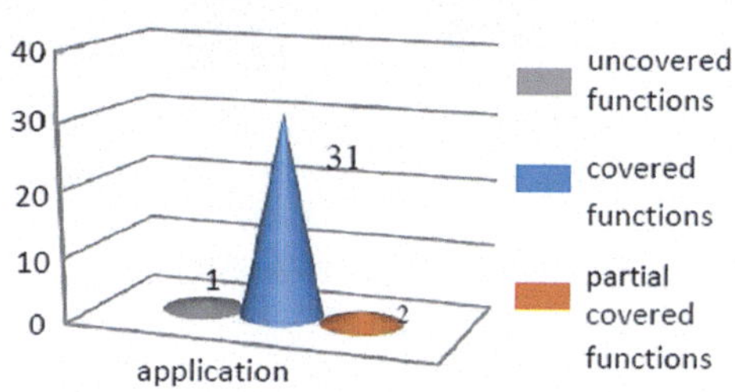


**Fig. 2** Function coverage

1 was not covered as shown in Fig. 4. The partial coverage and uncovered functions were the reason for the unexecuted 56 test cases.

The function coverage by different applications is compared in Fig. 5.

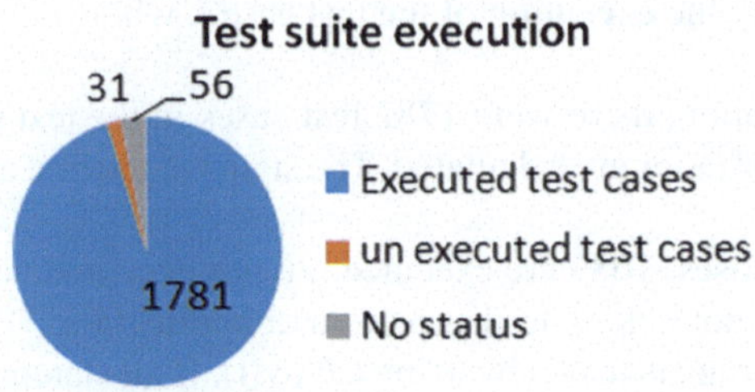


**Fig. 3** Test suite execution status of Application 2

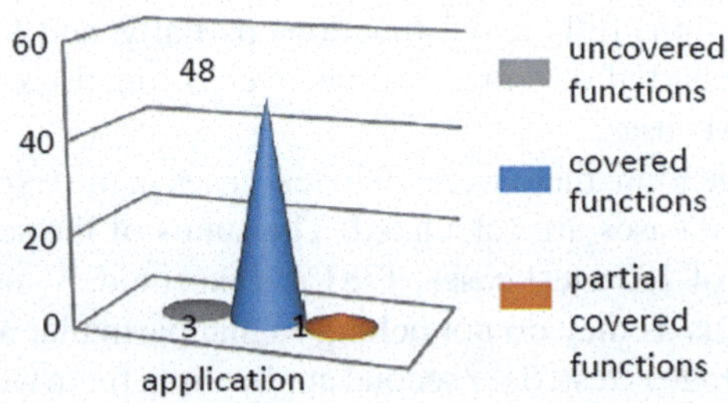


**Fig. 4** Function coverage

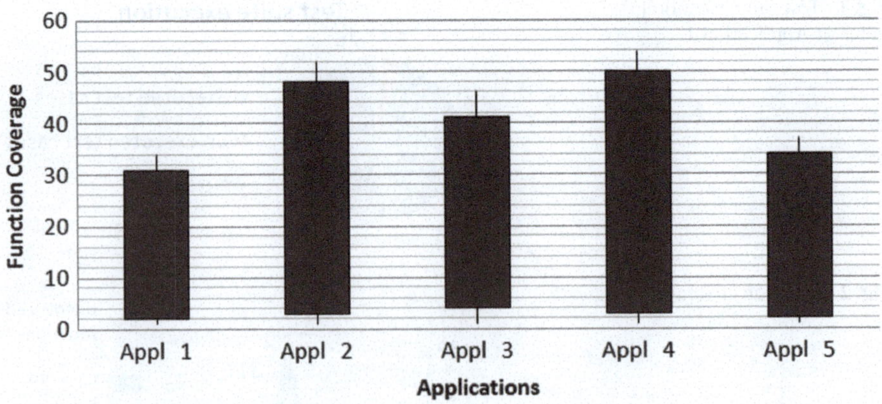


**Fig. 5** Function coverage comparison

## 6 Conclusion and Future Work

Presented tools and techniques that allow to dynamically collect call stacks in multithreaded GUI applications, including entries from the libraries that they use empirically, demonstrated the feasibility and effectiveness of using dynamically collected call stacks as a coverage criterion for GUI applications. The reduced test suite is used for further optimization by memetic algorithm.

Future work is to further generalize the results for coverage criteria that are effective for GUI testing scenarios and to have techniques that reduce the quantity of coverage requirements generated by a complete call stack data collection while still retaining call stack coverage's necessary qualities. Further, the effectiveness can be improved by memtic framework.

## References

1. Z. Zhu, Y.S. Ong, M. Dash, Wrapper-filter feature selection algorithm using a memetic framework. IEEE Trans. Syst. Man Cybern. Part B **37**(1), 70–76 (2007)
2. Z. Zhu, Y.S. Ong, M. Dash, Markov blanket-embedded genetic algorithm for gene selection. Pattern Recogn. **49**(11), 3236–3248 (2007)
3. D. Rui, X. Feng, S. Li, H. Dong, Automatic generation of software test data based on hybrid particle swarm genetic algorithm, in *IEEE Symposium on Electrical & Electronics Engineering (EEESYM)*, Mudanjiang, Kuala Lumpur (2012), pp. 670–673
4. G. Singh, D. Gupta, An integrated approach to test suite selection using ACO and Genetic Algorithm. Int. J. Adv. Res. Comput. Sci. Softw. Eng. (IIARCSSE) **3**, 1770–177 (2013)
5. A. Arcuri, L. Briand, A hitchhiker's guide to statistical tests for assessing randomized algorithms in software engineering, in *Software Testing, Verification and Reliability (STVR)* (2012)
6. M. Gendreau, A. Hertz, G. Laporte, New insertion and postoptimization procedures for the traveling salesman problem. Oper. Res. **40**, 1086–1094 (1992)
7. B. Korel, Automated software test data generation. IEEE TSE (1990)
8. K. Praditwong, M. Harman, X. Yao, Software module clustering as a multi-objective search problem. IEEE Trans. Softw. Eng. (2010)
9. P. Merz, B. Freisleben, Fitness landscapes and memetic algorithm design, in *New Ideas in Optimization*, ed. by D. Corne, M. Dorigo, F. Glover. McGraw Hill, London (1999)
10. F. Vavak, T. Fogarty, K. Jukes, A genetic algorithm with variable range of local search for tracking changing environments, in *Proceedings of the 4th Conference on Parallel Problem Solving from Nature*, ed. by H.M. Voigt, W. Ebeling, I. Rechenberg, H.P. Schwefel. Lecture Notes in Computer Science, vol. 1141 (Springer, Berlin, 1996)
11. J. Knowles, D. Corne, A comparative assessment of memetic, evolutionary and constructive algorithms for the multi-objective d-msat problem, in *2001 Genetic and Evolutionary Computation Workshop Proceeding* (2001)
12. N. Krasnogor, Self-generating metaheuristics in bioinformatics: the protein structure comparison case, in *Genetic Programming and Evolvable Machines*, vol. 5 (Kluwer Academic Publishers, 2004), pp. 181–201
13. S. McMaster, A.M. Memon, Call stack coverage for GUI test suite reduction. IEEE Trans. Softw. Eng. **34**, 99–115 (2008)
14. G. Rothermel, R. Untch, C. Chu, M. Harrold, Test case prioritization: an empirical study, in *Proceedings of International Conference on Software Maintenance* (IEEE Computer Society, 1999), pp. 179–188

15. V.R. Basili, R.W. Selby, Comparing the effectiveness of software testing strategies. IEEE Trans. Software Eng. **13**, 1278–1296 (1987)
16. A. Marchetto, M.M. Islam, W. Asghar, A. Susi, G. Scanniello, A multi-objective technique to prioritize test cases. Trans Softw. Eng. (2014)

# An Optimization Procedure for Quadratic Fractional Transportation Problem

**Nidhi Verma Arya and Preetvanti Singh**

**Abstract** In many real-life applications, people deal with various types of nonlinear programming problems. These nonlinear problems may provide solutions to some decision-making issues like constructing optimization model with fractional objective function such as profit/cost (financial and corporate planning) and inventory/sales (production planning marketing). Hence, fractional programming problems become one of the popular research topics. Fractional transportation problem is to transport various amounts of a single homogeneous commodity that are initially stored at various origins to different destinations in such a way that the total fractional transportation cost is minimized. In this paper, the researchers have provided study on one of the nonlinear programming problems known as quadratic fractional transportation problem. The objective of these problems is to minimize or maximize the ratios of physical and economical functions. As compared with the linear programming problems, the quadratic programming problem provides a superior representation of real-life distribution problem where the unit cost of transportation is not constant. In this paper, the researchers have proposed an algorithm to find optimal solution of such problems. The algorithm is illustrated with the help of numerical example which will provide validation and proof that the developed algorithm will help to make the transportation system more beneficial in many application areas.

**Keywords** Transportation problem · Nonlinear programming · Fractional programing · Optimization model · Algorithmic solution

## 1 Introduction

In real-life applications, a decision-maker often deals with optimization model with fractional objective function such as profit/cost (financial and corporate planning)

N. V. Arya (✉) · P. Singh
Faculty of Science, Dayalbagh Educational Institute, Dayalbagh, Agra, India
e-mail: nidhiverma162@gmail.com

P. Singh
e-mail: preetvantisingh@gmail.com



M. Pant et al. (eds.), *Computational Network Application Tools for Performance Management*, Asset Analytics,
https://doi.org/10.1007/978-981-32-9585-8_2

and inventory/sales (production planning marketing). Hence, fractional programming problems have become one of the popular research topics in operations research. Fractional transportation problem deals with transporting various amounts of a single homogeneous commodity that are initially stored at various origins to different destinations in such a way that the total fractional transportation cost is minimized.

Most of the studies in this field are on the solution methodology and its application. Sivri et al. [1] dealt with the transportation problem of minimizing the ratio of two linear functions subject to constraints of the convention transportation problem. A new algorithm in order to obtain an initial solution was also proposed for the problem which is similar to Vogel's approximation method. Charles et al. [2] proposed a stochastic programming model, while considering ratio of two nonlinear functions and probabilistic constraints.

A decomposition approach to solve a fuzzy transportation problem with linear fractional fuzzy objective function was proposed by Narayanamoorthy and Kalyani [3] where the fractional fuzzy transportation problem was decomposed into two linear fuzzy transportation problems. Gupta and Arora [4] developed a transportation problem with an objective function as the sum of a linear and fractional function.

The linear function represents the total transportation cost incurred in shipping goods from various sources to the destinations, and the fractional function presents the ratio of sales tax to the total public expenditure. Ekezie et al. [5] developed a transportation problem with an objective function as the sum of a linear and linear fractional function. Basu et al. [6] developed an algorithm for the optimum time-cost trade-off in fixed charge bi-criterion transportation problem. Prakash [7] proposed a transportation problem with objectives to minimize total cost and duration of transportation.

As compared with the linear fractional transportation problem, the quadratic transportation problem provides a superior representation of real-life distribution problem where the unit cost of transportation is not constant. In quadratic transportation problem, the cost coefficients are quadratic functions.

## 2 The Quadratic Fractional Transportation Problem: Mathematical Formulation

Let there be $M$ sources and $N$ destinations. $a_i (i = 1, \ldots, M)$ be the quantity of commodity available at the $i$th source, and $b_j (j = 1, \ldots, N)$ be the quantity of commodity required at the $j$th destination. $x_{ij}$ is the amount of the commodity transported from $i$th source to $j$th destination. Let $C_{ij}$ and $D_{ij}$ be two $(M \times N)$ cost matrices, where $C_{ij}$ is the unit actual shipping cost and $D_{ij}$ is the unit standard shipping cost. The quadratic fractional transportation problem can be stated mathematically as

$$\min z = \frac{\left[\sum_{i=1}^{M} \sum_{j=1}^{N} C_{ij} x_{ij}\right]^2}{\left[\sum_{i=1}^{M} \sum_{j=1}^{N} D_{ij} x_{ij}\right]^2} \tag{1}$$

Subject to constraints

$$\sum_{j}^{N} x_{ij} = a_i \quad (i = 1, \ldots, M) \tag{2}$$

$$\sum_{i=1}^{M} x_{ij} = b_j \quad (j = 1, \ldots, N) \tag{3}$$

Here

$$\sum_{i=1}^{M} a_i = \sum_{j=1}^{N} b_j (i = 1, \ldots, M; j = 1, \ldots, N) \tag{4}$$

$$x_{ij} \geq 0$$

The objective of this study is to develop an alternative solution methodology for the quadratic fractional transportation problem.

## 3 Algorithm

This section discusses the steps to solve the quadratic fractional transportation problem.

**Step 1**: Find the initial basic feasible solution to the problem by using VAM.

**Step 2**: The number of allocated cell should be $M + N - 1$. If not, then add $\in$ to an independent cell and proceed.

**Step 3**: Calculate the dual variables $u_i, u'_i, v_j, v'_j$ from the basic cells

$$u_i + v_j = C_{ij} \tag{5}$$

$$u'_i + v'_j = D_{ij} \tag{6}$$

**Step 4**: Calculate

$$C'_{ij} = C_{ij} - u_i - v_j \tag{7}$$

$$D'_{ij} = D_{ij} - u'_i - v'_j \tag{8}$$

for all nonbasic cells.

**Step 5**: Determine

$$M_{ij} = C'_{ij} \times E_{ij} \tag{9}$$

$$M'_{ij} = D'_{ij} \times E_{ij} \tag{10}$$

where $M_{ij}$ and $M'_{ij}$ are the changes in cost that occur for introducing a nonbasic cell with value $E_{ij}$ into the basis by making reallocation.

**Step 6**: Calculate $\Delta_{ij}$ for all nonbasic cells as

$$\Delta_{ij} = 2V_1\left(V_2 \times M_{ij} - V_1 \times M'_{ij}\right) \tag{11}$$

where $V_1 = \sum C_{ij}x_{ij}$ and $V_2 = \sum D_{ij}x_{ij}$

**Step 7**: If all $\Delta_{ij} \geq 0$, then current basic feasible solution is optimal, and stop else go to next step.

**Step 8**: Select most negative $\Delta_{ij}$ to make a closed loop and improve the solution $\Delta_{ij}$, and go to Step 2.

## 4 Numerical Example

The above algorithm is illustrated with the help of a goods shipping problem. A manufacturing unit has different types of processing sections in each of three work centres (*j*). The work centre *j* is receiving a fixed quantity of raw material (*i*), which has three different grades. The problem is to determine a feasible transportation system which minimizes the ratio of total actual shipping cost $C_{ij}$ and total standard shipping cost $D_{ij}$ of raw material. The problem can be stated as

$$\min z = \frac{\left[\sum_{i=1}^{3}\sum_{j=1}^{3} C_{ij}x_{ij}\right]^2}{\left[\sum_{i=1}^{3}\sum_{j=1}^{3} D_{ij}x_{ij}\right]^2}$$

subject to constraints

$$\sum_{j=1}^{3} x_{ij} = a_i \quad i = (1,\ 2,\ 3)$$

$$\sum_{i=1}^{3} x_{ij} = b_j \quad j = (1,\ 2,\ 3)$$

$$\sum_{i=1}^{3} a_i = \sum_{j=1}^{3} b_j$$

$$x_{ij} \geq 0$$

**Table 1** Data for the problem

| | Manufacturing units | | | $a_i$ |
|---|---|---|---|---|
| Work centres | $C_{11} = 9$<br>$D_{11} = 3$ | $C_{12} = 6$<br>$D_{12} = 2$ | $C_{13} = 8$<br>$D_{13} = 1$ | 10 |
| | $C_{21} = 5$<br>$D_{21} = 2$ | $C_{22} = 4$<br>$D_{22} = 1$ | $C_{23} = 5$<br>$D_{23} = 4$ | 8 |
| | $C_{31} = 6$<br>$D_{31} = 3$ | $C_{32} = 2$<br>$D_{32} = 3$ | $C_{33} = 9$<br>$D_{33} = 3$ | 6 |
| $b_j$ | 4 | 15 | 5 | |

**Table 2** Initial basic feasible solution is shown by bold values

| | | |
|---|---|---|
| 9/3 | 6/2<br>$x_{12} = \mathbf{9}$ | 8/1<br>$x_{13} = \mathbf{1}$ |
| 5/2<br>$x_{21} = \mathbf{4}$ | 4/1 | 5/4<br>$x_{23} = \mathbf{4}$ |
| 6/3 | 2/3<br>$x_{32} = \mathbf{6}$ | 9/3 |

Bold values represent basic feasible solution

**Table 3** Computed dual variables

| | | | |
|---|---|---|---|
| 9/3 | 6/2<br>$x_{12} = \mathbf{9}$ | 8/1<br>$x_{13} = \mathbf{1}$ | $u_1 = 8$<br>$u_1' = -1$ |
| 5/2<br>$x_{21} = \mathbf{4}$ | 4/1 | 5/4<br>$x_{23} = \mathbf{4}$ | $u_2 = 5$<br>$u_2' = 2$ |
| 6/3 | 2/3<br>$x_{32} = \mathbf{6}$ | 9/3 | $u_3 = 4$<br>$u_3' = 0$ |
| $v_1 = 0$<br>$v_1' = 0$ | $v_2 = -2$<br>$v_2' = 3$ | $v_3 = 0$<br>$v_3' = 2$ | |

Bold values represent basic feasible solution

The data is given in Table 1.

Applying VAM, the initial basic feasible solution of the problem is as shown in Table 2.

Calculated $u_i$, $v_j$ are written in the last row and column of the Table 3, respectively.

To determine the value of $E_{ij}$, loops are constructed to get

| $E_{ij}$ | $E_{11}$ | $E_{22}$ | $E_{31}$ | $E_{33}$ |
|---|---|---|---|---|
| | 1 | 4 | 1 | 1 |

**Table 4** Calculate $\Delta_{ij}$ for all non-basic cells

| | | |
|---|---|---|
| 9/3<br>$\Delta_{11} = -90{,}060$ | 6/2<br>$x_{12} = \mathbf{9}$ | 8/1<br>$x_{13} = \mathbf{1}$ |
| 5/2<br>$x_{21} = \mathbf{4}$ | 4/1<br>$\Delta_{22} = 21{,}158$ | 5/4<br>$x_{23} = \mathbf{4}$ |
| 6/3<br>$\Delta_{31} = -50{,}160$ | 2/3<br>$x_{32} = \mathbf{6}$ | 9/3<br>$\Delta_{33} = 29{,}640$ |

Bold values represent basic feasible solution

**Table 5** Optimal solution

| | | |
|---|---|---|
| 9/3<br>$x_{11} = \mathbf{1}$ | 6/2<br>$x_{12} = \mathbf{9}$ | 8/1<br>$\Delta_{13} = 90{,}850$ |
| 5/2<br>$x_{21} = 3$ | 4/1<br>$\Delta_{22} = 89{,}700$ | 5/4<br>$x_{23} = \mathbf{5}$ |
| 6/3<br>$\Delta_{31} = 11{,}500$ | 2/3<br>$x_{32} = \mathbf{6}$ | 9/3<br>$\Delta_{33} = 12{,}420$ |

Bold values represent basic feasible solution

Now, $C'_{ij}$, $D'_{ij}$, $M_{ij}$ and $M'_{ij}$ for all the nonbasic cells are determined using Eqs. (7), (8), (9) and (10)

| | | | | |
|---|---|---|---|---|
| $C'_{ij}$ | $C'_{11} = 1$ | $C'_{22} = 1$ | $C'_{31} = 2$ | $C'_{33} = 4$ |
| $M_{ij}$ | $M_{11} = 1$ | $M_{22} = 4$ | $M_{31} = 1$ | $M_{33} = 1$ |

| | | | | |
|---|---|---|---|---|
| $D'_{ij}$ | $D'_{11} = 4$ | $D'_{22} = -4$ | $D'_{31} = 3$ | $D'_{33} = 1$ |
| $M'_{ij}$ | $M'_{11} = 4$ | $M'_{22} = -16$ | $M'_{31} = 3$ | $M'_{33} = 1$ |

Calculating $\Delta_{ij}$ using Eq. (11), the improved solution is obtained (Table 4).

It can be seen that $\Delta_{11}$ is most negative so $x_{11}$ becomes entering variable. Now improve the solution by considering a closed loop and determine $\theta$. This gives the solution shown in Table 5. Again computing $u_i$, $v_j$ and $\Delta_{ij}$, it was found that all $\Delta_{ij} \geq 0$; hence, the solution is optimal.

## 5 Results and Conclusion

Initially, total cost $z_1 = 3.492$ after applying the algorithm, and the optimal solution was obtained as $x_{11} = 1$, $x_{12} = 9$, $x_{21} = 3$, $x_{23} = 5$ and $x_{32} = 6$ with $z_2 = 3.130$.

Applying the MODI method, the same optimum solution was found.

The main objective of this study was to develop an algorithm for obtaining the optimal solution of a quadratic fractional transportation problem. This algorithm makes use of $M_{ij}$ and $M'_{ij}$ which are the change in cost that occurs for introducing a nonbasic cell with value $E_{ij}$ into the basis by making reallocation for both costs. This computation can be easily extended to solve quadratic fractional transportation problem with fixed cost in (two dimension or three dimension).

## References

1. M. Sivri, I. Emiroglu, C. Güzel, F. Tasci, A solution proposal to the transportation problem with the linear fractional objective function, in *Proceedings of Modelling, Simulation and Applied Optimization (ICMSAO), 2011 4th International Conference on*, 1921 April 2011, Kuala Lumpur, pp. 1–9. https://doi.org/10.1109/icmsao.2011.5775530
2. V. Charles, V.S.S. Yadavalli, M.C.L. Rao, P.R.S. Reddy, *Stochastic fractional programming approach to a mean and variance model of a transportation problem* (Hindawi Publishing Corporation Mathematical Problems in Engineering, 2011), pp. 1–12
3. S. Narayanamoorthy, S. Kalyani, The intelligence of dual simplex method to solve linear fractional fuzzy transportation problem. Comput. Intell. Neurosci. 1–7 (2015)
4. K. Gupta, S.R. Arora, Linear plus linear fractional capacitated transportation problem with restricted flow. Am. J. Oper. Res. **3**(6), 581–588 (2013)
5. D.D. Ekezie, M.H. Ifeyinwa, J. Opara, Paradox in sum of a linear and a linear fractional transportation problem. Int. J. Appl. Math. Model. IJA2M **1**(4), 1–17 (2013)
6. M. Basu, B.B. Pal, A. Kundu, An algorithm for the optimum time-cost trade-off in fixed charge bi-criterion transportation problem bi-criterion transportation problem. Optim. J. Math. Program. Oper. Res. **30**(1), 53–68 (1994)
7. S. Prakash, A transportation problem with objectives to minimize total cost and duration of transportation. Opsearch **18**, 235–238 (1981)

# A Nature Inspired PID like Fuzzy Knowledge-Based Fractional-Order Controller for Optimization

**Ambreesh Kumar and Rajneesh Sharma**

**Abstract** Conventional PID (CO-PID) controllers have dominated industrial process control applications. Though their use in industry is still prevalent, new avenues have emerged with the advent of soft computing tools. Several soft computing techniques for implementing conventional PID control have been proposed, e.g., cruise control using genetic algorithm (GA), conical tank regulation using ANT colony optimization (ACO), PID control using multi-objective ACO, automatic voltage regulator system (AVR) using particle swarm optimization (PSO), DC motor control using GA, evolutionary programing (EP) and PSO. The fract-order PID controllers have an advantage over conventional PID controllers in terms of availability of additional tuning parameters. In this research work, the authors propose what may be termed "optimized" tuning method for FFPID controllers using a combination of GA and ant colony techniques on a fuzzy logic platform. The research work attempts to design a controller for integer-order and fract-order plants by unifying nature inspired optimization techniques with proportional–integral–derivative (PID) like fuzzy knowledge-based control. The controller employs genetic algorithms (GA) and ANT colony algorithms for offline tuning of fract-order PID controller. Subsequently, fuzzy knowledge-based PID formulation fine-tunes the controller. The authors propose a modified GA-ANT approach wherein the inputs to the ANT system are generated in an optimal manner by using GA. They have simulated it on two distinct plants: (i) DC motor and (ii) a standard fract-order system. Simulation results and comparisons thereof show its superiority and feasibility for control of fract-order plants.

**Keywords** Integer-order plant · Fract-order plants · Fuzzy knowledge-based control · Modified GA-ANT approach

---

A. Kumar
EC Department, Mewar University, Rajasthan, India
e-mail: kumar_amb@hotmail.com

R. Sharma (✉)
Division of Instrumentation and Control Engineering, NSIT, New Delhi, India
e-mail: rajneesh496@gmail.com



M. Pant et al. (eds.), *Computational Network Application Tools for Performance Management*, Asset Analytics,
https://doi.org/10.1007/978-981-32-9585-8_3

# 1 Introduction

Fractional-order systems can be represented as

$$G_f(s) = K_P + \frac{K_I}{s^{\lambda}} + K_D s^{\mu}; \quad \lambda, \mu \in (0, 1) \tag{1}$$

where $K_p$, $K_I$, $K_D$ are the parameters of the conventional PID, and $\lambda$ and $\mu$ are fract-order proportional–integral–derivative (FO-PID) controller parameters, respectively [1]. For analyzing any fract-order system (FOS), it needs to be approximated to an equivalent integer-order system (IOS). Several techniques have been reported in the literature for this conversion [2, 3].

Once this approximation has been made, the design of a FO-PID controller is straightforward using various optimization techniques and random search methods. Conventional PID (CO-PID) controllers have dominated industrial process control applications. Though their use in industry is still prevalent, new avenues have emerged with the advent of soft computing tools.

Several soft computing techniques for implementing conventional PID control have been proposed, e.g., cruise control using genetic algorithm (GA) [4], conical tank regulation using ANT colony optimization (ACO) [5], PID control using multi-objective ACO [6], automatic voltage regulator system (AVR) using particle swarm optimization (PSO) [7], DC motor control using GA, evolutionary programing (EP) and PSO [8, 9]. In [10], authors propose linear quadratic regulator and PID controller for inverted pendulum wherein the parameters of the PID controller are tuned using ACO.

As mentioned earlier, fract-order PID controllers have an advantage over conventional PID controllers in terms of availability of additional tuning parameters. Authors in [11] tune both CO-PID and FO-PID controllers by adjusting GM and PM for temperature control; in [12], authors have applied GA for tuning of seven and eight parameters of the FO-PID controller and test it on integer-order plants (IOP) with delay.

In [13], authors have performed control and stability studies on fractional-order chaotic systems, and in [14, 15], fract-order systems for IOPs and AVRs are tuned using PSO. Zamani et al. [16] presents the design of an $H_\infty$ optimal FO-PID controller. Tuning is performed using multiple random search techniques in [17, 18] for control of robotic manipulators and UAV autopilot. A FO-PID heart rate controller is designed in [19] and control of blood glucose levels in diabetes patients is developed in [20] using GA.

Fuzzy logic-based fract-order PID formulation provides better flexibility and control. It is suitable for the control of highly nonlinear systems and facilitates easy computations online. Robust fuzzy PID (FPID) controller for control of permanent magnet synchronous motor (PMSM) has been proposed in [21], and FPID controller for the inverted pendulum is described in [22]. Here, the authors have used ACO to estimate the initial parameters of the FPID.

In [23–25], FFPID controllers have been proposed where fract-order parameters are optimized using GA. Other notable approaches include sliding mode control, e.g., steam distillation process and PMSM for electric vehicles using PSO [26]. An FFPID approach using ACO for the control of IOP and FOP is detailed in [27]. Finally, a variable-order FFPID controller is discussed in [28].

In this paper, we propose what may be termed "optimized" tuning method for FFPID controllers using a combination of GA and ant colony techniques on a fuzzy logic platform. The controller is simulated on integer-order and fractional-order systems for validation. Based on minimization of the integral of the square of error, GA outputs a set of fract-order parameters as well as initial input parameter values for the ACO. Thereafter, ACO fine-tunes these initial fract-order parameters. In the final step, PID like fuzzy logic is used with error and derivative of error as inputs for generating a set of fract-order parameters. All the three fract-order parameter sets are algebraically combined to get the resulting nature inspired FFPID controller.

The key benefit is harnessing the generalization capability of fuzzy systems in tandem with optimality provided by nature inspired algorithms for generating a versatile fract-order controller. Section 2 gives brief details on the nature inspired algorithms used in this work, PID like fuzzy knowledge-based controller and our nature inspired fuzzy fractional controller. Section 3 details simulation results and associated discussions, and Sect. 4 concludes the paper.

# 2 Nature Inspired Algorithms for Fract-Order Systems

## *2.1 ANT Colony Optimization (ACO)*

ACO [29] belongs to the family of algorithms collectively bunched "nature inspired" wherein optimization is carried out on the behavioral pattern of ants. Ants practice an excellent way of optimizing the path they take for food search and other tasks. First, they select an arbitrary path, and then this path is marked for other ants by releasing pheromones.

Next step is to choose the best path based on the probability of pheromone trails. An interesting phenomenon is the disappearance of lower quality pheromones trails. Thus, only the best or most optimal path gets reinforced by repeated pheromone secretion by other ants. The algorithm has the following steps:

(i) A pheromone factor matrix $\tau$ is chosen for obtaining a good solution.

$$\tau = \{\tau_{pq}\} \text{ and } \tau_{pq} = \tau_i \ \forall \ (p, q) \tag{2}$$

$p$ and $q$ are nodes along the ant path.

(ii) Next, the probability that an ant will choose the node $q$ from node $p$ is evaluated as

$$P_{pq}(t) = \frac{[\tau_{pq}]^{\alpha}[\eta_{pq}]^{\beta}}{\sum[\tau_{pq}]^{\alpha}[\eta_{pq}]^{\beta}} \; \forall \; p, q \in T^1 \tag{3}$$

In each iteration, a solution is obtained using the probability $P_{pq}(t)$. In (2), $\eta_{pq} = \frac{1}{k_q}$ is a factor which is heuristic in nature; $\alpha$ and $\beta$ are constants which determine the influence of pheromone and heuristic values on the choice of the trail taken by an ant; and $T^1$ is the path decided by an ant at any given time. When a new trail is chosen, the weaker pheromone trails disappear. The quantity of pheromone on a path is

$$\Delta\tau_{pq}^{1} = \begin{cases} \frac{L^{\min}}{L^{1}} \; if \; p, q \in T^1 \\ 0 \quad \text{otherwise} \end{cases} \tag{4}$$

The structure formula [28] for updating of a pheromone is

$$\tau_{pq}(t) = \rho\tau_{pq}(t-1) + \sum_{1}^{N} \Delta\tau_{pq}^{1}(t) \tag{5}$$

where $N$ is the number of ants and the evaporation rate is $\rho \in (0, 1]$.

## 2.2 Genetic Algorithm

Genetic algorithm is a stochastic search technique based on human genome selection procedure and is classified as "evolutionary algorithm." GA uses the concept of natural selection and genetics and has been widely used for optimization tasks. GA is structured on the processes of natural selection, recombination and mutation of chromosomes. As with the case of any other nature inspired optimization algorithm, this technique follows the principle of survival of the fittest. The algorithm has the following steps:

(i) **Selection**: First a random choice of individuals from a population is done, and the fittest one is selected for crossover. Selection is done by evaluating a fitness function corresponding to each individual.

(ii) **Modification**: Modification is implemented by the process of crossover (recombination) or mutation. Crossover is the process of combining parent solutions and producing an offspring. The process of crossover and mutation attempts at generating a more fit set of individuals. Mutation prevents the algorithm from being trapped in a local minimum. Mutation maintains genetic diversity in the population. It introduces new genetic structures in the population by randomly modifying some of the individuals of the string.

The algorithm terminates when either a maximum number of generations have been produced or a sufficient fitness level has been achieved for the target population.

## 2.3 PID like Fuzzy Knowledge-Based Control (FKBC)

Fuzzy logic imitates human thinking and modeling of systems and processes. Implementing fuzzy logic-based control typically involves: (a) fuzzifying the inputs or converting crisp inputs to fuzzy membership functions; (b) coding human or process knowledge in terms of a rule base; (c) using fuzzy inputs along with rule base for inferring outputs called fuzzy inference system and (d) converting the aggregated fuzzy output from the fuzzy inference system to a crisp (usable) output by defuzzification.

Though any process or state variables can be chosen as input variables for the fuzzy logic-based control, a natural and more efficient method of implementing fuzzy knowledge-based control (FKBC) is to use error ($e$) and derivative of error ($\partial e$) as inputs to the fuzzy logic controller also termed as "PID like FKBC" in the literature. In this work, fuzzy membership functions (laid over the input variables universe of discourse) have been chosen as Gaussian, and the FIS is "Mamdani" [29]. Table 1 gives the rule base for the PID like FKBC for the variables $K_{\text{p}}$, $K_{\text{d}}$, $K_{\text{i}}$, $\lambda$, $\mu$. It is worthwhile to note that we have framed rules for not only the conventional PID parameters $K_{\text{p}}$, $K_{\text{d}}$, $K_{\text{i}}$ but also for the additional fractional-order parameters $\lambda$, $\mu$.

These rules have been framed based on empirical knowledge gained during simulations of fract-order PID control. Three fuzzy subsets are chosen, i.e., "Negative," "Zero" and "Positive" for the inputs $e$ and $\partial e$. The output variables $K_{\text{p}}$, $K_{\text{d}}$, $K_{\text{i}}$, $\lambda$ and $\mu$ have been fuzzified using five fuzzy subsets: NL (negative large), NLE (negative less), ZR (zero), PLE (positive less), PL (positive large). Defuzzification has been performed using the centroid method [30]. The plots for the membership functions laid over the inputs and outputs are shown in Fig. 1. This completes the design of the PID like FKBC.

## 2.4 Nature Inspired Fuzzy Fractional PID (NIFFPID)

In this work, we propose to unify all the three approaches outlined above. This is done by obtaining an algebraic sum of all the approaches, i.e., combining the PID like FKBC, ANT colony-based optimizer and the GA-based control. The aim here is to find the best possible values for the fractional PID parameters by using all the three approaches to aid each other in this process. The added advantage is that the inaccuracy of one of the approaches could possibly be covered by the others and the results indeed point to this. Complete structure of the proposed nature inspired fuzzy fractional PID controller is shown in Fig. 2.

As can be seen from the figure that each of nature inspired algorithms, i.e., GA and ACO output a set of fract-order parameters which are algebraically added to the parameters provided by the FKBC, and the combined strategy is applied to the plant being controlled.

**Table 1** Fract-order PID like FKBC rule base

| $K_P$ | | | $K_I$ | | | $K_D$ | | | $\lambda$ | | | $\mu$ | | |
|---|---|---|---|---|---|---|---|---|---|---|---|---|---|---|
| IF | AND | THEN | IF | AND | THEN | IF | AND | THEN | IF | AND | THEN | IF | AND | THEN |
| $e$ | ?$e$ | $K_p$ | $e$ | ?$e$ | $K_i$ | $e$ | ?$e$ | $K_d$ | $e$ | ?$e$ | | $e$ | ?$e$ | $\mu$ |
| Negative | Negative | Positive large | Negative | Negative | Negative large | Negative | Negative | Positive large | Negative | Negative | Positive large | Negative | Negative | Positive less |
| Negative | Zero | Zero | Negative | Zero | Negative large | Negative | Zero | Positive less | Negative | Zero | Positive less | Negative | Zero | Positive less |
| Negative | Positive | Positive less | Negative | Positive | Negative large | Negative | Positive | Positive large | Negative | Positive | Positive less | Negative | Positive | Positive large |
| Zero | Negative | Negative large | Zero | Negative | Negative large | Zero | Negative | Negative less | Zero | Negative | Zero | Zero | Negative | Zero |
| Zero | Zero | Negative large | Zero | Zero | Negative less | Zero | Zero | Zero | Zero | Zero | Zero | Zero | Zero | Zero |
| Zero | Positive | Positive large | Zero | Positive | Negative less | Zero | Positive | Positive less | Zero | Positive | Negative less | Zero | Positive | Positive less |
| Positive | Negative | Positive large | Positive | Negative | Positive less | Positive | Negative | Positive less | Positive | Negative | Positive less | Positive | Negative | Positive large |
| Positive | Zero | Positive less | Positive | Zero | Zero | Positive | Zero | Positive large | Positive | Zero | Positive large | Positive | Zero | Positive less |
| Positive | Positive | Positive large | Positive | Positive | Positive less | Positive | Positive | Positive large | Positive | Positive | Positive large | Positive | Positive | Positive large |

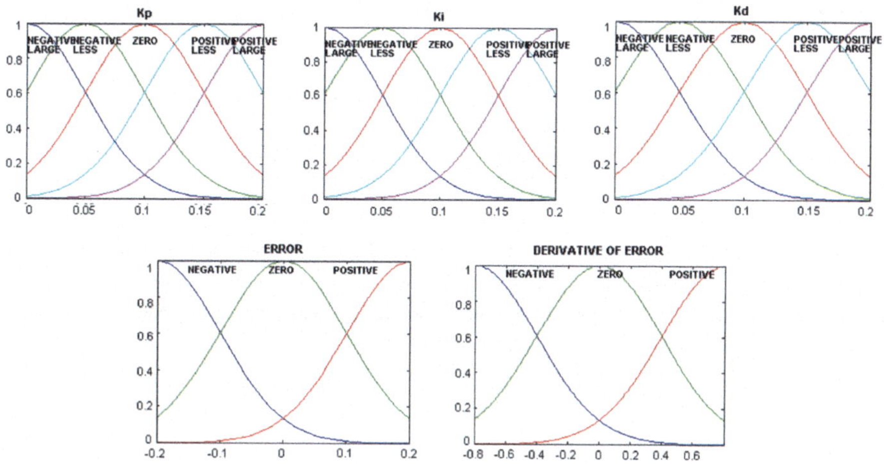


**Fig. 1** Membership functions for inputs: $e$ and $\partial e$; outputs: $K_{\mathrm{p}}$, $K_{\mathrm{i}}$, $K_{\mathrm{d}}$

**Fig. 2** Block diagram of NIFFPID controller

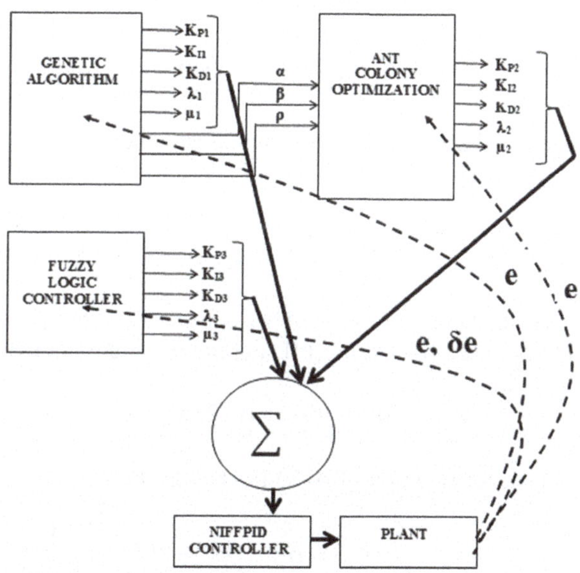


## 3 Simulation of Nature Inspired PID like FKBC

The proposed approach is tested on two systems:

### 3.1 DC Motor

The first plant considered is a DC motor having a transfer function

$$G_1 = \frac{-0.05963s^2 + 1.254s + 0.8736}{s^3 + 0.9708s^2 + 1.796s + 0.8736} \tag{6}$$

Unconstrained minimization with GA is used to evaluate the parameters of the fract-order PID controller and the same are fed as inputs to the ANT colony algorithm. Performance index chosen is the integral of square error (ISE). GA-based optimization yields the following parameters:

(i) Fract-order PID parameters

$$K_{p1} = 0.1833,\ K_{i1} = 1.6168,\ K_{d1} = 1.1348,\ L_1 = 0.0001,\ M_1 = 0.8712 \tag{7}$$

The GA controller transfer function is

$$F_{\text{GA\_ FOPID\_ 1}}(s) = 0.1833 + \frac{1.6168}{s^{0.0001}} + 1.1348s^{0.8712} \tag{8}$$

(ii) ANT colony initial parameter estimate

$$\alpha = 0.0187,\ \beta = 0.6283,\ \rho = 0.0780 \tag{9}$$

Using these values, the ANT colony algorithm (2) is implemented, and the ANT colony-based fract-order PID parameters are obtained:

$$K_{p2} = 0.11,\ K_{i2} = 0.18,\ K_{d2} = 0.19,\ L_2 = 0.01,\ M_2 = 0.05 \tag{10}$$

Transfer function of ACO fract-order PID is

$$F_{\text{ANT-FOPID\_ 1}}(s) = 0.11 + \frac{0.18}{s^{0.01}} + 0.19s^{0.05} \tag{11}$$

Finally, we merge the outputs of these fractional-order controllers, viz. GA, ANT and FKBC to generate our nature inspired fuzzy fractional PID (NIFFPID) controller with transfer function:

$$F_{\text{NIFFPID\_ 1}}(s) = 0.0871 + \frac{0.2445}{s^{0.0204}} + 2.0204s^{0.9242} \tag{12}$$

Figure 3 gives the responses obtained on the DC motor with different controllers. The NIFFPID controller proposed in this paper achieves a rise time of 0.27 s which

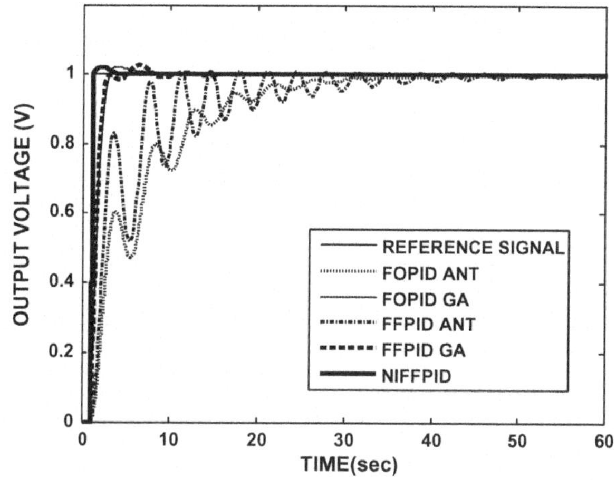


**Fig. 3** Step response of various controllers on DC motor

is significantly lower than the best rise time achieved by other controllers (FOPID, FFPID using GA) of 2.143 s. Our NIFFPID control achieves peak time of 1.102 s, settling time of 1.646 s and a peak overshoot of 0.022. These values point to pretty good time response performance.

## 3.2 *Fract-Order System*

The second case study is a fractional-order system with transfer function

$$G_2(s) = \frac{5}{s^{2.3}+1.3s^{0.9}+1.25} \tag{13}$$

Once again, GA is used to get the fract-order PID parameters:

$$K_{p2} = 2.3117,\ K_{i2} = 0.5424,\ K_{d2} = 0.9052,\ L_2 = 0.0172,\ M_2 = 0.9997 \tag{14}$$

Resulting GA-FOPID controller transfer function

$$F_{\text{GA-FOPID\_2}}(s) = 2.3117 + \frac{0.5424}{s^{0.0172}} + 0.9052s^{0.9997} \tag{15}$$

ACO initial parameters obtained are

$$\alpha = 0.3,\ \beta = 0.7,\ \rho = 0.1 \tag{16}$$

These parameters are used to generate an ACO fract-order PID controller

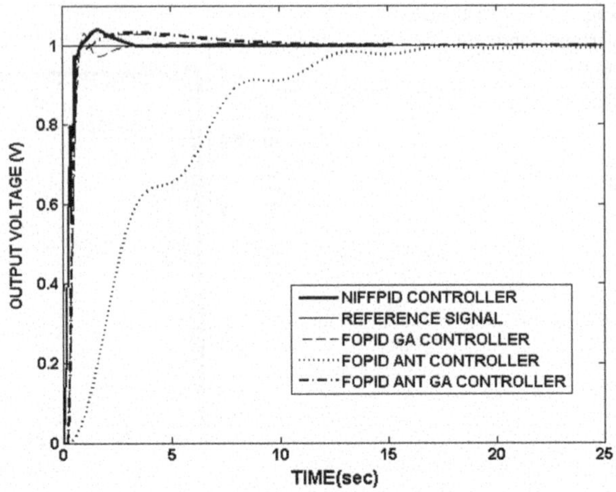


**Fig. 4** Step response of various controllers for fract-order system

$$K_{p2} = 0.06,\ K_{i2} = 0.02,\ K_{d2} = 0.40,\ L_2 = 0.13,\ M_2 = 0.2 \tag{17}$$

ACO transfer function of FOPID controller becomes

$$F_{\text{ANT-FOPID\_2}}(s) = 0.06 + \frac{0.02}{s^{0.13}} + 0.40s^{0.2} \tag{18}$$

We combine the three controller realizations to generate NIFFPID controller with transfer function:

$$F_{\text{NIFFPID\_2}}(s) = 2.4704 + \frac{0.6618}{s^{0.1484}} + 1.4052s^{0.9998} \tag{19}$$

Simulation results using different controllers on this plant are given in Fig. 4. Our NIFFPID controller (Fig. 4) is seen to achieve the best response parameters of rise time of 0.89 s and settling time of 3.00 s. Thus, an amalgamation of nature inspired approaches with fuzzy logic control technique, viz. GA, ACO and FKBC does lead to an improved controller response.

## 4 Conclusion and Future Work

An attempt has been made to hybridize two nature inspired algorithms in a PID like fuzzy setting. Our main objective is to use nature-based optimization for tuning of fuzzy logic-based fract-order PID controller. The methodology is implemented on two systems and performance compared with other soft computing-based fract-order controllers. Results indicate that our proposed controller gives better closed loop time response over other controllers.

In future, the authors would like to implement the proposed approach on some fract-order systems. We would also augment our methodology by employing type-2 fuzzy systems and self organizing fuzzy inference system structure.

## References

1. Y.Q. Chen, K.L. Moore, Discretization schemes for fractional-order differentiators and integrators. IEEE Trans. Circuits Syst. I Fund. Theory. Appl. **49**(3), 363–367 (2002)
2. D.Y. Xue, Y.Q. Chen, Sub-optimum $H_2$ rational approximations to fractional-order linear systems, in *IDETC/CIE Conference*, California (2005), pp. 1–10
3. A. Oustaloup, J. Sabatier, P. Lanusse, From fractional robustness to crone control. Fract. Calc. Appl. Anal. **2**(1), 1–30 (1999)
4. M.K. Rout, D. Sain, S.K. Swain, S.K. Mishra, PID controller design for cruise control system using genetic algorithm, in *International Conference on Electrical Electronics and Optimization Techniques (ICEEOT)*, Chennai (2016), pp. 4170–4174
5. K.V.L. Narayana, V.N. Kumar, M. Dhivya, R.P. Raj, Application of ant colony optimization in tuning a PID controller to a conical tank. Indian J. Sci. Technol. **8**(S2), 217–223 (2015)
6. I. Chiha, N. Liouane, P. Borne, Tuning PID controller using multiobjective ant colony optimization. J. Appl. Comput. Intell. Soft Comput. **11** (2012)
7. M.F. Aranza, J. Kustija, B. Trisno, D.L. Hakim, Tuning PID controller using particle swarm optimization algorithm on automatic voltage regulator system, in *IOP Conference Series: Materials Science and Engineering*,vol. 128 (2016), pp. 1–9
8. N.P. Adhikari, A. Gupta, PID controller tuning using soft computing techniques, in *All India Seminar on Biomedical Engineering*, Lecture Notes in Bioengineering (Springer, India, 2012)
9. N. Tandan, K.K. Swarnkar, PID controller optimization by soft computing techniques-a review. Int. J. Hybrid Inf. Technol. **8**(7), 357–362 (2015)
10. A. Jacknoon, M.A. Abido, Ant colony based LQR and PID tuned parameters for controlling inverted pendulum, in *International Conference on Communication, Control, Computing and Electronics Engineering*, Khartoum (2017), pp. 1–8
11. C.I. Muresan, Simplified optimization routine for tuning robust fractional order controllers. Am. J. Comput. Math. **3**, 7–12 (2013)
12. Y. Zhang, J. Li, Fractional-order PID controller tuning based on genetic algorithm, in *International Conference on Business Management and Electronic Information*, Guangzhou (2011), pp. 764–767
13. A. Soukkou, S. Leulmi, Controlling and synchronizing of fractional-order chaotic systems via simple and optimal fractional-order feedback controller. Int. J. Intell. Syst. Appl. **8**, 56–69 (2016). https://doi.org/10.5815/ijisa.2016.06.07
14. A.K. Mahmood, B.F. Mohammed, Design of fractional order PID controller based particle swarm. Diyala J. Eng. Sci. **7**(4), 42–93 (2014)
15. N.R. Raju, P.L. Reddy, Robustness study of fractional order PID controller optimized by particle swarm optimization in AVR System. Int. J. Electr. Comput. Eng. **6**(5), 2033–2040 (2016)
16. M. Zamani, M.K. Ghartemani, N. Sadate, Design of an $H_\infty$—optimal FOPID controller using particle swarm optimization, in CCC, Hunan (2007), pp. 435–440
17. D. Fani, E. Shahraki, Two-link robot manipulator using fractional order PID controllers optimized by evolutionary algorithms. Biosci. Biotechnol. Res. Asia **13**(1), 589–598 (2016)
18. G. Li,, C. Guo, Y. Li, W. Deng, Fractional-örder PID controller of USV course-keeping using hybrid GA-PSO algorithm, in *8th International Symposium Computational Intelligence and Design*, Hangzhou (2015), pp. 506–509
19. S.P. Arunachalam, S. Kapa, S.K. Mulpuru, P.A. Friedman, E.G. Tolkacheva, Intelligent fractional-order PID (FOPID) heart rate controller for cardiac pacemaker, in *IEEE Healthcare Innovation Point-Of-Care Technologies Conference*, Cancun (2016), pp. 105–108

20. M. Goharimanesh, A. Lashkaripour, A.A. Mehrizi, Fractional order PID controller for diabetes patients. JAMECH **46**(1), 69–76 (2015)
21. B.T. Zhang, Y. Pi, Robust fractional order proportion-plus-differential controller based on fuzzy inference for permanent magnet synchronous motor. IET Control Theory Appl. **6**(6), 829–837 (2012)
22. H. Boubertakh, M. Tadjine, P.Y. Glorennec, S. Labiod, Tuning fuzzy PID controllers using ant colony optimization, in *17th Mediterranean Conference Control and Automation*, Thessaloniki (2009), pp. 13–18
23. S. Das, I. Pan, S. Das, A. Gupta, A novel fractional order fuzzy PID controller and its optimal time domain tuning based on integral performance indices. J. Eng. Appl. Artif. Intell. **25**(2), 430–442 (2012)
24. V. Kumar, K.P.S. Rana, J. Kumar, P. Mishra, S.S. Nair, A robust fractional order fuzzy P + fuzzy I + fuzzy D controller for nonlinear and uncertain system. Int. J. Autom. Comput. 1–13 (2014)
25. R.H. Mohammed, F. Bendary, K. Elserafi, Trajectory tracking control for robot manipulator using fractional order-fuzzy-PID controller. Int. J. Comput. Appl. **134**(15), 22–29 (2016)
26. M. Tajjudin, N. Ishak, M.H.F. Rahiman, R. Adnan, Design of fuzzy fractional-order PI + PD controller, in *12th IEEE International Colloquium on Signal Processing & Its Applications (CSPA)*, Malacca City (2016), pp. 253–257
27. R. Singh, A. Kumar, R. Sharma, Fractional order PID control using ant colony optimization, in *1st IEEE International Conference on Power Electronics, Intelligent Control and Energy Systems*, Delhi (2016), pp. 1–6
28. L. Liu, F. Pan, D. Xue, Variable-order fuzzy fractional PID controller. ISA Trans. **55**, 227–233 (2015)
29. M. Dorigo, The ant system optimization by a colony of cooperating agents. IEEE Trans. Syst. Man Cybern. Part B **26**(1), 1–13 (1996)
30. K.S. Book Miller, B. Ross, *An Introduction to the Fractional Calculus and Fractional Differential Equation* (Wiley, New York, 1993)

# Neuro-Fuzzy-Rough Classification for Improving Efficiency and Performance in Case-Based Reasoning Retrieval

**Nabanita Choudhury and Shahin Ara Begum**

**Abstract** Case-based reasoning (CBR) is an artificial intelligence (AI) technique for solving problems. The very fact that CBR draws on past experiences to solve a new problem makes it intuitively appealing as humans also have the same problem-solving behavior. Another advantage of CBR over other conventional AI techniques is that it can work on a shallow knowledge base to start with. These make CBR an excellent method to solve real-life problems and useful in the field like medical diagnosis, engineering diagnosis, product selection, weather prediction, aerospace applications, etc. Classification plays a vital role in the retrieval of cases, as a correct classification results in a correctly retrieved case, which eventually results in a correct solution given by the CBR system. Typically, case retrieval is similarity-based and uses a $k$-nearest neighbor ($k$-NN) algorithm. Retrieval aims to find among the stored cases the best match for a given new case. Typically, CBR systems use the nearest neighbor algorithm as a similarity metric for retrieving cases. In this paper, the researchers use the machine learning workbench WEKA to combine well-known classifiers multilayer perceptron and fuzzy-rough nearest neighbor and compare the performance of $k$-NN with them. They have used benchmark medical data sets to carry out the evaluation process. The experimental results show that the combination of multilayer perceptron and fuzzy-rough nearest neighbor outperforms $k$-NN to a significant extent for classification, thus effectively improving the case retrieval efficiency and performance.

**Keywords** Case-based reasoning · Retrieval · Classification · Multilayer perceptron · Fuzzy-rough nearest neighbor

N. Choudhury (✉) · S. A. Begum
Department of Computer Science, Assam University, Silchar, Assam, India
e-mail: nabaniitaa@gmail.com

S. A. Begum
e-mail: shahin.ara.begum@aus.ac.in



M. Pant et al. (eds.), *Computational Network Application Tools for Performance Management*, Asset Analytics,
https://doi.org/10.1007/978-981-32-9585-8_4

# 1 Introduction

Case-based reasoning (CBR) is a paradigm of artificial intelligence (AI) used for solving problems. But unlike most of the other AI approaches, CBR solves new problems by utilizing the knowledge gained from solving the similar previous situations [1]. The very fact that CBR draws on past experiences to solve a new problem makes it intuitively appealing as humans also have the same problem-solving behavior. Another advantage of CBR over other conventional AI techniques is that it can work on a shallow knowledge base to start with [2]. These make CBR an excellent method to solve real-life problems. Over the years, CBR has particularly been found useful in various application fields like medical diagnosis, engineering diagnosis, product selection, weather prediction, aerospace applications, to name a few.

In a CBR system, the past situations as stored in a database are known as 'cases,' with each case being an individual experience. Given a new situation (case), the CBR system compares it with the existing cases in the case base and tries to find the nearest match. This is termed as case retrieval and is often considered to be the foundation and the most vital phase of CBR [3]. Retrieval aims to find among the stored cases the best match for a given new case. Typically, CBR systems use the nearest neighbor algorithm as a similarity metric for retrieving cases [4]. Decision trees and their derivatives are other retrieval techniques [5].

Classification plays a vital role in the retrieval of cases, as a correct classification results in a correctly retrieved case, which eventually results in a correct solution given by the CBR system. In this paper, a detailed comparative study is carried out using benchmark medical data sets, among well-known classifiers, viz. multilayer perceptron (MLP), fuzzy-rough nearest neighbor (FRNN), *k*-nearest neighbor (*k*-NN) and a combined form of MLP and FRNN.

In this study, it is observed that the classification accuracy increases by a significant amount when MLP and FRNN are combined, as compared to their individual performances. The rest of the paper is organized as follows. Section 2 provides a brief insight into the four phases of CBR, with a discussion on the relation between retrieval and classification. Section 3 outlines the classification techniques used in the present study. Section 4 evaluates the performance of MLP-FRNN combined in comparison with *k*-NN, MLP and FRNN. Section 5 presents the conclusion and future directions of the research.

# 2 Case-Based Reasoning

## *2.1 CBR Cycle*

The working of CBR can briefly be described as the four Re's [1], as depicted in Fig. 1:

- **Retrieve** the most similar case (s) from the case base

**Fig. 1** CBR cycle [1]

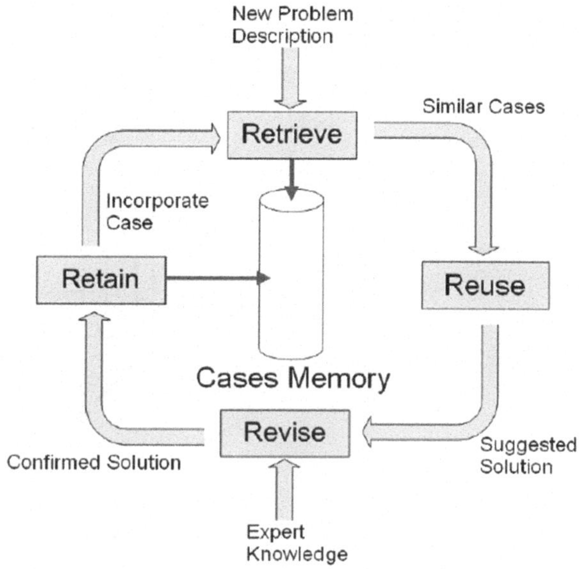


- **Reuse** the solution (s) of the retrieved case (s)
- **Revise** the solution to meet with the current problem situation
- **Retain** the current solution in the case base

Given a new problem situation (case), the CBR system first carries out a search in its case base for the nearest match. When found, the solution is either reused directly, or modified in accordance with the given situation. These two phases called reuse and revise are often known as an adaptation [5]. The confirmed solution is then retained in the case base. As seen from Fig. 1, the revise phase often needs the knowledge of domain experts, and automatic adaptation is still not much into practice for CBR systems. Most of the CBR systems that have been implemented in real-world situations, particularly in medicine avoid the adaptation phase and are retrieval only systems [6]. As a result, case retrieval is considered to be of utmost importance as the overall performance of CBR depends on it.

## 2.2 *Case Retrieval*

The most common retrieval technique for a CBR system is similarity-based retrieval [7] and is commonly implemented with *k*-NN [3]. Some of the other retrieval techniques include knowledge-guided approaches [5], adaptation-guided retrieval [8], order-based retrieval [9], diversity-conscious retrieval [10, 11], compromise-driven retrieval [12] and explanation-oriented retrieval [13, 14].

Figure 2 depicts the retrieval mechanism in terms of problem and solution spaces. Given an input problem, the nearest match is found in the case base. The closer

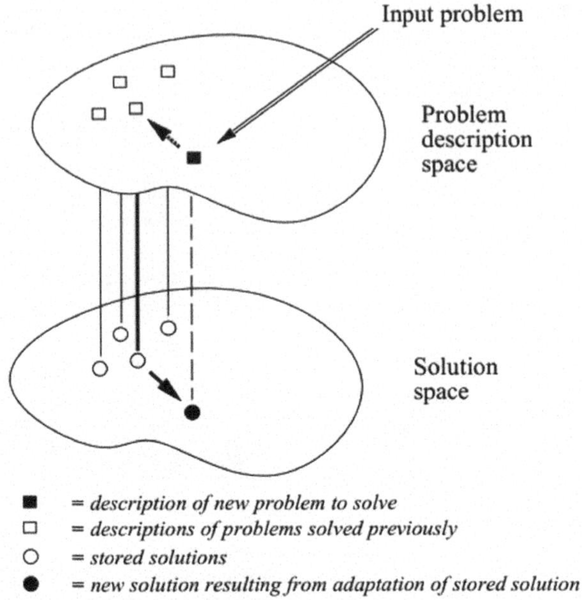


**Fig. 2** Problem and solution spaces [16]

the retrieved case from the existing case base, the lesser is the need of revising the solution.

CBR systems are often used for classification problems, e.g., in medical diagnosis or fault diagnosis. Jurisica and Glasgow [15] define a case-based approach for classification as follows: Given a new problem P (or a case), the aim is to retrieve a set of cases C similar to P and classify P based on C.

## 3 Classification Approaches

Classification is a supervised data mining method that assigns items or instances to a specific categorical attribute known as a class [17]. The present work focuses on three widely known classifiers, viz. *k*-nearest neighbor (*k*-NN), multilayer perceptron (MLP) and fuzzy-rough nearest neighbor (FRNN).

### *3.1 k-Nearest Neighbor*

Given an input case, the *k*-nearest neighbor algorithm computes *k* cases, which are nearest to the current case [18] as shown in Fig. 3. Typically, the similarity is computed using a Euclidean distance [4]. *k*-NN is a lazy learning method, and the chosen value of *k* determines the classification rate [19]. When *k*-NN is applied to a large

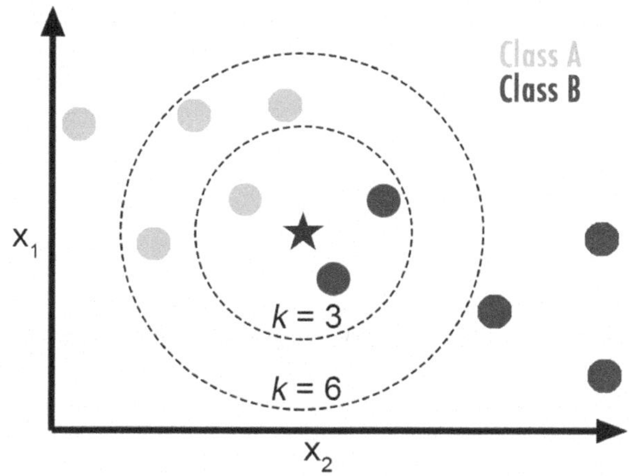


**Fig. 3** *k*-NN problem space [18]

database, enormous computation is needed, which becomes its major disadvantage. The number of computations also increases to a large extent when the number of feature dimensions is large [20].

## 3.2 Multilayer Perceptron

Artificial neural networks (ANN) are a branch of AI that work by mimicking the human brain [21, 22]. Multilayer perceptron (MLP) is a feedforward ANN that works as an excellent classifier with a back-propagation algorithm [23]. Figure 4 shows an MLP with $m$ nodes in the first layer, called the input layer, two hidden layers, and $p$ nodes in the output layer. One of the major drawbacks of MLPs is their

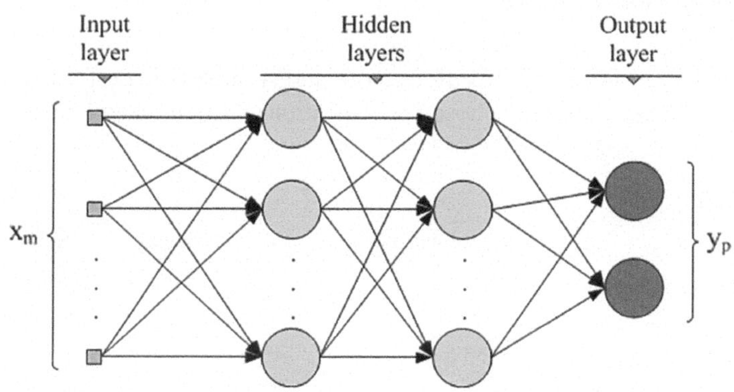


**Fig. 4** MLP with two hidden layers

slow pace [24]. Moreover, MLPs suffer from overfitting, when the network becomes very large [25].

### *3.3 Rough-Fuzzy Nearest Neighbor*

FuzzyNN introduced by Keller et al. [26] is an extension of the *k*-NN algorithm. It allows objects of different classes to belong to those with varied degrees of membership. It also considers the closeness of each neighbor with the given instance [27]. However, when knowledge is insufficient, the algorithm fails to work properly [28]. To overcome the disadvantages of conventional fuzzyNN, fuzzy-rough NN algorithm (FRNN) is proposed in the literature [29, 30].

But a slight modification of the FRNN algorithm proposed by Jensen and Cornelis [31] achieves better classification accuracy as it considers both lower and upper approximations of fuzzy-rough set theory for classifying test objects and combines the approximations with the classical approach.

## 4 Performance Evaluation

In a CBR system, given a new classification task, the retrieval accuracy depends on the classification made. So, in the present work, the classification problem has been chosen as the target application. The aim of this study is to show that when MLP and FRNN algorithms are combined, the classification accuracy increases to a significant extent. Table 1 details the basic information about the data sets used, obtained from the UCI ML repository [32].

### *4.1 Experimental Setup*

The WEKA Experimenter [25] is used to run and compare the performances of the following algorithms, with the chosen specifications as mentioned below:

**Table 1** Medical data sets

| Data sets | No. of instances | No. of attributes | No. of clases |
|---|---|---|---|
| Breast Cancer (Wisconsin) | 699 | 11 | 2 |
| Heart-Cleveland | 303 | 14 | 5 |
| Hepatitis | 155 | 20 | 2 |
| Hypothyroid | 3772 | 30 | 4 |
| Pima Indians diabetes | 768 | 9 | 2 |

**IB*k* (the *k*-NN algorithm available in WEKA)**:

- Window size = 0
- Distance function = Euclidean distance

**MLP**:

- No. of nodes in the hidden layer = (No. of attributes + number of classes)/2
- Learning rate = 0.3
- Momentum = 0.2

**FRNN** [33]:

- $k = 10$
- Algebraic T-norm: $T(x, y) = xy$.
- Similarity measure: $1 - \text{abs}(a(x) - a(y))/\text{abs}(a\_max - a\_min)$, where $x$ and $y$ are objects, $a$ is the given attribute, and $a\_max$ and $a\_min$ are the maximal and minimal occurring value of $a$.

**The combined algorithm MLP-FRNN**:
Stacking method is used to combine MLP and FRNN algorithms. It is an ensemble learning method that combines several base classifiers by means of a meta-classifier, which takes the output values of the base classifiers as its input [34, 35]. MLP and FRNN are used as the base classifiers and logistic function [36] as the meta-classifier.

## 4.2 *Results and Analysis*

The four algorithms mentioned above are compared with respect to the five medical data sets of Table 1. The comparison is made in terms of classification accuracy, which is the proportion of correctly classified instances, and is often assumed to be the best indicator of performance for classifiers. Ten-fold cross-validation is used for this. Table 2 details the results obtained. For each of the data sets, the highest value of classification accuracy is denoted in boldface.

**Table 2** Performance comparison in terms of classification accuracy

| Data sets | Classification accuracy | | | |
|---|---|---|---|---|
| | IBk | MLP | FRNN | Stacking MLP with FRNN |
| Breast Cancer (Wisconsin) | 95.13 | 95.58 | 95.74 | **96.95** |
| Heart-Cleveland | 76.24 | 77.9 | 81.15 | **81.38** |
| Hepatitis | 80.64 | **81.29** | 78.8 | 81.20 |
| Hypothyroid | 91.52 | 94.13 | 91.87 | **94.17** |
| Pima Indians diabetes | 70.18 | 74.75 | 69.07 | **75.01** |

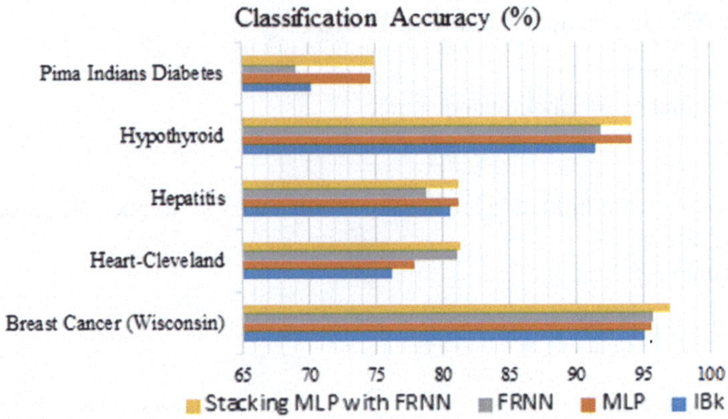


**Fig. 5** Performance comparison

From Table 2 and Fig. 5, it can be observed that except for Hepatitis data set, the combined algorithm scores better than the individual algorithms for all other four data sets in terms of percentage of correctly classified instances. Thus, it can be construed that when MLP is combined with FRNN, the classification improves to a significant extent.

## 5 Conclusions and Future Scope

In this paper, a neuro-fuzzy-rough classification approach has been presented, which performs better than the well-known classifiers, viz. *k*-NN, MLP and FRNN, in case-based reasoning retrieval. The combined approach is evaluated in comparison with the individual approaches using medical data sets obtained from the UCI ML repository. The experimental results demonstrate that the MLP-FRNN algorithm is an effective retrieval strategy that outperforms the classic nearest neighbor retrieval.

In the present work, a simple representation of cases is considered. The combined algorithm can be extended for more complex representations like object-oriented or hierarchical representations of cases. Further, the present work focuses on the medical data sets, keeping in mind the huge amount of application of CBR in medicine. Research can be carried out with the combined algorithm for a wider variety of data sets.

The algorithm can also be combined with genetic programing, another soft computing paradigm and well-known classifier. As CBR has widely been applied to classification tasks, e.g., to diagnose the presence of certain diseases, or to determine the type of an organism from the given attributes, further research can be carried out on more combinations of soft computing techniques for classification in the retrieval phase of CBR, to make it more efficient.

## References

1. A. Aamodt, E. Plaza, Case-based reasoning: foundational issues, methodological variations, and system approaches. AI Commun. **7**(1), 39–59 (1994)
2. S.C. Shiu, S.K. Pal, Case-based reasoning: concepts, features and soft computing. Appl. Intell. **21**(3), 233–238 (2004)
3. R.L. De Mantaras, D. McSherry, D. Bridge, D. Leake, B. Smyth, S. Craw, B. Faltings, M.L. Maher, M.T. Cox, K. Forbus, M. Keane, A. Aamodt, I. Watson, Retrieval, reuse, revision and retention in case-based reasoning. Knowl. Eng. Rev. **20**(3), 215–240 (2005)
4. D.W. Patterson, N. Rooney, M. Galushka, Efficient retrieval for case-based reasoning, in *FLAIRS Conference* (2003), pp. 144–149
5. S.K. Pal, S.C. Shiu, *Foundations of Soft Case-Based Reasoning*, vol. 8 (Wiley, Hoboken, 2004)
6. N. Choudhury, S.A. Begum, A survey on case-based reasoning in medicine. Int. J. Adv. Comput. Sci. Appl. **7**(8), 136–144 (2016)
7. B. Smyth, M.T. Keane, Adaptation-guided retrieval: questioning the similarity assumption in reasoning. Artif. Intell. **102**(2), 249–293 (1998)
8. B. Smyth, M.T. Keane, Experiments on adaptation-guided retrieval in case-based design, in *International Conference on Case-Based Reasoning* (Springer, Berlin, 1995), pp. 313–324
9. Bridge, D., Ferguson, A.: Diverse product recommendations using an expressive language for case retrieval, in *Advances in Case-Based Reasoning*, vol. 2416 (2002), pp. 43–57
10. B. Smyth, P. McClave, Similarity vs. diversity, in *Case-Based Reasoning Research and Development*, vol. 2080 (2001), pp. 347–361
11. D. McSherry, Diversity-conscious retrieval, in *Advances in Case-Based Reasoning*, vol. 2416 (2002), pp. 219–233
12. D. McSherry, Similarity and compromise. In: *Case-Based Reasoning Research and Development*, vol. 2689 (2003), pp. 291–305
13. F. Sormo, J. Cassens, A. Aamodt, Explanation in case-based reasoning—perspectives and goals. Artif. Intell. Rev. **24**, 109–143 (2005)
14. D. Doyle, P. Cunningham, D. Bridge, Y. Rahman, Explanation oriented retrieval, in *Advances in Case-Based Reasoning*, vol. 3155 (2004), pp. 157–168
15. I. Jurisica, J. Glasgow, Case-based classification using similarity-based retrieval, in *International Conference on Tools with Artificial Intelligence* (1996), pp. 410–419 (1996)
16. D.B. Leake, CBR in context: the present and future, in *Case-Based Reasoning, Experiences, Lessons & Future Directions* (1996), pp. 1–30
17. I. Bichindaritz, Data mining methods for case-based reasoning in health sciences, in *ICCBR (Workshops)* (2015), pp. 184–198
18. D.T. Larose, *Discovering Knowledge in Data: An Introduction to Data Mining* (Wiley, Hoboken, 2014)
19. G. Guo, H. Wang, D. Bell, Y. Bi, K. Greer, KNN model-based approach in classification, in *OTM Confederated International Conferences. On the Move to Meaningful Internet Systems* (Springer, Berlin, 2003), pp. 986–996
20. S.K. Pal, A. Pal (eds.), *Pattern Recognition: From Classical to Modern Approaches* (World Scientific, Singapore, 2001)
21. R.P. Lippmann, An introduction to computing with neural nets. IEEE Acoust. Speech Sig. Process. Mag. **61**, 4–22 (1987)
22. T. Kohonen, An introduction to neural computing. Neural Netw. **1**(1), 3–16 (1988)
23. D.W. Ruck, S.K. Rogers, M. Kabrisky, M.E. Oxley, B.W. Suter, The multilayer perceptron as an approximation to a Bayes optimal discriminant function. IEEE Trans. Neural Netw. **1**(4), 296–298 (1990)
24. A.G. Parlos, B. Fernandez, A.F. Atiya, J. Muthusami, W.K. Tsai, An accelerated learning algorithm for multilayer perceptron networks. IEEE Trans. Neural Netw. **5**(3), 493–497 (1994)
25. E. Frank, M.A. Hall, I.H. Witten, *The WEKA Workbench, Online Appendix for Data Mining: Practical Machine Learning Tools and Techniques*, 4th edn. (Morgan Kaufmann, Cambridge, 2016)

26. J.M. Keller, M.R. Gray, J.A. Givens, A fuzzy k-nearest neighbor algorithm. IEEE Trans. Syst. Man Cybern. **15**(4), 580–585 (1985)
27. J.C. Bezdek, *Pattern recognition with fuzzy objective function algorithms* (Plenum Press, New York, 1981)
28. M. Sarkar, Fuzzy-rough nearest neighbors algorithm. Fuzzy Sets Syst. **158**, 2123–2152 (2007)
29. H. Bian, L. Mazlack, Fuzzy-rough nearest-neighbor classification approach, in *22nd International Conference of the North American Fuzzy Information Processing Society* (IEEE, 2003), pp. 500–505
30. Q. Shen, A. Chouchoulas, A rough-fuzzy approach for generating classification rules. Pattern Recogn. **35**(11), 2425–2438 (2002)
31. R. Jensen, C. Cornelis, Fuzzy-rough nearest neighbour classification and prediction. Theor. Comput. Sci. **412**(42), 5871–5884 (2011)
32. M. Lichman, *UCI Machine Learning Repository* (University of California, School of Information and Computer Science, Irvine, CA, 2013). http://archive.ics.uci.edu/ml
33. R. Jensen, C. Cornelis, Fuzzy-rough nearest neighbour classification. Trans. Rough Sets **XIII**, 56–72 (2011)
34. D.H. Wolpert, Stacked generalization. Neural Netw. **5**(2), 241–259 (1992)
35. A.K. Seewald, How to make stacking better and faster while also taking care of an unknown weakness. In: *Nineteenth International Conference on Machine Learning* (2002), pp. 554–561 (2002)
36. S. le Cessie, J.C. van Houwelingen, Ridge estimators in logistic regression. Appl. Stat. **41**(1), 191–201 (1992)

# Better Performance in Human Action Recognition from Spatiotemporal Depth Information Features Classification

**Naresh Kumar**

**Abstract** The recent revolution of sensor-based depth information opens attracting scope to work for human activity recognition. The activities due to human being can have a great interest in every domain of real life where human is always a major factor. Activity recognition is having a key importance due to its advantages in several domains like surveillance systems at the airport, patient monitoring system, and care of elderly people. The variation in spatial and temporal parameters can present any activity efficiently. In the natural color vision, it is not efficient to give complete information because it represents flatness for every portion of the images. The author proposes the objective of this work to recognize daily life human activities by spatiotemporal depth information. This work is carried out by three phases which comprise preprocessing, feature extraction, and action classification. Actions may be performed by a single person or more than one person at a time. For this purpose, the Kinect sensor is used in the data collection phase. The spatiotemporal depth features are computed for recognition by support vector machine classifier. The research work of this problem is experimented on Intel i5 processor with clock speed 3.1 GHz under the windows 8 environment and processing work is performed by commercial software MATLAB 2015b. There are nine classes of human actions in the database described by RGB-D human activity recognition and video database, Cornell activity datasets, and Berkeley multimodal human action database. The accuracy of nine actions is 90.38%. The research work carried out here proves that using the proposed work, the research community and organizations can get better performance that is tough to achieve through the normal video frames of human activities.

**Keywords** Human action recognition (HAR) · Principal component analysis (PCA) · Spatiotemporal descriptors · Histogram of gradient (HOG) · Support vector machine (SVM)

---

N. Kumar (✉)
Department of Mathematics, Indian Institute of Technology Roorkee, Roorkee, India
e-mail: atrindma@iitr.ac.in



M. Pant et al. (eds.), *Computational Network Application Tools for Performance Management*, Asset Analytics,
https://doi.org/10.1007/978-981-32-9585-8_5

# 1 Introduction

Human is centered objective of all the happenings everywhere. The change in every domain creates keen interest for the researchers and common people to interpret the things. The still images are less promising than image sequences to ensure any prediction in the field of security, surveillance, and patient monitoring. In the context Ye et al.[1] presented a broad review of several metrologies from the depth information for human action recognition.

The sounding features of image sequences are to vary with space and time which becomes a key interest of researches. These features are termed as spatiotemporal features which are described by Harris 3D [2] Cuboid, Hessian, HOF [3], etc. Moreover, we introduced depth features [2, 4–6] also as the major part of this work.

## *1.1 Depth Map Information*

Depth maps are the image frames which have per pixel depth information extracted from natural images; i.e., the pixel value of the object is varying due to the lack of flatness. The varied pixel information in the different plane of the part of any object is classified by its depth information. The depth maps of the images can be created by taking images by different views and angles which become the source of depth image information [6].

Several depth sensors are available in the market to capture depth images, e.g., Kinect SDK launched by Microsoft in the year 2011. Human activities may be categorized in various sub-categories which include pose estimation, gesture classification, single person, and group activities with any object or communication in the context of social media analytics [7].

## *1.2 Research Motivation and Challenges*

Depth data provides the information with minimum noise which enhances the efficiency of the human action recognition system. Depth map-based recognition [1] of human activities opens a new door for researchers as it is being a novel technique of human activity recognition. Working with space–time interest point (STIP) for feature extraction, it creates a huge amount of multidimensional data which is very hard to process without rich processing devices.

The scope of research work is still open due to the lack of literature on depth map-based processing. Comparatively, high accuracy and cost-effectiveness ensure that depth information-based research is highly ranked. Human activity may involve as a single-person activity like gesture or action performed or two-person interaction, or it may also be a group activity as per the context. Our goal is to recognize all these

**Table 1** Depth datasets available on human actions

| Dataset | Modality | Metadata | Action class/ Video Seq. | Description |
|---|---|---|---|---|
| MSR action 3D | Depth map, skeletal joint | 10 subjects, 2–3 repetitions | 20/567 | Game context action, and full body |
| Chaleara multimodal | RGBD, skeletal | 20 subjects, 8–30 repetitions | 20/13558 | Multiple Indian gestures and ground truth |
| UTKinect action | RGBD, skeletal | 10 subjects, 2 repetitions | 10/200 | Indoor actions and variant view point |
| MSR action pair | RGBD, skeletal | 10 subjects, 2–3 repetitions | 12/360 | Action sequences of cues |
| UCLA multiview actions | RGBD, skeletal | 10 subjects, ao 3 view repetitions | 10/1475 | Indoor home activity |
| NTU action dataset | RGBD, Skeletal, Infrared | 40 subjects, 80 views | 60/56880 | Challenging data |
| CAD-60 | RGBD Videos | 4 subjects, 5 views | 12/16S0 | Indoor actions |

ongoing activities with the help of depth image frames taken from a depth camera or depth images created by some other means.

The real-life action recognition becomes an emergent challenge in multimodal group communication when the communication is randomly started and ended by the participant in parallel fashion. How to train the machine to determine the various modes of activities by many persons together. This always requires a multimodal feature descriptor to deal with inter-class ambiguity, intra-class variation, and occlusion. In Table 1, a review of available depth datasets is presented.

Reaming text of the work is organized as follows. The related work and system architecture of the proposed work are explained in Sects. 2 and 3, respectively. Experimental evaluations and result discussion are presented in Sects. 4 and 5. Finally, in Sect. 6, the work is concluded with future directions of natural vision limitations to get resolve by deep learning networks.

## 2 Related Work

Human action recognition attracts researchers till today because of its multimodal complexity due to the several environmental issues. The novel steps in video analytics is feature extraction spatiotemporal interest point (STIP) detector [8] which built a basic building block of interest points by Harris and Forester operators to resolve the occlusion and dynamic cluttered issues of environmental complex background, but this descriptor is not independent of motion, contract, and rotation of image. The spatiotemporal descriptor which is based on 3D gradients [2] optimized the depth parameters of activity analysis.

Key frame-based history of image motion (MHI), energy of image (MEI) [9, 10], for temporal segmentation is introduced which invariant of linear motion for achieving a benchmark for activities in natural vision. Many of the feature extraction techniques for HAR based on depth sequences are new which still require to establish a state of art. Depth map-based activities are resolved by the bag of 3D points which modeled view variant action graph of the human body [2, 11].

Local binary pattern features based on three-view fusion of depth motion map [12] is used recognition the human action. In [2] three views of motion characteristics of actions were used by DMMs and then *l1*-norm based regularisation method is used for classification which gives 90.5% accuracy with efficient computation. Similarly, [13] presents the state of art to project DMMs onto three orthogonal planes from HOG normal is computed for action recognition.

A feature descriptors random occupancy pattern (ROP) [14] which is robust to noise and less sensitive to occlusion and treats depth data as 4D volume [14] which is sampled by sparse coding further to improve the robustness. In [15], depth video-based STIP filter DSTIP is developed after that, spatiotemporal depth cuboid similarity feature (DCSF) is established a benchmark to describe for actions class that adaptable size of 3D cuboids. Histogram of normal orientation [16] in 4D space, time, and spatial geometry of joints gave a new benchmark for changing shape and motion, for activity recognition.

The methods applicable in the joint trajectory of depth sequence are developed [17] which accumulates several cues from sparse coding, max polling, etc. Further, it was introduced the pyramid of adaptive spatial–temporal cue that pertains spatial and temporal orders. Space–time features based on depth map treat the depth images as 2D video features. Several key points-based scale and view-invariant feature extraction techniques have been listed which characterized shape, motion parameters [3, 18] for SIFT, HOG, HOF, STIP and [19] introduced a hierarchical kernel descriptor for extracting layer-by-layer feature extraction.

However, the silhouette of depth data encodes 3D shapes and their geometric estimates simultaneously. In [16], it is resolved the issues of motion estimation at the joint by computing histogram-oriented normal (HON4D) treat the depth map as 4D data composed of shape and spatiotemporal information. The deformable changing structure can be captured easily for both space and time parameters.

After the motivation for 3D information on how computer generates spatial information [4] proposed a descriptor robust to occlusions and view and scale invariant based on $\tau$ test. Template matching transforms the 3D problem to 2D video sequences [10] which makes the projection in 2D plane. The entire video sequence is projected into orthogonal DMMs planes [13] from which histogram of gradient (HOG) is computed from each of the planes. This approach is view independent, but due to noise and occlusions it is hardly reliable. To address these issues, [11, 14] proposed space–time occupancy patterns (STOP) for action representation in depth maps by partitioning 4D video into 4D cells of space and time information.

# 3 Proposed Methodology

## 3.1 Histogram of Depth Map Information

This work is carried out by three phases which comprise preprocessing, feature extraction, and action classification. In the literature, several datasets are available that are presented in Table 1 and the sample the used dataset in this work is presented in Fig. 2a, b. The dataset used in this work is extracted from the standard dataset. In this phase, the features of the image sequence are computed to get classified for the specified objective (Fig. 1).

Feature extraction is the main phase of this work. The region of interest (RoI) is computed for every frame, which is further divided into $8 \times 5$ grids which is presented by grid image in Fig. 1. The architecture of the proposed human action recognition system is given in Fig. 1. Each pixel $p$ in depth map in represented by a triplet as $p = (x, y, d(x, y))$ where $d(x, y)$ is distance between pixel $x$ and $y$ which is set by Kinect sensor. Let $p = (x, y)$ be a point on the surface. We can compute normal vector $N$ at point $p$ by cross-product of tangent vectors to the plane. Tangent vectors $S_x$ and $S_y$ are given by (3.1) and (3.2) (Fig. 2).

$$S_x = \frac{\partial}{\partial x}\begin{bmatrix} x \\ y \\ d(x, y) \end{bmatrix}; \quad S_y = \frac{\partial}{\partial y}\begin{bmatrix} x \\ y \\ d(x, y) \end{bmatrix} \tag{3.1}$$

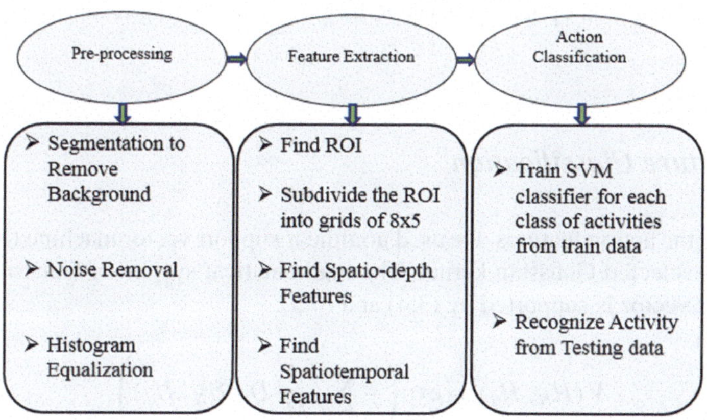


**Fig. 1** Human action recognition system architecture flow diagram

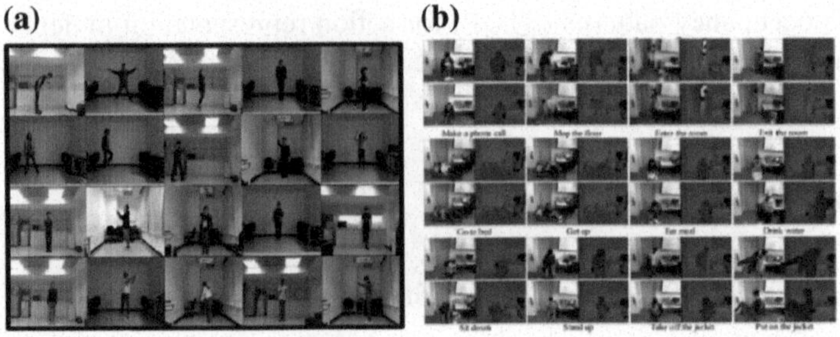

**Fig. 2** **a** Multimedia computing laboratory depth HAR dataset (left). **b** Dataset for human activities samples (right)

$$N = S_x \times S_y \quad \text{i.e. } N = \begin{bmatrix} -\frac{\partial(x,y,d(x,y))}{\partial x} \\ -\frac{\partial(x,y,d(x,y))}{\partial y} \\ 1 \end{bmatrix} \tag{3.2}$$

### 3.1.1 Spatiotemporal Features

The data modality of videos and images demands high-computational resources and storage architectures. One of the feasible efforts [9, 17, 20] in this direction is to use dictionary learning and sparse data which contain salient information. Direct features learning from video data gives the idea of feature descriptors that can extract the features changing with time and space in video analytics. Such features ensure to resolve the specified issues presented in [5, 20–22]. We used dense sampling which can extract the video block of the form $(x, y, t, \sigma, \tau)$, which contains the spatial and temporal information at regular position and scales. In this block, $\sigma$ and $\tau$ denote spatial and temporal parameters. The combination of dense sample features with histogram of oriented optical flow (HOOF) gives a promising result to support this work.

## *3.2 Feature Classification*

To classify the action features, we used nonlinear support vector machine (SVM) for which it is selected Gaussian kernel. The mathematical system of Gaussian kernel for support vector is supported by (3.4) and (3.5).

$$V(H_N, H_d) = \exp\left(-\sum_{c\epsilon C} \frac{1}{M_c} D_c(H_N, H_d)\right) \tag{3.4}$$

$$D_c(H_N, H_d) = \frac{1}{2}\sum_{i=1}^{V}\frac{(h_{\mathrm{Ni}} - h_{\mathrm{di}})^2}{h_{\mathrm{Ni}} + h_{\mathrm{di}}} \tag{3.5}$$

In (3.4) and (3.5), $H_N = \{h_{\mathrm{Ni}}\}$ and $H_d = \{h_{\mathrm{di}}\}$ are histogram of depth feature and dense sampling of optical flow features, respectively. Ac is mean value of the distances between all training samples with vocabulary size $V$ over channel $C$. Dc in (3.5) is the $\chi 2$ distance between the training feature vectors.

# 4 Experiments and Evaluations

The research work of this problem is experimented on Intel i5 processor with clock speed 3.1 GHz under the windows 8 environment and processing work is performed by commercial software MATLAB 2015b.

## *4.1 Data Collection and Preprocessing Phases*

The dataset of 20 videos which comprise nine daily life activities is created by Microsoft Kinect SDK XBOX 360 sensor which is easily available at very economical rate. This dataset is created on four to six persons with their different surrounding conditions.

It is indicated by Fig. 3 the environmental background is encoded red for one person in blue, for another person in green. Segmentation is performed to remove the background component from handshaking Fig. 3a, and then we get Fig. 3b which represents the noise-free human body only after a background removal. Morphological operation is followed by background removal to remove the noise with the opening and closing morphological operations. The effect of noise removal can be observed in Figs. 4b, 5, 6 and 7.

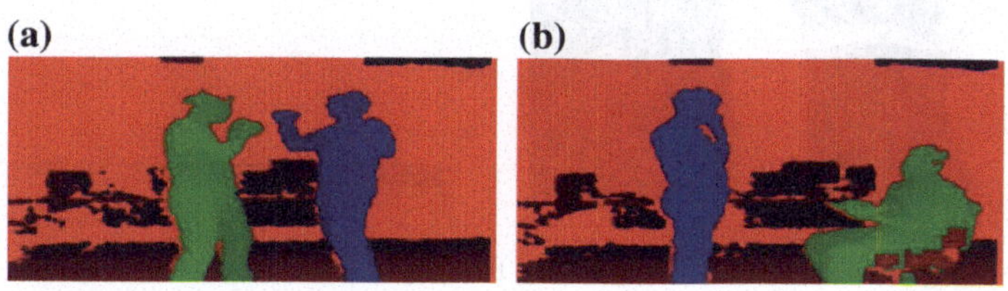


**Fig. 3** **a** Both fighting. **b** Sitting and standing

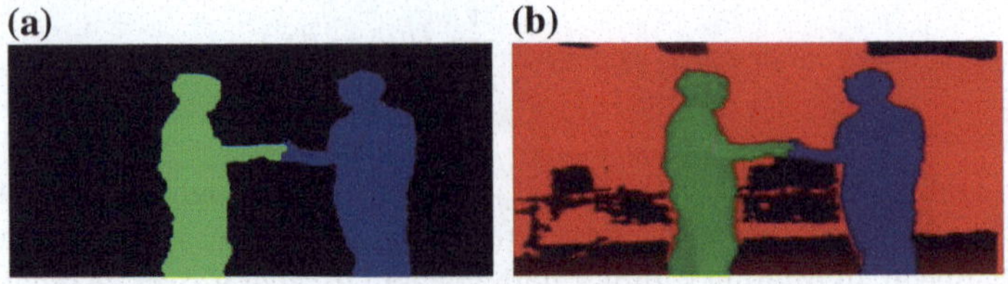


**Fig. 4** **a** Original image of handshaking. **b** Noise-free background removed image of Fig. 4a

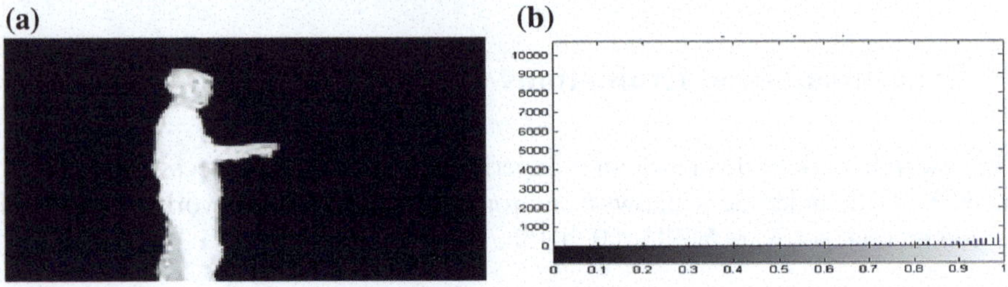


**Fig. 5** **a** Depth of green object (left). **b** Feature green histogram (right)

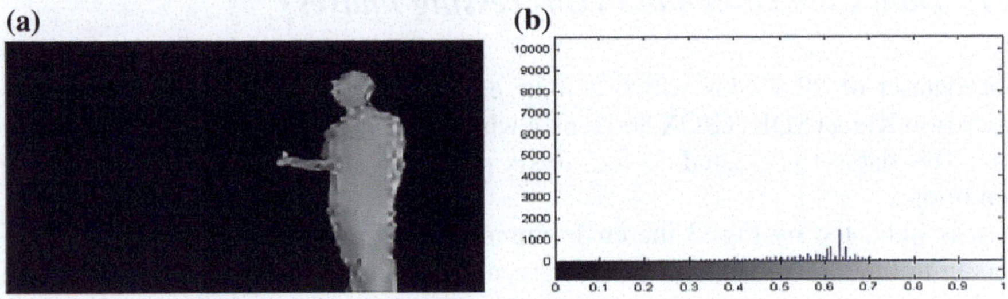


**Fig. 6** **a** Depth map blue object (left). **b** Feature blue histogram (right)

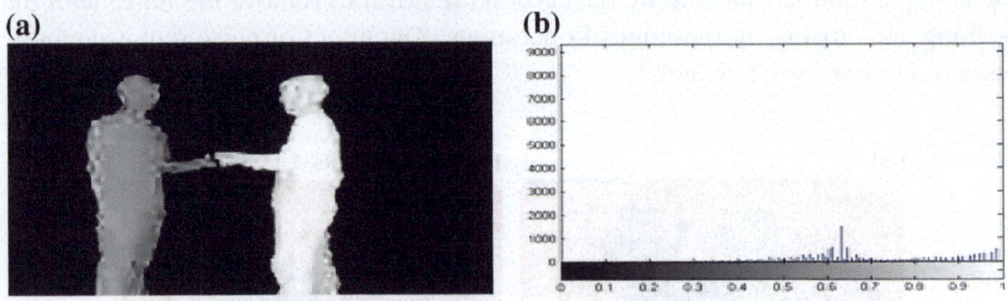


**Fig. 7** **a** Grayscale depth object (left). **b** Feature gray histogram (right)

## 4.2 Feature Extraction for Centroid and Spatiotemporal Points

The enhancement of noise-free objects follows feature extraction phase for spatio-depth and spatiotemporal feature extraction. Region of Interest (ROI) containing the information of actors is segmented into $8 \times 5$ grids. We take five bins and count the number of pixels in each bin of all the grids. Spatiotemporal features are computed as the difference of no. of pixels representing foreground object in several changing modes. Figure 9b represents the outcome features of spatiotemporal parameters (Fig. 8).

This is computed for all activities, in the successive difference of frames. The computation of the histogram of dense sampling of oriented optical flow (HOOF) features highlights this works as a promising accuracy (Fig. 9).

The metadata of feature sets to get classified by support vector machine is given in Table 2. The computation of feature vector utilized 200 grids for per-pixel information. Again in Tables 3 and 4, it is shown that the results of single-person activity like the action of discussing are very low (60%) since such activities are very much similar to other activities. This results the demand to work more efficient feature computation techniques.

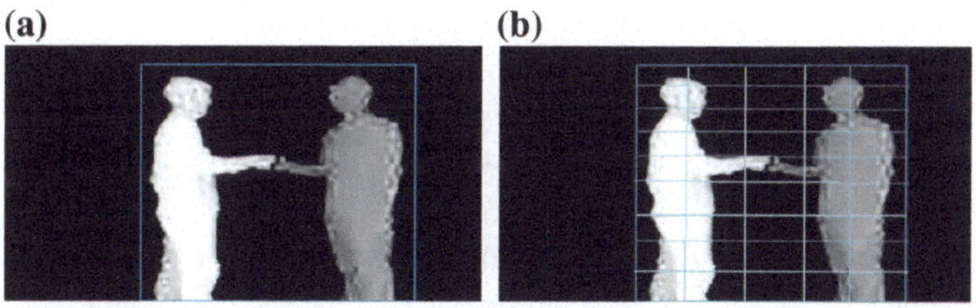


**Fig. 8** **a** RoI handshaking image (left). **b** Grid image (right)

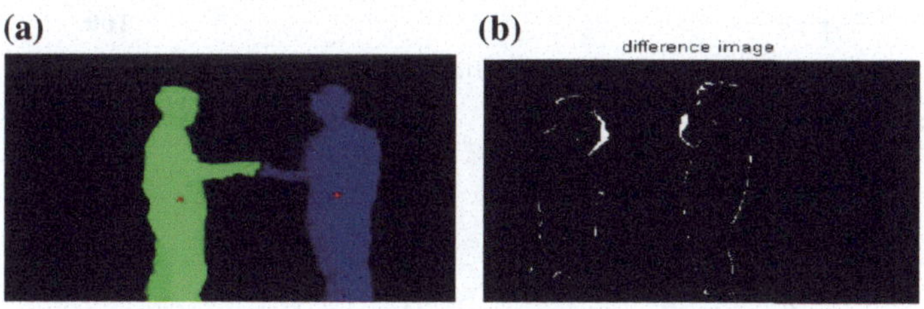


**Fig. 9** **a** Centroid feature of blue and green objects (left). **b** Spatiotemporal features points

## 5 Results and Comparative Analysis

Table 3 presents the confusion matrix of single-person activities such as 'dozing', 'typing', and reading books, etc. From the diagonal matching values of eight actions, it can be observed that some of activities are very hard to distinguish like discussing (6) in which accuracy is 60%; on the other hand, dozing (34) and typing (36) show success benchmark of our results with 100% accuracy.

Similarly, dense sampling of HOOF features is classified for two-person communication activities as represented in Table 2. The activity of passing bottle by person A to person B drinking is misclassified by (3) with waving for bye vice versa waving

**Table 2** Meta data feature vector computation

| Features | Values |
|---|---|
| Avg. depth of blue, green subject | 2 (1 each) |
| Distance between the centroids | 1 |
| No. of pixels in foreground | 1 |
| Frame differencing | 1 |
| ROI grids pixel distribution | 200 (8*5*5) |

**Table 3** Confusion matrix single-person activity

| S. No. | Labeled activity class | No. of video frames | Accuracy (%) |
|---|---|---|---|
| 1 | Dozing | 34 | **100** |
| 2 | Drinking | 35 | 91.4 |
| 3 | Mobile device wait | 30 | 83.3 |
| 4 | Talking phone | 35 | 88.5 |
| 5 | Reading book | 34 | 82.3 |
| 6 | Stretching | 11 | 81.8 |
| 7 | Typing | 35 | **100** |
| 8 | Discussing | 10 | 60 |

| Actions class | 1 | 2 | 3 | 4 | 5 | 6 | 7 | 8 |
|---|---|---|---|---|---|---|---|---|
| 1 | **34** | 0 | 0 | 0 | 0 | 0 | 0 | 0 |
| 2 | 0 | 32 | 0 | 2 | 0 | 1 | 0 | 0 |
| 3 | 0 | 2 | 25 | 1 | 2 | 0 | 0 | 0 |
| 4 | 0 | 3 | 0 | 31 | 1 | 0 | 0 | 0 |
| 5 | 1 | 3 | 0 | 1 | 28 | 1 | 0 | 0 |
| 6 | 0 | 2 | 0 | 0 | 0 | 9 | 0 | 0 |
| 7 | 0 | 0 | 0 | 0 | 0 | 0 | **35** | 0 |
| 8 | 0 | 0 | 0 | 0 | 0 | **4** | 0 | **6** |

**Table 4** Multiple action frame accuracy and confusion matrix

| S. No. | Labeled activity class | No. of video frames | Accuracy (%) |
|---|---|---|---|
| 1 | Fighting | 500 | **100** |
| 2 | Person passes bottle Person B drinks | 385 | 98.7 |
| 3 | Waving bye | 445 | 66.3 |
| 4 | Japanese greetings | 500 | **100** |
| 5 | Handshakes | 500 | 91 |
| 6 | Person A drops object Person B picks | 313 | **100** |
| 7 | Person A reads Person B stands | 301 | 67.8 |
| 8 | Sitting and talking | 724 | 100 |
| 9 | Person A walks to Person B | 400 | 89.7 |

| Actions class | 1 | 2 | 3 | 4 | 5 | 6 | 7 | 8 | 9 |
|---|---|---|---|---|---|---|---|---|---|
| 1 | **500** | 0 | 0 | 0 | 0 | 0 | 0 | 0 | 0 |
| 2 | 0 | **330** | 5 | 0 | 0 | 0 | 0 | 0 | 0 |
| 3 | 0 | 135 | **295** | 0 | 0 | 7 | 0 | 0 | 8 |
| 4 | 0 | 0 | 0 | **500** | 0 | 0 | 0 | 0 | 0 |
| 5 | 45 | 0 | 0 | 0 | **455** | 0 | 0 | 0 | 0 |
| 6 | 0 | 0 | 0 | 0 | 0 | **313** | 0 | 0 | 0 |
| 7 | 72 | 0 | 0 | 1 | 24 | 0 | **294** | 0 | 0 |
| 8 | 0 | 0 | 0 | 0 | 0 | 0 | 0 | **724** | 0 |
| 9 | 0 | 16 | 2 | 0 | 23 | 0 | 0 | 0 | **359** |

bye action is misclassified by (135) with bottle passing and drinking between two persons A and B (Table 3).

The action of handshaking is misclassified by (45) with fighting. The action of walking person A to B is misclassified with person A walking and person B drinking, waving bye and handshakes by (16), (2), and (23), respectively. Except all these scope of future research for this research our work is achieving novelty to recognize the actions of fighting, person A drops to person B picks and sitting and talking by 100% accuracy (Table 4). As represented in Table 3, 'dozing' and 'typing' are the most successfully (100%) classified single-person activities. Similarily, the activity 'discussing' requires more efforts to recognize as labeled row-8 have only 60% performance. The bold figures in Table 4 denote the better performance of our model for the specified multiple-person activities.

## 6 Conclusion and Future Directions

The conclusion can be drawn as a result of this research work and evaluations of depth map-based human activities recognition. The rate of recognition is higher than natural color vision-based recognition and computationally efficient for feature extraction. The standard SVM $x$-fold classifier with Gaussian kernel is used which assumed better than all other Bayesian classifiers, neural network, and decision tree for the feature classification.

The proposed architecture is invariant of lighting and illumination changes of environment. Moreover, we get 3D information which is not affected by varying texture and color. Deep learning features exploration for the group activities in unconstraint environment inspires this research for future directions.

The deep learning techniques are outperforming against highly complex and weakly unsupervised data. Moreover, this is highly stressed to cope up with dimensionality and various complexities of multiple actions in video data by exploiting deep network libraries with the help of recently developed fast optimization technologies efficient.

## References

1. M. Ye, Q. Zhang, L. Wang, J. Zhu, R. Yang, J. Gall, A survey on human motion analysis from depth data, in *Time-of-Flight and Depth Imaging. Sensors, Algorithms, and Applications* (Springer, Berlin, Heidelberg, 2013), pp. 149–187
2. C. Chen, K. Liu, N. Kehtarnavaz, Real-time human action recognition based on depth motion maps. J. Real-Time Image Proc. **12**(1), 155–163 (2016)
3. D.G. Lowe, Distinctive image features from scale-invariant keypoints. Int. J. Comput. Vision **60**(2), 91–110 (2004)
4. C. Lu, J. Jia, C.K. Tang, Range-sample depth feature for action recognition, in *Proceedings of the IEEE Conference on Computer Vision and Pattern Recognition* (2014), pp. 772–779

5. X. Yang, Y. Tian, Super normal vector for human activity recognition with depth cameras. IEEE Trans. Pattern Anal. Mach. Intell. **39**(5), 1028–1039 (2017)
6. C. Chen, R. Jafari, N. Ketharnavaz, A survey of depth and inertial sensor fusion for human action recognition. Multimedia Tools Appl. **76**(3), 4405–4425 (2017)
7. N. Kumar, A scheme of visual object tracking for human activity recognition in social media analytics, *in International Conference on Information, Communication and Computing Technology* (Springer, Singapore, 2017), pp. 194–204
8. I. Laptev, On space-time interest points. Int. J. Comput. Vis. **64**(2–3), 107–123 (2005)
9. G. Somasundaram, A. Cherian, V. Morellas, N. Papanikolopoulos, Action recognition using global spatio-temporal features derived from sparse representations. Comput. Vis. Image Underst. **123**, 1–13 (2014)
10. A.F. Bobick, J.W. Davis, The recognition of human movement using temporal templates. IEEE Trans. Pattern Anal. Mach. Intell. **23**(3), 257–267 (2001)
11. A.W. Vieira, E.R. Nascimento, G.L. Oliveira, Z. Liu, M.F. Campos, Stop: Space-time occupancy patterns for 3D action recognition from depth map sequences, in *Iberoamerican Congress on Pattern Recognition* (Springer, Berlin, Heidelberg, September 2012), pp. 252–259
12. C. Chen, R. Jafari, N. Kehtarnavaz, Action recognition from depth sequences using depth motion maps-based local binary patterns, in *2015 IEEE Winter Conference on Applications of Computer Vision (WACV)* (IEEE, New York, January 2015), pp. 1092–1099
13. X. Yang, C. Zhang, Y. Tian, Recognizing actions using depth motion maps-based histograms of oriented gradients, in *Proceedings of the 20th ACM International Conference on Multimedia* (ACM, New York, October 2012), pp. 1057–1060
14. J. Wang, Z. Liu, J. Chorowski, Z. Chen, Y. Wu, Robust 3D action recognition with random occupancy patterns, in *Computer Vision–ECCV 2012* (Springer, Berlin, Heidelberg, 2012), pp. 872–885
15. L. Xia, J.K. Aggarwal, Spatio-temporal depth cuboid similarity feature for activity recognition using depth camera, in *Proceedings of the IEEE Conference on Computer Vision and Pattern Recognition* (2013), pp. 2834–2841
16. O. Oreifej, Z. Liu, Hon4d: Histogram of oriented 4D normals for activity recognition from depth sequences, in *Proceedings of the IEEE Conference on Computer Vision and Pattern Recognition* (2013), pp. 716–723
17. X. Yang, Y. Tian, Super normal vector for activity recognition using depth sequences, in *Proceedings of the IEEE Conference on Computer Vision and Pattern Recognition* (2014), pp. 804–811
18. I. Laptev, M. Marszalek, C. Schmid, B. Rozenfeld, Learning realistic human actions from movies, in *IEEE Conference on Computer Vision and Pattern Recognition, 2008. CVPR 2008* (IEEE, New York, June 2008), pp. 1–8
19. L. Bo, K. Lai, X. Ren, D. Fox, Object recognition with hierarchical kernel descriptors, in *2011 IEEE Conference on Computer Vision and Pattern Recognition (CVPR)* (IEEE, New York, June 2011), pp. 1729–1736
20. Q.V. Le, W.Y. Zou, S.Y. Yeung, A.Y. Ng, Learning hierarchical invariant spatio-temporal features for action recognition with independent subspace analysis, in *2011 IEEE Conference on Computer Vision and Pattern Recognition (CVPR)* (IEEE, New York, June 2011), pp. 3361–3368
21. A. González, D. Vázquez, S. Ramos, A.M. López, J. Amores, Spatiotemporal stacked sequential learning for pedestrian detection, in *Iberian Conference on Pattern Recognition and Image Analysis* (Springer International Publishing, Berlin, June 2015), pp. 3–12
22. Y. Guo, Y. Li, Z. Shao, RRV: A Spatiotemporal Descriptor for Rigid Body Motion Recognition. arXiv preprint arXiv:1606.05729 (2016)

# Selecting Appropriate Multipath Routing in Wireless Sensor Networks for Improvisation of System's Efficiency and Performance

**Sukhchandan Randhawa and Sushma Jain**

**Abstract** Wireless sensor networks (WSNs) comprise high-density tiny-sized sensor nodes with a restricted range of communication, whose main task is to sense the target phenomena. These nodes are generally of small size and have computation, communication and sensing capabilities. However, sensor nodes have limited bandwidth, power, memory, processing resources and limited lifetime which impose challenges in design of efficient and performance-based communication protocol. Most of the existing multipath routing techniques have been designed on the basis of single-path routing protocol without handling network congestion. In this scenario, a single-path routing is not efficient and is prone to failure, due to the low battery power constraint which effects network lifetime. To solve this problem, the multipath routing technique is used nowadays which improves network lifetime, load balancing and data reliability. Researchers still find it difficult to choose the most appropriate and efficient multipath routing protocol from the existing research work of WSNs. This research work carried out depicts a broad methodical literature analysis of multipath routing in the area of WSNs in specific. The methodical analysis of multipath routing includes multipath routing protocols, their benefits, quality of service (QoS) parameters and also highlights the objective behind the development of each protocol category. Detailed analysis of this research area will assist the researchers to analyze the significant attributes of multipath techniques and to choose the most appropriate technique for multipath routing. Future research issues and orientations have also been presented in this research work.

**Keywords** Multipath routing · Wireless sensor networks · Networking · Quality of service · Routing

---

S. Randhawa (✉) · S. Jain
Thapar University, Patiala, India
e-mail: sukhchandan.95@gmail.com

S. Jain
e-mail: ssjain.thapar@gmail.com



M. Pant et al. (eds.), *Computational Network Application Tools for Performance Management*, Asset Analytics,
https://doi.org/10.1007/978-981-32-9585-8_6

## 1 Introduction

Wireless sensor networks (WSNs) consist of a large number of sensor nodes deployed in the region of interest for specific applications. These nodes are generally of small size and have computation, communication and sensing capabilities [1]. However, sensor nodes have limited bandwidth, power, memory, processing resources, and limited lifetime which impose challenges in the design of efficient communication protocol [2].

Most of the existing multipath routing techniques have been designed on the basis of the single-path routing protocol without handling network congestion [3]. In this scenario, single-path routing is not efficient and is prone to failure, due to the low battery power constraint which effects network lifetime and reduces the throughput in critical situations.

To cope up with the limitations of single-path, multipath routing has become a promising technique nowadays, which improves network lifetime, load balancing, and data reliability. This technique identifies multiple routes to transfer data from source to destination, which improves throughput and robustness of network transfer. Further, energy can be utilized efficiently by balancing the load across WSN which further improves network lifetime. The following are key benefits of multipath routing [4–7]:

(a) **Data Reliability**: In WSNs, reliable transmission of data is a challenging task. For reliable data delivery, multipath routing prevents node or link failure via two approaches: (i) transmitting multiple copies of the similar data on multiple routes to guarantee packet recovery from route failure and (ii) coding-based approach. In this approach, data packets are generated after adding some extra information and are transferred over different routes. At sink node, original packets are reconstructed based on extra information.

(b) **Increasing Fault Tolerance**: Energy efficient and reliable data delivery is required in such environments, where sensor nodes are equipped with low battery power. It results in additional routing overhead in case of node failure to identify the other possible routes which further results in higher energy consumption. To improve network lifetime, fault tolerance becomes an important aspect of routing protocol and can be achieved through multipath routing by transferring redundant information from source to destination through alternative paths which lead to minimum disruption of communication.

(c) **Load Balancing**: Network congestion can be easily avoided by performing load balancing of network traffic. In high-data-rate applications, network congestion is produced due to larger traffic load which affects the performance of WSNs. To improve network performance, network traffic is divided over many routes through multipath routing to decrease the chances of network congestion which leads to larger network lifetime and reduced energy consumption.

(d) **QoS Improvement**: An effective design of multipath routing protocol comprises of important QoS parameters such as end-to-end latency, data delivery ratio, and network throughput. QoS-based multipath routing protocol can easily distribute the network traffic by discovering different routes. For example, deadline-oriented data packets can be sent via higher data rate paths with minimum delay.

## 2 Related Survey

Gopi [8], Masdari and Tanabi [9], and Sha et al. [10] have done an innovative literature review in the field of multipath routing. Gopi [8] and Masdari and Tanabi [9] studied the problem of multipath routing in WSNs and presented a comprehensive taxonomy on the existing multipath routing protocols. Further, this research work explored the design and operation of different multipath protocols, and their performance has been compared on the basis of parameters like path disjointness, energy efficiency, delay, fault tolerance, and reliability.

Sha et al. [10] studied various multipath routing protocols and categorized into three classes: *non-infrastructure-based, infrastructure-based,* and *coding-based.* There is a necessity of methodical literature survey to evaluate and integrate the existing research presented in this field.

The rest of the paper is structured as follows: Sect. 2 describes the basic elements in designing multipath routing protocols. Section 3 presents the taxonomy of multipath routing protocols along with their comparison based on QoS. Section 4 classifies the multipath routing protocols into various categories. Section 5 concludes the paper and presents future research directions in multipath routing protocol.

## 3 Basic Elements in Designing Multipath Routing Protocols

Each multipath routing protocol comprises of many components to design multiple routes and transfer data over-identified routes. The following are the important components of an efficient multipath routing protocol [11–13]:

(a) **Path Discovery**: Different routes from source to destination are identified by making routing decisions using different parameters. Discovered paths can be classified as *partially disjoint, link-disjoint,* and *node-disjoint paths.*

- **Node-Disjoint Multipath**: There is no common node among the discovered paths, so one path is independent of another path failure. It offers larger aggregated network data, but it is difficult to identify the larger path due to the random deployment of nodes.
- **Link-Disjoint Multipath**: There is no link sharing among the routes, but some common intermediate nodes can be shared. Node failure in shared path can affect the other paths which use shared nodes due to interference.

- **Partially Disjoint Multipath**: There may be nodes or links can be shared among different routes. Node or link failure can affect many common routes.

(b) **Path Selection and Traffic Distribution**: It is also important to select the paths from total discovered paths based on the performance demands of the intended application. Further, multipath routing protocol distributes traffic over selected paths using different traffic management methods.

(c) **Path Maintenance**: Multipath routing protocol selects different optimal paths in case of path failure and discovery of path is started in three scenarios: (i) if all the active paths have failed, (ii) if certain number of active paths have failed, and (iii) if active path fails. Discovery of path after the failure of active node affects network performance and increases overhead.

# 4 Taxonomy of Multipath Routing Protocols

The comprehensive classification of the multipath routing protocols is shown in Fig. 1 and existing multipath routing protocols are classified into four categories *namely energy efficient, data transmission reliability, load balancing,* and *alternate path routing.*

## *4.1 Energy-Efficient Multipath Routing Protocols*

The main aim of energy-efficient multipath routing protocols is to choose the path which has minimum energy consumption. Different nodes have different energy usage, which creates problem while selecting the path because nodes with minimum energy value will drain out quickly and it affects the performance of network due to early death of nodes [14]. The protocols in this category are described [15–18] as follows:

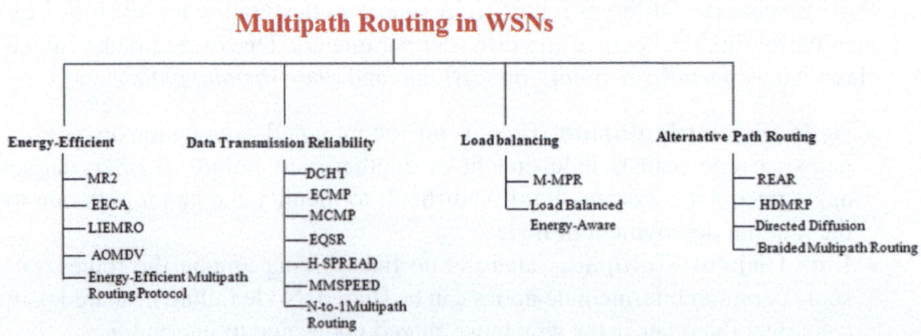


**Fig. 1** Taxonomy of multipath routing protocols

(a) **Maximally Radio-Disjoint Multipath Routing (MR2)**: It offers required bandwidth to multimedia applications via non-interfering paths which improve network lifetime. Only one route is created for a particular session using incremental approach. In case of reduction in bandwidth or network congestion, an additional path can be created. Only selected nodes will be in active state while other nodes (free or idle) will put into passive state (sleep mode) that saves energy and results in improved network lifetime.
(b) **Energy-Efficient and Collision-Aware Multipath Routing Protocol (EECA)**: To avoid collisions among discovered routes, broadcast nature of wireless communication is used in EECA. Further, EECA regulates transmitting power of node with the assistance of information of node position which reduces energy consumption, improves average packet delivery ratio, and reduces average end-to-end delay. It is assumed that the location of destination node is also known by each node.
(c) **Low-Interference Energy-Efficient Multipath Routing Protocol (LIEMRO)**: It identifies the multiple interference-minimized node-disjoint routes between source to destination to improve latency, network lifetime and packet delivery ratio. Further, based on quality of every path LIEMRO distributes traffic over multipaths through load balancing. Multiple interference-minimized node-disjoint routes reduce route coupling effect.
(d) **Energy-Efficient Multipath Routing Protocol**: This protocol is used to identify multiple node-disjoint paths between source and destination. Ad hoc on-demand distance vector multipath (AODVM) approach is used in this protocol to construct the route using overhearing neighboring nodes' transmissions, in which receiver constantly remains in the receive state and leads to energy efficiency.
(e) **Energy-Efficient Adaptive Multipath Routing**: This protocol using minimum energy routes in which energy of nodes is drained out quickly and finds alternate paths, which also saves energy consumption.

## *4.2 Data Transmission Reliability Multipath Routing Protocols*

To improve the reliability of the network, multiple copies of the same data should be sent through different paths and redundancy of data improves the probability of data delivery. The protocols in this category are described [14, 15, 19–28, 29] as follows:

(a) **H-SPREAD**: This protocol identifies the extra paths and dividing the message into small messages using "one message per node" property. Every time neighborhood will be informed about the identification of new alternate path and increases the number of disjoint paths per node which improves message delivery ratio.

(b) **N-to-1 Multipath Routing Protocol**: This protocol identifies node-disjoint multipaths between source and destination and tree is traversed to transmit data which improves reliability of network without focusing on energy consumption.
(c) **Multipath Multispeed Protocol (MMSPEED)**: SPEED-based protocol creates more than one path from source to destination and offers multispeed transmission. An additional path and QoS speed can be set to improve the network performance for every speed. To avoid congestion and reduce the packet loss rate, MMSPEED sends packets by considering the end delay parameter. Further, this protocol offers multiple delivery speed options for timely delivery of packets.
(d) **Multi-constrained QoS Multipath Routing (MCMP)**: This protocol considers QoS requirements such as reliability and delay while transferring data from source to destination through braided routes. This protocol selects path with minimum number of hops for data transmission to save energy consumption. Further, MCMP reduces overhead for resource-limited sensor nodes and provides required level of QoS.
(e) **Energy Constrained Multipath Routing (ECMP)**: This protocol is an extension of MCMP which uses geo-spatial path selection constraints to optimize energy consumption. ECMP chooses a route which has maximum energy efficiency and minimum number of hops and fulfills QoS requirements.
(f) **Delay-Constrained High-Throughput Protocol for Multipath Transmission (DCHT)**: For multipath video streaming over WSN, DCHT is used in which multiple disjoint paths are utilized to improve throughput and reliability of network.
(g) **Energy-Efficient and QoS-based Multipath Routing Protocol (EQSR)**: This protocol uses the concept of service differentiation to transfer high traffic over the network by balancing energy consumption and maximizes network lifetime and reduces end-to-end delay. EQSR predicts the best next hop through the paths construction phase using signal-to-noise ratio, node available buffer size, and residual energy.

## *4.3 Load Balancing-Based Multipath Routing Protocols*

The main goal of load balancing-based multipath routing protocols is to optimize network traffic and divert traffic through alternate paths when link becomes over-utilized to avoid congestion and bottlenecks. The protocols in this category are described [15, 24, 30] as follows:

(a) **Meshed Multipath Routing (M-MPR)**: In [31], M-MPR-based protocol is proposed to provide many options to transfer the data packet. Some mobile nodes are used to broadcast the information about the location of node. A query message is used to identify the meshed routes. A receiver replies to sender with confirmation message after receiving the query. Every receiver node can receive a maximum of two queries to avoid loops in meshed routes.

(b) **Load Balanced Energy-Aware**: This protocol uses poll–reply communication model to transfer data and balance load efficiently. Minimal hop distance-based multiple paths are constructed from source to destination while poll messages are flooded and receiver sends the acknowledgement. Further, mesh structure is used for multipath routing for data reply to reduce network congestion.

## 4.4 Alternative Path Routing Protocols

To increase resiliency to route failures, alternative multipath routing can be used. Alternative multipath routing discovers and maintains multiple paths between the source and destination. If a path is failed during transmission, then alternative path can be used to provide fault tolerance. The protocols in this category are described [13, 14, 19, 20, 32] as follows:

(a) **Directed Diffusion**: This protocol offers support for source node to broadcast a query toward the intermediate nodes for data transfer. In this protocol, every node is aware of data transmission and interprets data of their interest without forwarding directly to next nodes.

(b) **Braided Multipath Routing Protocol**: This protocol transfers data along routes and constructs small alternate paths in case of failure, and it is also called braided multipath. Alternate paths do no involve any node from main path for transferring data from source to destination.

(c) **Reliable Energy-Aware Routing Protocol (REAR)**: Routing paths are created using residual energy capacity of every node to improve reliability of data transfer. After successful transfer of data, REAR provides acknowledgement.

(d) **HDMRP: An Efficient Fault-Tolerant Multipath Routing**: In this protocol, root neighbors are called *sub-roots* while sink neighbors are called *root nodes*. To construct multiple energy-node-disjoint paths in this protocol, route request (RREQ) message propagation is used. Routing table is also maintained by every non-root node to store record of every discovered path. Master nodes use controlled intersection by permitting them to forward numerous RREQ messages to their neighbors.

## 4.5 QoS-Based Comparison of Multipath Routing Protocols

The existing multipath routing protocols have been compared based on different QoS parameters (path disjointedness, energy efficiency, delay, fault tolerance, and reliability) as described in Table 1.

**Table 1** QoS-based comparison of multipath routing protocols

| Protocols | Path disjointedness | Energy-efficient | Delay | Fault tolerance | Reliability |
|---|---|---|---|---|---|
| H-SPREAD | Node-disjoint | No | No | No | Yes |
| N-to-1 | Node-disjoint | No | No | No | Yes |
| MMSPEED | Partially disjoint | No | Yes | No | Yes |
| MCMP | Partially disjoint | No | Yes | No | Yes |
| ECMP | Partially disjoint | Yes | Yes | No | Yes |
| DCHT | Node-disjoint | No | Yes | No | Yes |
| EQSR | Node-disjoint | Yes | Yes | Yes | No |
| M-MPR | Node-disjoint | No | No | No | No |
| LBEA | Partially disjoint | Yes | No | No | Yes |
| REAR | Node-disjoint | Yes | No | No | Yes |
| Directed diffusion | Node-disjoint | Yes | No | Yes | No |
| HDMRP | Node-disjoint | No | No | Yes | No |

# 5 Classification of Multipath Routing Protocols

The multipath routing protocols have been classified into three categories which are based on infrastructure, non-infrastructure, and coding as shown in Fig. 2.

## *5.1 Infrastructure-Based Multipath Routing Protocols*

This protocol constructs and maintains the multiple paths from source to destination, and there is a need of a particular topology to create an efficient path. For example, to create a multipath in spanning tree, in which tree is traversed to discover multiple paths. Node-disjoint multiple paths are identified based on position, location,

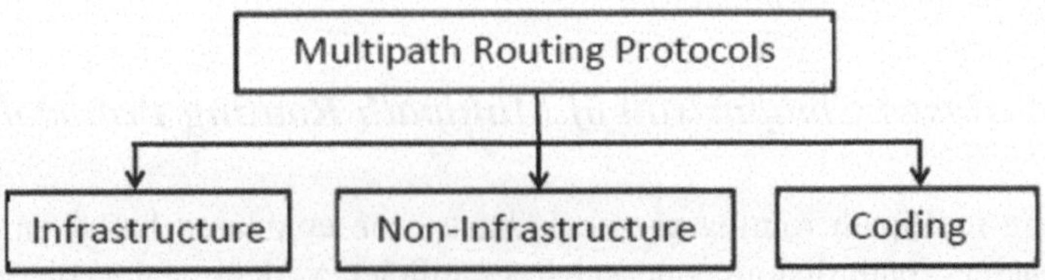


**Fig. 2** Classification of multipath routing protocols

and capability of a node to avoid collision. It also provides alternative route which can reduce failure recovery time. This protocol is categorized into three categories: *energy-aware (already discussed in Sect. 3.1), hierarchy-based,* and *ant-based* which are described as follows:

(a) **Hierarchy-Based Multipath Routing Protocols**: These protocols construct the infrastructure in which effective multipaths are discovered by creating hierarchical relationship. Wang et al. [33] developed a protocol which uses set of relay nodes to improve reliability of data. Based on the position of node in the hierarchy, relay nodes are selected. Further, it avoids the bottleneck nodes which have minimum energy efficiency to improve throughput of network.
(b) **Ant-Based Multipath Routing Protocols**: The ants have capability to identify the shortest path between then nest and food source. In [34], the author proposed AntNet algorithm (MR-ACS)-based multipath routing protocol, in which ants search the path in parallel and *forward ants* applies meta-heuristic approach to middle nodes to construct the paths. Ant ignores the middle node if it is visited by some other node and searches for other nodes; otherwise, ant checks the closeness of sensor node to the sink and pheromone is updated accordingly. De et al. [35] proposed an ant colony optimization and dynamic clustering-based multipath routing protocol to identify the multipath through three phases: (i) in the first phase, based on signal strength and residual energy, cluster head (CH) is selected, (ii) ant-based approach is used to identify the path between sink node and CH in the second phase, and (iii) CH selects the dynamic route for transferring the data in the final phase.

## 5.2 *Non-infrastructure-Based Multipath Routing Protocols*

Those protocols which construct multipaths to transmit data from source to destination without considering any infrastructure are called non-infrastructure multipath routing protocols. Every intermediate node uses local information to make decisions to transmit data instead of finding prior information of the next hop. Data can be transmitted to other nodes also, instead of sink node because node makes its own decision about forwarding packets, but packet will always be forwarded toward the direction of sink.

This type of routing has many benefits: (i) path is created while forwarding the packet, so there is no need of path maintenance, (ii) data is transmitted to the destination using randomized routing mechanism to improve load balancing, and (iii) dynamic packet state is used for transfer of data in which every data packet contains an important information about conditions of network. Geography-based multipath routing protocol considers the information about location of node.

The position of destination node, neighboring node, and source node is used to make routing decision. Further, when data packet is received by intermediate node, then it will forward the data packet to the neighbor node which is closest to the destination.

### *5.3 Coding-Based Multipath Routing Protocols*

Coding-based routing uses encryption and decryption techniques to provide the security to the data packets transfers over the network. At source node, the data packets are divided into fragments and add redundancy to the fragments before transferring through the discovered paths. After receiving the required number of fragments, the original data will be reconstructed at the destination using decoding process. Different types of coding schemes are: *XOR-based coding, network coding,* and *erasure coding* with different efficiency of compression and decompression.

In [35], authors proposed erasure coding-based multipath routing protocol uses on-demand routing algorithm to create a path from source to destination whenever is required which leads to energy saving. Further, message will broadcast over the network to create multipaths. Destination node replies with route reply message when it receives the request message.

In [36], network coding-based multipath routing protocol is proposed to improve data security and reliability. Further, based on better coding opportunity and path reliability, paths are switched dynamically which improve the network throughput. In [20], another multipath routing protocol is proposed to improve network lifetime. Similar coding technique is used to transmit data as in REER but along with energy efficient technique. In this technique, two batteries are used and one battery can get a chance to recover during rest period, which improves energy savings.

## 6 Conclusions: Future Research Directions

The research papers have been studied on multipath routing from existing research work in WSNs. In this research paper, the results have been analyzed in various ways like types of multipath routing protocols and QoS-based comparison of multipath routing protocols have been presented. Contrast and assessment of types of multipath routing protocols in WSN can aid to select the adequate technique. Possible future directions can be:

- Due to the availability of fewer resources at each node, there is a need of proper deployment of network in challenging and hostile environments, frequent changing network topology, and providing required level of fault tolerance.
- Message broadcasting or flooding to the whole network introduces large communication overhead.

- Sending the same data packet from different discovered paths consumes a lot of energy at each data routing node and increases the network traffic significantly.
- Energy-efficient multipath routing protocols are prone to malicious attacks.
- Non-infrastructure-based multipath routing protocols provide a high rate of reliability in the presence of channel errors; however, they do not provide a way to detect the failed nodes.
- In the coding-based multipath routing protocols, simultaneous transmission of data from node-disjoint paths causes high data packet loss and affects the transmission performance.
- Failure in the consecutive nodes due to several obstacles can decrease the effectiveness of the coding scheme.

## References


1. M.Z. Hasan, H. Al-Rizzo, F. Al-Turjman, Survey on multipath routing protocols for QoS assurances in real-time wireless multimedia sensor networks. IEEE Commun. Surv. Tutor. **31**(3), 32–54 (2017)
2. J. Jinfang, G. Han, H. Guo, L. Shu, J.J. Rodrigues, Geographic multipath routing based on geospatial division in duty-cycled underwater wireless sensor networks. J. Netw. Comput. Appl. **59**, 4–13 (2016)
3. H. Junxiao, O. Yang, Globally-aware allocation of limited bandwidth in multipath routing based on queueing performance, in *2017 IEEE Wireless Communications and Networking Conference (WCNC)* (IEEE, New York, 2017), pp. 1–6
4. S. Yanjing, J. Sun, F. Zhao, Z. Hu, Delay constraint multipath routing for wireless multimedia ad hoc networks. Int. J. Commun. Syst. **29**(1), 210–225 (2016)
5. S.K. Singh, T. Das, A. Jukan, A survey on internet multipath routing and provisioning. IEEE Commun. Surv. Tutorials. **17**(4), 2157–2175 (2015)
6. S. Sharma, S.K. Jena, Cluster based multipath routing protocol for wireless sensor networks. ACM SIGCOMM Comput. Commun. Rev. **45**(2), 14–20 (2015)
7. S. Sarkar, R. Datta, A secure and energy-efficient stochastic multipath routing for self-organized mobile ad hoc networks. Ad Hoc Netw. **37**, 209–227 (2016)
8. P. Gopi, Multipath routing in wireless sensor networks: A survey and analysis. IOSR J. Comput. Eng. **16**(4), 27–34 (2014)
9. M. Masdari, M. Tanabi, Multipath routing protocols in wireless sensor networks: A survey and analysis. Int. J. Futur. Gener. Commun. Netw. **6**(6), 181–192 (2013)
10. K. Sha, J. Gehlot, R. Greve, Multipath routing techniques in wireless sensor networks: A survey. Wirel. Pers. Commun. 1–23 (2013)
11. H. Al-Hamadi, R. Chen, Redundancy management of multipath routing for intrusion tolerance in heterogeneous wireless sensor networks. IEEE Trans. Netw. Serv. Manage. **10**(2), 189–203 (2013)
12. P.V. Krishna, S. Vankadara, G. Vedha, A. Bhiwal, A.S. Chawla, Quality-of-service-enabled ant colony-based multipath routing for mobile ad hoc networks. IET Commun. **6**(1), 76–83 (2012)
13. L. Wang, Y. Yang, W. Zhao, Network coding-based multipath routing for energy efficiency in wireless sensor networks. EURASIP J. Wireless Commun. Netw. **1**, 115 (2012)
14. B. Deb, S. Bhatnagar, B. Nath, ReInForM: Reliable information forwarding using multiple paths in sensor networks, in *28th Annual IEEE International Conference on Local Computer Networks, 2003. LCN'03. Proceedings* (IEEE, New York, 2003), pp. 406–415
15. A. Premita, M. Katiyar, A review on power efficient energy- aware routing protocol for wireless sensor networks. Int. J. Eng. Res. Technol. (IJERT) (2012)

16. M. Maimour, Maximally radio-disjoint multipath routing for wireless multimedia sensor networks, in *Proceedings of the 4th ACM Workshop on Wireless Multimedia Networking and Performance Modeling* (ACM, New York, 2008), pp. 26–31
17. M. Radi, D. Behnam, A.R. Shukor, A.B. Kamalrulnizam LIEMRO: A Low-Interference energy-efficient multipath routing protocol for improving QoS in event-based wireless sensor networks, in *2010 Fourth International Conference on Sensor Technologies and Applications (SENSORCOMM)* (IEEE, New York, 2010), pp. 551–557
18. Y. Ming Lu, W.S.W. Vincent, An energy-efficient multipath routing protocol for wireless sensor networks. Int. J. Commun. Syst. **20**(3),747–766 (2007)
19. B. Yahya, B.-O. Jalel, REER: Robust and energy efficient multipath routing protocol for wireless sensor networks, in *Global Telecommunications Conference, 2009. GLOBECOM* 2009 (IEEE, New York, 2009), pp. 1–7
20. W.B. Jaballah, N. Tabbane, Multi path multi speed contention window adapter. Int. J. Comput. Sci. Netw. Secur. **9**(2), 113–118 (2009)
21. W. Lou, Y. Kwon, H-SPREAD: A hybrid multipath scheme for secure and reliable data collection in wireless sensor networks. IEEE Trans. Veh. Technol. **55**(4), 1320–1330 (2006)
22. A.R. Rezaie, M. Mirnia, CMQ: Clustering based multipath routing algorithm to improving QoS in wireless sensor networks. Int. J. Comput. Sci. Issues **3**, 156–160 (2012)
23. F. Emad, C.-G. Lee, E. Ekici, MMSPEED: Multipath Multi-SPEED protocol for QoS guarantee of reliability and timeliness in wireless sensor networks. IEEE Trans. Mob. Comput. **5**(6), 738–754 (2006)
24. R. Sumathi, M.G. Srinivas, A survey of QoS based routing protocols for wireless sensor networks. J. Inf. Process. Syst. **8**(4), 589–602 (2012)
25. A. Jayashree, G.S. Biradar, V.D. Mytri, Review of multipath routing protocols in wireless multimedia sensor network—A Survey. Int. J. Sci. Eng. Res. **3**(7), 1–9 (2012)
26. S. Li, C.L. Raghu Neelisetti, A. Lim, Delay-constrained high throughput protocol for multipath transmission over wireless multimedia sensor networks, in *2008 International Symposium on a World of Wireless, Mobile and Multimedia Networks, WoWMoM 2008* (IEEE, New York, 2008), pp. 1–8
27. A. Ghaffari, N. Firuz, H.R. Bannaeian, Remp: Reliable and energy balancing multi-path routing algorithm for wireless sensor networks. World Appl. Sci. J. **15**(5), 737–744 (2011)
28. R. Vidhyapriya, P.T. Vanathi, Energy efficient adaptive multipath routing for wireless sensor networks. IAENG Int. J. Comput. Sci. **34**(1), 56–64 (2007)
29. X. Hong, M. Gerla, H. Wang, L. Clare, Load balanced, energy-aware communications for mars sensor networks, in *Aerospace Conference Proceedings, 2002*, vol 3 (IEEE, New York, 2002), pp. 3–3
30. P. Hurni, T. Braun, Energy-efficient multi-path routing in wireless sensor networks, in *International Conference on Ad-Hoc Networks and Wireless* (Springer, Berlin, Heidelberg, 2008), pp. 72–85
31. J. Wu, S. Dulman, P. Havinga, T. Nieberg, Multipath routing with erasure coding for wireless sensor networks, in *Proceedings SAFE and ProRISC* (2004), pp. 181–188
32. B.-O. Jalel, B. Yahya, Energy efficient and QoS based routing protocol for wireless sensor networks. J. Parallel Distrib. Comput. **70**(8), 849–857 (2010)
33. X. Wang, C. Che, L. Li, Reliable multi-path routing protocol in wireless sensor networks, in *Proceedings of the 2010 International Conference on Parallel and Distributed Computing, Applications and Technologies* (IEEE Computer Society, 2010), pp. 289–294
34. Y. Jing, M. Xu, W. Zhao, B. Xu, A multipath routing protocol based on clustering and ant colony optimization for wireless sensor networks. Sensors **10**(5), 4521–4540 (2010)
35. S. De, C. Qiao, W. Hongyi, Meshed multipath routing with selective forwarding: an efficient strategy in wireless sensor networks. Comput. Netw. **43**(4), 481–497 (2003)
36. W. Lou, An efficient N-to-1 multipath routing protocol in wireless sensor networks, in *IEEE International Conference on Mobile Adhoc and Sensor Systems Conference, 2005* (IEEE, New York, 2005), pp. 8–17

# A Classification of ECG Arrhythmia Analysis Based on Performance Factors Using Machine Learning Approach

**Rekh Ram Janghel and Saroj Kumar Pandey**

**Abstract** Electrocardiogram is a diagnostic tool that makes a record of the muscular and electrical activities of the heart for showing that data as a trace on a piece of paper, which is then carefully studied and interpreted by a clinical assistant. Classification of ECG signals on performance factors like sensitivity, specificity and accuracy using machine learning techniques can provide substantial input to doctors for essential and effective treatment of the patient. Arrhythmia refers to the condition when the heart beats improperly. Irregular, fast or slow beating of heart comes under arrhythmia. It is caused due to improper working of electrical impulses of the heart. In this research work, various machine learning techniques were made use for the purpose of classification of normal and arrhythmic beats. The major objective of this work is automated classification of normal and irregular beats. Introduced approach deals with a good volume of standard ECG time-series data as inputs to various machine learning classifiers such as Naïve Bayes, support vector machine, ada-boost, random forest, decision tree and k-nearest neighbor classifiers. MIT-BIH arrhythmia database has been made use for the purpose of examining the best classification performance, and one of the most popular datasets of the same database has been taken for training and testing purposes. This comprises of an exact 47 records of thirty minutes each and forty percent of the entire records were those of cardiac patients. Three major performance evaluation parameters have been examined by the researchers on distinct machine learning algorithms. They are accuracy, sensitivity and specificity. A confusion matrix has been made use for describing all these measurements as false positive [FP], false negative [FN], true positive [TP] and true negative [TN]. The efficiency and potential of different methods of arrhythmia detection are demonstrated, and numerous comparisons with various other conventional machine learning techniques are also made. The researchers calculated the sensitivity, specificity and accuracy and found the best result using decision tree classifier with 88.2% accuracy.

R. R. Janghel (✉) · S. K. Pandey
National Institute of Technology, Raipur, Chhatisgarh, India
e-mail: rrjanghel.it@nitrr.ac.in

S. K. Pandey
e-mail: sarojpandey23@gmail.com

 
M. Pant et al. (eds.), *Computational Network Application Tools for Performance Management*, Asset Analytics,
https://doi.org/10.1007/978-981-32-9585-8_7

**Keywords** Support vector machine · Arrhythmia classification · Random forest

## 1 Introduction

Electrocardiogram is a kind of clinical test or tool that helps us in sensing the abnormalities of the heart by quantifying the muscular functions and electrical activities of the heart. These electrical activities can simply be referred to very minute electrical impulses that can be spread through the muscle of the heart.

An ECG machine has the ability to identify such types of impulses, record all the electrical activities of the heart and depict that data on a piece of paper which can be studied and interpreted by any clinical assistant. Electrocardiogram also assists in finding a reason for the symptoms or any kind of chest pain and thus aids in detecting the abnormal beat [1].

ECG is the account of the electrical property of the heartbeats and has turned out to be a standout among the most imperative apparatus in the determination of heart illnesses. Because of the high death rate of heart ailments, early discovery and exact separation of ECG flag are fundamental for the treatment of patients. Early and exact identification of ECG arrhythmia encourages specialists to identify different heart maladies. Arrangement of ECG signals utilizing machine learning systems can give a generous contribution to specialists to affirm the determination.

Arrhythmia refers to the condition when the heart beats improperly. Irregular, fast or slow beating of heart comes under arrhythmia. It is caused due to improper working of electrical impulses of the heart. Depending upon the irregularity, there are usually 14–15 types of arrhythmias [2] (Fig. 1).

With the aim to minimize the manual work of detecting the abnormal rhythms in the electrocardiogram signals, we have applied some machine learning algorithms for automated detection of irregular beats. The beats that are detected as abnormal are then shown to a cardiologist for any analysis [3]. The introduced techniques operate with a huge volume of standard ECG time-series data as inputs to different machine learning techniques such as Naïve Bayes, support vector machine, decision tree, ada-boost, random forest and k-nearest neighbor.

Considering the flow of the remaining sections, this paper is organized as follows. Section 2 describes the literature review of several classification techniques. Section 3 describes the dataset description, and Sect. 4 explains the experiment results. Conclusions and future work are presented in Sect. 5.

## 2 Literature Review

The existing studies and various researchers have investigated the domain of automated computerized ECG for effective diagnosis of heart diseases. This review,

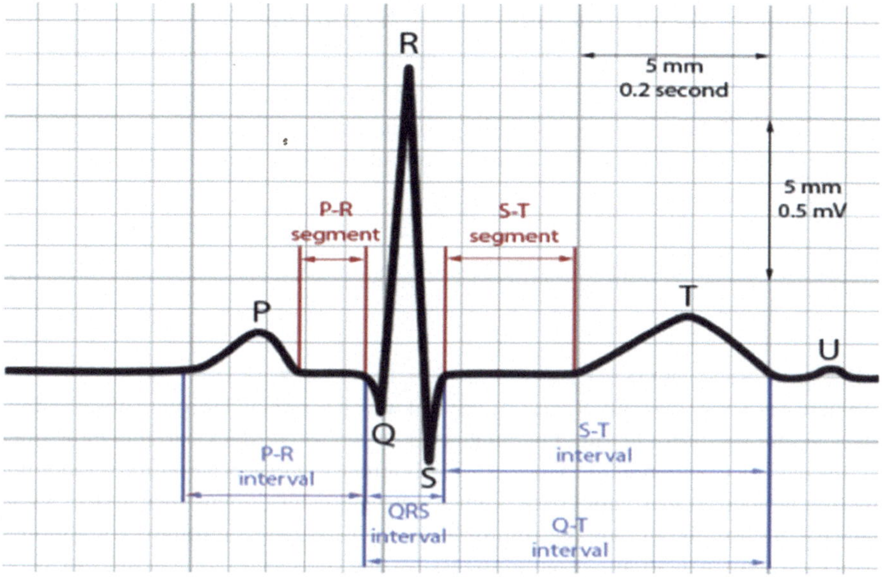


**Fig. 1** Representation of normal ECG signal

therefore, is an attempt to critically explore the literature in the area of different algorithms and machine learning techniques in ECG analysis.

## *2.1 Naïve Bayes-Based Technique*

The Naïve Bayesian classifier (NBC) is a basic and viable strategy for classifier calculation [3]; it is a calculation in view of a grouping of information and using Bayes hypothesis on the bunched information [4]. This model gauges the class likelihood by accepting that the qualities of one class are restrictively autonomous from another class. Gullible Bayes calculation has gotten an incredible consideration in view of its straightforwardness and viability in execution, and additionally it is very handy in everyday issues. Here, we have utilized the Naïve Bayes classifier for the regulated task, in the way that we have considered just the information gave by delineation of a similar class. This technique applies the most extreme probability to evaluate the likelihood of information, and in simplified manner we can state Bayes hypothesis as [5]:

$$\text{Posterior} = \frac{\text{prior} * \text{likelihood}}{\text{evidence}} \tag{1}$$

Naive Bayes provides good results in various complicated real-world scenarios such as fault detection and alert correlation intrusion. It works well for large datasets.

## 2.2 Support Vector Machine-Based Technique

The basic idea in support vector machines (SVMs) [4] is to obtain the optimal hyperplane between data values corresponding to the distinct classes. For a given set of learning data ($x_j$, $y_j$) for $i = 1, \ldots, m$, the formulation of optimization issue for the SVM is given as:

$$\min_{\omega,\tau,b} J(\omega, \tau) = \frac{1}{2}\omega^T \omega + c\sum_{j=1}^{N} \tau_j \tag{2}$$

Such that $y_j(\omega^T \varphi(x_j) + b) \geq 1 - \tau_j, j = 1, \ldots, m, \tau_j \geq 0.$

where $c$ is a positive regularization constant which is selected through observation, $\omega$ is a weight vector for learning parameters, $\tau_j$ is a positive slack variable indicating the distance of $x_j$ with regard to the decision boundary, and $\varphi$ is a nonlinear mapping function applied to map input data point $x_j$ into a greater dimensional space. SVM may be written applying Lagrange multipliers $\alpha \geq 0$. Lagrange multipliers' solution is given by solving a quadratic programing issue. The support vector machine decision function can be given as

$$g(x) = \sum_{x_j \in \mathrm{SV}} \alpha_j y_j K(x, x_j) + b \tag{3}$$

where $K(x, x_j)$ is a kernel function and defined as

$$K(x, x_j) = \varphi(x)^T \varphi(x_j) \tag{4}$$

The Gaussian radial basis function is applied in this work. It is defined as $K(x, z) = \mathrm{e}^{-\gamma||x-z||2}$, and implementation of the SVM classifier is done using LIBSVM [6].

## 2.3 Decision Tree-Based Technique

This classification technique is one among the most commonly used and pragmatic techniques for analytic inference. This technique is particularly used for estimating functions that are discrete-valued and are immune to corrupted information and have the ability to learn different varied expressions [7].

Decision tree learning is a technique in which the function to be learned is represented in the form of a tree. Sets of if-then rules are used to represent learning trees to improve understanding. Such learning methodologies are the most prevalent of inductive inference algorithms and have been applied successfully to a variety of functions ranging from learning to analyze the risk of loan credits of applicants to training to diagnose medical cases. Learning in decision trees is one-step look ahead (hill climbing), heuristic, non-backtracking search throughout the space of all possible decision trees [8]. The main motive of this training is recursively dividing information into subgroups. Training in decision trees proceeds in the following way:

- Selection of an attribute followed by a formulation of logical test on same.
- Every outcome of the test is branched, and subsets of instances of training data which satisfy those outcomes are moved to corresponding child nodes.
- The algorithm is then run recursively on each of the child nodes.
- A base condition specifies when to define a leaf node.

## 2.4 *Random Forest-Based Technique*

According to Breiman, the random forests algorithm is defined [9] as follows:

A set of decision tree technique defined as $\{h(x, Y_k), k = 1, \ldots\}$ is termed as random forests classifier. Here, $Y_k$ represents identically and randomly distributed vectors, and each of the tree casts a single vote for the most probable class at input $x$. Steps for constructing a decision tree in the forest are as follows:

- Selection of $T$ number of trees to be grown is done.
- Selection of $f$ number of features for splitting each node is done. If $F$ denotes the set of features in input data, then the condition: $f < F$ must get satisfied. During the formation of the forest, the subset of features $f$ is kept constant.
- The $T$ number of trees is grown according to the following basis:

Construction of a bootstrap specimen of size $n$ is done followed by a selection of a specimen of $S_n$ for growing a tree. For growing a tree at every node, a random selection of $m$ features is done for finding the best split. Without any pruning, the tree is developed to a maximal extent.

- For evaluating votes from each of the tree in the forest, a majority voting scheme is applied for classifying a specimen $X$.

Performance of classification using random forests algorithm reckon on the diversity of trees in it. This is achieved by selecting features randomly at each node of the tree followed by the usage of that attribute that has the maximum level of learning. Hence, between any two trees in the forest, the correlation is lowered which in turn helps in increasing the performance of the algorithm [10].

## 2.5 K-*Nearest Neighbor (*K-*NN)-Based Technique*

The weighting process is done for every attribute individually. For instance, the first attribute values in whole data are revised and updated corresponding to the $K$-NN scheme. This process is repeated for the second value of attributes, and the process goes on. The process that determines an attribute value of a single data specimen can be understood in the following manner: Let us take $n$ as a label of data specimen and $t$ as the attribute index. That is we search a new value for the $t$th value of the $n$th data specimen. The first thing we do is calculating the distances of all attribute values of the same data specimen, in this case $n$th data specimen, to this value of the attribute. A easy absolute difference is taken as a measure of distance:

$$d(x_n(t), x_n(m)) = |x_n(t) - x_n(m)| \tag{5}$$

where $x_n(t)$ is the $t$th attribute of $n$th data specimen, $x_n(m)$ is the $m$th attribute of $n$th data specimen. The nearest $k$ attribute values are taken after calculating the distances, and their mean is calculated as:

$$\text{mean}(t) = \frac{1}{k} \sum_{\text{attr}_n \in \text{attr}_k, i=1}^{k} \text{attr}_i \tag{6}$$

where $\text{attr}_i$ shows the value of $i$th attribute in the $k$-nearest neighbor attribute values, and $k$ is the number of nearest values to the related attribute value $t$. These estimates are done to take this mean value as the new value of related value. That is, $t$th value of the $n$th data specimen is updated with this mean value. The process is done for all attribute values of the same data specimen similarly [7].

## 2.6 Multilayer Perceptron-Based Technique

MLP neural networks have been used as classifiers. It basically comes under the class of feed word networks. They contain several layers in which one is the input layer of source nodes, some hidden layer(s) of computational nodes (termed neurons) and a single layer for output [11]. In learning algorithms, back-propagation (BP) algorithm still comes under the most famous algorithms [12].

## 2.7 Ada-Boost-Based Technique

The ada-boost ensemble method [13] is also known as adaptive boosting. It is one of the most extensively used boosting algorithms for producing a form of committee by combining multiple base classifiers, which outperforms any base classifier. The boosting runs on the principle of sequential training of the base classifiers and applying a weighted appearance of the dataset for training every base classifier, where the weighting coefficient corresponding to every data value relies on the performance of the previous classifiers. Precisely, misclassified values by one of the base classifiers are assigned greater weights for training the classifier that comes next in the sequence. After all the classifiers are trained, we use a weighted majority voting scheme for combining their predictions [14].

To train a new classifier, we use a dataset in which coefficients of weights get adjusted in accordance with the performance of the previously trained classifier, hence giving more weight to the misclassified data values at every stage of the ada-boost algorithm [15]. Finally, after training the required number of classifiers, a committee is formed by combining them using those coefficients that assign weights to distinct base classifiers. A detailed study on the ada-boost technique is available in [13].

## 3 Dataset Description

In this paper, we have made use of MIT-BIH arrhythmia database for examining the classification performance of the rhythms and one of the most popular datasets of the same database has been taken for training and testing purposes. This comprises of an exact 47 records of thirty minutes each and forty percent of the entire records were those of cardiac patients. Depending on the position of placement of leads, the records comprised of various kinds of signals like: V1, V2, V4, V5 and [16]. Prior to all, 70–30 splitting of the data will be done. Then, we pick up the ML2 signals, and for every record, segmentation of the signal will be done such that the length of each chunk is 720–720. As we already knew that the sampling rate is 360, 360 segments before the *R*-peak value and 360 segments after the same ensured that almost three beats will be there in one chunk, and the classification of the central beat was to be done against 15 possible arrhythmic labels.

The dataset has very standard values, so there was no need to apply band-pass filters or anything. The signal values were normalized (so that it can be tested on any other ECG signal whose sampling rate is also 360) and then joined up forming an array of signal blocks, with each block having 720-length ECG and the input training set was made ready. For output values in the training set, *R*-peak values along with their label were provided in the annotations file and were used.

## 4 Experiment and Results

### *4.1 Performance Measurement Using Confusion Matrix*

The three major performance measure parameters, i.e., sensitivity, accuracy and specificity have been examined by the researchers on several machine learning methods. A confusion matrix has been made use for describing all these measurements as false positive [FP], false negative [FN], true positive [TP] and true negative [TN].

True positive observation is likely to occur when the result depicts arrhythmia with the help of classifier, and this result matches with the observation of the physician. True negative observation occurs when the result depicts the absence of arrhythmia with the help of classifier, and this result matches with the observation of the physician. False positive happens in a scenario where the classifier shows the presence of arrhythmia and the physician has not observed any arrhythmia. False negative is the vice versa of false positive. The term classification accuracy can be described as the entire number of truly classified instances, i.e., (TN + TP) divided by all the instances (TP, TN, FP, FN).

For binary classification,

$$\text{Accuracy} = \frac{\text{TP} + \text{TN}}{\text{TP} + \text{TN} + \text{FP} + \text{FN}} \tag{7}$$

Sensitivity can be described as the ratio of correctly classified instances to the addition of TP and FN. It is also called the true positive rate.

$$\text{Sensitivity} = \frac{\text{TP}}{\text{TP} + \text{FN}} \tag{8}$$

Specificity can be referred to as the ratio of correctly classifying the negatives to the sum of FP and TN

$$\text{Specificity} = \frac{\text{TN}}{\text{FP} + \text{TN}} \tag{9}$$

### *4.2 Performance Comparison of Different Methods*

See Table 1 and Fig. 2.

## 5 Conclusion and Future Work

In this paper, we have proposed a novel approach on machine learning for the active classification of arrhythmia using ECG signals from the MIT-BIH arrhythmia database. We used several machine learning classifiers like Naïve Bayes, SVM, decision tree classifier, random forest classifier, ada-boost, *k*-nearest neighbor and multilayer perceptron-based technique for the classification of ECG dataset. We calculated the sensitivity, specificity and accuracy and found the best result using decision tree classifier with **88.2%** accuracy.

The future work tends to enhance the arrangement precision utilizing machine learning strategies by playing out the preprocessing to include extraction on the MIT-

**Table 1** Experimental analysis for machine learning approaches

| Classification algorithms | Training dataset | Test dataset | Sensitivity (%) | Specificity (%) | Accuracy (%) |
|---|---|---|---|---|---|
| Naïve Bayes | 76,801 | 28,385 | 49.14 | 45.74 | 48.18 |
| Ada-boost | 76,801 | 28,385 | 84.36 | 80.77 | 83.30 |
| MLP | 76,801 | 28,385 | 99.23 | 34.55 | 80.18 |
| *K*-NN | 76,801 | 28,385 | 83.36 | 47.34 | 72.75 |
| Random forest | 76,801 | 28,385 | 93.95 | 19.54 | 72.05 |
| **Decision tree** | **76,801** | **28,385** | **98.14** | **64.38** | **88.20** |
| SVM-linear | 76,801 | 28,385 | 84.94 | 47.33 | 73.86 |
| SVM-RBF | 76,801 | 28,385 | 95.58 | 39.74 | 79.13 |

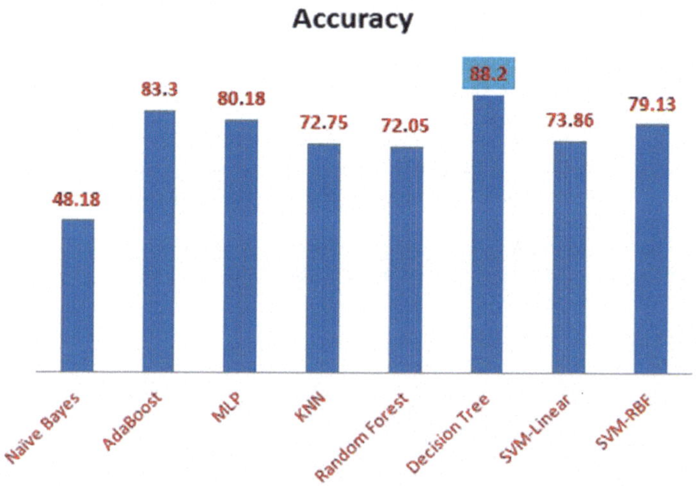


**Fig. 2** Accuracies of the machine learning methods

BIH database. We have likewise utilized various feature determination techniques on ECG dataset. We discovered better characterization comes about with the included choice.

## References

1. M.E.A. Bashir et al., Highlighting the current issues with pride suggestions for improving the performance of real time cardiac health monitoring, in Lect. Notes Comput. Sci. (including Subser. Lect. Notes Artif. Intell. Lect. Notes Bioinformatics), vol. 6266 LNCS (2010), pp. 226–233

2. G. Schreier, P. Kastner, W. Marko, An automatic ECG processing algorithm to identify patients prone to paroxysmal atrial fibrillation. Comput. Cardiol. (February 2001), pp. 133–135
3. G. Guidi, M. Karandikar, Classification of arrhythmia using ECG data
4. P.P. Tiwari, S. Vivekanandan, Identification of Epilepsy by Naïve Bayes classifier and analysis using back propagation network. **2**(4), 112–115 (2012)
5. K. Puntumapon, W. Pattara-atikom, Classification of cellular phone mobility using Naive Bayes model. IEEE Veh. Technol. Conf., pp. 3021–3025 (2008)
6. C.J.C. Burges, A tutorial on support vector machines for pattern recognition. Data Min. Knowl. Discov. **2**(2), 121–167 (1998)
7. C. Chang, C. Lin, LIBSVM: A library for support vector machines. ACM Trans. Intell. Syst. Technol. **2**, 1–39 (2013)
8. K. Polat, S. Güneş, The effect to diagnostic accuracy of decision tree classifier of fuzzy and *k*-NN based weighted pre-processing methods to diagnosis of erythemato-squamous diseases. Digit. Sign. Process. Rev. J. **16**(6), 922–930 (2006)
9. J.R. Quinlan, Induction of decision trees. Mach. Learn. **1**(1), 81–106 (1986)
10. L. Breiman, Random forests. Mach. Learn. **45**(1), 5–32 (2001)
11. A. Özçift, Random forests ensemble classifier trained with data resampling strategy to improve cardiac arrhythmia diagnosis. Comput. Biol. Med. **41**(5), 265–271 (2011)
12. A. Ebrahimzadeh, M. Ahmadi, M. Safarnejad, Classification of ECG signals using Hermite functions and MLP neural networks. J. AI Data Mining (JAIDM) **4**(104), 55–65 (2016)
13. H. Demuth, M.H. Beale, M.T. Hagan, H.B. Demuth, Neural Network ToolboxTM User's Guide R2017a, MathWorks (2015), p. 446
14. R.E. Schapire, A short introduction to boosting. Society **14**(5), 771–780 (2009)
15. X.D. Zeng, S. Chao, F. Wong, Ensemble learning on heartbeat type classification, in *Proceedings of the 2011 International Conference on System and Science Engineering. ICSSE 2011* (June 2011), pp. 320–325
16. G.B. Moody, R.G. Mark, A.L. Goldberger, PhysioNet: A web-based resource for the study of physiologic signals. IEEE Eng. Med. Biol. Mag. **20**(3), 70–75 (2001)

# An Efficient Semiautomatic Active Contour Model of Liver Tumor Segmentation from CT Images

**Ankur Biswas, Paritosh Bhattacharya and Santi P. Maity**

**Abstract** Computed tomography (CT) image is one of the most extensively used imaging modalities for revealing and analyzing tumors as it has a higher spatial resolution, faster imaging speed relatively lower cost compared to MRI. The liver tumor volumetry requires the tumor segmentation in three dimensions which is performed manually tracing the tumor regions on slices which are tiresome and prolonged also, and the volume of manual demarcation is subjective. The major challenging task in liver tumor segmentation is due to the significant variation in location, shape, intensity and texture. This makes it difficult to develop a universal computer algorithm that is applicable for all cases. In this paper, an efficient semiautomatic technique for segmentation of liver tumor from CT images is proposed. The technique is based on semiautomated segmentation approach based on active contour segmentation using the level set method. The proposed approach consists of mainly four stages. In the first stage, the region of interest (ROI) image is initialized, which contains the liver tumor region in the CT image extraction using seed points; in the second stage, resampling and segmentation of ROI is done for reducing the noise and enhancing the boundaries; in the third stage, threshold values adjustment and seed point calculations are carried out; and in the fourth stage, the post-processing is done to extract and refine the liver tumor boundaries. The proposed technique is compared with the region growing algorithms that require filling holes and removing small connected components that can be achieved by using binary morphological operations: opening to remove small connected components and closing to fill holes. The liver tumors detected by the scheme were compared with those manually traced by experts, used

A. Biswas (✉)
Tripura Institute of Technology, Narsingarh, Tripura, India
e-mail: abiswas.tit@gmail.com

P. Bhattacharya
National Institute of Technology, Agartala, Tripura, India
e-mail: pari76@rediffmail.com

S. P. Maity
Indian Institute of Engineering Science and Technology, Shibpur, Howrah, West Bengal, India
e-mail: spmaity@yahoo.com

 
M. Pant et al. (eds.), *Computational Network Application Tools for Performance Management*, Asset Analytics,
https://doi.org/10.1007/978-981-32-9585-8_8

as the ground truth results. The study was evaluated on two datasets of tumors. The proposed scheme obtained the Dice similarity coefficient 0.938 and the Jaccard similarity coefficient 0.883. The mean surface distance, the median surface distance and the maximal surface distance were 0.025, 0.712 and 2.828 mm, respectively. With the proposed scheme, the time requisite is reduced significantly and proves to be helpful to the observer in better visualizing the probable tumors inside the liver. The proposed method represents the 3D reconstruction of segmented tumors within the liver.

**Keywords** Computed tomography (CT) · Active contour · Level set · Dice similarity coefficient · Jaccard similarity coefficient

## 1 Introduction

Computed tomography (CT) image is one of the most extensively used imaging modalities for revealing and analyzing tumors. It has a higher spatial resolution, faster imaging speed and relatively lower cost compared to MRI [1] and an important tool for detecting variance in the texture and shape of the liver and visible lesions that perform as biomarkers for preliminary disease finding and succession in primary as well as secondary hepatic tumor disease [2].

Primary tumors mainly, breast, colon and pancreas cancer during the approach of disease extend metastases to the liver which is why the liver and its lesions require routine analysis in primary tumor staging. Moreover, the liver is the primary site of tumor disease such as Hepatocellular carcinoma (HCC). HCC is the sixth most common disease and the third most regular reason for fatality relating malignancy around the world [3].

HCC comprises a heritably and molecularly high category of cancers that commonly happen to a chronically damaged liver. The stepwise change to HCC is linked with significant changes in tissue architecture incorporating an expansion of cells and a change in vascular supply (arterialization). These quantifiable changes in tissue architecture give the premise to the non-intrusive detection of HCC in imaging [4], yet in addition prompt variable factor structures and shapes.

The basic evaluation criterion of the tumor response toward the treatment is the size of the tumor. Liver tumor segmentation and volumetry facilitate medical experts to find out the tumor growth rate with respect to time and the efficacy of cancer management. The information collected can be utilized to assess the response of the patient toward treatment and, if needed, settle in the therapy.

It is shown that volume measurement (3D) offers the best manifestation of the tumor response out of tumor size including one-dimensional, two-dimensional and volumetric measurements [5]. The liver tumor volumetry requires the tumor segmentation in three dimensions. This task can be performed manually by tracing the tumor regions on slices which are tiresome and prolonged. Moreover, the volume of manual demarcation is subjective.

The major challenging task in liver tumor segmentation is due to the significant variation in location, shape, intensity and texture. This makes it difficult to develop a universal algorithm that is applicable for all cases [1]. Hence, in this paper, a semiautomated segmentation method is proposed which is based on level set method that produces output in 3D view and obtains robust segmentation results.

The proposed technique is compared with previous segmentation methods in terms of region growing algorithm, and the results are evaluated with ground truth and achieved a significant result in terms of the Dice similarity coefficient and the Jaccard similarity coefficient. The remainder of the paper is organized as follows: Sect. 2 provides the necessary background and related work covering the aspects of region growing algorithms. While Sect. 3 describes the methodological framework of the proposed approach, Sect. 4 deals with the segmentation results and discussion, and Sect. 5 presents the concluding remarks and future scope.

## 2 Previous Work

In this section, several interactive and automatic methods using different algorithms that have been developed to segment the liver and liver lesions in CT volumes are discussed.

### *2.1 Region Growing (Connected Threshold)*

The algorithm starts with a single pixel (seed) and new pixels are added slowly. It is initialized by setting a seed point (pixel) from which the region starts growing using SetSeed() strategy which is instated with a point in the distinctive region of the anatomical structure (liver) requires to be segmented. Later, the algorithm is left to set up a foundation to choose whether a specific neighboring pixel ought to be incorporated into the current region or not.

The standard utilized by the filter depends on user-provided range of intensity values. Lower threshold (min) and upper threshold (max) values ought to be given. For $I()$ being the image and $X$ being the position of the picky neighbor pixel which is considered for addition in the region, the region growing algorithm incorporates those pixels, whose intensities are within the range of interval,

$$I(X) \in [\min, \max] \tag{1}$$

It finally stops if no more pixels can be added. Invocation of the update() method on the writer triggers the execution of the pipeline.

## 2.2 Region Growing (Confidence Connected)

The second method in this class of region growing segmentation algorithm confidence connected permits to certainly determine the threshold bounds in view of the basic measurements of the current region. To start with, the algorithm registers the mean, $\mu$ and standard deviation, $\sigma$ of intensity values for every one of the pixels currently incorporated into the region. A user given factor '*k*' is utilized to multiply the standard deviation and characterize a range around the mean and assessed from the seed points, $\mu \pm k\sigma$.

Neighbor pixels whose intensity values fall inside the range are acknowledged and incorporated in the region. At the point when no more neighbor pixels are found that fulfill the criterion, the algorithm is considered to have completed its first iteration. By then, the mean and standard deviation of the intensity levels are recomputed utilizing every one of the pixels currently included in the region. This mean and standard deviation characterize a new intensity range that is used to visit current region neighbors and assess whether their intensity falls within the range. This iterative process is rehashed until no more pixels are included or the most extreme number of iterations is come to. The accompanying condition delineates the inclusion criterion used by this filter,

$$I(X) \in [\mu - k\sigma, \mu + k\sigma] \tag{2}$$

where $I()$ is the image and $X$ is the position of the particular neighbor pixel being considered for inclusion in the region.

## 2.3 Iterative Watershed

In watershed technique, the grayscale image is considered to be reminiscent of a topological surface with valleys and mountains. This region growing algorithm is like flooding catchment basins that represent local minima from the image. Ridge lines around them are created by flooding the basins that separate different regions [6].

As medical images mostly have elevated noise variance, there is a threat of over segmentation due to the presence of high density of local minima. In order to prevail over this issue, many watershed strategies use marker points which are placed inside and outside the tumor by the user in order to indicate where to start flooding. The watershed strategy is subsequently applied to the GVF field transformation of the image.

This gives an initial segmentation called level 0. The iterative watershed strategy uses the resultant boundary as a set of markers, and the strategy is applied over again. These results in segmentation are called level 1, consisting of one region consisting of pixels inside the tumor, one fuzzy region and one region outside the tumor. Next,

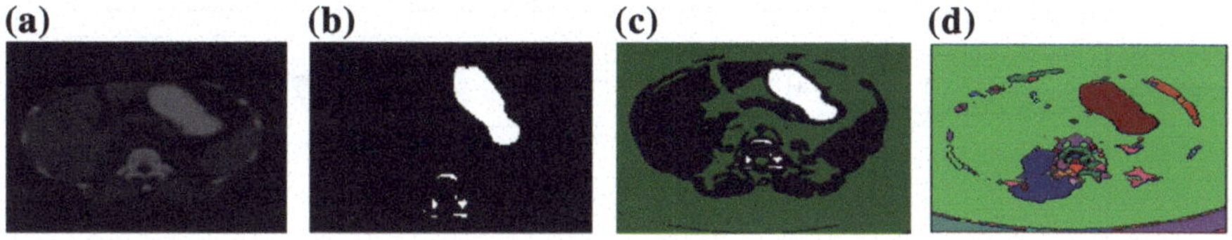


**Fig. 1** Segmentation result applied on CT image of patient extracted from MIDAS repositories [7]. **a** Original image, **b** threshold connected, **c** confidence connected, **d** watershed

**Table 1** Parameters required

| Segmentation type | Parameters | Value |
|---|---|---|
| Connected threshold | Lower threshold | 100 |
| | Upper threshold | 170 |
| Confidence connected | Number of iterations | 0 |
| | Multiplier | 2 |
| | Initial neighborhood radius | 1 |
| | Replace value | 1 |
| | Multiplier | 4 |

the boundaries are again indicated as additional sets of markers, and the watershed method is applied one last time, resulting in level 2.

Level 2 consists of one region inside the tumor, three fuzzy regions and one region outside the tumor. The fuzzy regions are, going from outside to inside, increasingly likely to belong to the tumor. The second most outer boundary in level 2 was found to be the closest to the reference boundary. Figure 1 shows the result of liver segmentation CT images using different region growing algorithms (Table 1).

## 3 Proposed Approach

This section describes the different steps in the proposed approach. The task of the proposed approach can be subdivided into four main stages: (1) Initialization of the region of interest (ROI) image which contains the liver tumor region in the CT image extraction using seed points. (2) The ROI resample and separation for reducing the noise and enhancing the boundaries. (3) Threshold values assessment and seed points estimation (4). The post-processing stage.

It is applied to extract and refine the liver tumor boundaries. The proposed approach is performed on MIDAS dataset on liver and liver tumor CT images including the expert manual segmentation referred here as ground truth. The main idea is to apply semiautomatic segmentation on the tumor detected from the CT image. The flow diagram of the proposed approach is shown in Fig. 2.

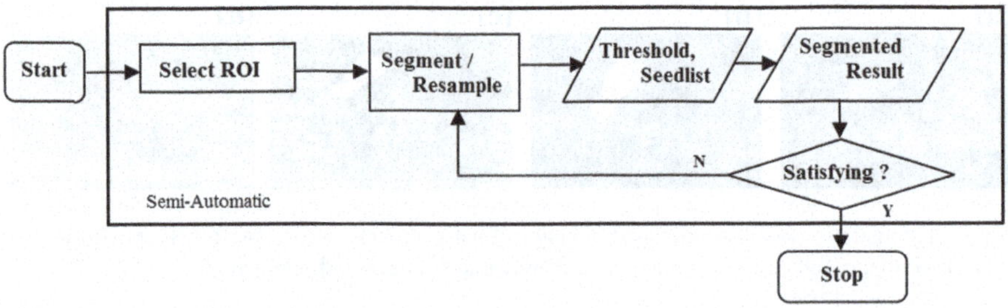


**Fig. 2** Flow diagram of the proposed approach

## *3.1 Methodology*

Firstly, the seed points inside the tumor are evaluated. Based on the seed points, the 3D region of interest (ROI) relating the tumor is determined. In the second step, this ROI is resampled setting the appropriate parameters for reducing the noise and enhancing the structures of the liver tumor by using an anisotropic diffusion algorithm. Noise present in the image can reduce the capacity of the filter to grow large regions.

The noise-reducing technique is handled by a modified curvature diffusion equation that not only removes the noise from the image but also preserves the major structures that include the boundaries as well. The noise-reduced image is then passed to enhance the boundaries of the segmented image. In the third step, once the ROI is segmented, the lower and upper threshold values on the separated image are adjusted to set the initial seed points for active contours to grow.

Pixels whose value lie within the lower threshold (min) and upper threshold (max) are included in the region of segmentation, and any pixel whose value is out of these ranges are excluded. Setting values, i.e., min and max too close together is often restrictive for the region to grow and setting them too extreme apart may cause the region to engulf the image. The output received at this stage is a binary image having zero-value pixels all over except the extracted region.

The intensity value set inside the region is selected. The seed points selected is allowed to grow until boundaries are reached. Finally after the output is obtained, the image requires some post-processing for 3D visualization. Figure 3 shows the intermediate steps of the proposed approach for getting the final 3D output of tumors.

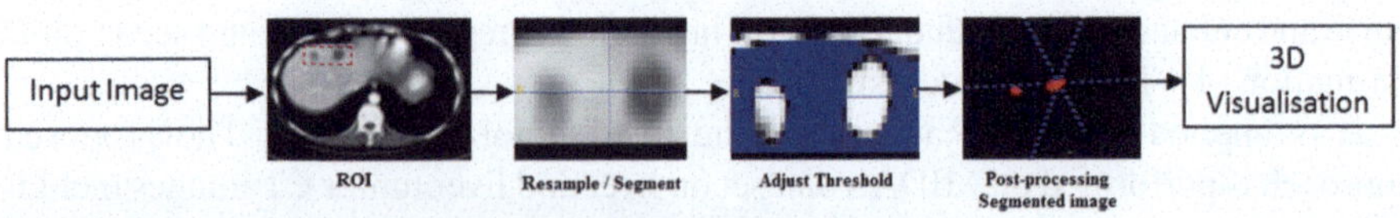


**Fig. 3** Intermediate steps of the proposed approach

## 4 Experimental Results

In this section, the intermediate results of the proposed scheme for two examples case were shown in Fig. 4. A comparison between the semiautomatic liver tumor segmentation and the ground truth manual liver tumor segmentation by experts (MIDAS dataset) is also illustrated in Fig. 5. The liver tumor volume was computed from the segmented regions.

### *4.1 Evaluations*

The performance of the proposed method is assessed by means of the quality metrics established in the grand challenges for liver and lesion segmentation by [2, 8] and following statistical performance measures are utilized. These statistics are premeditated based on the guiding principle and the evaluation software [9]. Additionally, overlap percentage, Jaccard index [10–12], Dice [11, 13] and surface distance (mean, median and max) are reported. Metrics are applied to binary-valued volumes, so a metric computed on the lesions, for example, considers only lesion objects as foreground and everything else as background.

The main metric is the Dice score, where the Dice score is in the interval [0, 1]. A perfect segmentation yields a Dice score of 1. Here, the proposed method is

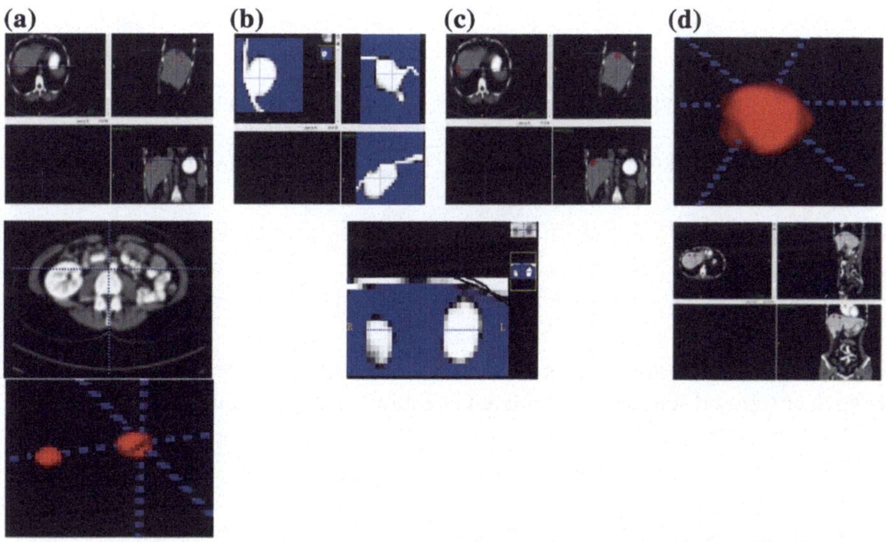


**Fig. 4** Result using the proposed approach of semiautomatic segmentation applied on CT images of two patients extracted from MIDAS repositories [7]. **a** Original image of liver with ROI selected, **b** ROI resampling, **c** segmented tumor using level set, **d** final 3D view of tumor after post-processing

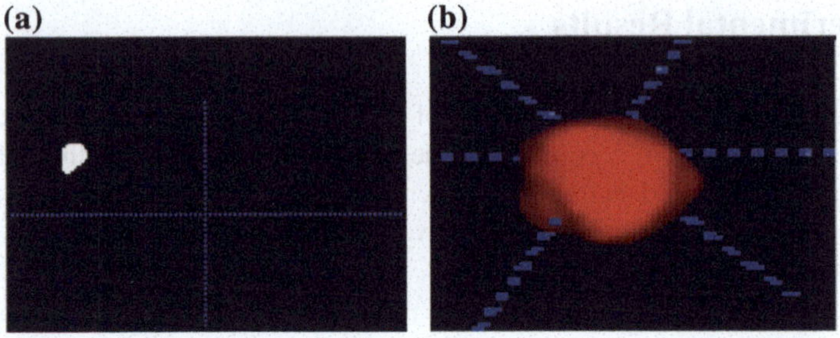


**Fig. 5** Comparison of (**a**) ground truth and (**b**) actual image using proposed method

**Table 2** Quantitative segmentation results with scores as reported in the original papers of the liver on different datasets and other clinical CT and MR-DWI datasets

| Previous approach | Dataset | VOE (%) | RVD (%) | ASD (mm) | MSD (mm) | DICE (%) |
|---|---|---|---|---|---|---|
| U-Net as in [14] | 3DIRCAD | 39 | 87 | 19.4 | 119 | 72.9 |
| Li et al. [15] (liver-only) | 3DIRCAD | 9.2 | −11. 2 | 1.6 | 28.2 | – |
| Chartrand et al. [16] | 3DIRCAD | 6.8 | 1.7 | 1.6 | 24 | – |
| Li et al. [17] (liver-only) | 3DIRCAD | – | – | – | – | 94.5 |
| Ben-Cohen et al. [18] (liver-only) | Own clinical CT | – | – | – | – | 89 |
| Cascaded U-Net | MR-DWI | 23 | 14 | 5.2 | 135.3 | 87 |
| Cascaded U-Net | Clinical CT | 22 | −3 | 9.5 | 165.7 | 88 |
| Cascaded U-Net + 3D CRF | Clinical CT | 16 | −6 | 5.3 | 48.3 | 91 |

compared with other approaches are tabulated in Table 2, while the results obtained using the proposed scheme are tabulated in Table 3 and graphically shown in (Fig. 6).

# 5 Conclusions and Future Scope

With growing demand in the usage of CT images of the liver as a single exam tips to imperious demands for exploring researches in the automated process of liver

**Table 3** Evaluation of results of the proposed scheme on two different datasets

| | Overlap percentage | Jaccard | Dice | Volume similarity | False negative | False positive |
|---|---|---|---|---|---|---|
| Dataset 1 | 0.901 | 0.82 | 0.901 | 0.052 | 0.075 | 0.122 |
| Dataset 2 | 0.938 | 0.883 | 0.938 | 0.048 | 0.021 | 0.067 |
| | Hausdorff distance | Mean surface distance | Median surface distance | Std surface distance | Max surface distance | |
| Dataset 1 | 4.905 | 0.025 | 0.712 | 0.513 | 2.828 | |
| Dataset 2 | 3.354 | 0.021 | 0.906 | 0.144 | 1 | |

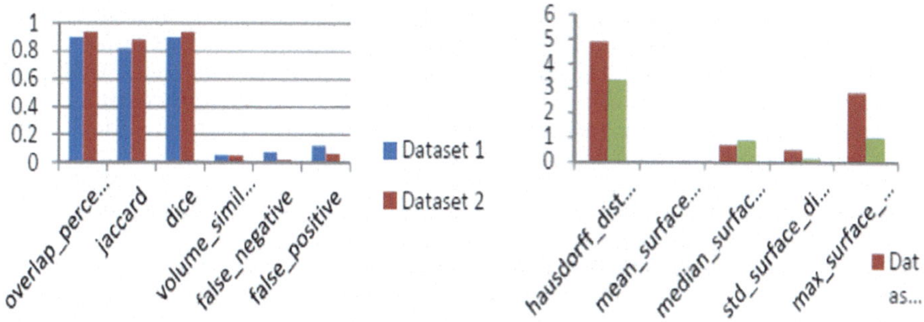


**Fig. 6** Graphs showing of results of the proposed scheme on two different datasets

tumor segmentation. But many studies and researches have already been reported for this challenging task. In this paper, a semiautomatic scheme for CT images of liver tumor segmentation is developed whose experimental results have been compared and shown that the proposed method is perfect and efficient as compared to manual ground truth segmentation.

By exploring the segmentation and evaluation results, it can be concluded as follows: First, its accuracy is comparable or improved than the other existing semi-automatic methods. Second, the region grows in 3D. Thus, the user only needs to pick seed points once and does not need to initialize the method for every slice. It involves very little manual operation in initial seed selection. With the proposed scheme, the time requisite is reduced significantly for the segmentation of liver tumor.

Finally, the extraction of liver tumors from the CT series, 3D visualization of the tumor can be helpful to the observer in better visualizing the probable tumors inside the liver and the liver itself which is usually completed as going through a slice by slice basis on CT series, which can be both tedious and time consuming. The proposed method represents the 3D reconstruction of segmented tumors within the liver. Hence, it can be helpful for the radiologists for the analysis of liver tumor on CT images.

The idea of this paper can be easily extended to other organs mainly brain, breast to locate the tumors and to additional imaging modalities, such as MRI and X-rays.

Once it is applied to brain MRI, it will facilitate computer-aided disease diagnosis structurally, such as narrowness of the cerebral aqueduct and foramina means that they can become blocked, for example, by blood following a hemorrhagic stroke. The proposed methodology can also be applied to locate fractures on bones from medical images.

## References

1. B.N. Li, C.K. Chui, S. Chang, S.H. Ong, A new unified level set method for semi-automatic liver tumor segmentation on contrast enhanced CT images. Expert Syst. Appl. **39**(10), 9661–9668 (2012)
2. T. Heimann, B.V. Ginneken, M.A. Styner, Comparison and evaluation of methods for liver segmentation from CT datasets. IEEE Trans. Med. Imaging **28**(8), 1251–1265 (2009)
3. J. Ferlay, H.R. Shin, F. Bray, D. Forman, C. Mathers, D.M. Parkin, Estimates of worldwide burden of cancer in 2008: Globocan 2008. Int. J. Cancer **127**(12), 2893–2917 (2010)
4. European Association for the Study of the Liver, Easl-eortc clinical practice guidelines: management of hepatocellular carcinoma. J. Hepatol. **56**(4), 908–943 (2012)
5. S. Ray, R. Hagge, M. Gillen, M. Cerejo, S. Shakeri, L. Beckett, T. Greasby, R.D. Badawi, Comparison of two-dimensional and three-dimensional iterative watershed segmentation methods in hepatic tumor volumetrics. Med. Phys. **35**(12), 5869–5881 (2008)
6. L.N. Tran, M.S. Brown, J.G. Goldin, X. Yan, Comparison of treatment response classifications between, unidimensional, bidimensional and volumetric measurements of metastatic lung lesions on chest computed tomography. Acad. Radiol. **11**(12), 1355–1360 (2004)
7. NLM: Imaging Methods Assessment and Reporting, http://hdl.handle.net/1926/586
8. X. Deng, G. Du, M. Styner, 3D Segmentation in the clinic: A grand challenge II-liver tumor segmentation, in *MICCAI Workshop*, 2007, (2007), pp. 7–15
9. A. Taha, A. Hanbury, Metrics for evaluating 3D medical image segmentation: Analysis, selection, and tool. BMC Med. Imag. (2015)
10. R. Cardenes, R. de Luis-Garcia, M. Bach-Cuadra, A multidimensional segmentation evaluation for medical image data. Comput. Methods Programs Biomed. **96**(2), 108–124 (2009)
11. A.Q. Al-Faris, U.K. Ngah, N.A.M. Isa, I.L. Shuaib, MRI breast skin-line segmentation and removal using integration method of level set active contour and morphological thinning algorithms. J. Med. Sci. **12**(8), 286–291 (2012)
12. K.H. Zou, S.K. Warfield, A. Baharatha, C. Tempany, M.R. Kaus, S.J. Haker et al., Statistical validation of image segmentation quality based on a spatial overlap index. Acad. Radiol. **11**(2), 178–189 (2004)
13. K.H. Zou, W.M. Wells, R. Kikinis, S.K. Warfield, Three validation metrics for automated probabilistic image segmentation of brain tumours. Stat. Med. **23**(8), 1259–1282 (2004)
14. O. Ronneberger, P. Fischer, T. Brox, U-net: Convolutional networks for biomedical image segmentation, in *MICCAI: LNCS,* vol. 9351 (Springer, Berlin, 2015), pp. 234–241
15. G. Li, X. Chen, F. Shi, W. Zhu, J. Tian, D. Xiang, Automatic liver segmentation based on shape constraints and deformable graph cut in CT images. IEEE Trans. Image Process. **24**(12), 5315–5329 (2015)
16. G. Chartrand, T. Cresson, R. Chav, A. Gotra, A. Tang, J. DeGuise, Semi-automated liver CT segmentation using Laplacian meshes, in *ISBI* (IEEE, New York, 2014), pp. 641–644
17. C. Li, X. Wang, S. Eberl, M. Fulham, Y. Yin, J. Chen, D.D. Feng, A likelihood and local constraint level set model for liver tumor segmentation from CT volumes. IEEE Trans. Biomed. Eng. **60**(10), 2967–2977 (2013)

18. A. Ben-Cohen, I. Diamant, E. Klang, M. Amitai, H. Greenspan, Fully convolutional network for liver segmentation and lesions detection, in *International Workshop on Large-Scale Annotation of Biomedical Data and Expert Label Synthesis, LNCS*, vol. 10008 (Springer, Berlin, 2016), pp. 77–85

# A Classification-Based Summarization Model Using Supervised Learning

**M. Esther Hannah**

**Abstract** Classification-based summarization model using ID3 and multivariate (CBS-ID3MV) approach produces summaries from the text documents through the process of classification. Extracting the features that are important from a text is one of the most basic tasks. A feature is a set of attributes which captures important qualities of the text document. The approach is to develop a summarizer that takes into account text features from each sentence, for the purpose of classifying summary sentences. The CBS-ID3MV model is trained with DUC 2002 training documents, and the proposed approach's performance is measured at several compression rates on the data corpus. The results got by the proposed framework works better when compared with other summarizers after evaluation using ROUGE metrics.

**Keywords** Training · Classification · Information retrieval (IR) · Decision trees · Feature extraction · Summarization · Regression

## 1 Introduction

Of the many statistical and machine learning methods used, HMM, fuzzy, neural networks, etc., have made an impact in the research on summarization [1–3]. Extracting the features that are important from a text is one of the most basic tasks in any information retrieval (IR) problem. A feature is a set of attributes which captures important qualities of the text document [4, 5].

In this work, a method of summarization is viewed as a problem of classification where the input sentences are classified either as '*summary*' or '*not-a-summary*' sentence [6]. It is found that the decision tree method augmented by multiple linear regressions to classification proves to be the right candidate for the text summarization process, thus enabling us to produce better summaries [7, 8].

The classification-based summarization (CBS-ID3MV) framework generates high-quality summaries. It is done by identifying relevant sentences from the text

---

M. Esther Hannah (✉)
St. Joseph's College of Engineering, Chennai, India
e-mail: hanmoses@gmail.com



M. Pant et al. (eds.), *Computational Network Application Tools for Performance Management*, Asset Analytics,
https://doi.org/10.1007/978-981-32-9585-8_9

document supervised learning. The paper is categorized as follows: Sect. 2 discusses some of the existing work related to text summarizations techniques. Section 3 proceeds to explain the proposed framework. Section 4 brings out the evaluation set-up and discusses the results with Sect. 5 giving a conclusion by providing scope for future work.

## 2 Related Work

Classification is a data mining and a knowledge management technique used in grouping similar data objects together [9]. It is a set of supervised learning algorithms that classifies data objects into their pre-defined class labels. A number of classification algorithms exist in literature, and decision trees are the one of the popular methods due to its ease of its implementation [10, 11, 12]. The problem of classification and its learning approach is discussed in the next subsection.

### *2.1 The Classification Problem*

Classification, being one of the most popular supervised learning technique, learns a classifier model by using a set of training data set [4, 13]. Figure 1 shows a typical supervised learning framework. The classifier model is built from learning from the instances present in the training data. Classification requires sufficient training in order to get accurate results [14–16]. The testing data set is used in the evaluation of the trained classifier model. Thus, model construction and model usage are the two important phases of any classification approach.

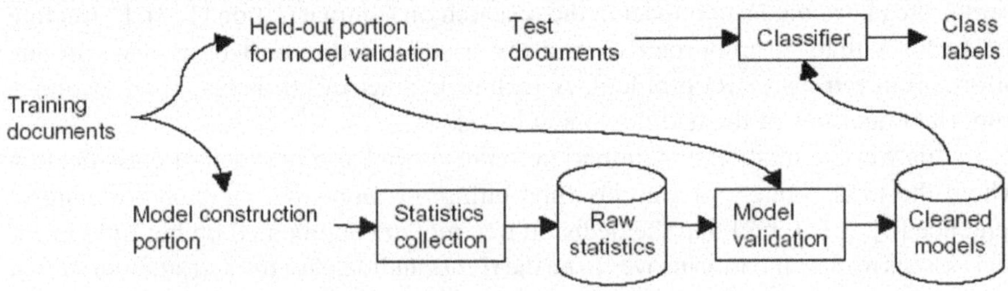


**Fig. 1** Supervised learning model

# 3 Classification-Based Summarization Using ID3 and MV

The CBS-ID3MV framework implements an extractive way to summarization where decision trees are used to classify sentences to be part of summary to be generated. The CBS-ID3MV makes use of multiple linear regression technique for giving weights for the attributes used in the training data set generation.

The proposed framework uses decision tree induction for summarizing text documents [17, 18]. Four layers are present in the proposed framework which are pre-processing, feature link, MV-based classification and the summary presentation.

The pre-processing layer performs pre-processing by cleaning the data and removing noise. The feature link layer extracts features such as sentence length, resemblance with title, theme-based words, numerical data, presence of a noun, frequency of terms and similarity between one sentence and every other sentence. Each feature value is normalized between 0 and 1 as given in Table 1.

The following subsection gives the strengths of the multivariate approach in feature weighing.

## 3.1 Multiple Linear Regression

The regression model has one intercept and '$n$' slopes, and therefore, it defines a n-dimensional regression plane in a $(n + 1)$-dimensional space of $(X^{(1)}, X^{(2)}, \ldots, X^{(n)}, Y)$ [19, 20]. Multivariate Regression Model uses a multiple linear regression technique which will connect a response variable $Y$ to several predictors $X^{(1)}, X^{(2)}, \ldots, X^{(n)}$.

This model assumes more independent variables (IVs) and one dependent variable (DV). The approach is capable of identifying the value denoting the relation between a text and its manually summarized form. Observed are $mx1$ response vector $Y$ and an $mx(n + 1)$ predictor matrix $X$, where $m$ is the number of sentences in the document and $n$ is the number of features extracted for each sentence [21, 22].

The dependent and the independent vectors become the input to the MV-based system [23]. A constant weight is got as the result of the regressions, which denotes the relation between a text document and its summarized version.

**Table 1** Feature value notation

| Feature value | Category | Notation |
|---|---|---|
| 0–0.2 | Very low | VL |
| 0.21–0.4 | Low | L |
| 0.41–0.6 | Average | A |
| 0.6–0.81 | High | H |
| 0.8–1.0 | Very high | VH |

Thus, by using multivariate on a set of independent vectors, a set of weights corresponding to the independent vectors can be learnt. This learnt set of weights is used in producing informative training data set.

### *3.2 MV-Based Classification Layer*

The CBS-ID3MV model utilizes supervised learning using decision trees, which is a powerful tool of multi-variable analysis. Decision trees can substitute for other existing forms of analysis, namely the traditional statistical forms such as artificial neural networks and HMM in search of business intelligence [24].

The approach starts with extracting features which are then augmented with weights learnt from multivariate, for every sentence of the input text document using the decision tree induction. The 'status' for these sentences are denoted as INT for an '*summary*' sentence and NOT-INT for a '*not_a_summary*' sentence based on the generated summary document.

### *3.3 Presentation of Summary*

The function of this layer is to produce a summary for an input text. Providing information-rich summaries are the role of this layer, where the produced summaries are as close to the model summaries. The compression ratios for the summaries are maintained as 10%, 20% and 30% as required by the user.

## 4 Experimental Set-up

40% documents from the DUC2002 data set is used for testing the system, while 60% of it is used to train the system. Model summaries provided by DUC2002 were used to evaluate our system. Each document has minimum of 10 sentences and maximum of 30 sentences. The total number of sentences in the corpus is 1260 with 288 documents.

### *4.1 Results*

The CBS-ID3MV model is evaluated for various compression ratios using ROUGE metrics [3, 25–27]. We have tested the system using the ROUGE-1 obtaining the recall, precision and F-score results as shown in Table 2.

**Table 2** CBS-ID3MV model results

| F-score | Number of documents | | |
|---|---|---|---|
| Summarizer value | Recall | Precision | F-score |
| <0.3 | 9 | 8 | 6 |
| 0.3–0.4 | 23 | 16 | 13 |
| 0.4–0.5 | 126 | 115 | 121 |
| 0.5–0.6 | 111 | 117 | 125 |
| ≥0.6 | 19 | 32 | 29 |

**Table 3** Recall, precision and F-score for 10, 20 and 30% CR

| Metrics | CBS-ID3MV | | |
|---|---|---|---|
| CR | 10% | 20% | 30% |
| Recall | 0.539 | 0.5653 | 0.5877 |
| Precision | 0.6768 | 0.6793 | 0.6892 |
| F-score | 0.6 | 0.6171 | 0.6344 |

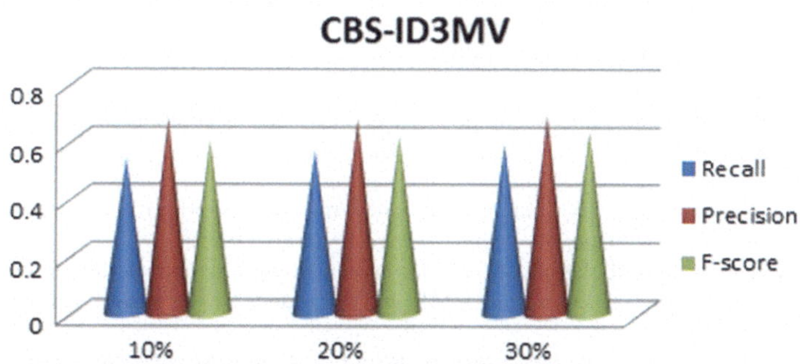


**Fig. 2** CBS-ID3MV results for 10, 20 and 30% compression ratios

The results of CBS-ID3MV model for the various compression ratios, namely 10, 20 and 30%, are shown in Table 3, and it is graphically shown in Fig. 2.

## *4.2 Discussion*

It is can be shown from Table 2 that the CBS-ID3MV framework shows a better precision and recall since the features that are used as attributes for training the model are unique and are sufficient for presenting the most important portions of a document [28, 29]. Though the recall has decreased slightly at 10% CR, the precision, recall and F-score increased as the compression ratio increased 20% and later to 30%.

## 5 Conclusions

In this article, the use of classification algorithm is investigated for the task of automatic text summarization. The classification-based summarization using ID3MV (CBS-ID3MV) approach is applied on English articles present in the DUC2002 corpus. The feature selection and extraction techniques utilized will give researchers the opportunity on feature-based type of text document and also based on the language. Currently, we have designed the system only for the English language, which can in future handle other languages also.

## References

1. C.Y. Lin, Training a selection function for extraction, in *Proceedings of the Eighth International Conference on Information and Knowledge Management*, Kansas City, Missouri, United States (1999), pp. 55–62
2. H.P. Edmundson, New methods in automatic extracting. J. Assoc. Comput. Mach. **16**(2), 264–285 (1969)
3. C.-Y. Lin, Rouge: A package for automatic evaluation of summaries, in *Proceedings of the ACL-04 Workshop*, pp. 74–81 (2004)
4. D.R. Radev, E. Hovy, K. McKeown, Introduction to the special issue on summarization. Comput. Linguist. **28**(4), 399–408 (2002)
5. G.D. Clifford, Singular value decomposition & independent component analysis for blind source separation, HST582 J/6.555 J/16.456 J Biomedical Signal and Image Processing Spring (2005)
6. Y. Freund, R.E. Scaphire, Experiments with anew boosting algorithm, in *Proceedings of the Thirteenth International Conference on Machine Learning* (1996)
7. Esther Hannah, A hybrid classification-based model for automatic text summarization using machine learning approaches: CBS-ID3MV, Int. J. Product Development, Vol. 23, Nos. 2/3, 2019, pp 201-211.
8. S. Mitra, K.M. Konwar, S.K. Pal, Fuzzy decision tree, linguistic rules and fuzzy knowledge-based network: generation and evaluation. IEEE Trans. Syst. Man Cybern. **32**(4), 328–339 (2002)
9. E. El-Qawasmeh, Categorizing received email to improve delivery. Int. J. Comput. Syst. Sci. Eng **26**(2), 115–121 (2011)
10. T.N. Phyu, Survey of classification techniques in data mining, in *Proceedings of the International Multi Conference of Engineers and Computer Scientists* (International Association of Engineers, 2009), pp. 727–731
11. M.N. Anyanwu, S.G. Shiva, Comparative analysis of serial decision tree classification algorithms. Int. J. Comput. Sci. Secur. (IJCSS) **3**(3), 231 (2009)
12. H. Milde, L. Hotz, J. Kahl, S. Wessel, Qualitative model-based decision tree generation for diagnosis in real world industrial application, in *Industrial and Engineering Applications of Artificial Intelligence and Expert Systems* (1999)
13. S.P. Yong, Ahmad I.Z. Abidin, Y.Y. Chen, A neural based text summarization system, in *Proceedings of the 6th International Conference of Data Mining* (2005)
14. H.P. Luhn, The automatic creation of literature abstract. IBM J. Res. Dev. **2**, 159–165 (1958)
15. M.A. Fattah, F. Ren, Automatic text summarization, in *Proceedings of World Academy of Science, Engineering and Technology*, vol. 27 (2008), pp. 192–195
16. Inderjeet Mani, Gary Klein, David House, Lynette Hirsctman, Therese Firmin, Beth Sundheim, SUMMAC: a text summarization evaluation. Nat. Lang. Eng. **8**(1), 43–68 (2002)

17. J. Kupiec, J. Pedersen, F. Chen, A trainable document summarizer, in *Proceedings of the Eighteenth Annual International ACM Conference on Research and Development in Information Retrieval (SIGIR)*, Seattle, WA (1995), pp. 68–73
18. A.D. Kulkarni, C.D. Cavanaugh, Fuzzy neural network models for classification. Appl. Intell. **12**(3), 207–215 (2000)
19. C.Y. Lin, E.H. Hovy, The potential and limitation of sentence extraction for summarization, in *Proceedings of the HLT/NAACL Workshop on Automatic Summarization*, Edmonton, Canada (2003)
20. J. Chen, D. Chen, O. Lemon, A feature-based detection and tracking system for gaze and smiling behaviors. Int. J. Comput. Syst. Sci. Eng. **26**(3), 207–2014 (2011)
21. J.M. Conroy, D.P. O'leary, Text summarization via hidden Markov models, in *Proceedings of SIGIR'01* (2001), pp. 406–407
22. H.-H. Huang, Y.-H. Kuo, H.-C. Yang, Fuzzy-rough set aided sentence extraction summarization, in *Proceedings of the First International Conference on Innovative Computing, Information and Control* (2006)
23. K. Svore, L. Vanderwende, C. Burges, Enhancing single document summarization by combining RankNet and third-party sources, in *Proceedings of the Joint Conference on Empirical methods in Natural Language Processing and Computational Natural Language Learning* (2007), pp. 448–457
24. T.K. Landauer, P.W. Foltz, D. Laham, Introduction to latent semantic analysis. Discourse Processes **25**, 259–284 (1998)
25. S.K. Pal, P. Mithra, Case generation using rough sets with fuzzy representations. IEEE Trans. Knowl. Data Eng. **16**(3), 293–300 (2004)
26. L. Suanmali, M.S. Binwahlan, N. Salim, Sentence features fusion for text summarization using fuzzy logic, in *Proceedings of Ninth International Conference for Text Summarization Using Fuzzy Logic* (2009), pp. 142–146
27. J.R. Quinlan, Induction of decision trees. Mach. Learn. **1**(1), 81–106 (1986)
28. E. Hannah, S. Mukherjee, A classification based summarization (CBS) model for summarizing text documents. Int. J. Inf. Commun. Technol. **6**(3/4) (2014)
29. J. Kupiec, J. Pedersen, F. Chen, A trainable document summarizer, in *Proceedings SIGIR '95* (1995), pp. 68–73

# Low-Cost and Energy-Efficient Smart Home Security and Automation

**Amit Kumar Singh, Siddharth Agrawal, Shreyansh Agarwal and Deepanshu Goyal**

**Abstract** With the advancement of technology, smart home systems are developing rapidly. In the recent years, the world's centralized principle is to automate each conceivable thing for simplicity in life, providing security, saving electricity, and time. With the development of technology, many research projects have been developed regarding smart home automation to improve lifestyle of human. Smart home automation is an emerging concept that allures the synergy of several areas of engineering and science. A smart home automation, which is smart, is the technology used to make all electronic equipment around the home act smart or intelligent; that is to say, smart home has highly advanced automatic systems for lighting, temperature control, security, and continuous monitoring. Smart home systems incorporate a communication network that integrates new technologies for improving human's quality of living as well as connects the electronic and electrical appliances by allowing them to be remotely monitored, controlled, and accessed. The research work carried out deals with the idea of implementing an interactive home automation and security system using a low-cost flexible home control monitoring system developed using Raspberry Pi with Internet connectivity for accessing and controlling devices by means of smart home application. The project is combined with both hardware and software technologies for multiplatform control system. The implemented system can be regarded as comfortable, secured, economic, energy-efficient, flexible, and reliable.

**Keywords** Smart home automation · Internet of things · Raspberry Pi · Wi-Fi · Android application · Web server · Sensors · Apache · Microcontroller

---

A. K. Singh · S. Agrawal · S. Agarwal (✉) · D. Goyal
Institute of Infrastructure Technology Research and Management, Ahmedabad, Gujarat, India
e-mail: shreyanshag@gmail.com

A. K. Singh
e-mail: amitkumar@iitram.ac.in

S. Agrawal
e-mail: siddharthagrawal99@yahoo.com

D. Goyal
e-mail: deepanshu.goyal.14e@iitram.ac.in



M. Pant et al. (eds.), *Computational Network Application Tools for Performance Management*, Asset Analytics,
https://doi.org/10.1007/978-981-32-9585-8_10

# 1 Introduction

In the recent years, the world's centralized principle is to automate each conceivable thing for simplicity in life, providing security, saving electricity, and time. With the development of technology, a tremendous rise in research projects has been seen regarding smart home automation to improve lifestyle of human. Smart home automation is an emerging concept that allures the synergy of several areas of engineering and science. A smart home automation, which is smart, is the technology used to make all electronic equipment around the home act "smart" or "intelligent"; that is to say, smart home has highly advanced automatic systems for lighting, temperature control, security, and continuous monitoring [1, 2].

The coded signals are sent through wiring of the house to the outlets which are programmed to be operated like electronic devices and appliances. Smart home can provide an interface to automatically control appliances via telephone lines, Wi-Fi, Internet, and android application. The literature review reveals that the developments in making the home smart is being from the beginning and has gained a great from the rudimentary level [3].

The literature survey shows that from 1920 onwards invention of home appliances was made, so that the people are benefitted and the devices will save a lot of time; later approximately 1996, the invention of computer kitchens were made which was very expensive but has led to the development of making home smarter. Now, with the Internet of Things (IOT) the smart homes have become much more smarter and are able to perform each and every tasks and also provide security.

# 2 Advantages of Home Automation System

The advantages of home automation system are as follows:

- **Convenience** Smart homes provide users to remotely access systems like heaters, air conditioners, light, music, and multimedia devices throughout the home, for example, turning on all the lights without getting up. By using mobile phone or portal device, switching wireless home security alarm system on/off or using voice recognition to control and monitor the household appliances. These common tasks are streamlined by the smart home technologies.
- **Energy Management and Savings** Smart homes are designed with such aspects which makes less usage of energy. The electronic devices are linked with the mobile applications, through which we can continuously monitor the devices, and we can switch the appliances which are running unnecessarily. Management and savings of energy are one of the key features which make smart home more popular. All of these automated tasks, along with energy-efficient, reliable, and modern electrical appliances, combine to save on natural gas, water, and electricity, thereby reducing the strain on natural resources which are drastically reducing. Thus, it provides an

efficient system for conservation of natural resources and thus helps in sustainable development.

- **Wireless Home Security** Home automation systems have many security benefits. They grant access by allowing user to keep an eye on the home from a remote location giving complete satisfaction [4]. Some home automation systems let user to interact with home security system, by providing user ability to turn on/off the system remotely. Some home automation systems provide alert phone calls, text messages, or emails in case of any unusual movements that occur in the house.
- **Accessibility** For senior members, elderly or disabled residents, a smart home is integrated with accessibility technologies [5]. The voice commands can perform tasks like operating the light controls, telephones, computers, and lock doors. With the home automation, it is possible to set time for tasks like when the garden needs to be watered and opening of curtains based on the intensity of light.

For all these reasons, developments and advancements are made in smart home technology.

# 3 Implementation

The project design system consists of five stages which are connected to both Raspberry Pi and application. The first sub-system in smart home automation is the main door security [6]. Smart home security has been designed and implemented through two interfaces which are microcontroller and mobile application. The second sub-system is lighting control system which includes the internal house lighting and the ceiling lighting outside the house. The third sub-system is maintaining ambient temperature of the rooms to get a pleasant and comfortable environment. The fourth sub-system is controlling of curtains through mobile applications. The fifth sub-system is smoke or fire sensing for the security purpose of the house.

## *3.1 Hardware*

**Wi-Fi Receiver** The Wi-Fi receiver shown in Fig. 1 is used to receive signals from a wireless device such as router, and further, it translates the signal so that the user can access the Internet any time when they are in the range of a Wi-Fi.

**Fig. 1** Wi-Fi receiver

**Fig. 2** RasPi Cam NoIR

**Fig. 3** PIR sensor

**RasPi Cam NoIR** The RasPi NoIR has all the features which are generally offered by the normal or regular camera, except it does not incorporate infrared, but in spite of not having the infrared, it has a feature which is able to see things in the dark. RasPi NoIR Cam is specially design for the Raspberry Pi and has 5 megapixel (2592 × 1944) resolutions. The Pi NoIR camera is shown in Fig. 2.

**PIR** The PIR sensor as shown in Fig. 3 is a motion sensor which consists of components such as Fresnel lens, an infrared, and supporting detection circuitry. The Fresnel lens which is mounted on the sensor focuses on any IR present around it toward the IR detector. As infrared heat is generated by the human body, as a result this radiation gets picked by the motion of human in the range of up to 6–7 m [7].

**Raspberry Pi** The Raspberry Pi 3 shown in Fig. 4 and specification makes use of Broadcom BCM2837 SoC with a 1.2 GHz 64-bit quad-core ARM Cortex-A53 processor, with 512 KB shared L2 cache and 1 GB LPDDR2 RAM at 900 MHz. It also has Bluetooth 4.1, 4 USB ports, 40 GPIO pins, HDMI port, Ethernet port, 3.5 mm audio jack, display interface [8, 9].

## *3.2 Software*

- **Raspbian** Raspbian is a free operating system based on Debian optimized for the Raspberry Pi hardware. It is called Raspbian because it is a combination or blend of Raspberry and Debian. Raspbian uses PIXEL as its main desktop environment. It is composed of a modified LXDE desktop environment and the Openbox stacking window manager with a new theme and few major changes.
- **Python** Python is a widely accepted and used dynamic, interpreted, general purpose, high-level programming language [10]. It mainly focuses on code readabil-

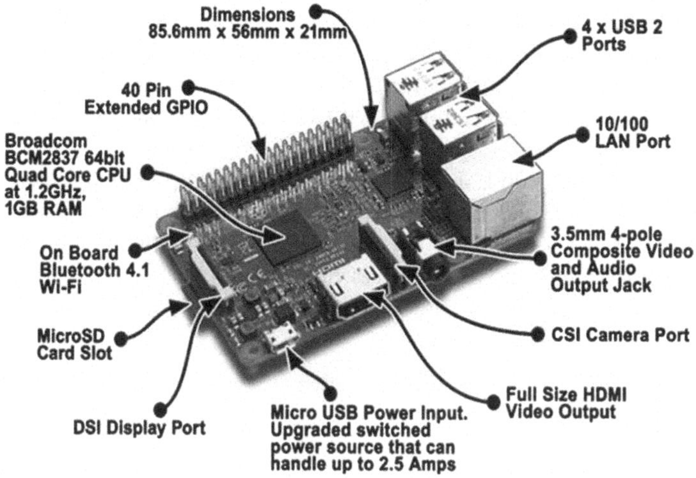


**Fig. 4** Raspberry Pi

ity, and syntax helps in reducing number of lines for expressing similar concepts compared to other languages such as C++ or Java.

In our project, we have used python as its libraries, like time, GPIO, subprocess, and Pi camera is sufficient for fulfilling our task and is comparatively easy to understand both for writing and reading compared to the libraries offered in other languages. Python is also used as it can easily receive transmitted data on a server, do the required modifications or tasks accordingly, and send the data back to the server for wireless control.

- **Apache** The Apache is universally the most used web server software based on the NCSA HTTP server. It is developed and maintained by an open community of developers under the auspices of the Apache Software Foundation. Apache is used in the project, as it is free and open-source software. It was installed in the Raspberry Pi for hosting a server on it, so that it can be used to transmit and receive data wirelessly over Wi-Fi or Internet.
- **PHP** Hypertext Preprocessor (PHP) is used for web development scripting language, and it is also used as a general-purpose programming language. PHP code can be embedded into HTML code too. PHP code is processed by a PHP interpreter in the web server. The web server accumulates the results from the interpreted and executed PHP code, with the generated web page.
- **SQL** Structured Query Language is a special-purpose domain-specific language used in programming and designed for managing data. SQL was installed on Raspberry Pi so as to maintain database for user id and password of the users who can control the equipment using application.
- **HTML/CSS** Hypertext Markup Language (HTML) is the most standard markup language for creating web pages and web applications. It describes the structure of a web page semantically. HTML was used to create web pages on the server. Cascading Style Sheets (CSS) is used for aesthetics of the web page.

- **JAVA** It is basically a combination of computer software which provides a system for developing application software and deploying it in a cross-platform computing environment. We have used Java for back-end programming of application along with android Software Development Kit (SDK). The application was developed in Android Studio.
- **XML** Extensible Markup Language (XML) is a markup language that defines a set of rules for encoding documents in a format; that is, both human-readable and machine-readable.XML was used in the front-end development of the application, i.e., the layout, design, and aesthetics of the application.

## 4 Execution of Project

In order to implement the project, the first step will be to ensure that the required software is installed, and the hardware components required are functioning properly. While working with Raspberry Pi, ensure that the Raspberry Pi is protected from any kind of static charge, and for this purpose, antistatic wrist band and antistatic Raspberry Pi case can be used.

### *4.1 Main Door Security*

The PIR and RasPi cam will be mounted on the door, as shown in Fig. 5, and the PIR will detect the presence of human. If the presence of a human is detected, then the camera will be activated (will click photographs at regular intervals which can

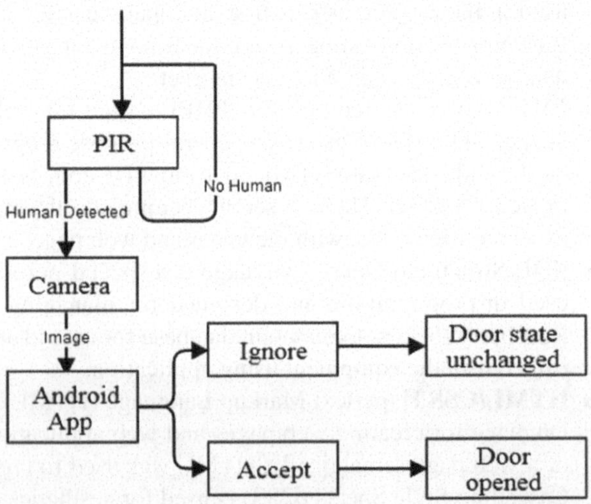


**Fig. 5** Flowchart for main door security

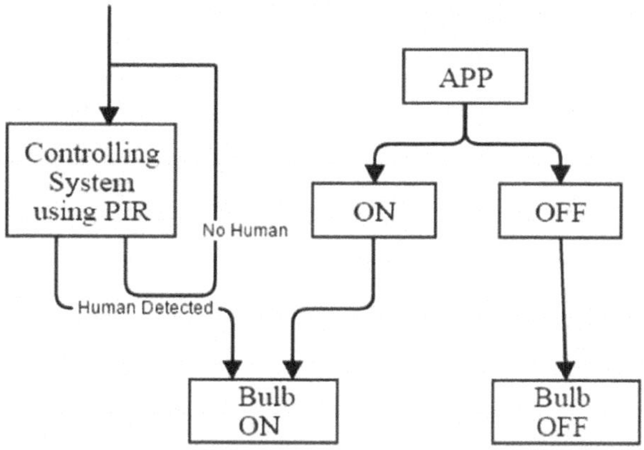


**Fig. 6** Flowchart for light automation

be specified by user). The image will be sent to the application with an alert message displaying "There is someone at the door, please take a look!" On clicking that alert message, the user will automatically be switched to the door section of the application where he or she will be able to see the image. Below the image, there will be an option to open the door or to ignore it.

## *4.2 Light Automation System*

The controlling system will use PIR(s) and IR sensors to detect the presence of human in a room. If the presence is detected, then the bulb will be ON and vice versa. However, the bulb can also be controlled using the application. The flowchart depicting is shown in Fig. 6.

## *4.3 Temperature Control*

The temperature sensor will sense the temperature and send the data to application. The user will be given an option for setting ambient temperature. Now according to the current temperature and the ambient temperature, air conditioner or heater will be turned ON. The user will also be provided for an option for turning on/off temperature control. The flowchart illustrating the above description is shown in Fig. 7.

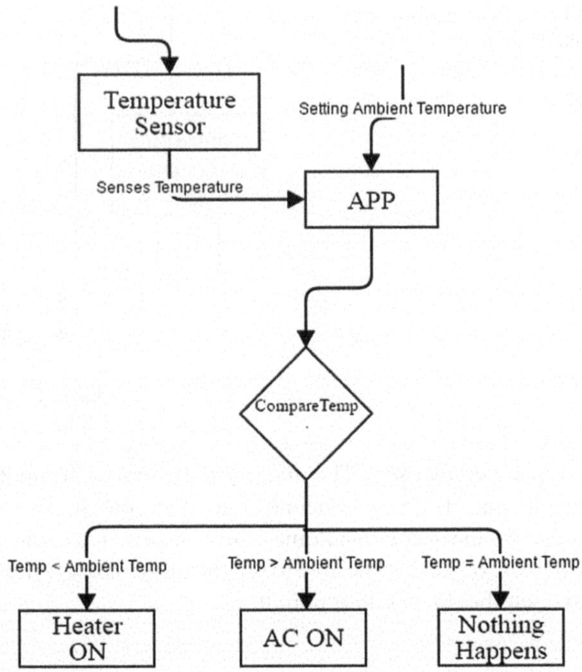


**Fig. 7** Flowchart for temperature control

## 4.4 *Fire Sensing and Protection*

For smoke and fire sensing, smoke sensor (MQ-2 gas sensor) and flame sensor are used, respectively, as shown in Fig. 8; if smoke is detected but flame is not detected, then an alert notification will be sent to the application, and a buzzer will be triggered. On clicking the notification, the user will be sent to the fire or smoke sensing page of the application where he or she will be provided an option for switching on/off all electronic devices. Also, in the case when both smoke and flame is sensed, then sprinkler will also be activated with all the other things mentioned above.

## 4.5 *Overview of Application*

The first page of the application will be a login page; in this, the user has to login with the specified username and password. After that in the next page, various image buttons will be there for going to the pages of different rooms (like drawing room, master's bedroom, children bedroom, kitchen), gallery, fire or smoke sensing, settings page, and the door. On clicking these buttons, the user will be directed to their respective pages.

**Fig. 8** Flowchart for re-sensing and protection

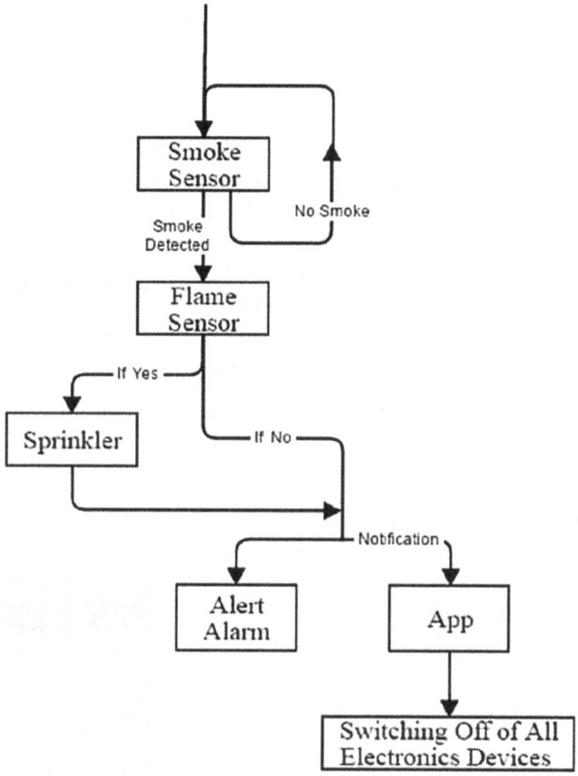


In the page for rooms, there will be several toggle buttons for turning fan, ac, light, etc., on/off. On clicking the door and fire or smoke sensing, their respective pages will be open where the required options will be there as described above. The feature of the application is shown in Fig. 9.

The first page that appears just after the login page is shown in Fig. 10, through this the user could navigate the entire home. Figure 11 shows the screen by which the user could control the lighting, fan, air conditioner, night lamp, etc., depending upon the things required in that part of the home.

## 5 Results

The actual setup is shown in Fig. 12. The implementation of the setup shows different LED's each depicting different electronic equipment as mentioned below it.

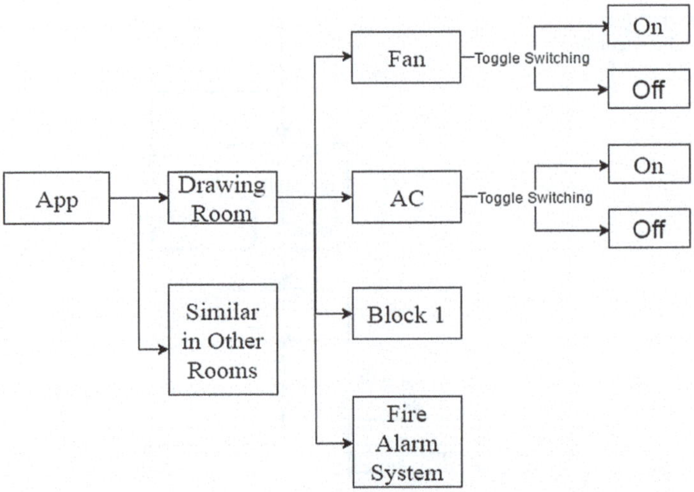


**Fig. 9** Overview of application

**Fig. 10** First screen of mobile application

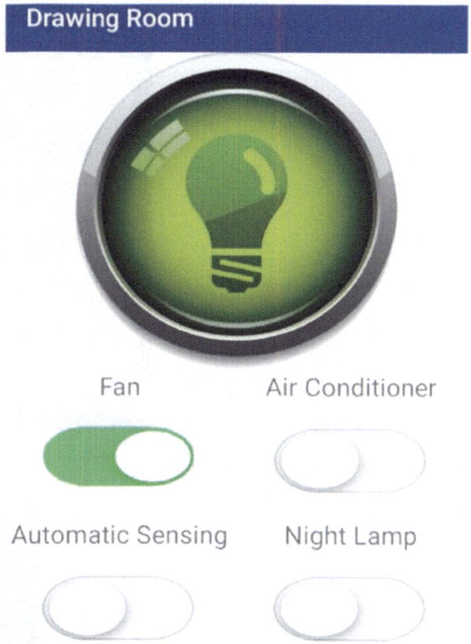


**Fig. 11** Smart home controlling screen

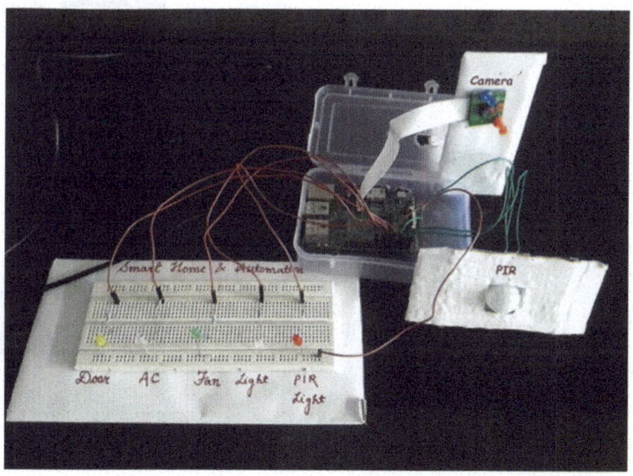


**Fig. 12** Setup

## *5.1 Main Door Security*

Figure 13 shows the activation of the camera and PIR when someone appears at the door. The indication of activation of PIR is shown by the LED labeled "PIR LIGHT." The image taken by the camera is sent to the application, and the user is given the option to open the door or to ignore the notification as shown in Fig. 14.

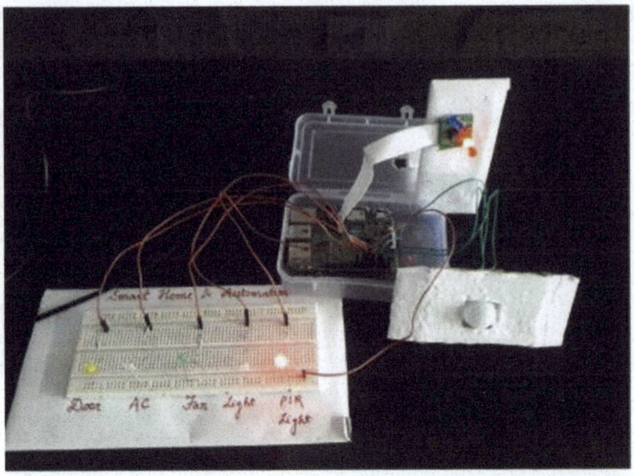


**Fig. 13** Activation of PIR and camera

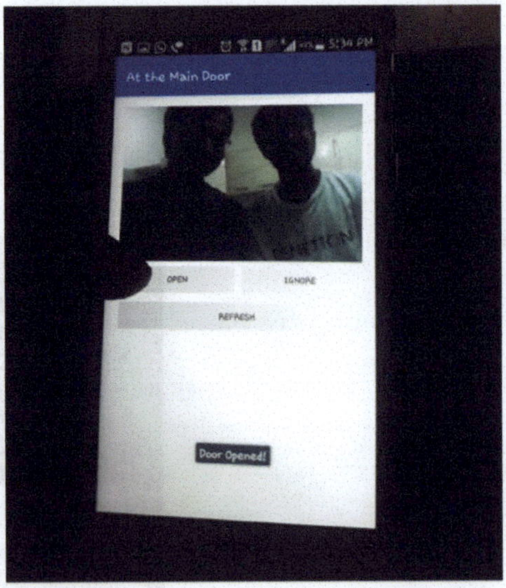


**Fig. 14** Application showing clicked image

## 5.2 *Controlling Electrical Equipment*

The electrical equipment like fan, light, air conditioner can be controlled using the application as shown in Figs. 15 and 16.

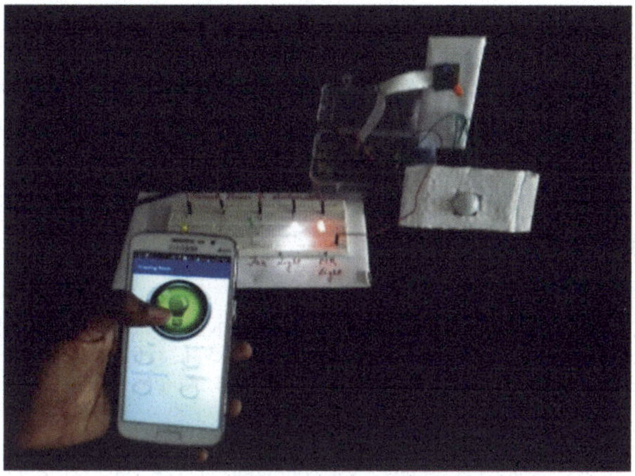

Fig. 15 Controlling light

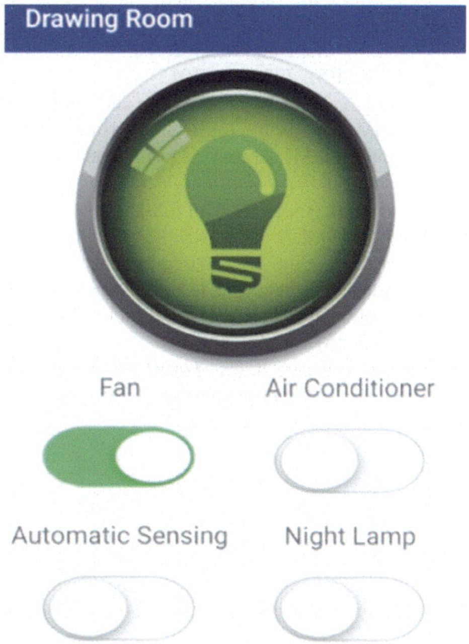


Fig. 16 Controlling fan

## 6 Conclusion and Future Scope

The implementations of the subsystems mentioned above have been successfully implemented by using Raspberry Pi microcontroller, and the results are displayed above a real-time implementation of home automation. The implementation also indicates that the smart home will also be secured, as it sends the alert message to the owner directly.

The implementation of the remaining subsystems of the project is in progress which can be further expanded to many other areas like Burglar alarm and theft protection, automated doors using face detection. The application which is currently developed for android can be further developed for other platforms.

## References


1. S. Suresh, K. Vadivukkarasi, Multifunction sensor node for home intelligent system and Raspberry Pi gateway. IJAER. **10**(7), 17163–17170 (2015)
2. M. Sripan, X. Lin, P. Petchlorlean, M. Ketcham, Research and thinking of smart home technology, in *International Conference on Systems and Electronic Engineering (ICSEE'2012)*, Phuket (Thai-land), 18–19 Dec 2012
3. A.S. Dar, S.B. Dhage, V.V. Jamadar, H.S. Kasar, J. Sheikh, Smart home automation system. Proc. Int. J. Res. Appl. Sci. Eng. Technol. (IJRASET) **5**(4) (2016)
4. M. Manasa, M. Vanitha, Smart home automation security and energy efficient wireless system through GSM. Proc. Int. Adv. Res. J. Sci. Eng. Technol. (IARJSET) **3**(7) (2016)
5. P.B. Rao, S.K. Uma, Raspberry Pi home automation with wireless sensors using smart phone. IJCSMC **4**(5), 797–803 (2015)
6. J. Bangali, A. Shaligram, Design and implementation of security systems for smart home based on GSM technology. Int. J. Smart Home **7**(6), 201–208 (2013)
7. A. Anbarasi, M. Ishwarya, Design and implementation of smart home using sensor network, in *Proceedings of International Conference on Optical Imaging Sensor and Security*, Coimbatore, Tamil Nadu, India, 2–3 July 2013
8. M.M. Patel, M.A. Jajal, D.B. Vataliya, Home automation using Rasp-berry Pi. Int. J. Innovative Emerg. Res. Eng. **2**(3) (2015)
9. S. Ganesh, S. Venkatash, P. Vidhyasagar, S. Maragatharaj, Raspberry pi based in-teractive home automation system through internet of things. Int. J. Res. Appl. Sci. Eng. Technol. (IJRASET) **3**(III) (2015)
10. TIOBE Software Index, *TIOBE Programming Community Index Python* (2015). http://www.tiobe.com/index.php/paperinfo/tpci/Python.html

# An Improvised Model for High-Security License Plate Detection and Recognition for Indian Vehicle to Enhance Detection Accuracy

**Tarun Jain, Vivek Kumar Verma, Payal Garg and Mahesh Jangid**

**Abstract** In the present time of data advancement, there is the collection of innovation utilized by the diverse branches of the legislature for observation checking. Recently, India has launched a new license plate format according to the Central Motor Vehicles (CMV) rules, 1989, in which each number plate is assigned using a unique permanent consecutive identification number and a hologram system. A chromium-based hologram has been placed, and "IND" in blue is inscribed using hot stamping foil. Almost all the states of India have started implementing this new format of number plates called high-security registration plate scheme (HSRP). At this point of time, the Indian traffic system needs a robust automatic license recognition system which may work according to the new HSRP format. In this research work, the authors first discuss the issues and challenges in identification of number plate using automatic recognition system with respect to Indian scenario and further propose a robust method for automatic detection of license plate. The proposed system uses a strong preprocessing technique for improving the identification accuracy up to 97%. The proposed system has a limitation that it does not bring up the number plate recognition in a real-time application yet which may be considered as a future work.

**Keywords** Vehicle number plate recognition · HSRP license plate · Image localization · Character segmentation

T. Jain (✉) · V. K. Verma · M. Jangid
Manipal University Jaipur, Jaipur, India
e-mail: tarunjainjain02@gmail.com

V. K. Verma
e-mail: vermavivek123@gmail.com

M. Jangid
e-mail: mahesh.jangid@jaipur.manipal.edu

P. Garg
G L Bajaj Inst. of Engineering and Technology, Greater Noida, India
e-mail: payalsmile86@gmail.com



M. Pant et al. (eds.), *Computational Network Application Tools for Performance Management*, Asset Analytics,
https://doi.org/10.1007/978-981-32-9585-8_11

## 1 Introduction

In India, according to the CMV rules, a new license plate format has launched in which a unique permanent identification number with a hologram inside is assigned for each plate. In this, a chromium-based hologram is placed, and "IND" in blue color is described using hot stamping foil. High-security registration plate scheme (HSRP) [1, 2] is a new format and almost all the states have implemented this scheme.

Indian traffic control system requires a strong fully automated license plate identification system at current scenario according to HSRP format. For this, we proposed a strong method for automatic identification of license plate under Indian environment.

## 2 License Plates in India

In the present time of data innovation, there is an assortment of innovation utilized by the diverse branches of the legislature for observation checking. As a piece of the activity arrangement, there are a large number of cameras the nation over close to the roadside and stopping for observation checking. Programmed license plate recognition assumes a vital part in different genuine applications, for example, programmed stopping region, security control of confined ranges movement law requirement, and programmed to gathering.

In India, the number plate of the vehicle made up of white foundation using dark closer view shading for autos and for the business vehicle number plate utilized yellow color as foundation and dark color as frontal area shading. Vehicles having a place with remote offices contain white color lettering on a light blue color foundation. Vehicles of military have one of a kind numbering framework, as in this, an initial character is an upward-pointing bolt.

In 2011, "the high-security registration plate scheme (HSRP)" was propelled. It contains chromium-based 3D image with "IND" in blue color and is engraved by utilizing hot stamping foil and an interesting permanent consecutive identification number [3]. In India, the vehicle number plate contains nation code, state code, locale district code, and sort of vehicle lastly the real enlistment number as shown in Fig. 1.

**Fig. 1** HSRP license plate format

All HSRP has a laser recognizable proof number carved at first glance, which cannot be eradicated and has extraordinary for each HSRP all through India. This laser number is joined with all the applicable data about the vehicle like registration number, make, model, engine number, and chassis number.

This information is electronically spared in the database of the government. This laser number aided in deciding if the number plate is bona fide or not, and along these lines help in distinguishing the credibility of the vehicle being referred to the system.

HSRP is settled on the vehicles utilizing temper obvious, non-removable, and non-reusable snap locks which make it to a great degree hard to expel the number plate once it has been joined making it troublesome for lawbreakers to take vehicle and supplanting the HSRP with common number plates.

The HSRP likewise has a white or yellow intelligent sheet covered on its surface making the vehicle more unmistakable amid night consequently maintaining a strategic distance from mishaps. There are just four sizes of HSRP and the registration numbers are emblazoned unmistakably on it making them profoundly coherent. This helps the law implementation organizations to control down wrongdoing in different ways.

The final product is a number plate which has a brilliant complete and unparalleled looks improving your vehicle look even. This paper shows a technique for the improvement of a HSRP license plate identification and number recognition framework intended for the dissimilar distinctive applications as shown in Fig. 2.

A license plate recognition framework for the most part comprises of fundamental two parts: first license plate localization and last characters' division and recognition [2].

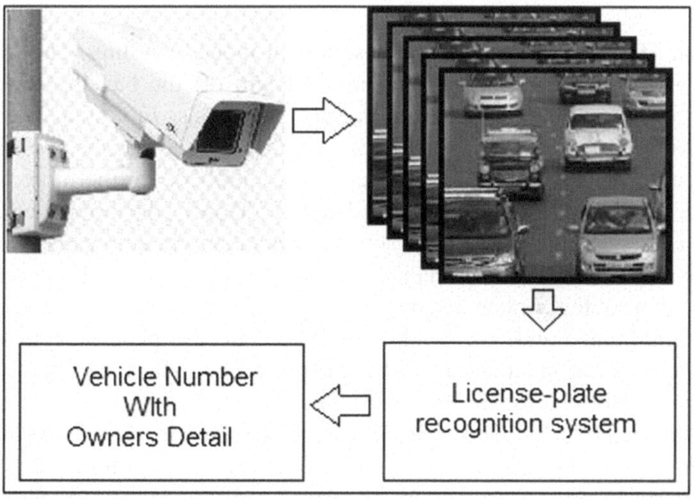


**Fig. 2** License plate recognition process

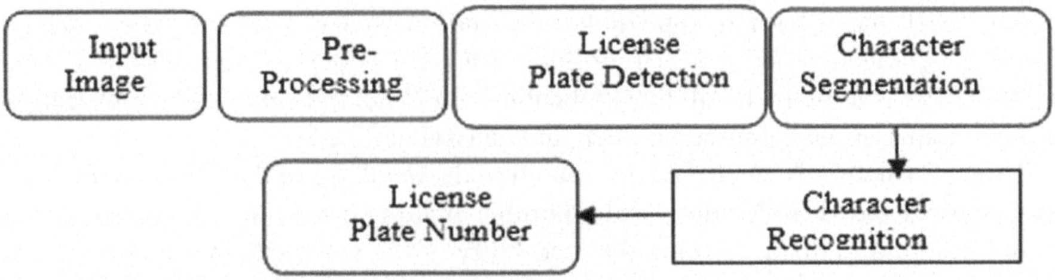


**Fig. 3** System model for license plate number recognition

The framework model of the proposed vehicle license plate recognition is appeared in Fig. 3. Given various edges of a movement video as information image, we initially portion from unique edges by processing the movement data in a locale of intrigue. Before the discovery process, we have to apply a few pre-handling for de-noising of the image as images are preprocessed to evacuate clamor and improve image differentiate. By intertwining numerous components to create a saliency outline, changed visual consideration demonstrate and can identify the position of the license plate.

Once the license plate locale is separated from the first image, it can be additionally divided into singular character pieces. At the last phase, optical character recognition is the electronic transformation of images or printed content into machine-encoded content or text.

## 3 Challenges

Recognition of vehicle permit is immense test in image handling. The reason can be closed as the accompanying perspectives. Right off the bat, the state of auto plate license plate might be different in various nations. In China, license plate is joined with Chinese characters, English characters, and numbers. However, in Europe, license plate incorporates characters and numbers. Furthermore, all things considered, the license plate might be mutilated too. Thirdly, the luminance condition may shift a considerable measure in auto images taken via auto camera either too brilliant or excessively dim luminance may definitely influence the precision and increment the trouble for plate discovery.

Each of elements builds the level of trouble of license plate recognition. Then again, as the application situations of license plate recognition are unique, the specialized prerequisites on the license plate recognition are additionally extraordinary. For example, the arrangement of license plate recognition must contemplate the higher prerequisites on vehicle speed factor in expressway, contrasted and that in the standard way. In the arrangement of license plate recognition, it is difficult to enhance both the exactness and speed of recognition simultaneously.

The reasons lie not just in the defect of the recognition's strategies, yet in addition to the detection of equipment. We delimit ourselves to plates with clear letters and numbers. This implies that we forget the plates tainted with much messy or fluffy in light of the fast. Furthermore, this framework is appropriate with the Indian HSRP plate. It cannot perceive the other countries plate, because the license plates are entirely unexpected in different nations.

## 4 Related Work

In the prior work, recognition of license plate for various applications under different conditions has introduced. Since the 1990s, automatic license recognition issue is being research territory and a portion of the examination still in preparation for Indian condition [2, 12]. A large portion of the initial methodologies depended on highlight of geometrical elements and limit lines. At first, information images are preprocessed to enhance the visual value and after that being handled to improve limit line data and components discovery.

Then this procedure executed by utilizing calculations, for example, channel, and outcomes in the shaped of images which are edges based. First it was changed over to its double partner for preprocessing and afterward handled by some standard methodologies, as Hough change to recognize lines. By and large couples of parallel lines recognized were considered as a license plate [4].

In addition to this one approach, class was proposed with variety in view of the image for their morphology operations of components [5]. This sort of method accentuation on features of vehicle plate images such that their splendor, complexity, edges, and symmetry is considered. On the closeness of these elements, this sort of techniques utilized to recognize the comparative features in comparative images and find the situation of number plate locales. Another third classification method was proposed by different creators for several recognitions of character procedures.

This kind of techniques depends on measurable components of the image [6–8]. In starting in these methodologies, content locales were identified utilizing measurable components of the content, for example, number of edges in the entire image, fluctuation of dim image pixels, edge densities in the area of intrigue. This sort of approach was usually utilized for finding content in the objective images and perceiving hopeful numbers in the plate ranges as it incorporates letters in order and numerals [9–11].

As more, as of few methodologies are additionally proposed in view of the counterfeit consciousness and genetic calculations [13]. These frameworks by and large utilized the elements like for edge recognition and edge-based insights and after that utilizing artificial intelligence strategies to recognize the area of the number plate region [14].

# 5 Proposed Model

In common situation movement, camera captures vehicle images in various points and condition which needs pre-handling for exact recognizable proof of the vehicle owner. While image acquisition process, there are grater probability to captures noise as well as in the image which need to identify and evacuate before the real handling. In this way, few of the preprocessing license plate is actualized, for example, dark shading transformation, enlargement and disintegration, skew adjustment.

Gray Conversion

This framework handles image of input in dim tone taking pixels power esteems between (0–255) and utilizing sift holding method shading image changes over from RGB to gray tone.

Dilation and Erosion

Viewpoint issue of examined image because of mistake in securing process is known as skewed image. Skew revision and identification are required to adjust the content characters in the entire image, and it is fundamental preprocessing step.

## 5.1 Number Plate Detection

In license plate recognition, the vital piece of focus is license plate detection; it restrains the pursuit space of the recognition part, so it can be figured quicker. In today's life, license plate recognition is a vital subject. There are these days many engine vehicles out and about to be made out. It is of great importance to separate the engine vehicles for a great deal of uses. For instance for activity observing, robotized tolling frameworks, speed control and street prizing, open well-being and security. In this work, we proposed method in view of edge thickness.

For finding area of intrigue, i.e., number plate, the entire image is fragmented to numerous squares in view of edge esteem. In the wake of changing, an image from original to gray tone is partitioned into little squares for assessing the component thickness. In number plate, the essential geometric element is that it holds a few of vertical edges. In this approach, it indicates step-by-step process of identification of applicant image from the entire image.

Each piece of the image filter from left best to the correct base for vertical stroke thickness and later this chose squares consider for the tallness and width proportion extent. At the keep going chose squares tried on the geometrical components of number plates removed from the image, for example, force estimation of foundation and forefront as often as possible change.

In license plate region identification sometimes in a few images, there is more than one applicant region identified. From the hopefuls, the genuine license plate must be chosen on the second and third element extraction license plate.

## 5.2 Recognition of Number Plate

In the second piece of the work, removed number plate image needs to change into content which is editable. That one is utilized by end goal of transformation of content of images into comparing the characters which are editable. For this reason, optical character recognition (OCR) framework is utilized. Image must be sectioned into singular character image prior to the acknowledgment of character.

***Character segmentation***: In number plate to disconnect the characters from each other, numerous methods have been utilized; the removed license plate is resized into a standard edge format measure. At this layout, all positions of character are given ahead of time. The correct area is ascertained for the characters in the wake of resizing. This technique is very powerful and contains very high precision rate. If there should arise an occurrence of move in removed license plate, then the outcomes in foundation are rather than characters.
***Character recognition***: At first, a database is made for all 26 English letters in order to maintain synchronization with template of new license plate format text styles. These are letter sets/digits that we consider to be perfect ones. The letter sets/digits are put away all together beginning from first textual style sparing vectors for all the twenty-six letters in order and after that beginning it with the new textual style. There is no restriction to the textual styles that can be put away; however, there exists a trade-off between the extent of database and exactness (Fig. 4).

A gray-level image or binary image input for segmented character can directly liken with a standard template designed based on the captured database. Based on the similarity factors, a prototype similarity matching process is applied for the character recognition of the segmented letters and numerals. The pattern matching method applied over the entire segmented image and the final recognize characters are integrated for the further processing.

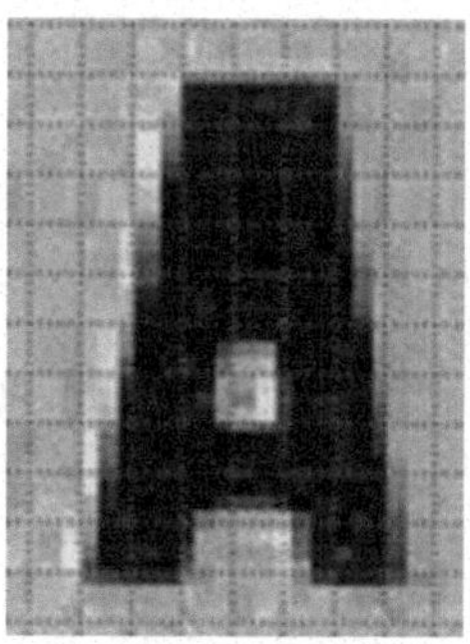

**Fig. 4** Template for letter A

**Table 1** Benchmark testing results

| No. of images | Resolution | Average object distance from camera (m) | Correct detection | Incorrect detection |
|---|---|---|---|---|
| 100 | 720 × 480 | 2–5 | 99 | 1 |
| 100 | 540 × 320 | 5–8 | 99 | 1 |
| 100 | 360 × 280 | 8–15 | 95 | 5 |

## 6 Result Analysis

In this area, we assess the proposed technique for acknowledgment of high-security registration plate. For execution, we utilized MATLAB as a testing tool. The execution assessment of the framework did on the information images taken under various conditions. For the benchmark testing of the system, an image database has prepared for three different classes. As based on the distance from the CCTV camera, three different image classes have been prepared.

The proposed technique communicated here in this paper is tried on 300 unique images, and the achievement rate of plate put is gotten up to 98% and recognition of character came to 99% so this outcome demonstrates the high proficiency approach.

In order to examine the efficacy of the procedure, the system for the actual function is verified. Following are some of the actual shooting of the car brand image as well as the natural scene around the body which includes the license plate in different provinces background of different plates. Vehicle handling may be stationary or vehicle speed at 40 km/h. or less movement. Against the car under a variety of circumstances, license plate positioning experiments are carried out and the results are shown in Table 1.

## 7 Conclusion

In this paper, an approach for the automatic vehicle number plate recognition has been proposed to validate a powerful scheme for the best result in this framework and getting rate of almost 97%. Major challenges of the system in Indian environment has been discussed and attempted to rectify as much. This type of system depends on the phases of intermediate processing that involves with different image processing techniques.

In a few applications, system requires a success rate of approximately 100%, since requires the license plate numbers of each vehicle for general applications. Proposed system has a limitation that it does not bring up the number plate recognition in a real-time application yet, but the accuracy has been tested on the real-time scenario of the Indian traffic road system.

## References


1. H.K. Gianey, A. Goyal, Localization and recognition of high security registration plate for Indian vehicle. Int. J. Comput. Organ. Trends **4**(2), 16–19 (2014)
2. V. Sathya, J. Abdul Samath, Implementation of fuzzy logic with high security registration plate (HSRP) for vehicle classification and checking in toll-plaza, in *International Conference on Advanced Information Technology academy and Industry Research collaboration* (2012), pp. 297–306
3. Y. Tang, C. Zhang, R. Gu, P. Li, B. Yang, Vehicle detection and recognition for intelligent traffic surveillance system. Multimedia Tools Appl. **76**(4), 5817–5832 (2017)
4. M. Ghazal, H. Hajjdiab, License plate automatic detection and recognition using level sets and neural networks, in *1st International Conference on Communications, Signal Processing, and their Applications* (IEEE, 2013), pp. 1–5
5. T.D. Duan, T.L.H. Du, T.V. Phuoc, N.V. Hoang, Building an automatic vehicle license-plate recognition system, in *International Conference in Computer Science* (2005), pp. 59–63
6. Sahar S. Tabrizi, Nadire Cavus, A hybrid KNN-SVM model for Iranian license plate recognition. Procedia Comput. Sci. **102**, 588–594 (2016)
7. M.T. Qadri, M. Asif, Automatic number plate recognition system for vehicle identification using optical character recognition, in *IEEE 2009 International Conference on Education Technology and Computer* (2009), pp. 335–338
8. J. John, K.V. Pramod, K. Balakrishnan, Handwritten Malayalam character recognition with a novel gradient based feature descriptor and a comparative study using SVM and ELM. Int. J. Adv. Eng. Techol. Sci. **2**(3), 13–20 (2016)
9. S. Chakraborty, R. Parekh, An improved template matching algorithm for car license plate recognition. Int. J. Comput. Appl. **118**(25) (2015)
10. L. Janowski, P. Kozłowski, R. Baran, P. Romaniak, A. Glowacz, T. Rusc, Quality assessment for a visual and automatic license plate recognition. Multimedia Tools Appl. **68**(1), 23–40 (2014)
11. M.S. Sarfraz, A. Shahzad, M.A. Elahi, M. Fraz, I. Zafar, E.A. Edirisinghe, Real-time automatic license plate recognition for CCTV forensic applications. J. Real-Time Image Proc. **8**(3), 285–295 (2013)
12. S. Saha, S. Basu, M. Nasipuri, iLPR: an Indian license plate recognition system. Multimedia Tools Appl. **74**(23), 10621–10656 (2015)
13. H. Samma, C.P. Lim, J.M. Saleh, S.A. Suandi, A memetic-based fuzzy support vector machine model and its application to license plate recognition. Memetic Comput. **8**(3), 235–251 (2016)
14. R. Baran, A. Glowacz, A. Matiolanski, The efficient real-and non-real-time make and model recognition of cars. Multimedia Tools Appl. **74**(12), 4269–4288 (2015)

# Process Efficient Artificial Neural Network-Based Approach for Channel Selection and Classification of Seizures

**T. Rajesh Kumar, K. Geetha, G. Remmiya Devi and S. Barkath Nisha**

**Abstract** The rate of neurological and psychiatric disorders is increasing rapidly in our day-to-day life, and epilepsy is one of the common neurological disorders in brain which is a constant, persistent brain disorder characterized by abnormal electrical activity in the brain. A single seizure cannot be predicted as epilepsy, because it is a condition of two or more arbitrary seizures. Seizures can also result in the loss of consciousness. The origin of seizures may be due to high electrical discharges from a collection of brain cells. Therefore, the development of accurate computer-aided diagnostic system for the classification of brain disorders is strongly desired. There is a significant interest in the research community for the development of reliable EEG-based automated tools. With the advancement of new signal processing techniques and mathematical algorithms in EEG analysis, supporting methods in medical decision and diagnosis can be developed to avoid tedious analysis of voluminous records and obtain clarity about the brain pathology. The importance of epileptic seizure detection is increasing due to the higher statistical occurrence of epileptic seizures in our normal day-to-day life activities. The epileptic seizure event must be appropriately detected to avoid its unexpected occurrences in the future. Hence in order to make this process as efficient as possible, this research work proposed an ANN-based intelligence method epileptic seizure classification and detection technique. The research work also includes result and discussion section to provide validation for the proposed methodology. The results showed that feedforward BPNN classifiers resulted in satisfactory classification accuracy percentages. This method affords reliable computerized methodology for appropriate EEG signal classification and better decision-making for epileptic seizure diagnosis in clinical practice.

**Keywords** Artificial neural network (ANN) · Feedforward network (FFN) · Seizure

T. Rajesh Kumar (✉) · G. Remmiya Devi · S. Barkath Nisha
Sri Krishna College of Technology, Coimbatore, India
e-mail: rajeshkumarprofessor@gmail.com

K. Geetha
Hindusthan College of Engineering and Technology, Coimbatore, India



M. Pant et al. (eds.), *Computational Network Application Tools for Performance Management*, Asset Analytics,
https://doi.org/10.1007/978-981-32-9585-8_12

## 1 Introduction

The rate of neurological and psychiatric disorders is increasing rapidly in our day-to-day life due to mental burden, neurological and behavioural disorders. Among the various neurological brain disorder, epilepsy is a constant, persistent brain disorder which is characterized by abnormal electrical activity in the brain. It is characterized predominantly by recurrent and unpredictable interruptions of normal brain function [1]. Epilepsy is identified by recurrent seizures. Diagnosis of epilepsy is done by analyzing electroencephalogram (EEG) signals as well as patient behaviour [2]. A single seizure cannot be predicted as epilepsy, because it is a condition of two or more arbitrary seizures. The occurrence of an epileptic seizure can be observed from abrupt muscular movements and changes in the mental state.

Seizures can also result in the loss of consciousness. The origin of seizures may be due to high electrical discharges from a collection of brain cells. The period of seizures can differ from short lapses of muscle jerks to prolonged disturbances.

The types of seizure also include focal seizure otherwise known as partial seizures and generalized seizures. The source of seizures may also be stress, insomnia, skipping of meals, exposure to heavy flashing lights, or higher consumption of alcohol in focal seizures; the epileptic process initiates in a section of the brain, and the individual may not be aware of undergoing epilepsy.

Basically, the occurrence of seizures may start in frontal and temporal lobes of the brain. These types of seizures can last only for a few minutes and may transform into generalized seizures. A specific type of focal seizure is known as Jacksonian seizure, where there may be short trembling movements. This seizure starts from a finger and then progresses towards the whole hand.

In generalized seizures, the epileptic seizure may occur in both halves of the brain. This type of seizure can also occur for a short duration that no one can notice. The seizures may be broadly classified into five types namely, absence seizures, tonic-clonic seizures, atonic seizures, tonic seizures, myoclonic seizures.

In tonic–clonic seizures, the individual falls down, but during generalized seizure, the individual does not fall down. In myoclonic seizure, the individual just shakes a part of the body.

Partial seizures are further segmented into simple partial seizures and complex partial seizures. The consciousness is sustained in simple partial seizures, while the consciousness is lost in complex partial seizures. The problems with epileptic seizure patients involve depression and memory loss. Depression may occur when the patients are administered epileptic medicine.

Therefore, the development of accurate computer-aided diagnostic system for the classification of brain disorders is strongly desired. There is a significant interest in the research community for development of reliable EEG-based automated tools. With the advancement of new signal processing techniques and mathematical algorithms in EEG analysis, supporting methods in medical decision and diagnosis can be developed to avoid tedious analysis of voluminous records and obtain clarity about the brain pathology. Clients can use their service as much as they need to, based on their requirements [3]. This work, therefore, investigates and develops a neural network-based diagnostic system for use in these automatic neurological event detection systems.

## 2 Proposed Methodology

This process can be divided into

(1) Measurement of EEG.
(2) Preprocessing.
(3) Feature extraction.
(4) Classification.

### *2.1 Measurement of EEG*

While measuring the EEG, the electrodes are connected to head. During measurement, the artefacts should be avoided. Hence, the participants should be in a relaxed mode. Finally, the signals are recorded in raw form. EEG signals provide rich information about the electrical activity of the human brain [4]. The EEG signals were recorded with the help of Ag/AgCl electrodes. These electrodes were placed at the positions of 6 points of Fp1, Fp2, F3, F4, F7, F8, and 8 points of T3, T4, T5, T6, C3, C4, P3, P4 and 2 points of O1, O2 loci of the international 10–20 System (Fig. 1). In a sample recording, the potential at each electrode is recorded relative to the potential

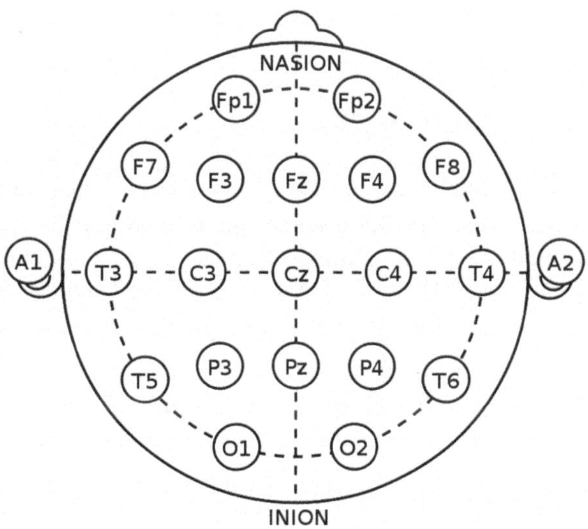


**Fig. 1** International 10-20 system

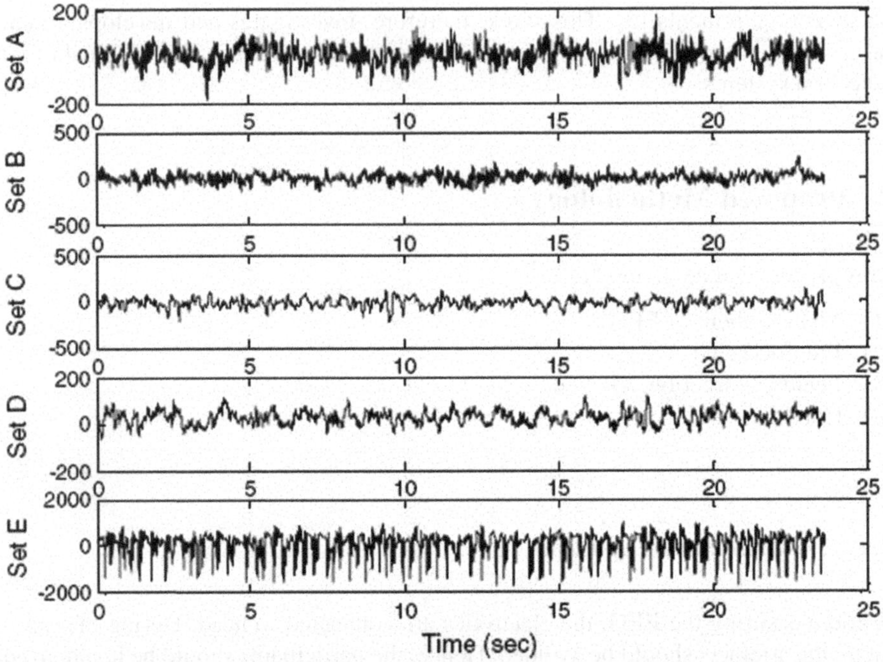


**Fig. 2** Discrete wavelet transforms of a sample EEG signal using DB2

at any one of the reference electrodes. Referential as well as bipolar recordings were used for visually reviewing EEG as shown in Fig. 2.

In 10–20 system of electrodes, F stands for Frontal, C stands for Central, P stands for Parietal, T stands for Temporal, O stands for Occipital and the last A stands for Earlobe references.

### 2.2 *Preprocessing*

The received data are usually large in size because of the high sampling frequency. Hence, preprocessing becomes more important. The most important preprocessing method is filtering. During filtering, raw EEG signals are filtered at a desired frequency band. However, the resulting filtered signals are still large to train ANNs.

### 2.3 *Feature Extraction and Classification*

Two datasets $X = \{x(1,1), \ldots, x(a,b)\}$ and $Y = \{y_1, \ldots, y_a\}$ were assumed, where

$X$—EEG measurements,
$Y$—corresponding classification of the target,
$a$—total number of trials recorded in the experiments,
$b$—number of EEG channels.

For the channel selection process, artificial neural network is implemented.

## 3 Artificial Neural Network

Artificial intelligence (AI) is the simulation of human intelligence on a machine, so as to make the machine efficient to identify and use the right piece of knowledge at a given step of solving a problem. artificial neural network is one of the disciplines in the area of AI. Presently research on artificial neural networks is being performed in a great number of disciplines, ranging from neurobiology to energy engineering applications [5].

ANN is a computer model representing the biological brain. Neurons are the basic building blocks of human brain; it works as a group of interconnected processing units with weighted connections. The activities of electrical signals can be obtained by firing millions of neurons in brain [6]. These interconnections which combine to produce an output of signal to solve a certain problem based on the input signals have received. An artificial neural network composes an input layer and multiple hidden layers with an output layer.

A feedforward neural network (FFNN) are among the most used neural networks for modeling of various non-linear problems in engineering [7]. It is a network comprising of different layers of processing units. One layer input is feed to the next layer in forward manner with a set of connection strengths or weights. By a suitable choice of architecture for a feedforward network, it is possible to perform several pattern recognition tasks. The constraint on the number of input patterns is overcome by using a two-layer feedforward network with nonlinear processing units in the output layer.

An ANN performs in two different modes of operation, learning or training and testing. The first mode learning is an adaptive process which includes the weights associated with all the interconnected neurons change in order to give the optimal response to all the observed stimuli in the process. Neural networks can be implemented in two ways, supervised or unsupervised.

While considering these two cases, the first stage is learning stage, and here the associated weights are frozen when the network reaches the required performance, whereas the last stage in this network is saved, and it is applied to classify a new unseen input data. In the testing process, an input signal is obtained which is processed to produce an output. If the system has successfully learnt it, then it is capable of producing the actual output, and it is almost the best one obtained in the learning stage which is shown in Fig. 3.

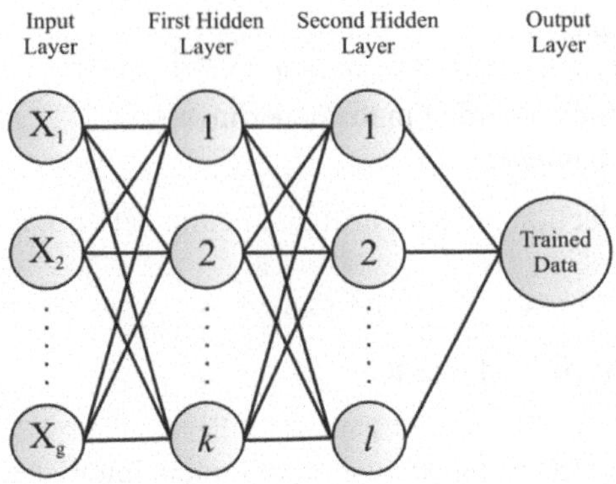


**Fig. 3** Feedforward neural network architecture

**Table 1** Training set and validation sets of the EEG data obtained from the patients at epileptic and normal condition

| Class | Training set | Validation set |
|---|---|---|
| Epileptic | 102 | 88 |
| Normal | 198 | 112 |

## 4 Result and Discussion

The procedure for ANN-based prediction is shown as follows:

*Step* 1: The EEG data obtained from the patients are considered as input data (Table 1).

*Step* 2: The 300 data of the EEG signals are fed to ANN and trained. The output of the epileptic is assigned '1', the output of normal are assigned '0'.

Figure 4 shows the best validation performance of the proposed system. From the results, it is clear that the proposed method affords higher performance rate accommodating less epochs and MSE rate. The function trains the network according to the training parameters. Two main reasons of such improvement in the classification results are separability and adaptivity [8]. Number of epochs to achieve the goal was 60; the regression value is found to be 0.99996; and the training time is 18 s.

## 5 Conclusion

In this work, an ANN-based method has been proposed for effective classification of EEG recordings as normal and seizure. Initially, the neural network has been trained with an effective LM training algorithm to obtain the results in an optimal number of epochs. The results showed that feedforward BPNN classifiers resulted in satisfactory classification accuracy percentages. This method affords reliable computerized

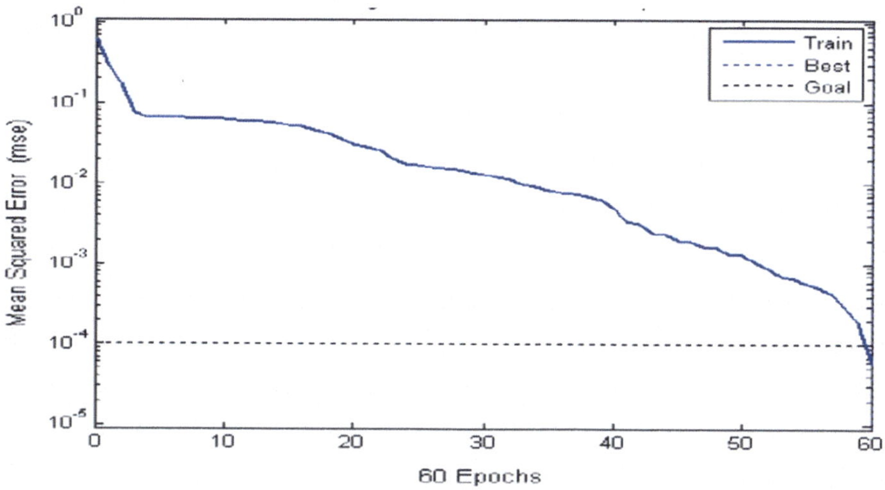


**Fig. 4** Training of ANN

methodology for appropriate EEG signal classification and better decision-making for epileptic seizure diagnosis in clinical practice.

## References


1. R.S. Fisher, W.V.E. Boas, W. Blume, C. Elger, P. Genton, P. Lee, J. Engel Jr., Epileptic seizures and epilepsy: definitions proposed by the International League Against Epilepsy (ILAE) and the International Bureau for Epilepsy (IBE). Epilepsia. **46**(4), 470–472 (2005)
2. T.N. Alotaiby, S.A. Alshebeili, T. Alshawi, I. Ahmad, F.E.A. El-Samie, EEG seizure detection and prediction algorithms: a survey. EURASIP. J. Adv. Sig. Process. **2014**(1), 183 (2014)
3. T. Rajesh Kumar, G. Remmiya Devi, K. Abinaya, N.N. Deepika, S. Priyadharshini, An integrated density based traffic load balancing system in a cloud environment. Pak. J. Biotechnol. **14**(4), 623–627 (2017)
4. N. Hamzah, N.A.M. Syukur, N. Zani, F.H.K. Zaman, EEG signal classification to detect left and right command using artificial neural network (ANN). J. Fundam. Appl. Sci. **9**(4S), 193–209 (2017)
5. A. Al-Shehri, Artificial neural network for forecasting residential electrical energy. Int. J. Energy. Res. **23**(8), 649–661 (1999)
6. B.J.A. Rani, A. Umamakeswari, Electroencephalogram-based brain controlled robotic wheelchair. Indian. J. Sci. Technol. **8**(S9), 188–197 (2015)
7. N. Vuković, & Z. Miljković, Robust sequential learning of feedforward neural networks in the presence of heavy-tailed noise. Neural. Networks. **63**, 31–47 (2015)
8. R. Ameri, A. Pouyan, V. Abolghasemi, EEG signal classification based on sparse representation in brain computer interface applications, in *2015 22nd Iranian Conference on Biomedical Engineering (ICBME)*, pp. 21–24. IEEE. (2015, November)

# The Presence of Anti-community Structure in Complex Networks

**Pawan Kumar and Ravins Dohare**

**Abstract** It has recently been argued that the complex networks do posses the anti-community structure along with the community structure. Anti-community structure is as useful as the community structure itself to uncover the topological and functional arrangement of the nodes in complex networks. In this article, we introduce the concept of anti-community structure called maximal $p$-anti-community and a corresponding algorithm to identify them in complex networks. We also investigate a number of characteristics of the anti-communities vis-a-vis those of communities in detail in a class of real-world networks. A key feature observed in anti-communities is that they are highly overlapped in contrast to the communities. We have addressed the possible causes of such a high overlapping in anti-communities. The analysis reveals that the anti-community structure is as essential as the community structure itself to comprehend the structure of real networks.

**Keywords** Anti-community · Maximal-$p$-anti-community · Strength · Anti-interaction coefficient · Algorithm

## 1 Introduction

Complex networks have become an essential tool to interpret the hidden patterns or structures in the natural systems. Community structure has been used quite frequently in the past to understand the complex networks and classify them into cohesive groups called "communities" or "clusters" [1–5]. It is then natural to ask why these groups be cohesive. What kind of topology of a network can be revealed if the groups are taken to be sparse? This is what motivates us to look for the groups in complex networks where nodes have fewer in-neighbors and larger out-neighbors. Such groups are termed as

P. Kumar · R. Dohare (✉)
Centre for Interdisciplinary Research in Basic Sciences, Jamia Millia Islamia, New Delhi, India
e-mail: ravinsdohare@gmail.com

P. Kumar
e-mail: pkumariitd@gmail.com



M. Pant et al. (eds.), *Computational Network Application Tools for Performance Management*, Asset Analytics,
https://doi.org/10.1007/978-981-32-9585-8_13

"anti-communities" or "anti-clusters" [6, 7]. Anti-communities have applications in such as social networks [8], food webs, and protein–protein interaction networks [9].

Till date, there are no efforts to formalize the concept of anti-community. Newman used the modularity minimization technique [10] to get the anti-communities in networks. It is, however, limited to detect the bipartitivity of a network. Recently, Chen et al. [7] devised the label propagation-based algorithm for anti-community detection (LPAD) in complex networks. Similar to the label propagation algorithm [11], LPAD initially assigns different labels to all the nodes. Then, label of each node propagates to its non-neighbors to form anti-communities. But LPAD is unable to detect the overlapping nature of the anti-communities. Nodes in real networks naturally share multiple groups as communities or anti-communities.

In this paper, we introduce the notion of an anti-community as a maximal $p$-anti-community and a corresponding algorithm to uncover them in complex networks. Our algorithm is capable of detecting the overlapping anti-communities. We have discussed the characteristics of anti-communities versus their counterparts in detail on a class of real-world networks with varied characteristics. A crucial feature of anti-communities that we observed is that they are highly overlapped in contrast to the communities. We have tried to reveal the possible causes for such higher overlaps.

## 2 Definitions

Let $G$ be a simple graph with vertex set $V(G)$ and edge set $E(G)$. The adjacency matrix representation of $G$ is $A = (a_{uv})_{n\times n}$, where $n$ is the order of $G$(i.e., the number of vertices in $G$) and $a_{uv}$ is 1 if there is an edge between $u$ and $v$, otherwise 0. For $T \subseteq V(G)$, a subgraph $C$ of $G$ is said to be *induced* by $T$, written $G[T]$, if $V(C) = T$ and $E(C) = \{uv \in E(G) \mid u, v \in T\}$. The only difference between a subgraph and an induced subgraph is that the former may not contain all the edges incident upon its vertices while the later does. Let $C$ be an induced subgraph of $G$. From now onward, a subgraph means an induced subgraph for us. Let $v$ be a vertex in $C$. A neighbor of $v$ in $C$ is called an *internal* neighbor of $v$. A neighbor of $v$ not in $C$ is called an *external* neighbor of $v$. The *internal* degree of $v$ is defined as $d_C^{\text{int}}(v) = \sum_{u\in C} a_{uv}$ and the *external* degree of $v$ is defined as $d_C^{\text{ext}}(v) = \sum_{u\notin C} a_{uv}$. The degree of $v$, $d(v)$ is then the sum of its internal and external degrees. The *internal* degree of $C$, denoted as $d_G^{\text{int}}(C)$, is the sum of the internal degrees of all of the vertices of $C$. Similarly, the *external* degree $d_G^{\text{ext}}(C)$ of $C$ is the sum of the external degrees of all the vertices of $C$. The *total* degree or degree of $C$, denoted as $d(C)$, is the sum of its internal and external degrees [12]. The *neighborhood* of $C$, written $N_G(C)$, is the set of all external neighbors of the vertices of $C$.

**Definition 1** Let $G$ be graph and $C$ a subgraph of $G$ with $n(C) \geq 2$. Then, the *strength* of $C$ is defined as

$$s(C) = \frac{d^{\text{int}}(C) - d^{\text{ext}}(C)}{d(C)} \tag{1}$$

We define the strength of a single non-isolated vertex to be $-1$. Then for any subgraph $C$, $p(C) \in [-1, 1]$. If $p(C) = -1$, then $C$ is an independent set and if $p(C) = 1$, then $C$ is a component or a union of components.

**Definition 2** A connected induced subgraph $C$ of a graph $G$ with strength $s(C) = p > 0$ is called a *p-community* $G$. An induced subgraph $C$ of a graph $G$ with strength $s(C) = p < 0$ is called a *p-anti-community* of $G$.

Since a $p$-anti-community may be contained in a larger $p$-anti-community, it immediately forces us to define the largest possible $p$-anti-community for a particular value of $p$. We define it as follows.

**Definition 3** A $p$-anti-community $H$ of a graph $G$ is said to be a *maximal p-anti-community* if for $\emptyset \neq T \subseteq G - V(H)$, $s(H \cup G[T]) > p$.

Intuitively, intra-anti-community nodes would have anti-relationship. We quantify this anti-relationship by the parameter anti-interaction coefficient which we define as below.

**Definition 4** Let $H$ be a subgraph of a graph $G$ and $v$ be a non-isolated vertex in $G$ such that $v \notin N_G(H)$. Then, the anti-interaction coefficient of $v$ with $H$, denoted by $\eta(v, H)$, is defined as

$$\eta(v, H) = 1 - \frac{\sum_{u \in N_G(H)} a_{uv}}{\sum a_{uv}}$$

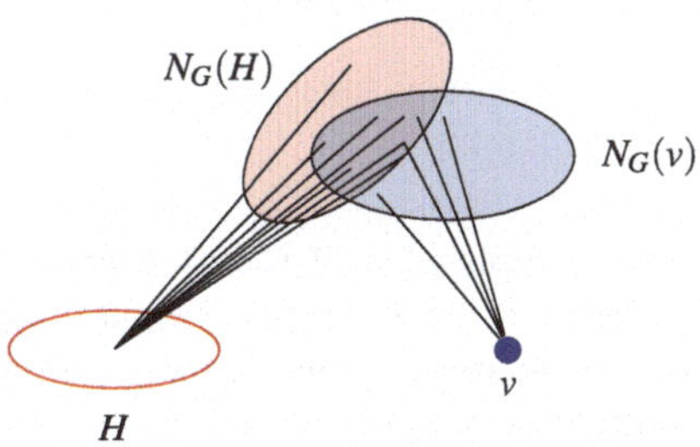


The anti-interaction coefficient of an isolated node taken to be 1 as such vertices would immediately join any anti-community. Then, we have $0 \leq \eta(v, H) \leq 1$. The lower and upper bounds are achieved when $N_G(v) \subseteq N_G(H)$ and $N_G(v) \subseteq V(G) - N_G(H)$, respectively.

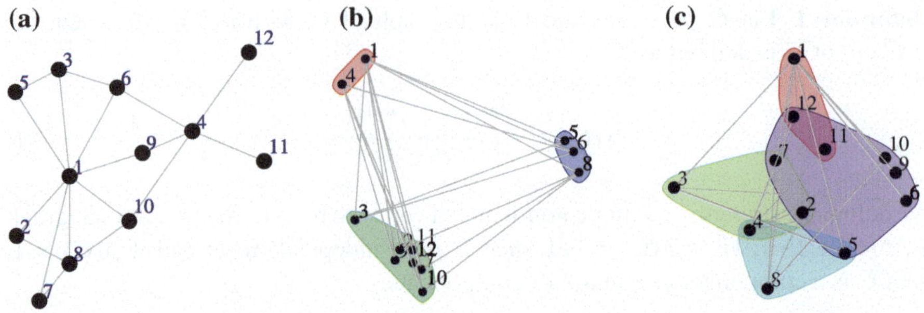


**Fig. 1** **a** A graph with unknown anti-community structure. **b** An LPAD partition of the graph into anti-communities. **c** An optimal partition with four overlapping maximal $-1$-anti-communities

Let us see how the anti-interaction coefficient can play the pivotal role for location of the vertices among the groups to get the optimal partition of a graph into anti-communities. Consider the graph given in Fig. 1a. Its anti-community structure is unknown to us. The LPAD algorithm produced three anti-communities (shades red, green, and blue) of the graph given in Fig. 1b. However, none of the three anti-communities is optimal. This is because the partition can be refined by rearranging the nodes among the groups. For example, the vertex 1 can sit together with the group {11, 12} better than with 4 as $\eta(1, 4) = 2/5$ and $\eta(1, \{11, 12\}) = 1$. On the other hand, the vertices 11 and 12 can better go with the group {5, 6, 8} (the blue one) instead of with the group {2, 3, 7, 9, 10} as

$$\eta(11, \{2, 3, 7, 9, 10\} = 0 \quad \text{and} \quad \eta(11, \{5, 6, 8\}) = 1$$
$$\eta(12, \{2, 3, 7, 9, 10\} = 0 \quad \text{and} \quad \eta(12, \{5, 6, 8\}) = 1$$

Doing all such necessary rearrangements, we get the new partition as shown in Fig. 1c.

## 3 Algorithm

Our algorithm works on the simple idea of repeated inclusion of potential nodes in the groups (anti-communities) starting with a single node. The groups grow as long as their strengths do not increase. Once an anti-community is found, a new node is chosen from the remaining nodes as a seed for the next anti-community. The algorithm stops when there are no more nodes available for seed. The algorithm is presented below.

**Algorithm 1** Algorithm to find maximal p-anti-communities in a network

**Input:** A graph $G$
**Output:** maximal $p$-anti-communities of $G$
1: Mark all nodes as *uncovered*.
2: While there are *uncovered* nodes in $G$, select $u$ as one of the *uncovered* nodes. Otherwise, stop.
3: Let $H \leftarrow \{u\}$ and $p \leftarrow 1$.
4: Choose $P$ as the set of those non-neighbors of $H$ whose *anti-interaction coefficient* with $H$ is greater than the average anti-interaction coefficient of all the non-neighbors of $H$ with $H$. Then choose $P_{ind}$ as the largest independent subset of $P$.
5: Set $H_{new} \leftarrow H \cup P_{ind}$ and $p_{new} \leftarrow strength(H_{new})$.
6: If the $p_{new} > p$, print $H$, mark all the nodes in $H$ as *covered* and go to step 2. Otherwise, set $H \leftarrow H_{new}$ and $p \leftarrow p_{new}$ and go to step 4.

# 4 Application

In this section, we discuss the application of our algorithm to detect the anti-community structure of a class of real-world networks in comparison with the community structure. We also throw some light on a few characteristics of anti-communities and their possible causes.

## 4.1 *r-partite Graphs*

A graph $G$ is said to be an $r$-partite graph if $V(G) = \cup_{i=1}^{r} V_i$, where $\emptyset \neq V_i \subset V, \forall i$ and $V_i \cap V_j = \emptyset$, for $i \neq j$. An $r$-partite graph $G$ is said to be a complete $r$-partite graph if for any two vertices $u$ and $v$ lying in distinct partitions of $G$, $uv \in E(G)$. Complete $r$-partite graphs are the best models possessing the non-overlapping anti-community structure. Any good anti-community detection algorithm must be able to detect all the partitions as the anti-communities. This is because the partitions are unique. However, in incomplete $r$-partite graphs, there may be certain nodes which belong to multiple partitions. Any algorithm ought to be able to detect such multiple memberships of the vertices. However, so far only a handful of algorithms have been devised to detect the anti-communities and none of those is capable of detecting the overlapping anti-communities. Our algorithm detects the partitions of a complete $r$-partite graph uniquely as well as the overlaps in the non-complete $r$-partite graphs.

## 4.2 *Zachary Karate Club*

Consider the Zachary karate club network [13]. The algorithm SLPA [14] detects two communities as shown in Fig. 2. We then applied anti-community detection algorithm

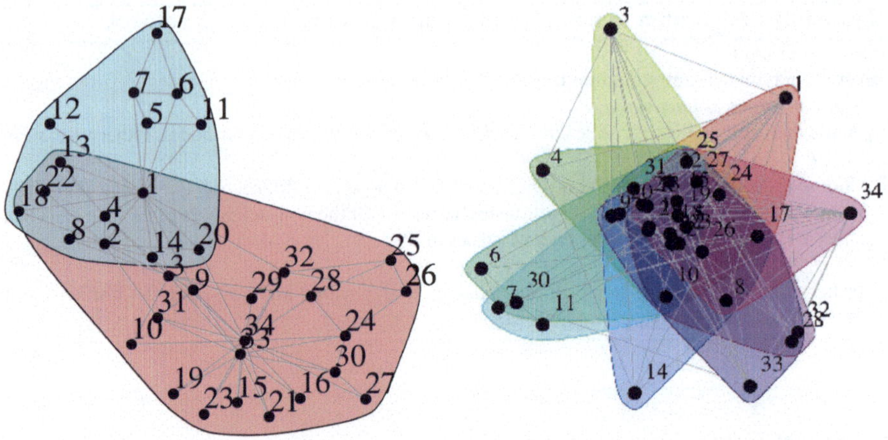


(a) Communities detected by SLPA (b) Maximal −1-anti-communities.

**Fig. 2** Communities and anti-communities in the Zachary Karate Club network

proposed in this paper to uncover the anti-community structure of the network. It revealed 11 anti-communities as maximal −1-anti-communities. The overlaps among the anti-communities were much higher than the community overlaps.

## 5 Anti-community Versus Community Characteristics

Now, we look at the overall characteristics of the anti-communities versus their counterparts in a class of real-world networks.

### *5.1 Vertex Overlap Distributions*

Next, we present the distributions of the overlaps of nodes in the anti-communities in a class of real-world networks. For a network, we define $P_v(k)$ as the fraction of the vertices of the network sharing $k$ communities for $k = 1, 2, 3, ...,$ etc. Then, $\{P_v(k)\}_{k \geq 1}$ represents the vertex overlap distribution of a network. The shape of the distribution will help us understand the kind of vertices responsible for high overlaps. We plotted the $\{P_v(k)\}_{k \geq 1}$ for all the networks listed in Table 1. The plots are shown in Fig. 3. All the plots are bimodal against the general intuition that higher number of nodes share low number of anti-communities (Table 2).

**Table 1** Properties of networks, communities, and anti-communities. Here, $n$ is the number of vertices and $e$ the number of edges, $cc$ the clustering coefficient of the network, $k_c$ and $k_a$ are, respectively, the number of communities and anti-communities, $<n_c>$ and $<n_a>$ are, respectively, the average orders of the communities and anti-communities

| Networks | $n$ | $e$ | $cc$ | $k_c$ | $k_a$ | $<n_c>$ | $<n_a>$ | References |
|---|---|---|---|---|---|---|---|---|
| *E. Coli* (version 1.1) | 423 | 519 | 0.209 | 70 | 98 | 15.5 | 270.6 | [15] |
| Yeast U. Alon | 688 | 1078 | 0.091 | 88 | 96 | 19.2 | 433.3 | [16] |
| Budapest | 1015 | 989 | 0.442 | 578 | 123 | 23.8 | 804.9 | [17] |
| Network Scientists | 1589 | 2742 | 0.878 | 462 | 848 | 13 | 594.5 | [6] |
| Yeast PPI | 2361 | 6646 | 0.200 | 489 | 302 | 25.3 | 1306.1 | [18] |
| Power Grid | 4941 | 6594 | 0.106 | 1069 | 1497 | 16.3 | 2288.1 | [19] |
| HEP | 8361 | 15,751 | 0.636 | 2275 | 2754 | 20.0 | 3595.4 | [1] |
| Astro-physics | 14,845 | 119,652 | 0.715 | 2023 | 5965 | 57.0 | 3810.9 | [1] |

**Table 2** Average number of anti-communities per vertex ($<z_a>$) versus the average number of communities per vertex ($<z_c>$) in different networks. It is observed that $<z_a>$ is much higher than $<z_c>$ and this difference increases with the network order

| Network | $<z_a>$ | $<z_c>$ |
|---|---|---|
| Yeast U. Alon | 61.1 | 1.4 |
| Budapest | 98.4 | 1.1 |
| Political blogs | 130.8 | 1.2 |
| Network scientists | 317.3 | 1.1 |
| Yeast PPI | 167.3 | 2 |
| Power grid | 692.3 | 1.7 |
| HEP | 1182.1 | 1.4 |
| Astro-physics | 1503.3 | 3.0 |

## 5.2 *Degree Versus the Number of Shared Anti-communities*

To uncover the bimodal nature of the vertex overlap distributions of the networks, we look into the number of anti-communities of a vertex with respect to its degree. We plot the degree versus the number of shared anti-communities for all the networks given in Table 1. The plots (see Fig. 4) indicate that the nodes are divided into two classes—one whose anti-community share is higher than the average number of anti-community share(see the portion above the blue horizontal line, which represents the average number of anti-community share) and those whose anti-community share is below the average anti-community share(see the portion below the blue horizontal

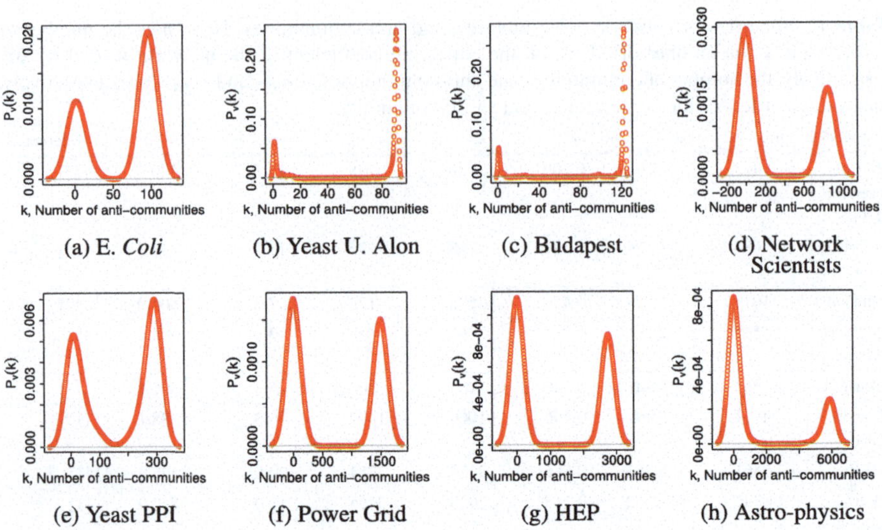


**Fig. 3** Vertex overlap distributions of different networks. The vertex overlap distribution, $P_v(k)$ is the fraction of vertices sharing $k$ anti-communities. $P_v(k)$ has bimodal shape for all the six networks in this figure. Similar results are obtained on many other real networks

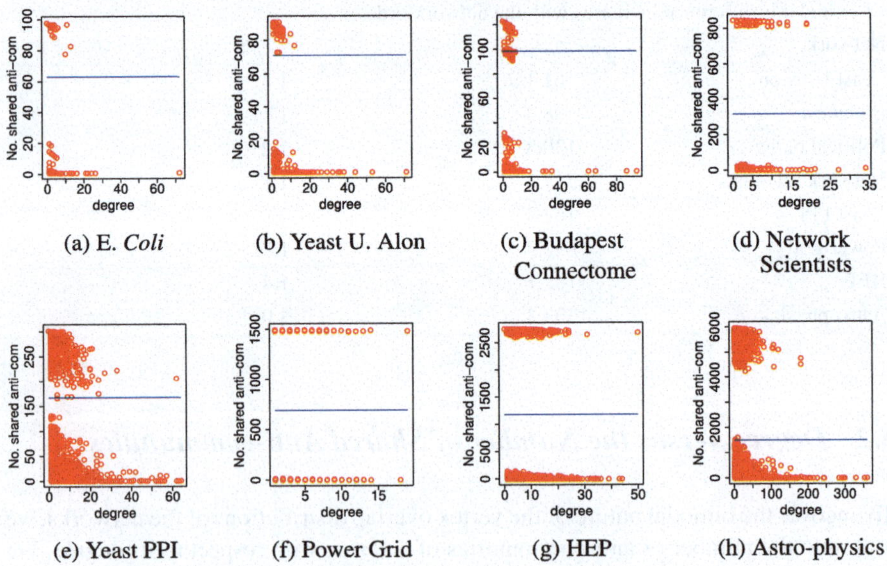


**Fig. 4** Degree versus number of shared anti-communities of different networks

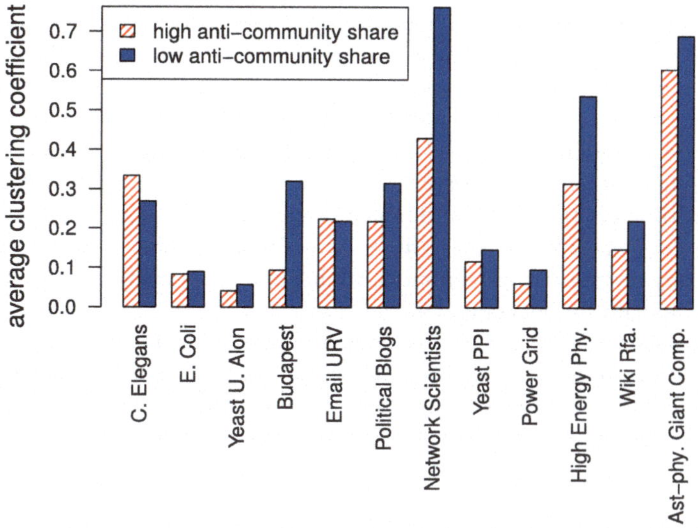


**Fig. 5** Average clustering coefficient of two classes of nodes. We can infer from here that the vertices with high anti-community share have low average clustering coefficient while those with low anti-community share have high average clustering coefficient. This seems to be a significant cause for the bimodal shape of the vertex overlap distributions in Fig. 3

line). This is in line with the bimodal nature of the plots of Fig. 3. Then, we compute the clustering coefficients of the two classes of nodes. What we find is that the vertices with above the average anti-community share possess the low clustering coefficient while the ones with below average anti-community share possess the high clustering coefficient (see Fig. 5). This seems to be a significant cause for the bimodal shape of the vertex overlap distributions in Fig. 3.

## 6 Conclusion

We have proposed a new structure-based definition of anti-community called maximal $p$-anti-community in complex networks. We have then presented an algorithm to find maximal $p$-anti-communities in a network using the concept of anti-interaction coefficient. The algorithm works perfectly on the complete $r$-partite graphs, where each anti-community is a non-overlapping set of mutually non-adjacent vertices. When the graph is not a complete $r$-partite graph, the vertices are free to join multiple groups. A novel part of our algorithm is that it detects the overlapping anti-communities automatically. Tests of the algorithm on a class of real-world networks highlight the characteristics of the anti-communities vis-a-vis those of the communities. For example, it is observed that the number of anti-communities in all the networks we have considered are much higher than the number of communities within them. The average anti-community orders are also higher than the average community orders. Another crucial characteristics of the anti-community is that they are highly overlapped in comparison to their counterparts. Lastly, the vertex overlap distributions of different networks emerge to be in bimodal shapes. This corresponds to the two classes of the vertices—the ones with low anti-community share and those with the high anti-community share. The reason behind bimodal shape of the vertex overlap distribution plots is the difference in the clustering coefficients of the vertices. We infer that the vertices with high anti-community share (memberships) have comparatively low clustering coefficient, while the vertices with low anti-community share have high clustering coefficient.

The analysis reveals that the anti-communities are equally necessary to uncover the hidden structure of real-world complex networks. The opposite characteristics of anti-communities may provide us complementary statistics about real-world complex networks. In future, we shall explore the anti-community structure in weighted and directed networks.

**Acknowledgements** This work is supported by the project grants received from SERB, DST, Govt. of India and was carried out at the Centre for Interdisciplinary Research in Basic Sciences, Jamia Millia Islamia, New Delhi.

## References

1. M.E.J. Newman, The structure of scientific collaboration networks. Proc. Nat. Acad. Sci. **98**(2), 404–409 (2001)
2. M. Girvan, M.E.J. Newman, Community structure in social and biological networks. Appl. Math. **99**, 7821–7826 (2002)
3. J.Q. Jiang, A.W.M. Dress, G. Yang, A spectral clustering-based framework for detecting community structures in complex networks. Appl. Math. Lett. **22**, 1479–1482 (2009)
4. A. Lancichinetti, S. Fortunato, J. Kertesz, Detecting the overlapping and hierarchical community structure of complex networks. New J. Phys. **12** (2010)
5. R. Nadakuditi, M. Newman, Graph spectra and the detectability of community structure in networks. Phys. Rev. Lett. **108**(188701) (2012)
6. M.E.J. Newman, Finding community structures in networks using the eigenvectors of matrices. Phys. Rev. **74** (2006)
7. L. Chen, Q. Yu, B. Chen, Anti-modularity and anti-community detecting in complex networks. Inf. Sci. **275**, 293–313 (2014)
8. B. Baesens, V. Van Vlasselaer, W. Verbeke. *Fraud Analytics Using Descriptive, Predictive, and Social Network Techniques: A Guide to Data Science for Fraud Detection* (Wiley, New York, 2015). Google-Books-ID: OZwvCgAAQBAJ
9. E. Estrada, D.J. Higham, N. Hatano, Communicability and multipartite structures in complex networks at negative absolute temperatures. Phys. Rev. E **78**(2), 026102 (2008)
10. M.E.J. Newman, M. Girvan, Finding and evaluating community structure in networks. Phys. Rev. E **69**(2), 026113 (2004)
11. U.N. Raghavan, R. Albert, S. Kumara, Near linear time algorithm to detect community structures in large-scale networks. Phys. Rev. E, **76** (2007)
12. S. Fortunato, Community detection in graphs, **486**, 75–174 (2010)
13. W.W. Zachary, An information flow model for conflict and fission in small groups. J. Anthropol. Res. **3**, 452–453 (1977)

14. J. Xie, B.K. Szymanski, X. Liu, *SLPA: Uncovering overlapping Communities in Social Networks via a Speaker-Listener Interaction Dynamic Process*, pages 344–349. (IEEE, 2011)
15. S.S. Shen-Orr, R. Milo, S. Mangan, U. Alon, Network motifs in the transcriptional regulation network of *Escherichia coli*. Nat. Genet. **31**(1), 64–68 (2002)
16. R. Milo, S. Shen-Orr, S. Itzkovitz, N. Kashtan, D. Chklovskii, U. Alon, Network motifs: simple building blocks of complex networks. Science **298**(5594), 824–827 (2002)
17. B. Szalkai, C. Kerepesi, B. Varga, V. Grolmusz, The budapest reference connectome server v2.0. Neurosci. Lett. **595**, 60–62 (2015)
18. B. Dongbo, Y. Zhao, L. Cai, H. Xue, X. Zhu, L. Hongchao, J. Zhang, S. Sun, L. Ling, N. Zhang, G. Li, R. Chen, Topological structure analysis of the protein–protein interaction network in budding yeast. Nucleic Acids Res. **31**(9), 2443–2450 (2003)
19. D.J. Watts, S.H. Strogatz, Collective dynamics of small world networks. Nature **393**, 440–442 (1998)

# A Hybrid ACO-SVM Approach for Detecting and Classifying Malaria Parasites

**Damandeep Kaur and Gurjot Kaur Walia**

**Abstract** The major growth in computing technology has done wonders for the medical field. Being a significantly favourable research domain, many algorithms have been proposed in the near past to detect the presence of malaria parasites. The target of this work was to originate a technique which detects the parasites of malaria easily and classifies in just a few seconds. A hybrid ant colony optimization and support vector machine approach is developed for this task. In this work, ant colony optimization was used for the detection of the boundaries of microscopic images of malaria parasites and by using multi-class support vector machine, classification of malaria parasites is achieved. In SVM various parameters were taken (HSV colour values, auto correlogram, colour moments, mean amplitude, area and wavelet moments), which are used to build different classes or groups. The performance of this approach is verified by simulation results.

**Keywords** Malaria · Ant colony optimization · Edge detection · Support vector machine

## 1 Introduction

Plasmodium of mosquito's category is accountable to cause malaria. The biting of female mosquitoes generally known as anopheles results in the entrance of malaria-causing parasites into the human blood circulatory system leading to diseased people. In accordance with the reports presented by World Health Organization (WHO), cause of one million deaths every year is none other than malaria and the proportion of people getting infected is much higher [1]. After entering into the bloodstream of a patient, the process life cycle of a parasite of malaria also starts. During this process, parasites flourish and reproduce themselves. The red blood cells (RBCs) are utilized as hosts and are destroyed thereafter. There are four major species of malaria parasites infecting humans which are all the plasmodiums of different kinds namely

D. Kaur (✉) · G. K. Walia
ECE Department, GNDEC, Ludhiana, India
e-mail: giansinghkhalsa@gmail.com



M. Pant et al. (eds.), *Computational Network Application Tools for Performance Management*, Asset Analytics,
https://doi.org/10.1007/978-981-32-9585-8_14

vivax, falciparum, malariae and ovale. In tropical and subtropical areas, *Plasmodium vivax* parasites are widely available and have a strict clinical substantiation [2].

## 2 Literature Survey

V. Vapnik et al. (1995) was the first who proposed support vector machine algorithm [3]. Dorigo M. et al. (1996) proposed the first ACO algorithm, called the Ant System [4]. C. D. Ruberto et al. (2002) had given a grammatical approach to segmentize the cells [5]. It gives more precise results when it comes in comparison with other methods like watershed algorithm. Element having hemispherical disk shape is used to improve the compactness and round shape of the red blood cells in this method, whereas flat disk-shaped element was operated to separate overlapping cells. For the distribution, project models which rely on grammatical operator and coloured histogram similarity are implied. Even the above approaches basically give great results, but they are highly influenced by the quality of the given image. It is important to analyse that the process is slowing down due to both hue and saturation images. Dorigo and Stutzle [6] are the first who propose the ant colony algorithm [7]. The algorithm ACO imitates the behaviour of a original ant colony. The basic family unit of ants is ant colony, around which ants spent their whole life. Ants are so smart that they will find the shortest possible path starting from a food source and ending at their nest through decryption of the pheromone information. Always the ants continuously deposit the pheromone on the track so that the path from source to destination is made available for the following ants. When it comes to turning left or right, random path is taken. Half of the ants choose to turn left and the others will choose the opposite path of turning right. Pheromone density is more on shorter paths. The shortest path is chosen following the similar pathway as that of the other ants in search of the food. Ant colony optimization (ACO) is inspired from the true and real phenomenon of deposition of pheromone on the ground so as to mark some preferable track that should be adopted by other ants and that's why it is called nature-inspired optimization algorithm. S. F. Toha and U. K. Nagah (2007) proposed an algorithm based on low time consumption [8]. Pi fuzzification algorithm and fuzzy c-mean clustering are used. In their work, they use the various soft computing tools which give the efficient results for any malaria detection techniques. They propose an automated system followed by histogram equalization, image segmentation and then counting parasites which were extracted by morphological operations. The threshold values from 1 to 255 are inputted for image segmentation. The basic steps of digital image analysis are used in their work. D. J. Bacon et al. (2007) in their paper stated that the role of automatic visual enquiry becomes very important when the computational power increases [9]. K. Mitiku et al. (2007) in their paper stated that manual detection methods are hardly practiced in developing nations due to their excessive cost, specific infrastructure requirements and complications in handling [10]. Makkapati and Rao (2009) presented a schematic, which is based on HSV colour space model [11]. This method of significance is basically determined by finding range of the hue and threshold value of saturation. The background is represented by the dark colour in this type of image. The hue range is in between 360°. Every segment of the hue is made of 60°. To find the number of pixels in a particular hue segment, these segments are used. They propose a method which can determine the relevant thresholds, which are dynamic in nature for a given image. With the colour variability the performance is analysed. Here, with the help of hue range they determine the background. After the determination of back ground pixels, the remaining pixels are used to determine the parasitic type. The parasites are determined on the basis of their colour variations. G. Diaz et al. (2009) states that, in order to enhance and change the manmade screening of specimen tools, for example, artificial intelligence and image processing are vital [12]. The time span required to count the parasites is declined when digital image analysis comes into practice. An enhancement in the performance of parasite density quantification is noticed when the time period is reduced. It was represented for quantifying parasites in stained thin blood films. While proposing this method, the image was freed from luminance differences and in order to categorize pixels as erythrocyte or background, RGB colour space is practised. Identification of erthrocytes is done in the classification process through bank of classifiers which were trained. N. Alexander and Drakely (2010) give an explanation about the demerits of the digital image analysis method of processing, in which user intervention is must, which results into more time consumption and larger inter and intra-observer variability [13]. I. Ljungstrom et al. (2011) had given a statement on an effective, efficient and as a substitute to these methods, which involves thin blood smear embedded with stains of Giemsa to be processed under visual microscopic quantification [14]. With the continuation of the staining process, the parasites of the falciparum of plasmodium are highlighted and erythrocytes and parasites are differentiated from each other. Also, visual analysis is more time consuming including more theoretical and complicated processing resulting in larger inter and intra-observer variability. K. M. Khatri et al. (2013) had given a statement that the optimal saturation thresholding method involves an ideal threshold for major bimodal distributions, but at the same time, no proper results for unimodal distributions of unimodal is given. Most of the pixels are related to the background while only a few numbers of pixels belong to the parasites. This results into big and wide peaks of histogram, hence giving the unimodal distribution as a result [15]. W. Y. Guo et al. (2014) had given a theory that for the optimal saturation thresholding method mainly classic image segmentation is used in applications based on the selection of the discriminant criterion, to enhance the separability of the resulting classes in grey levels [16].

## 3 Methodology

There are some steps which are used to fulfil the objectives of the proposed work:

Step 1. The medical images of malaria are inputted.

Step 2. The Malaria images contain some noises and errors; so to remove these noises here image pre-processing step is performed. Here, the microscopic images of malaria are firstly filtered using spatial filtering. Spatial filtering is the technique which adds values of particular pixels to neighbourhood pixels.

Step 3. In this step, the pre-processed images are implemented to the Ant Colony Optimization, so that the edges of the image are achieved.

Step 4. After getting the edges of an image, the colour of the image is enhanced.

Step 5. These enhanced images are applied to the multi-class support vector Machine method to achieve the class of the parasite present in an image.

### 3.1 *Ant Colony Optimization*

For segmentation of the malaria images basic tool of ant colony optimization is implied. The segmentation of the malaria images is followed by the filtering. Filtering is done with the help of spatial filters. Filtering is an important factor in processing of image. Filters are used to reduce the unacceptable noise from image so that to provide more accurate results. Spatial filters are those in which each value of pixel $I(u, v)$ is changed by an intensity pixel function of neighbourhood $(u, v)$ [17].

### 3.2 *Support Vector Machine: Basic Mathematics*

$n$ number of training samples are given in Eq. (1), where $t$ is the training input for each sample (Eq. 2). Here, one of two values is the labelling of the class (Eq. 3).

$$\{a_i, b_i\}, \quad i = 1 \ldots .n \tag{1}$$

$$a_i \in S^t \tag{2}$$

$$b_i \in \{-1, 1\} \tag{3}$$

$S^t$ All hyper planes are parameterized by a vector $(c)$ and a constant $(d)$, which is shown in Eq. (4)

$$c.a + d = 0 \tag{4}$$

The hyper planes which separate the data (i.e. $(c, d)$) are shown in the form of function in Eq. (5)

$$f(a) = \text{sign}(c.a + d) \tag{5}$$

The above function classifies the training data correctly.

Now $(c, d)$ is the representation of hyper planes which is expressed by all pairs, i.e.$(\lambda c, \lambda d)$ where $\lambda \in S^{+}$. So, canonical hyper planes are those by the distance, 1 they separate the hyper planes from each other. These hyper planes are shown in the form of equation as given below:

$$a_i.c + d \geq +1 \quad \text{when } b_i = +1 \tag{6}$$

$$a_i.c + d \leq -1 \quad \text{when } b_i = -1 \tag{7}$$

Or it can be represented as,

$$b_i(a_i.c + d) \geq 1 \quad \forall i \tag{8}$$

These hyper planes have the "functional distance" $\geq$ 1. This distance cannot be compared by the Euclidean distance or the geometric distances.

For the given hyper planes, $(c, d)$, $(\lambda c, \lambda d)$ gives the same hyper plane value. The function distance given to the data points has different values. Magnitude $c$ is normalized so that between the data points and hyper planes distance will be obtained. The distance is given below:

$$k((c, d)a_i) = \frac{b_i(a_i.c + d)}{||c||} \geq \frac{1}{||c||} \tag{9}$$

The hyper planes are obtained in such a manner that the data points having less distance between them, that distance is maximized. This can be done with the help of Lagrange multiplier (Fig. 1).

$$C(\alpha) = -\sum_{i=1}^{n} \alpha_i + \frac{1}{2}\sum_{i=1}^{n}\sum_{j=1}^{n} b_i b_j \alpha_i \alpha_j \left(b_i b_j\right) \tag{10}$$

$$\sum_{i=1}^{n} b_i \alpha_i = 0 \tag{11}$$

$$0 \leq \alpha_i \leq A \quad (\forall i) \tag{12}$$

$\alpha$ is the Lagrange multiplier having a non-negative value with the vector $n$, where $A$ is a constant.

Matrix $(G)_{ij} = b_i b_j \left(a_i a_j\right)$ is defined which introduces new given equations:

$$C(\alpha) = -\alpha^R 1 + \frac{1}{2}\alpha^R G\alpha \tag{13}$$

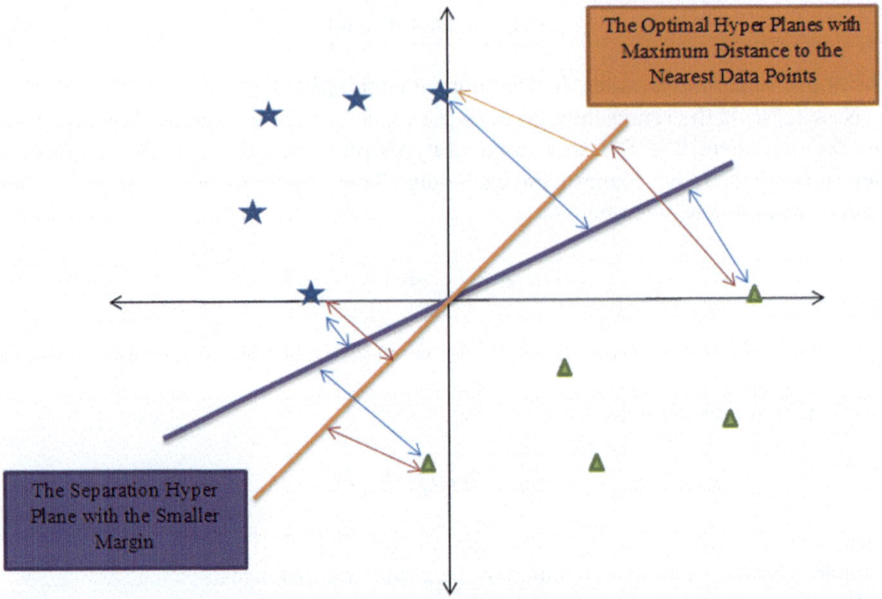


**Fig. 1** Hyper plane selection which maximizes margins

$$\alpha^R y = 0 \tag{14}$$

$$0 \leq \alpha \leq A1 \tag{15}$$

After the derivation of the above equations, the hyper planes are shown as below:

$$C = \sum_i \alpha_i b_i a_i \tag{16}$$

$C$ is the training examples having linear combinations.

$$\alpha_i (b_i (c.a_i + d) - 1) = 0 \quad \forall i \tag{17}$$

$\alpha_i = 0$ when the functional distance is greater than 1, .i.e. when $(c.a_i + b) > 1.c$ contributes by the closest data points. The training examples having $\alpha_i > 0$ are termed as 'support vectors'. These support vectors are used to define the optimal hyper planes.

To achieve the classification process, these operations should be performed:

1. Segmentation

Segmentation is where the contiguity constraint is mentioned the data in series clustered in a particular manner. 1, 2, ..., $N$ are the measured intensity labelling; then according to depth, $J$ segments are sought, then in some of $N - 1$ gaps, $J - 1$ 'markers' are used in between the measurements of neighbour $J$ segments block data, which is used in contiguous manner. The unconstraint case clustering is more as compares to the possible partitions number. Many algorithms were used the semi-exhaustive and exhaustive search within the search space which is reduced previously. Identification of the $h_i$ segment is given below:

$$h_j = \{\{a_{l,1}, \ldots, a_{1,K}\}, \ldots, \{a_{l,1}, \ldots, a_{l,K}\}, \ldots, \{a_{n,j,1}, \ldots, a\}\}_j \tag{18}$$

where $a_{l,k} \in K^n$ is a data which is to be measured.

$$\begin{aligned} l &= 1, 2, \ldots, n_j, \quad \text{Where } n_j \text{ is the intensity number in } h_j \text{ segments,} \\ k &= 1, 2, \ldots, K, \quad \text{Where } K \text{ is the signal number;} \\ j &= 1, 2 \ldots, J, \quad \text{Where } J \text{ is the segment number.} \end{aligned}$$

When the segments are distributed to a particular class, some of the classification is solved.

$$h_j \to C_i \tag{19}$$

Here from the mean of segment, the square derivations of group sum are minimized and the data set is partitioned into $J$ groups, i.e. dispersion occurs. There are various methods which are used to follow the above-mentioned approach:

(i) For the dynamic programming, the solution of any problem is obtained recursively.
(ii) In statistical criteria, a subtle difference is noticed; a marker is placed at those points and there is a window moved along, the data of fixed width is observed (S. S. Savkare and S. P. Narote 2012).

2. Feature Extraction

The selected features have an effect on the classifier's overall performance. The choice of characteristic will be utilized in a selected data class trouble which is crucial as the differentiate itself. Most oftenly for training reason and the process of identification features offering difference in regular and inflamed cells are used. These characteristic features are based on colour, geometry and statics of an image.

The above set of parameters having geometrical functions is described below:

1. Area is a number of pixels present on a particular area of interest.
2. Compactness is the ratio of $parameter^2$ by area.

For unfold inflamed cellular or ordinary cellular, the saturation value of histogram is used. For the ordinary cell, the histogram spreads over the area but for infected cell, it lies on the right side.

$$s = \frac{1}{\sigma^2} \sum_{q=0}^{N-1} (q - \bar{q})^3 \tag{20}$$

$$s_d = \left( \sum_{q=0}^{n-1} (q - \bar{q}) \right)^{1/2} \tag{21}$$

where $s$ is the skewness and $s_d$ is the standard deviation;

$H(q)$ = Histogram of first order;

$q$ = Amplitude value at each pixel;

$N$ = Value of upper limit of amplitude which is quantized in nature.

These above described parameters are used for extracting the features from an image. Saturation and grey-level histograms are used by statistical features, which are primarily based on such type of evaluations. These histogram values are based on various parameters like, angular momentum, mean value standard deviation and skewness.

3. SVM Classifier

In this Section, it is clear that SVM can give the excellent results. The linear classifiers work on principle of differentiation between two margins. For *M* dimensional feature space having *N* dimensional input vector *i*, the decision function is defined as:

$$D(i) = \omega^P \varphi(i) + a; \text{ Including the function } \varphi(i).$$

where $(i) = [\varphi_1(i), \varphi_2(i), \ldots, \varphi_L(i)]$;

$\omega$ is the weight factor having value $\omega = [\omega_1, \omega_2, \ldots, \omega_k]^P$;

$a$ is the bias weight.

Here, the values of weights are arranged in decreasing order. Here, those values which are having the higher priorities are selected to form a class and further used as classifier. The basic idea of SVM is that it maximizes the distance of margin which is used for the classification between the two types. The simple SVM algorithm is used for classifying the two classes whereas the multi-class SVM used to distinguish between the parasites present in a blood sample (T. Markiewicz and S. Osowski 2006).

## 4 Results and Discussion

The SVM multi-class classifier is used to differentiate between the parasites present. In the whole task, total of 200 images were used to process through this automatic system. In which for training and testing properly, nearly 25 images of each parasite were used. Area and standard deviation value of RGB of each parasite are different from other parasites. The wavelet movements of the *Plasmodium malariae* parasite are approximately 7.08679, for *Plasmodium falciparum* the value is 6.76997, 6.69667 for *P. vivax* and 8.05647 for the *Plasmodium ovale*. The output results of the above approach are shown in Figs. 2, 3, 4, 5 and 6.

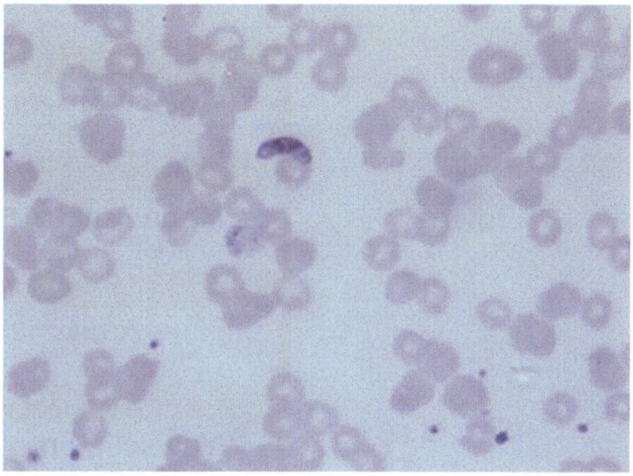

**Fig. 2** Input image

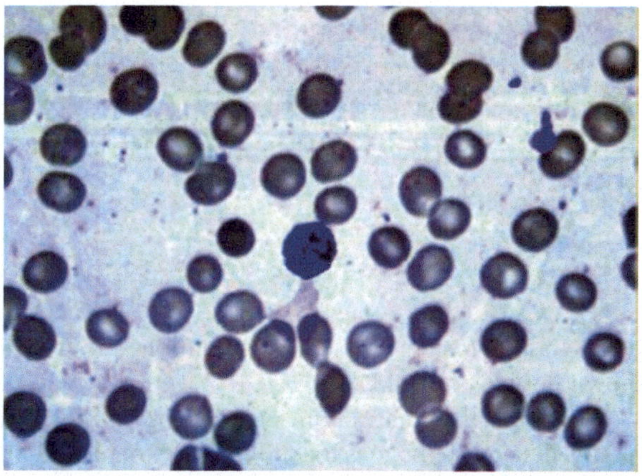

**Fig. 3** Contrast enhanced

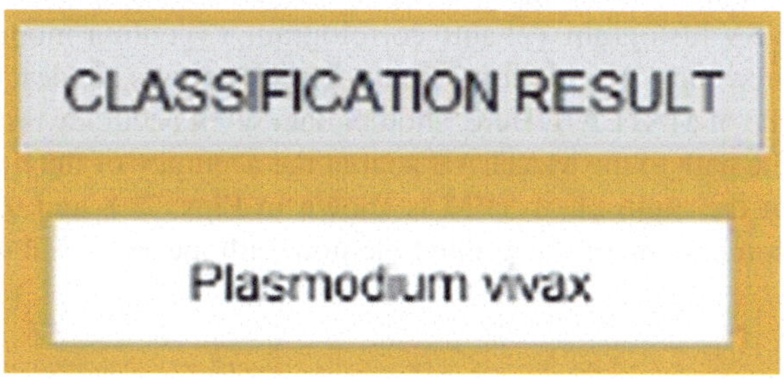


**Fig. 4** Classification results

**Fig. 5** Output values of the image parameters

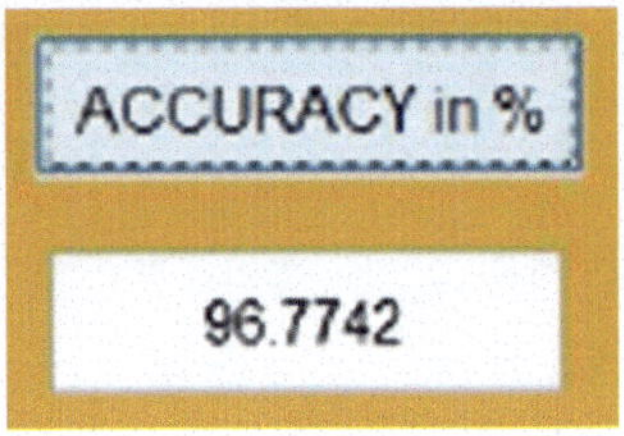


**Fig. 6** Accuracy data

The output results of the above-mentioned four parasites are shown in the GUI as shown in Figs. 7, 8 and 9.

Here, first the image is inserted using *imread* command in MATLAB 2010a. Firstly, the query image is loaded from the malaria data set. After pressing the colour enhancement push button, the output of that image is shown on the features column. The inserted image is compared to the bases of the below-mentioned features: (1) HSV histogram, (2) auto correlogram, (3) colour moments, (4) mean amplitude, (5) area and (6) wavelet moments. These features are described in the different function file of MATLAB. Here, another data set of accuracy is also created and then provided the path to the MATLAB so that the accuracy of the image is calculated. The output of the multi-class SVM is shown in Figs. 7, 8 and 9. Table 1 gives details of the comparison of the manual method with the proposed method.

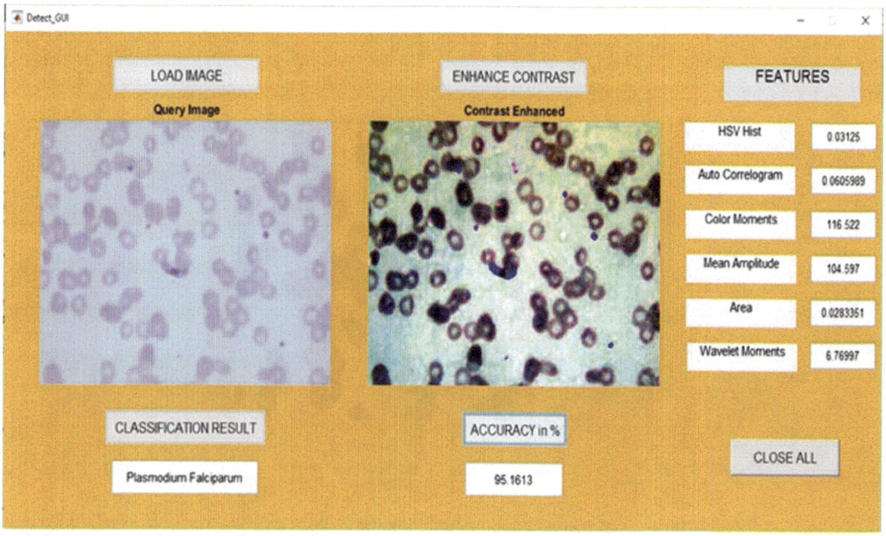


**Fig. 7** Output results for *Plasmodium falciparum*

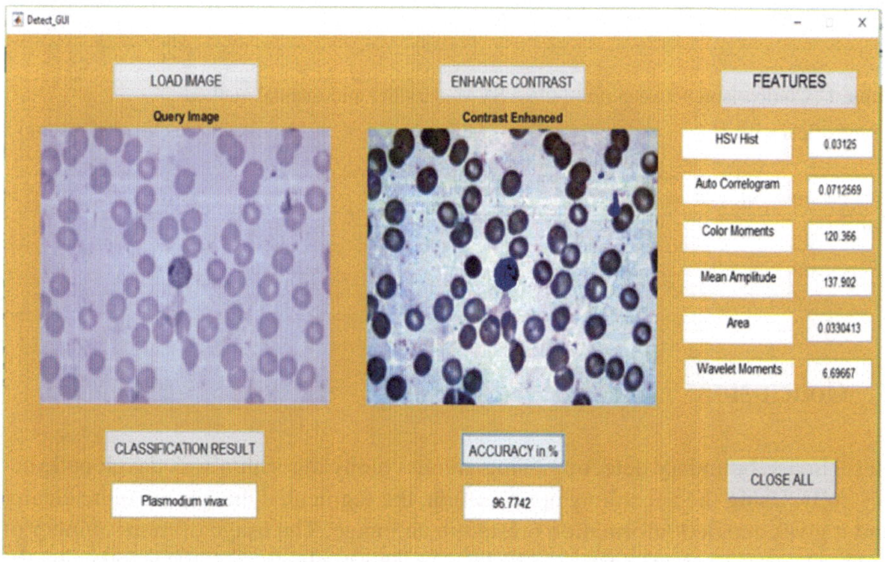


**Fig. 8** Output results for *Plasmodium vivax*

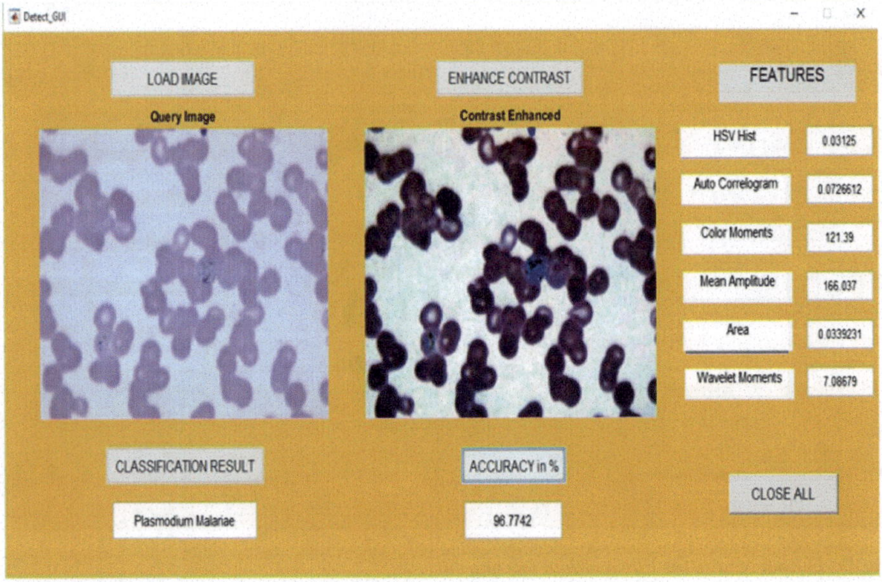


**Fig. 9** Output results for *Plasmodium malariae*

**Table 1** Comparison between multi-class SVM classifier and manual method

| Type of parasite | Accuracy in % (Multi-class support vector machine) | Accuracy in % (Manual results) [1] |
|---|---|---|
| *Plasmodium falciparum* | 95.1613 | 90 |
| *Plasmodium vivax* | 96.7724 | 88 |
| *Plasmodium malariae* | 94.7724 | 92 |
| *Plasmodium ovale* | 95.1724 | 86 |

## 5 Conclusion

Here, image boundary detection using an ant colony algorithm was developed successfully. Using the ant colony optimization, the segmented images are quite clearer and it gives detailed information present in an image. The usage of more number of artificial ants gives more accurate results [17]. This method can be extended using the parallel ACO and hybrid ACO algorithms which can give more clean and accurate results.

The proposed automatic device is also used for categorizing the malaria parasites which are all plasmodiums of the four different types namely falciparum, ovale, malariae and ovale. Overlapping cells are separated through watershed work which is the next step after segmentation. Geometrical and applied mathematics options area unit extracted from every mobile and it is provided to SVM classifier which is binary so as to check whether erythrocytes are infected or regular. Features like colour and geometrical are extracted and are the given to multi-class SVM for classification to identify lifestyles degree of parasite of malaria. Kernels of SVM including HSV histogram, RGB colouration moments, place and wavelet moments are used on two hundred snapshots. Multi-class classifier of SVM (i.e. RBF kernel) gives 96.42% accurate result properly to identity the rate of existence level of parasite of malaria.

So from the description given, it is clear that the proposed system is very essential in the modern world for extracting the parasites present in the blood smears without the human labour. The proposed work also reduces the time requirement and gives excellent results in just a few seconds.

**Acknowledgements** Both the authors would like to specially thank Dr. Naveen Kakkar who is the Incharge of Hematopathology in the Department of Pathology at Christian Medical College and Hospital situated in Ludhiana, Punjab. He helped in providing the images required for work.

## References

1. J.E. Arco, J.M. Gorriz, J. Ramirez, I. Alvarez, C.G. Puntonet, Digital image analysis for automatic enumeration of malaria parasites using morphological operations. Expert Syst. Appl. **42**, 3041–3047 (2014)
2. M. Rougemont, M.V. Saanen, R. Sahli, H.P. Hinrikson, J. Bille, Detection of four plasmodium species in blood from humans by 18S rRNA gene subunit-based and species-specific real-time PCR assays. J. Clin. Microbiol. **42**, 5636–5643 (2004)
3. B. Bhattacharya, D.P. Solomatine, Machine learning in soil classification, in *International Joint Conference Neural Network*, 2015
4. M. Dorigo, G.D. Caro, L.M. Gambardella, Ant algorithms for discrete optimization. Artif. Life **5**, 137–172 (1999)
5. C.D. Ruberto, A. Dempster, S. Khan, B. Jarra, Analysis of infected blood cell images using morphological operators. Image Vis. Comput. **20**, 133–146 (2002)
6. M. Dorigo, T. Stutzle, *Ant Colony Optimization* (The MIT Press, Cambridge, 2004)
7. C.R. Reeves, *Modern Heuristic Techniques for Combinatorial Problems* (Wiley, New York, 1993)
8. S.F. Toha, U.K. Ngah, Computer aided medical diagnosis for the identification of malaria parasites, in *International Conference Signal Processing Communication Networking ICSCN'07* (2007), pp. 521–522
9. D.J. Bacon, R. Jambou, T. Fandeur, World antimalarial resistance network (WARN) II: in vitro antimalarial drug susceptibility. Malaria J. (2007)
10. K. Mitiku, G. Mengistu, B. Gelaw, The reliability of blood film examination for malaria at the peripheral health unit. Trop. Med Int. Health (2000)
11. V.V. Makkapati, R.M. Rao, Segmentation of malaria parasites in peripheral blood smears images, in *International Conference Acoustics Speech Signal Processing*, (2009), pp. 1361–1364
12. G. Diaz, F.A. Gonzalez, E. Romero, A semiautomatic method for quantification and classification of erythrocytes infected with malaria parasites in microscopic images. J. Biomed. Inf. **42**, 296–307 (2009)
13. N. Alexander, D. Schellenberg, B. Ngasala, M. Petzold, C. Drakeley, C. Sutherland, Assessing agreement between malaria slide density readings. Malaria J. **9**, 1–12 (2010)

14. I. Ljungstrom, H. Perlmann, M. Schichtherle, A. Scherf, M. Wahlgen, Editors methods in malaria research (2004)
15. K.M. Khatri, V.R. Ratnaparkhe, S.S. Agrawal, A.S. Bhalchandra, Image processing approach for malaria parasite identification. Int. J. Comput. Appl., 5–7 (2013)
16. W.Y. Guoa, X.F. Wang, X.Z. Xia, Two dimensional Otsu's thresholding segmentation method based on grid box filter. Optik—Int. J. Light Electron Opt. **125**, 1234–1240 (2014)
17. D. Kaur, G. Kaur, Edge detection of malaria parasites using ant colony optimization, in *International Conference, Computing Control ISPCC 2017*, (Accepted)

# Performance Enhanced and Improvised Approach to Reduce Call Drops Using LTE-SON

**Divya Mishra and Anuranjan Mishra**

**Abstract** In today's world, cellular phone has become an important necessity and essential part of everyday life. Call drop is a phenomenon in which the ongoing conversation is terminated abruptly in-between. With the introduction of technologies like 3G and 4G and services like voice and data, and stiff competition among the telecommunication companies, the volume of call drop cases has increased many folds. Unexpected call drop is one of the biggest issues in telecom industry in our country and worldwide. Researchers, telecom operators and industry have proposed many solutions which were implemented as a solution to dropped calls minimization in mobile network. All the solution proposed so far has their own pros and cons, and no one solution could be considered as a comprehensive successful solution which has been deployed till now. This research work carried out is an attempt to identify and describes the reasons for call drop. The research work further provides analysis on the problem encircling the issue of call drop at every stage of wireless technology. This research work presents the journey of Global System for Mobile Communications (GSM) to Long-Term Evolution (LTE) on the basis of their merits and demerits and finds out the reasons to move to next emerging technology. Then, the author focuses on their proposed work, i.e., self-organizing network (SON), is most capable to improve voice call quality, reduces call drop factors, and degrades the capital and operational expenditure on the basis of their architecture and installation features.

**Keywords** Call drop · Global system for mobile communication · Long-term evolution · Self-organizing network · Centralized SON

This chapter draws heavily from my previous work published as Mishra and Mishra [1], and is reproduced here with my permission.

D. Mishra (✉) · A. Mishra
Noida International University, G.B Nagar, Noida, U.P, India
e-mail: divya_rbl2@yahoo.com

A. Mishra
e-mail: amc290@gmail.com



M. Pant et al. (eds.), *Computational Network Application Tools for Performance Management*, Asset Analytics,
https://doi.org/10.1007/978-981-32-9585-8_15

# 1 Introduction

In today's world, a cellular phone is the most important economical status symbol of human life. Without it, our daily life is impacted and uncompleted. But we cannot use it only as a toy because its uneasy services and weak signal strengths and cracked voice call quality impacted our work life. There are many situations when we need an emergency phone call, but weak signal strengths and even no signals do not be supportive during traveling because of different networks stands up on the way and ongoing call is not transfer smoothly to neighbor cells. Our voice call can be dropped in the middle of our important conversation. So that there are many recommended techniques proposed earlier by different intellectuals [2], but till now call drop existed and according to the survey of TRAI [2], 62% mobile subscribers facing this problem in different areas.

Cell phone market is increasing day by day having different attractive features on the basis of upcoming wireless technologies and sells expensive cell model to subscribers for using its best features; one of them is voice call quality and network speed also. Most subscribers are unaware of their backend core network technology which is based on their network infrastructures and installed operational algorithm on it to give life to expensive phone. In other words, cell phone infrastructure is not improving very fast as the subscriber rate [1]. The resultant feedback is the most people are struggling with low call quality and call drop issue. And they feel like cheating.

According to TRAI [2], around 62% of users are struggling with the issue of unexpected call termination and poor voice call quality. To justify this situation, the Indian Government established the interactive voice response (IVR) system in different areas to take the feedback response from users directly to check the voice call quality. The final result is discussed and shared with telecom vendors to examine the problem and sort out the issue as soon as possible. But the existed IVR system is only a way to collect live data from users not a call drop solution.

Call drop is unexpected situations when in the ongoing communication is disturbed and finally call is terminated. TRAI allowed only 2% or lesser call drop ratio. Telecom department conducted the survey [2, 1] and find out the 112 crore mobile connections which are in live condition. It means customer speed is increasing day to day, but unfortunately, telecom infrastructure is not focusing to improve itself with upcoming wireless technology according to the ratio of customers that would be able to manage the handovers and radio traffic load to distribute to spare resources and increased the trust of customers on telecom vendors.

Call drop impacted the quality of services and quality of experience in rural and urban both areas; because of the digital divide, a call is not transferred to neighbor cell properly in time and an ongoing call is broken down. TRAI conducted the drive test time to time in different areas to dig out the reasons of call drop as live factors. It does not depend on an algorithm, so it cannot be a permanent solution to minimize the call drop. Call drop does not only reduce the overall performances of a network, but it adds cost on monthly billing cycle [1]. It increases the cost of infrastructure because we need more mobile towers to optimize the load of radio traffic and increases the operational cost to maintain the network performance manually. Not only subscribers even telecom vendors also impacted by this issue.

Our research paper proposed the self-organizing network (SON) architecture which is implemented with LTE, LTE-A, and upcoming technology IMT-2020. Initially, SON is the part of LTE and is developed by 3GPP and NGMN, but now there are many networks which are continuously spending the time in research of this field to enhance and improve the SON features that can fight with implementation challenges of SON algorithm in the real platform [1]. SON is a concept and automatically controlled by key functions of optimization algorithms. It reduces the manual interference, reduces the capital expenditure and operational expenditure of network, and controls the network parameters according to need [3].

## 2 Related Work

TRAI [2] conducted the drive test time to time in different areas to measure the network parameters and dig out the reasons of call drop as live factors using different types of tools and softwares; most of the calls could be dropped due to reasons of electromagnetic effects, irregular user behavior, and abnormal network response.

| Drop call causes | Occurrence (%) |
|---|---|
| Electromagnetic causes (RF related) | 51.4 |
| Irregular user behavior | 36.9 |
| Abnormal network response | 7.6 |
| Others | 4.1 |

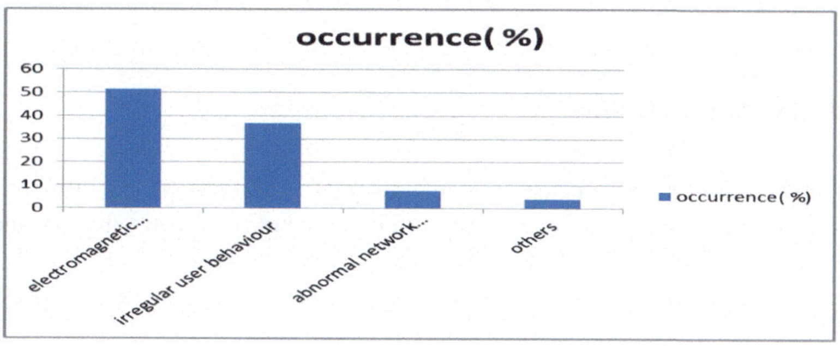


Author of [4] worked on the queuing priority channel assignment in his research paper that can be helpful in reducing call drop; in his approach, priority is given to continuing call rather than new entering call. Queues are used as buffer to store secondary call and entertain later. The cons of this approach are the high consumption of bandwidth.

The prioritization scheme can give a better result in comparison to single scheme with the combination of measurement-based prioritization scheme, guard channel prioritization scheme, queue handoff calls, call admission control protocol, and use auxiliary station [2, 5, 6, 7]. Many telecom vendors use TDMA-based dynamic channel allocation at the time of overloaded radio traffic [2, 8]. A research scholar [9] proposed the bandwidth degradation scheme where bandwidth allocation to various subscribers is adjusted dynamically as required to optimize the utilization of bandwidth for other calls.

The intellectual of [10] worked on adaptive bandwidth reservation scheme to reserve the bandwidth in all neighboring cell to reuse by another subscriber at the time of handoff. In [11], Andreas Lobinger and Szymon Stefanski have done a great job in LTE network. His research work is based on self-optimization algorithm to control the traffic load and handover automatically.

## 3 Reasons for Call Drop

Call drop ratio (CDR) is allowed only 2% or lesser according to TRAI. It means only two call drop out of 100. There might be lot of reasons of call drop such as-

### *3.1 Congestion on Network*

New subscribers are added fast by the telecom service provider, but less focus is being paid on increasing infrastructure. Thereby, operating existing infrastructure is taking place at the threshold level and the resultant call drop factors increases and reduces the customer trust on network.

### *3.2 High Radio Traffic*

Radio traffic rises on the occasion of the festival, and there is no infrastructure developed so far to control that situation. Finally, we get poor voice quality and call drop.

## 3.3 *Cells Overlap*

Cells overlap is also an important factor of call drop. Whenever different cells overlap with each other and unable to handle handover, the call would be dropped.

## 3.4 *Weak Coverage*

There are some areas where signal strength is very feeble because of tunnels, high mountains, in-building areas. Impacted consumers are getting compelled to installed radio frequency boosters to boost up their mobile signals that is not specific for any frequency band and unintentionally only promote the whole GSM band of all service providers and the resultant feedback is interference in signals. According to TRAI [2] survey, currently, over 250 illegal boosters installed in Delhi.

## 3.5 *During Traveling*

The subscriber gets call drop while roaming because one cell passes the ongoing call to another cell. During this process, if a neighbor cell having the weak signals and coverage area, the call drop occurs.

## 3.6 *Hardware Issues*

The hardware issue is a major concern in the mobile era. Subscriber rate is increasing rapidly, but the updated towers with robust technology are not maintaining by vendors. So the compatibility between cell phone and towers is not working appropriately. For example, 5G phone is launched in the market, but the 5G has not existed yet. So we are unknown the technology updated and buy expensive phone model.

## 3.7 *Weather*

Mobile signals cannot be impacted by the wind, but rain is a killer of mobile signals, because water has the power to block the radio signals between the mobile tower and your cell phone.

# 4 GSM to LTE

Global System for Mobile Communication (GSM) is a worldwide accepted wireless standard for mobile communication. It is developed by ETSI (European Telecommunications Standards Institute) in 1991 to describe the protocols for 2G technology. GSM has roaming contract over 219 countries and territories to maintain the mobility worldwide with our single phone with a single number on the single billing cycle. Approximate 90% people across the world uses GSM technology for wireless conversation [12, 13]. After 2G, many extended and improved technologies have come which are distinguished with each other such as 2.5G, 3G, 4G, LTE, LTE-A, and 5G.

Post-adoption of LTE technology mobile operators will expect to achieve reduced operational cost, service disruption, and maximize subscriber usage to find out the best-optimized solution to improve the quality of service and enhanced user experience.

## *4.1 1G*

First-generation technology was purely analog and introduced in the 1980s in the USA using the Motorola DynaTAC mobile phone which was very big in size and heavy in weight. 1G used analog radio signal for voice calling while for connecting with the tower it used digital signal [14]. Post-adoption of 2G technology, 1G is almost replaced by a 2G network.

## *4.2 2G*

GSM is common wireless standard for all countries that is the main reason why GSM subscribers can travel in GSM network across the world that has the roaming contract with other countries. When 2G is released in 1991 by Finland, it was the biggest revolution in the mobile world. 2G offers voice calling, SMS, MMS, services to subscribers. Data speed is up to 64 kbps. 2G needs strong coverage area for conversation. Nowadays, some operators have decided to shut down the 2G network finally and move to next-generation technology [11].

## *4.3 2.5G*

2.5G offers GPRS to the mobile subscriber that is a unique gift to mobile users. Now, speed is 64–144 kbps attached with small pixel camera and we could have downloading mp3 songs using Internet service. Basically, 2.5G is the mediator between 2G and 3G [15].

## 4.4 3G

3G mobile cellular system or Universal Mobile Telecommunications (UMT) system is developed and maintained by 3rd Generation Partnership Project (3GPP) in 2001 [16, 15]. Its data transmission speed is 144 kbps–3.1 Mbps. UMT uses wideband code division multiple access (WCDMA) radio access technologies to offer more spectral capacity and bandwidth to mobile operators. Consequently, nowadays we are using faster web browsing, video conferencing, 3D online gaming, mobile TV on our smartphone.

UMT is also referred to as freedom of mobile access (FOMA), but it needs separate network architecture. Even some legacy components of GSM networks are reused. The main improved subsystem is radio access network (RAN) which is called UTRAN in UMT standard. The full form of UTRAN is UMT terrestrial radio access network. In new UTRAN, BTS is called Node-B and BSC is called RNC and our MS also has a new name, i.e., user equipment (UE). Node-B is responsible for all functions required for sending and receiving data over the air interface. Now, the challenge is high bandwidth for data service [17].

## 4.5 4G/LTE

3GPP in 2010 evolved a new wireless standard in release 8 and 9 named as Long-Term Evolution (LTE) to remove the multipath fading of radio signals. In place of a single signal over the complete carrier bandwidth (5 MHz), LTE uses orthogonal frequency-division multiplexing (OFDM) which transmits the data over many narrowband carriers of 180 kHz each. In place of one single transmission, a data stream is divided into many data streams for transmitting simultaneously, i.e., MIMO transmission which minimizes the multipath effect even data rate in comparison to UMT is similar in the same bandwidth. There are many bandwidths for LTE from 1.25 MHz up to 20 MHz. In a 20 MHz carrier, data rates up to 100 Mbit/s show a very good signal quality [15].

The second change in LTE is it completely depends upon flat IP approach. It has the capability to handle all legacy network calls. The LTE network architecture is totally different from a legacy network. Now, Node-B is more improved in functionality and is called eNodeB. The data speed is 100 Mbps–1 Gbps that is real-time speed to download and upload or watching videos from the Internet. LTE is highly secured and offers new cell phone services at low cost. It is also capable to handle seamless handover, whenever a cell phone left one cell area and moves to another cell area during the ongoing conversation, which reduces the unexpected termination of calls.

## 5 LTE-SON

As above said, UMT is simplified and improved by LTE, now the focus on LTE. LTE needs self-optimized functions that need less manual work and effort to optimize the network parameters automatically according to need and offer the quality of service and quality of experience to users and reduces the expenditure cost.

The new approach is called LTE-SON (self-organizing network). It is initially developed by 3rd Generation Partnership Project (3GPP) and Next-Generation Mobile Network (NGMN) [18]. SON has been introduced by 3GPP during releases 8, 9, and 10, and first of all, Japan and USA have been adopted this concept in 2009/10 [19, 20].

As shown in Fig. 1, SON is controlled by three robust functionalities, i.e., self-configuration, self-optimization, and self-healing [21, 22]. To optimize the network resources, these features have some algorithms and corresponding functions to offer the automatic services to users. Self-configuration is the pre-operational stage where newly installed eNodeBs are configured by automatic procedures to find basic parameters and download the required software for operation. Self-configuration is also used in the automatic failure recovery mechanism which is also called cell outage case [23].

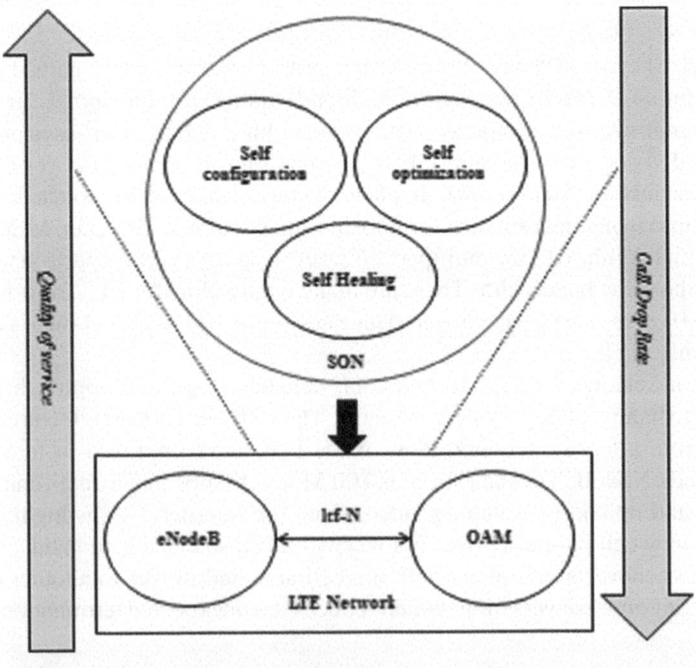


**Fig. 1** Block diagram of SON concept with LTE

Self-optimization is an operational stage where SON algorithm functions optimized all the network resources without any human effort using different robust algorithms such as coverage and capacity optimization, energy savings, interference reduction, mobility robustness optimization, mobility load balancing optimization, and RACH optimization algorithm. It sets the network parameters according to need automatically [24].

The third self-healing feature works in the operational stage to identify and rectify the network fault automatically without manpower. The network fault can be related to corresponding software or hardware equipment which could be solved automatically by triggering appropriate recovery actions, e.g., cell outage detection and cell outage recovery [23].

SON functions can be installed over the LTE infrastructure in only two locations, i.e., eNodeB and OAM, or individually in only one location of these and make the category of centralized, distributed, and hybrid SON. LTE-SON improved the quality of service and quality of experience to users and decreases the call rate. It solves all the network problems self and reduces the capital expenditure (CapEx) and operational expenditure (OpEx) also. But the challenges are to right implementation of this approach to telecom operators. SON is a very robust concept to reduce call drop. There are many service providers who have also accepted and installed this concept with LTE network to enhance the end-user's quality of service (QoS) and quality of experience (QoE).

There are three faces of SON architecture.

i. Centralized
ii. Distributed
iii. Hybrid

These categories are based on the location where the SON algorithm is implemented such as OAM, eNodeB, or in both. As the name refers, in centralized SON, the SON algorithm is implemented in OAM, whereas in distributed, the SON algorithm is implemented in eNodeB, and in hybrid, the SON algorithm is implemented in both parts OAM and eNodeB. In hybrid SON, a complex part of the algorithm is implemented in OAM and easy and quick part is implemented in eNodeB. Nomor research depicts the hybrid architecture is very flexible in comparison to other because it supports all types of optimization cases between different vendors through X2 interface [23].

## *5.1 Centralized SON*

In centralized SON architecture, all the optimization algorithm functions are stored in OSS level and manage all the network parameters from there as shown in Fig. 2. The merit of this approach is all the network parameters globally optimized at once, and coordination between OSS and eNodeB is easy. The main advantage of a centralized approach is features which are added in OSS level not in nodes, so maintenance

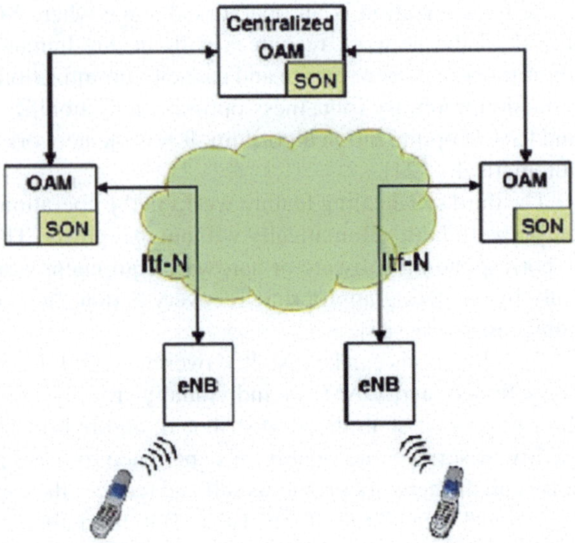


**Fig. 2** Centralized SON architecture

by the third party is easy. The cons of this approach are single-point failure, and processing time is higher.

## 5.2 *Distributed SON*

In this approach, functions and algorithms are installed in network elements (eNodeB). The messages are interchanged directly between nodes are possible and easy. This is a very dynamic and quick approach. The cons of this approach to install the functions in all nodes individually for a third party are a challenging task as shown in Fig. 3.

## 5.3 *Hybrid SON*

In hybrid SON, some part of the algorithm is run on OSS level and another part is run on eNodeB. So the pros and cons also inherited from both centralized and distributed approach as shown in Fig. 4.

As addressed above, this SON concept is very necessary for future mobile infrastructure to optimize whole mobile network automatically without any interruption. As shown in Fig. 5 [8], The SON concept increased the customer experience index while decreases the wireless operational cost of the network. If customer experience index is increasing per year, it means a quality of service is also improved and call drop would be reduced. According to Nokia 50%, call drop reduction is pos-

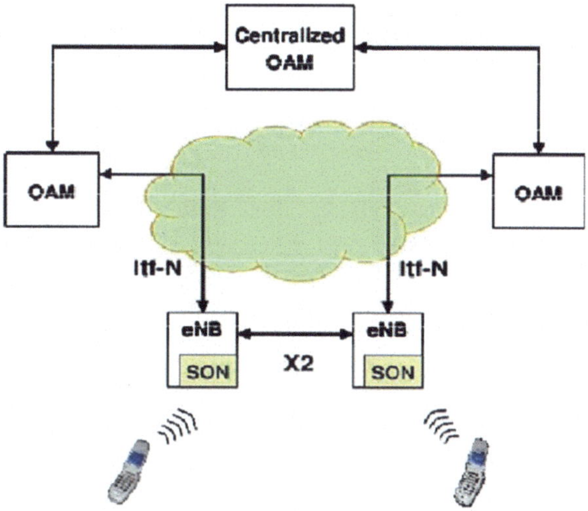


**Fig. 3** Distributed SON architecture

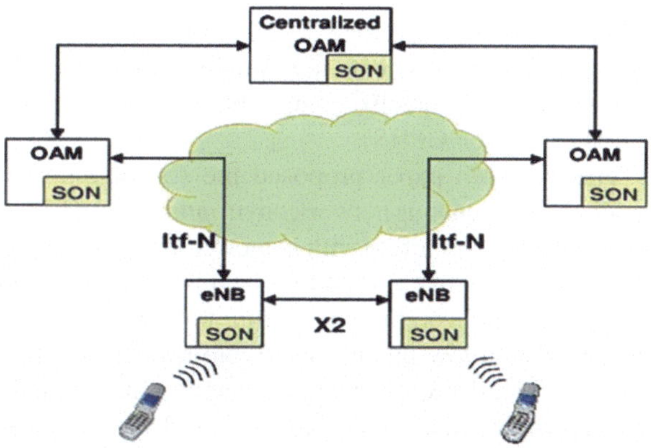


**Fig. 4** Hybrid SON architecture

sible through using SON technology in a multi-vendor environment. This graph is implemented by Nokia in May 2015.

# 6 Conclusion and Future Work

Many researchers, telecom vendors, and even telecom government authority tried to resolve the call drop problem in existing network technology with an optimized utilization of network resources but still, no reliable and optimized future-proof solution has discovered which improved the telephonic conversation quality as expected. Unexpected call termination problem has become complex with a rapid growth of wireless technology and urgent requirement of network resources for new mobile

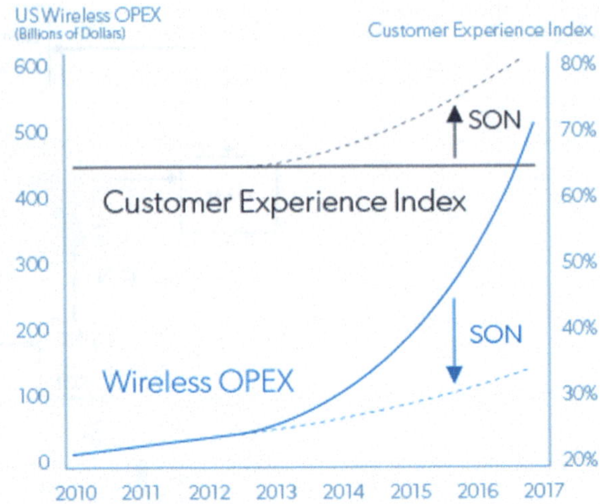


**Fig. 5** Improvement of user experience through SON

connection. The new added smartphone connection required robust automated technology for strong coverage signals in splitting cells' coverage area (macro, micro, pico, and femto cells) with high quality of service at low cost without any intervention which would be also compatible with coexisting wireless technology (2G, 3G, 4G, 5G and even GPRS).

This research paper proposed the self-organizing network system in a multi-vendor heterogeneous network environment with LTE infrastructure. SON is a part of LTE, but it is compatible with legacy GSM technologies also. Some authors depicted it as a cost-effective model in telecom industry because it reduces the operational expenditure and capital expenditure both with the optimized utilization of network resources with low manpower. Radio traffic on cells and numbers of unsuccessful handovers are decreased by implementing SON functions in a mobile network. SON reduced the manual work and increased the operational efficiency by the various algorithm functions such as handover optimization, mobility load balancing algorithm, and automatic neighbor relation function. SON can increase the revenue of telecom operators with upcoming technology because total revenue depends on network operational efficiency [20].

Despite widespread intensive research, SON has many challenges that remain to investigate and improve in R&D of SON algorithm to make it more suitable and cost-effective in existing and upcoming telecom infrastructure. SON algorithm implementation complexity and its dedicated backhaul interface between eNodeBs and configuration server need more research work in real implementation platform [16].

Our future research work will be focused on implementation challenges of SON with upcoming 5G technology without any dedicated backhaul complexity where newly added eNodeB will boot up in UE mode first and then connect to a neighbor eNodeB in operation state.

## References


1. D. Mishra, A. Mishra, Self-optimization in LTE: An Approach to Reduce Call Drops in Mobile Network, in *Futuristic Trends in Network and Communication Technologies* ed. by P.K. Singh et al. FTNCT 2018, CCIS 958 (Springer Nature Singapore Pte Ltd. 2019), pp. 382–395. https://doi.org/10.1007/978-981-13-3804-5_28
2. Telecom Regulatory Authority of India: Technical Paper on Call Drop in Cellular Networks, http://www.trai.gov.in/web-123/Call-Drop/Call_Drop.pdf (2016)
3. H. Gacanin, A. Ligata, Wi-Fi self-organizing networks: challenges and use cases. IEEE Commun. Mag. 158–164 (2017)
4. Y.-B. Lin, S. Mohan, A. Noerpel, Queuing priority channel assignment strategies for pcs handoff and initial access. IEEE Trans. Veh. Technol. **43** (1994)
5. I.A.M. Balapuwaduge, L. Jiao, V. Pla, Channel assembling with priority-based queues in cognitive radio networks: strategies and performance evaluation. IEEE Trans. Wirel. Commun. **13**, 630–645 (2014)
6. C.H. Monica, K.V.L. Bhavani, A bandwidth degradation technique to reduce call dropping probability in mobile network systems. Telkomnika Indonesian J. Electr. Eng. **16**, 303–307 (2015)
7. S. Shiokawa, M. Ishizaka, Call admission scheme based on estimation of call dropping probability in wireless network. 0-7803-7589-0/02/$17.00 ©2002 IEEE (2002)
8. X.J. Li, P.H. J. Chong, A dynamic channel assignment scheme for TDMA-based multihop cellular networks. IEEE Trans. Wirel. Commun. **7** (2008)
9. Nokia buys Eden Rock for self-organizing networks (German), http://www.zdnet.de/88235891/nokia-kauft-eden-rock-fuer-self-organizing-networks/
10. J. Moysen, L. Giupponi, From 4G to 5G: self-organized network management meets machine learning. arXiv:1707.09300v1 [cs.NI] (2017)
11. A. Lobinger, S. Stefanski, T. Jansen, Coordinating handover parameter optimization and load balancing in LTE self-optimizing networks, in *2011 IEEE 73rd Vehicular Technology Conference (VTC Spring)* (2011)
12. SNS Research: https://www.vanillaplus.com/2016/11/28/23993-son-revenue-expected-to-grow-to-more-than-5bn-by-end-of-2020-says-sns/
13. M. Sauter, from GSM to LTE an introduction to mobile networks and mobile broadband. Wireless Moves, Germany. ISBN: 978-0-470-66711-8
14. C. Oliveira, J.B. Kim, T. Suda, An adaptive bandwidth reservation scheme for high-speed multimedia wireless networks. IEEE J. Sel. Areas Commun. 858–874 (1998)
15. A. Dahlén, A. Johansson, F. Gunnarsson, J. Moe, T. Rimhagen, H. Kallin, Evaluations of LTE Automatic Neighbor Relations. 978-1-4244-8331-0/11/$26.00 ©2011 IEEE9
16. S. Khara, S. Saha, A.K. Mukhopadhyay, C. Kumar Ghosh, Call dropping analysis in a UMTS/WLAN integrated cell. Int. J. Inf. Technol. Knowl. Manage. (2010)
17. GPP, Evolved Universal Terrestrial Radio Access (E-UTRA) and Evolved Universal Terrestrial Radio Access (E-UTRAN); Overall description; Stage 2, 3rd Generation Partnership Project (3GPP), TS 36.300, Sep. 2008. (Online). http://www.3gpp.org/ftp/Specs/html-info/36300.htm
18. NGMN Alliance, Next Generation Mobile Networks Use Cases related to Self Organising Network, Overall Description (May 31st 2007)
19. M. Nohrborg: Self-organizing network. http://www.3gpp.org/technologies/keywords-acronyms/105-son (2017)
20. NEC Corporation, Self Organizing Network: "NEC's proposals for next-generation radio network management" white paper (2009)
21. Cisco, SON and the LTE Challenge: How to Get More for Less White Paper. https://www.cisco.com/c/en/us/solutions/collateral/service-provider/son-architecture/white-paper-c11-733194.pdf (2015)
22. Nokia Siemens Networks, Self-Organizing Network (SON) Introducing the Nokia Siemens Networks SON Suite—An Efficient, Future-Proof Platform for SON. http://cwi.unik.no/images/c/c3/SON_white_paper_NSN.pdf

23. S. Feng, E. Seidel, *Self-Organizing Networks (SON) in 3GPP Long Term Evolution*. (Nomor Research GmbH, Munich, Germany, 20th of May 2008)
24. S. Hämäläinen, H. Sanneck, C. Sartori, LTE Self-Organizing Networks (SON). ISBN: 9781119970675

# Performance Evaluation of Various Transmission Control Protocols in NS2

**Palak Bansal, Kritika Agrawal and Ankita Gupta**

**Abstract** Rapid transfer of data of high magnitude is a necessity to meet the demand of today's high-speed communication networks. The currently prominent implementation of TCP protocol is insufficient for the high bandwidth-latency product networks that are available to users. The current TCP Reno protocol implementation fails to utilize the available bandwidth optimally and requires an exceptionally small bit error rate (BER) for it to maintain that rate. A substantial amount of bandwidth is left unused in such networks. Moreover, congestion control is required so that the stability of the network is maintained. TCP Reno's congestion policy is not suitable in today's technology as it might take more than a few hours to recover that congestion window. Many variants of TCP protocols have been suggested which follow more aggressive approach than the current implementation like loss-based metrics algorithm and delay-based algorithm for congestion control. Loss metric based determine congestion by loss of a packet; and delay metric focuses on delay as a sign of congestion. The research work presents a comparative study and performance analysis factors in terms of congestion window size growth and fairness (throughput in terms of bytes transferred per second) of TCP Reno, Scalable TCP and TCP Cubic which are loss-based metrics algorithm, and TCP Vegas which is a delay-based algorithm for congestion control. According to the observation and analysis performed using simulation, Scalable TCP among TCP Reno, TCP Vegas and TCP Cubic performs better in terms of the congestion window corresponding with respect to time and can be considered as a good option. In terms of fairness, TCP Cubic and Scalable TCP, both are more aggressive than TCP Reno and TCO Vegas. To conclude for aggressiveness and packet loss, Scalable TCP is the best option among the TCP variants taken for performance analysis and evaluation.

---

P. Bansal (✉) · K. Agrawal · A. Gupta
Department of Computer Science, Jaypee Institute of Information Technology, Noida, India
e-mail: palakbansal94@gmail.com

K. Agrawal
e-mail: 1995.kritika@gmail.com

A. Gupta
e-mail: ankita.gupta.mail@gmail.com



M. Pant et al. (eds.), *Computational Network Application Tools for Performance Management*, Asset Analytics,
https://doi.org/10.1007/978-981-32-9585-8_16

**Keywords** Transmission control protocol · Congestion control · Network simulator · TCP Reno · Scalable TCP · TCP Vegas · TCP Cubic

## 1 Introduction

Large amount of data is required to be transferred quickly over high-speed networks. TCP Reno [1] is most widely accepted and implemented transport protocol. But it is not able to scale well to data rate of 100 Mbps and more. Despite large bandwidth being available, TCP Reno is not able to completely utilize it. TCP Reno was designed when the value of data rate used to be in a few kbps. Congestion control is required so that the stability of the network is maintained. TCP Reno's [2] additive-increase/multiplicative-decrease (AIMD) policy for congestion back-off is too rapid and it might take more than a few hours to recover that congestion window size as explained by Floyd [3]. Recovery time is too large for TCP Reno. Average congestion window varies with inverse square root of probability of loss [4]. TCP Reno detects congestion by packet loss. For high-speed network links, very low packet drop probability is required, which is unreasonable to achieve.

Many variants of the TCP are proposed with changes on the sender side. Those variants are more aggressive than the TCP Reno. Some of the variants follow loss-based metric, and some follow delay metric. Loss metric based determine congestion by loss of a packet; and delay metric focuses on delay as a sign of congestion. Delay metric based make full use of state of network which is given by packet delay. Some variants involving updating the congestion control condition on the sender side are TCP Vegas [5], Scalable TCP [3], TCP Cubic [6], TCP Africa [7], etc. We are simulating TCP Reno, TCP Scalable, TCP Vegas and TCP Cubic using NS2 [8] as a network simulator and analysing them using graphical analysis for this paper.

The rest of the paper is organized in the following manner: Tools used for simulating and analysis are explained in Sect. 2, followed by related work details in next Sect. 3, and then working and congestion control algorithm of TCP Reno are explained in Sect. 3.3, which is then followed by Scalable TCP, loss-based algorithm in Sect. 3.4, TCP Cubic, implemented in Linux and a loss metric based in Sect. 3.5 and TCP Vegas, delay-based algorithm in Sect. 3.6. These algorithms are then followed by their implementation and testing details in next Sect. 4. Section 5 consists of details of performance evaluation followed by conclusions and future work in Sects. 6 and 7, respectively. Finally, the last section consists of the references used for the paper.

## 2 Tools

This section consists of the description of the tools which were used for implementing congestion control algorithms and analyzing it. Since a lot of traffic is generated in the actual network of Internet, it was necessary to imitate the actual network. To emulate the behaviour of the computer network, network simulator is being used.

### *2.1 Simulator*

NS2 [9], second version of network simulator, is used for simulating TCP variants. It is a simulation tool that is event-driven and helps in emulating dynamic nature of actual network like Internet. Different protocols (TCP, TCP Vegas, UDP, etc.) and queues (drop tail, etc.) can be simulated using NS2, and traffic may be generated according to the protocols simulated. The network of simulation may be wired or wireless. Tcl is the script used for creating a simulation file in NS2. The Tcl script is executed with the command ns along with the name of the file and input arguments, if required. NS2 consists of mainly two languages: C++ and Object-Oriented Tool Command Language (OTcl). While simulating, internal mechanism is defined by C++ and events are configured and assembled by OTcl. TclCL is used for linking C++ and OTcl.

### *2.2 Simulation Results*

Simulation results may be text-based as well as animation-based. To interpret the results, tools NAM and Xgraph are being used. A network object is created as output in NAM. Topology is created and coded in Tcl file is emulated using NAM, which helps to interpret flow of the packets in the network. Observations are recorded in trace file. The trace file is being used for plotting the graph and analyzing the results.

## 3 Related Work

TCP Reno [1], the traditional and most accepted TCP, was developed around 1990. There are various improvements proposed for TCP Reno in [2, 10], etc. Many new are variants which are proposed of TCP Reno, which changes the algorithm of congestion control and are more aggressive than TCP Reno. These variants follow different approaches for detecting congestion in the network and implementing congestion control. Some of the variants follow packet loss-based approach to detect congestion as HSTCP [11], Scalable TCP, TCP Cubic, etc. Some variants follow delay approach like TCP Vegas, TCP Fast [12]. Some protocols like TCP Africa have been proposed which follow both approaches: packet loss based and delay based to be able to utilize the benefit of both approaches. These protocols follow loss of packet approach under particular conditions and delayed approach under other conditions.

## 3.1 TCP Africa

TCP Africa [7] is neither a completely loss-based protocol nor delay-based protocol. It is a hybrid one. Delay metric is used by it to determine the network congestion level, and it acts accordingly. If congestion is absent, then it follows fast mode; and in congestion presence, it follows slow mode of TCP Reno. It grabs the unutilized bandwidth quickly, but it becomes slow when the next congestion event is induced. It uses a parameter $\alpha$ which determines the sensitivity of protocol to delay. This parameter is generally taken as greater than 1.

## 3.2 HSTCP

HSTCP [11] is a variation of TCP Reno which also uses packet loss as an indication of the congestion in network. Three new parameters are being used in this protocol: High_Window, which indicates the highest size of congestion window; Low_Window, which tells about the minimum congestion window required for HSTCP's new response function to work; and High_P, the probability of packet drop in HSTCP. If size of congestion window is less than or equal to Low_Window, then slow mode of TCP Reno is followed; otherwise, if size of congestion window exceeds Low_Window, then response function of high-speed TCP is followed.

## 3.3 TCP Reno

TCP Reno [2] congestion control algorithm consists of four components: slow start, congestion avoidance, fast retransmit, and fast recovery. Sender using TCP Reno is in any of the following phases:

- Slow start
- Congestion avoidance
- Fast retransmit and fast recovery.

Congestion is detected if either timeout occurs or triple acknowledgement is received. Whenever congestion is detected or acknowledgement is received, the next phase of Reno is decided by checking the current phase and congestion status.

**Slow Start**

Congestion window is increased by most Sender Maximum Sender Size (SMSS) whenever an acknowledgement is received for new packet sent. In slow start phase, congestion window is generally doubled for every round trip. When congestion window exceeds the threshold value (ssthresh), Reno goes to congestion avoidance phase.

**Congestion Avoidance**
In congestion avoidance phase, packet loss or timeout size of congestion window is increased by 1 full-size segment per RTT.

Congestion window is updated until acknowledgement is received for every new packet sent as:

$$\text{cwnd} = \text{cwnd} + \text{SMSS} * \text{SMSS}/\text{cwnd} \tag{1}$$

Whenever timeout occurs, the value of ssthresh is updated. In case of receiving triple acknowledgement, Reno enters fast retransmit phase.

**Fast Retransmit and Recovery**
A timer is being maintained for every packet sent. If a sender receives acknowledgement after timeout occurs, then it is considered that the packet is lost. But, it might take too long to realize that a packet is lost and take action accordingly. Fast retransmit phase uses duplicate acknowledgements to detect that a packet is lost. When multiple acknowledgment packets (generally 3) are received of the same sequence number, TCP considers that the packet is lost and retransmits it.

## *3.4 Scalable TCP*

Scalable TCP [3] follows multiplicative-increase/multiplicative-decrease (MIMD) policy for updating congestion window. The phases and the congestion detection occurrences of TCP Scalable are same as that of TCP Reno. But its implementation differs from TCP Reno as follows:

When packets are acknowledged and there is no congestion, congestion window value is updated by 0.01, i.e.,

$$\text{cwnd} = \text{cwnd} + 0.01 \tag{2}$$

When congestion is detected (triple acknowledgement or timeout), then congestion window value is reduced to 0.875 of its value; that is, it is reduced by 0.125 times of its value. i.e.,

$$\text{cwnd} = \text{cwnd} - 0.125 * \text{cwnd} \tag{3}$$

Scalable TCP reduces the problem of recovery time of congestion window to a constant time rather than being dependent on the size of the congestion window, as in the case of TCP Reno.

### 3.5 TCP Cubic

TCP Cubic [6] is an improved variant of BIC-TCP as sometimes BIC becomes too aggressive specifically in networks with low speeds. The phases and congestion detection occurrences are similar to TCP Reno. A value $W_{max}$ is noted when the first packet loss occurs. Cubic might be in TCP mode, concave or convex regions depending upon the value of the congestion window. If cwnd < $W_{max,}$ then it is in concave region, and if cwnd > $W_{max,}$ then it is in convex region.

Congestion window update is given as:

$$\text{cwnd} = C(t - K)^3 + W\text{max} \tag{4}$$

$$K = (W\text{max}\beta/C)^{1/3} \tag{5}$$

where

- $C$ cubic parameter
- $t$ time elapsed since last reduction of window
- $\beta$ decrease factor.

### 3.6 TCP Vegas

TCP Vegas [5] follows delay metric to determine the congestion of the network. Vegas is based on the idea that bytes in the transit of connection are directly related to the throughput of connection. The used bandwidth by connection is compared with the bandwidth available of the network; in order utilize available bandwidth and avoid congestion. In Vegas Base, RTT is one of the main factors used to determine the expected value of throughput.

$$\text{Throughput}_{\text{Expected}} = \text{cwnd}/\text{BaseRTT} \tag{6}$$

where cwnd is congestion window's current size.

Then, actual value of throughput is calculated by measuring the number of bytes transmitted and dividing it by RTT value. This calculation is done once per round trip time.

Value of difference ($D$) between actual and expected throughput is calculated.

$$D = \text{Throughput}_{\text{Expected}} - \text{Throughput}_{\text{Actual}} \tag{7}$$

Two thresholds $x$ and $y$ are defined such that $x < y$. If $D < x$, then congestion window is increased linearly for next RTT, and if $D > y$, then congestion window is decreased for the next RTT. If $x < D < y$, then no change in congestion window is done.

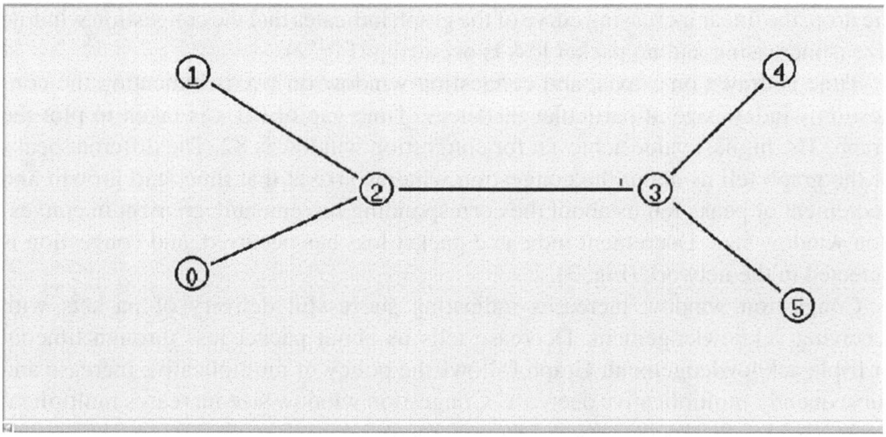


**Fig. 1** Topology used for analysis of TCP variants

## 4 Implementation and Testing

TCP variants [13, 14] are simulated in NS2 [8] with using their default parameters for Scalable TCP, TCP Reno and TCP Vegas; for TCP Cubic, default parameters are set as beta = 0.125, max_increment = 16, fast_convergence = 1 and bic_value = 410. The topology [15] used for doing analysis is as follows (Fig. 1).

Topology consisting of six nodes is being used to simulate the network. Nodes marked as 0 and 1 are being used as TCP senders, and 4, 5 are being used as TCP receivers. Nodes 2 and 3 served as bottlenecks in the network. Links from nodes 0 and 1 to 2 have a bandwidth of 2 Gbps and delay of 10 ms. Links from 2 to 3 have a bandwidth of 1 Gbps with a delay of 200 ms. Links from 4 to 5 and 6 are similar to 0 to 1 link.

Details of simulation are stored in trace files (.tr) and their graph is plotted using Xgraph. Analysis is done in the form of congestion window size versus time and fairness [16]. For this implementation, queue size is set to 10 for connection between nodes 2 and 3, and packet size is set to 550 bytes. Simulated network is tested up to 550 bytes of packet size, and analysis is done accordingly.

## 5 Performance Evaluation

### *5.1 Congestion Window Size Growth*

*X*-axis indicates time with interval of 10 s. *Y*-axis indicates the size of congestion window. The graph first increases and then decreases indicating packet loss. The sharp drop is due to the multiplicative-decrease policy followed by TCP Reno. After the drop, the linear increasing curve of the graph indicates that the congestion window size is increasing and no packet loss is occurring (Fig. 2).

Time is drawn on *x*-axis, and congestion window on *y*-axis indicating the congestion window size at particular instances. Time gap of 0.1 s is taken to plot the graph. The highest value achieved for congestion window is 82. The different peaks of the graph tell us about the congestion window size at that time, and growth and decrement of peaks tell us about the corresponding increment/decrement in congestion window size. Decrement indicated packet loss has occurred, and congestion is detected in the network (Fig. 3).

Congestion window increases indicating successful delivery of packets with receiving acknowledgement. Decrease tells us about packet loss through timeout or triple acknowledgement. Graph follows the policy of multiplicative increase and subsequently multiplicative decrease. Congestion window size increases multiplicatively till 55 s, then decreases and then increases again (Fig. 4).

Congestion window of TCP Vegas grows and attains a value of 33 at 5 s. Then, a packet drop takes place and the value of congestion window becomes 19. The earlier lost packet is retransmitted successfully; followed by the successful transmission of new packets which leads to an increase in the size of congestion window. Positive slope after 5 s indicates that packet loss is not taking place (Fig. 5).

For the implementation considered, congestion window size of TCP Vegas does not vary much as compared to TCP Reno; the difference is really less. No packet loss after 10 s for the simulation taken could be one of the reasons for this observation. Values of congestion window of Scalable TCP are much higher than that of TCP Reno; even when there is a packet loss in scalable and congestion window decreases, there is no packet loss at the same time on TCP Reno. This shows the aggressiveness

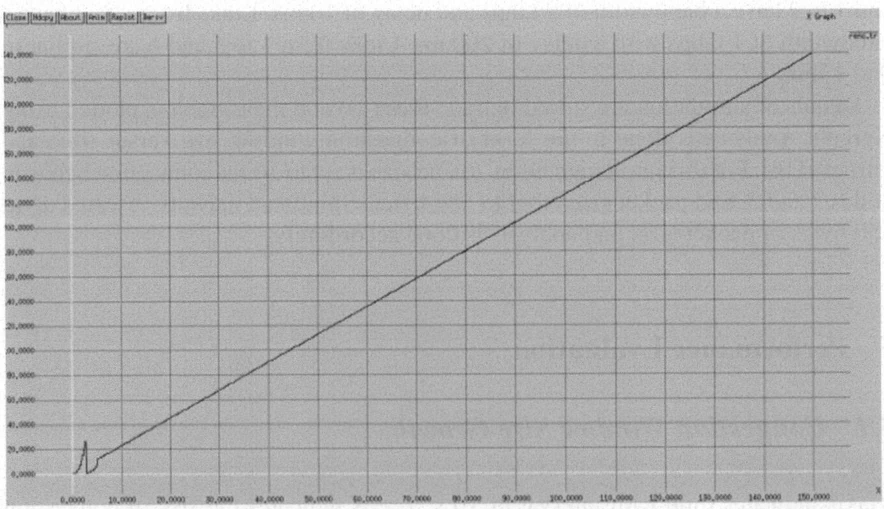

**Fig. 2** Congestion window versus time for TCP Reno in NS2

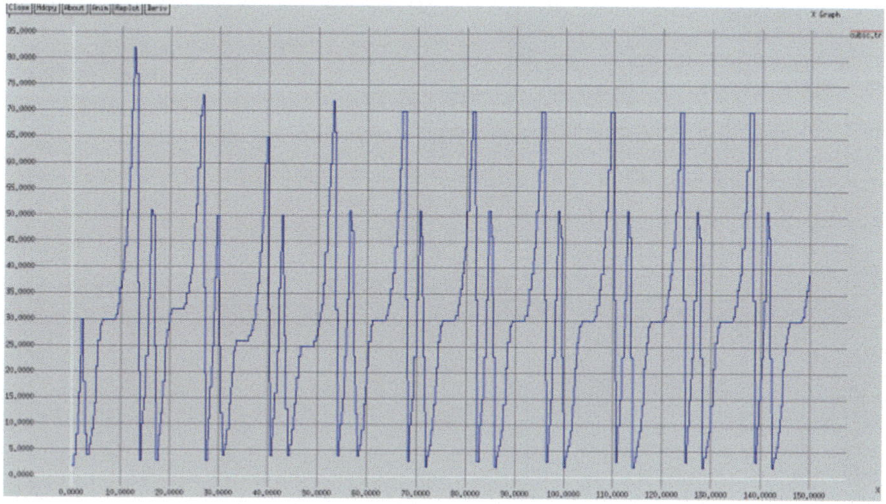

**Fig. 3** Congestion window versus time for TCP Cubic in NS2

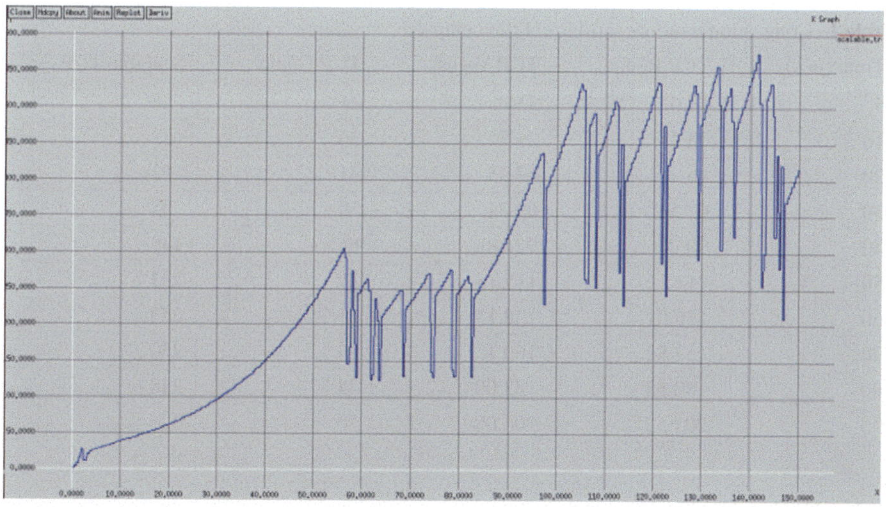

**Fig. 4** Congestion window versus time for TCP Scalable in NS2

of the Scalable TCP. Values of congestion window for TCP Cubic are less than TCP Reno, but they increase at almost by same level despite TCP Cubic window having less value (Table 1).

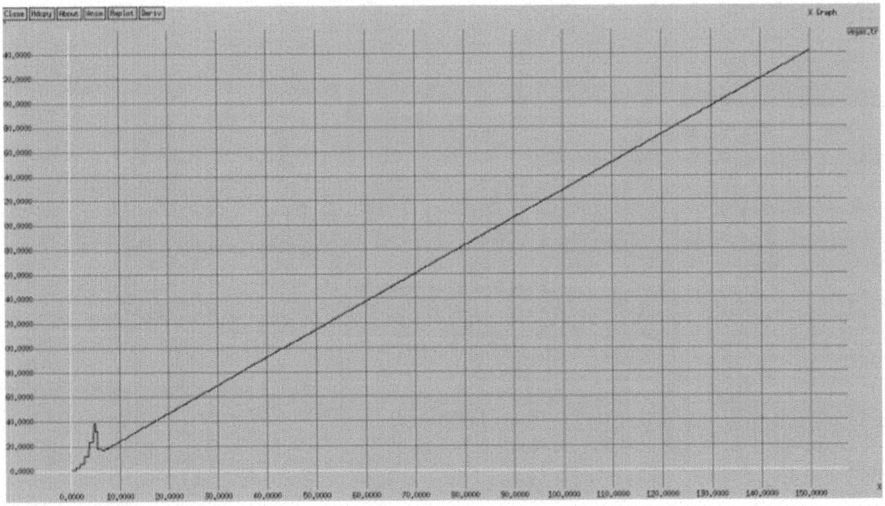

Fig. 5 Congestion window versus time for TCP Vegas in NS2

Table 1 Congestion window at different time elapsed

| Time (in s) | TCP Reno | TCP Vegas | TCP Cubic | Scalable TCP |
|---|---|---|---|---|
| 5 | 13.07 | 33 | 21 | 28 |
| 10 | 23.48 | 24.7 | 36 | 39 |
| 20 | 46 | 47.35 | 31 | 62 |
| 30 | 67.53 | 69.24 | 50 | 95 |
| 40 | 90.27 | 92.18 | 65 | 149 |
| 50 | 113.12 | 115.14 | 27 | 233 |
| 60 | 136.01 | 138.11 | 21 | 253 |
| 70 | 157.82 | 160.1 | 23 | 230 |
| 80 | 180.65 | 183.09 | 44 | 248 |
| 90 | 203.52 | 206.08 | 30 | 326 |

## 5.2 *Fairness*

For analyzing fairness [16] of TCP variants with TCP Reno, link from node 0 to node 4 is simulated using TCP Cubic, Scalable TCP, TCP Vegas one by one, and the link from node 1 to node 5 is simulated using TCP Reno.

For evaluating fairness, throughput in terms of bytes transferred per second is taken as a parameter. Throughput or bytes transferred per second is plotted on *y*-axis against time in seconds is plotted on *x*-axis.

The cubic curve (red curve) depicts the throughput variation with time for TCP Cubic and Threno (green curve) depicts the variation for TCP Reno. Initially, both start with throughput at low value and later on (at 5 s) value gets increased, varying TCP Cubic's value more than TCP Reno. 171 packets are dropped during this scenario (Fig. 6).

In Fig. 7, Scalable TCP's throughput values are plotted by curve scalable (red curve) and TCP Reno's throughput is plotted by Reno (green curve). Throughput of Scalable TCP increases more than TCP Reno. While simulating scenario is depicted in Fig. 7, 61 packets are dropped.

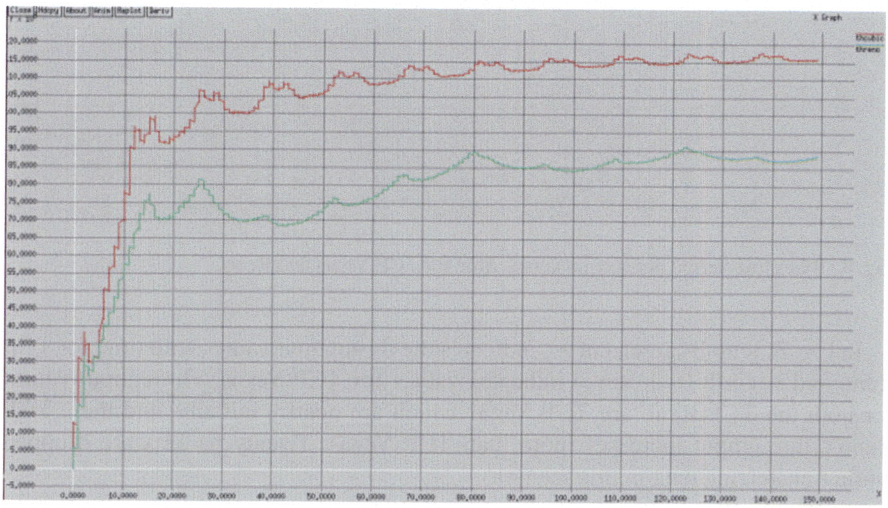


**Fig. 6** Bytes transferred per second versus time for TCP Cubic and Reno

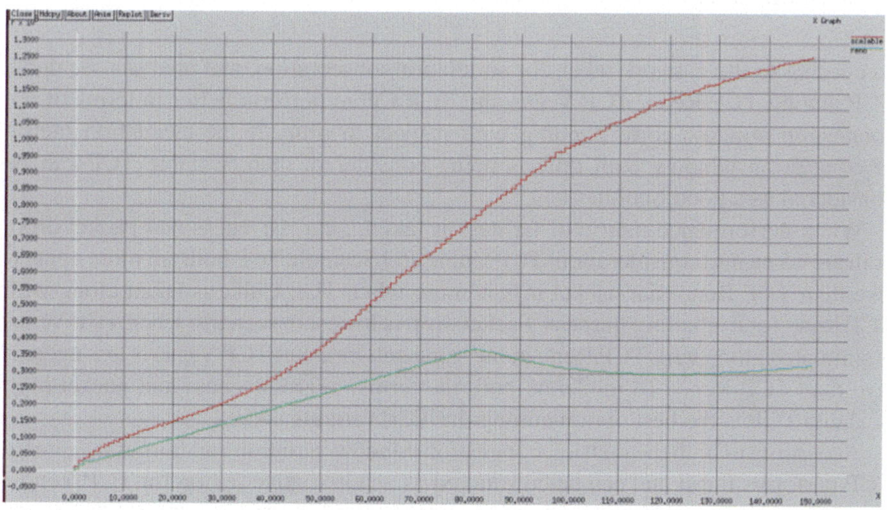


**Fig. 7** Bytes transferred per second versus time for TCP Scalable and Reno

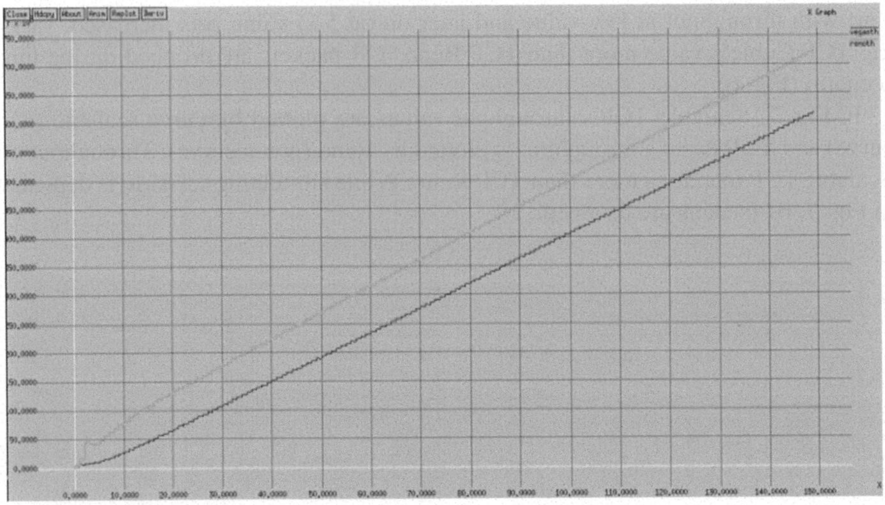

**Fig. 8** Bytes transferred per second versus time for TCP Vegas and Reno

In Fig. 8, renoth (green curve) indicates the throughput values with time for TCP Reno and vegasth (red curve) indicates values for TCP Vegas. Throughput values for both the TCP Reno are TCP Vegas which are nearby initially, and then, TCP Reno's throughput increases more than TCP Vegas. Twenty packets are dropped while transferring data in this scenario.

## 6 Conclusion

According to the network taken for simulation, observation, and analysis, Scalable TCP among TCP Reno, TCP Vegas and TCP Cubic perform better in terms of the congestion window corresponding with respect to time. If the evaluation metric of congestion window with time is being considered, then Scalable TCP can be considered as a good option.

When performance metric of fairness is taken, aggressiveness and packet drop, both are taken into consideration. TCP Cubic and Scalable TCP both are more aggressive than TCP Reno, but packet loss is more when TCP Cubic is taken along with TCP Reno for evaluating fairness. Packet drop is lowest in scenario when TCP Vegas is simulated along with TCP Reno in the same network, but TCP Vegas is less aggressive than TCP Reno. To moderate both the terms, aggressiveness and packet loss, Scalable TCP is the best option among the TCP variants taken.

According to both the metrics, congestion window variation and fairness, Scalable TCP performs finest and can be considered as an alternative option for TCP Reno.

## 7 Future Work

This analysis can be extended to other protocols as TCP Fast, TCP Africa, etc. TCP is currently not implemented in NS2; thus, it can be implemented in C++ and then linked to NS2 followed by its simulation. Other performance metrics may be considered for evaluation as safety, reliability, etc., for complete analysis of an alternative option for TCP Reno.

## References


1. J., Van, Congestion avoidance and control. ACM SIGCOMM Comput. Commun. Rev. **18**(4). ACM (1988)
2. A. Mark, V. Paxson, E. Blanton, TCP congestion control. No. RFC 5681 (2009)
3. T. Kelly, Scalable TCP: improving performance in highspeed wide area networks. ACM SIGCOMM Comput. Commun. Rev. **33**(2), 83–91 (2003)
4. P. Jitendra, et al., Modeling TCP throughput: a simple model and its empirical validation. ACM SIGCOMM Comput. Commun. Rev. **28**(4), 303–314 (1998)
5. L.S. Brakmo, S.W. O'Malley, L.L. Peterson, *TCP Vegas: New Techniques for Congestion Detection and Avoidance*, vol. 24(4) (ACM, 1994)
6. S. Ha, I. Rhee, X. Lisong, CUBIC: a new TCP-friendly high-speed TCP variant. ACM SIGOPS Operat. Syst. Rev. **42**(5), 64–74 (2008)
7. R. King, R. Baraniuk, R. Riedi, TCP-Africa: an adaptive and fair rapid increase rule for scalable TCP, in *Proceedings IEEE INFOCOM 2005 24th Annual Joint Conference of the IEEE Computer and Communications Societies*, vol. 3. (IEEE, 2005)
8. Tutorial for Linux in NS2, http://netlab.caltech.edu/projects/ns2tcplinux/ns2linux/tutorial/. Last accessed 2017/05/27
9. Introduction to NS2, http://www.ns2blogger.in/p/introduction-to-ns2.html. Last accessed 2017/05/03
10. S. Floyd, H. Balakrishnan, M. Allman, Enhancing TCP's loss recovery using limited transmit (2001)
11. S. Floyd, High speed TCP for large congestion windows (2003)
12. D.X. Wei, et al., FAST TCP: motivation, architecture, algorithms, performance. IEEE/ACM Trans. Network. **14**(6), 1246–1259 (2006)
13. A. Sawarkar, H. Saraswat, Performance analysis of TCP variants. Int. J. Comput. Sci. Netw. Secur. (IJCSNS) **16**(4), 102 (2016)
14. K., Ravi, G. Singh, Various TCP options for congestion evasion. Feedback **4**(4) (2015)
15. P. Subramanya et al., Performance evaluation of high speed TCP variants in dumbbell network. IOSR J. Comput. Eng. **16**(2), 49–53 (2014)
16. A Quantitative Measure of Fairness and Discrimination for Resource Allocation, http://www1.cse.wustl.edu/~jain/papers/ftp/fairness.pdf. Last accessed 2017/06/30

# Identifying Optimal Path to Boost Performance of Distribution Chain System Using Queueing Models

**Jitendra Kumar and Vikas Shinde**

**Abstract** Queueing model is a more effective tool to analyze the performance of distribution chain system which emphasize on quality of service (QoS). Single-channel system and multi-channel system are developed which perform the functioning of procurement of product, maintaining the stock level of products, transportation of products, and finally distribution of products to the customers. This process is done by each company, although the complexity of such exercise may vary from company to company. Performance measures provide the better potential and success of distribution system. In this research work, the authors explore the performance analysis of distribution chain system by M/M/1 and M/M/C queuing model. They examine the distribution chain system pattern via path analysis as single queue with single server model, single queue with multiple server model, and multiple queues with multiple server model. The authors have carried out the various performance measures as average queue length, response time, and waiting time corresponding to store, packing, and transportation by adopting different paths. The aim of this research work is to obtain the optimal path which provides the delivery of item as early as possible to the customer. In this context, the authors have presented the design of different service channels and evaluated their performance. Numerical illustrations have also been provided as a means of validation of the research work. The proposed model enhances lower inventories, higher productivity, lower cost, shorter lead time, higher profit, and customer satisfaction by adopting supply chain system.

**Keywords** Queueing models · Queue length · Response time · Waiting time and optimal path

---

J. Kumar (✉) · V. Shinde
Department of Applied Mathematics, Madhav Institute of Technology & Science, Gwalior, MP, India
e-mail: jkmuthele@gmail.com

V. Shinde
e-mail: v_p_shinde@rediffmail.com



M. Pant et al. (eds.), *Computational Network Application Tools for Performance Management*, Asset Analytics,
https://doi.org/10.1007/978-981-32-9585-8_17

# 1 Introduction

Queueing model is a more effective tool to analyze the performance of distribution chain system which emphasize on quality of service (QoC). Single-channel system and multi-channel system are developed which perform the functioning of procurement of product, maintaining the stock level of products, transportation of products, and finally distribution of products to the customers. This process is done by each company, although the complexity of such exercise may vary from company to company. Performance measures provide the better potential and success of distribution system. The aim of this investigation is to identify the optimal path in order to achieve effective service. Since the last few decades, researchers have been paid their attention to examine the performance of distribution chain system by using queueing models. Viswanadhan [1] discussed analytical model for evaluating the average lead time. Agrawal et al. [2] established a methodology for managing capacity, inventory, and shipment for an assortment of retail products produced by multiple vendors. Scott et al. [3] investigated the total cost-benefit which achieved by suppliers and warehouses through the increased global visibility provided by an integrated system. Bruce et al. [4] evaluated different characteristics of the textile industry and identified the perspectives of lean, quick, and legality (a combination of these) within existing supply chain. Kerbachea et al. [5] proposed a three-stage supply chain model which contains sale, production, and purchase logistics planning. Bhaskar and Lallement [6] identified the optimal path for least response time for the delivery of products to the destination. Sahraeian et al. [7] examined a supply chain network design (SCND) model with the consideration of strategic and operational decision, which determines plant and distribution centers (DC) as well as product shipment, however, the shipment has to wait in the queue for the transportation from plants to distribution centers. Mokaddis et al. [8] developed supply chain system, which involving a single manufacturer and several retail outlets. The manufacturer makes several products in batches and stores than in different warehouses after production. Taherdoost et al. [9] analyzed the three-echelon inventory model for supply chain system. Zhou et al. [10] considered a two-stage tandem network with Markov arrival process (MAP) to derive performance measure of the supply chain, such as inventory level and unfill rate. Jakhar [11] used supply chain network as an integrated method of structural modeling. Kumar and Shinde [12] established modeling approach to analyze the network for five-input, five-stage for better delivery of items. Kvasnicova et al. [13] compared known definitions and classifications of e-services. Xu et al. [14] examined the online seller's e-service offerings and customer cumulative ratings and demand.

The present modeling approach will able to compute the performance of distribution chain system using queueing models. Queueing models evaluate the optimal number of order service points (servers) to ensure a cost-effective business model. To compute the minimum response time, waiting time, and average queue length depend on order to customer to be delivered with particular cases for the response time for the delivery of product from source to final destination (customers) through some stages by using queueing models. The rest of the paper is organized as follows: notations and queueing models described in Sects. 2 and 3. Section 4 developed the model along with various performance indices like utilization of system with single and multi-server and obtained performance analysis for the average queue length, average response time, and average waiting time by using M/M/1 and M/M/C queueing model in Sects. 5 and 6. Section 7 obtained nodes corresponding to different stages with single-server, multi-server queue model and also finds out the best optimal path corresponding to network. Numerical illustrations have been mentioned in Sect. 8. Finally, Sect. 9 presented the conclusion for the best optimal path.

## 2 Notations

$n$ = Number of customers in the system (in queue plus in service),
$k$ = Number of parallel servers,
$\lambda$ = Arrival rate per order to customer for any things,
$\mu$ = Service rate per order to customer for any things,
$C$ = Number of Servers to reach things to customers corresponding to order,
$C\mu$ = Serving rate when $C > 1$ in a system,
$P_n$ = Steady-state probability of exactly $n$ customers in the system,
$\rho$ = The utilization factor ($= \lambda/(C\mu)$) (the expected factor of time the server is busy that is, service capability being utilized on the average arriving customers),
$P_0$ = Steady-state probabilities of all idle servers in the system,
$L_q$ = Average queue length,
$R_t$ = Average Response time order to customer for any things,
$W_t$ = Average waiting time for next order to customer.

## 3 Model Description

Different structures of queueing model have been discussed. Customers requiring services are generated over time by an input source. This service mechanism is described in three ways:

3.1 Single queue with single server model
3.2 Single queue with multiple server model
3.3 Multiple queues with multiple server model

The single queue, multiple queues and multiple queues with multi servers are illustrated in Figs. 1, 2 and 3.

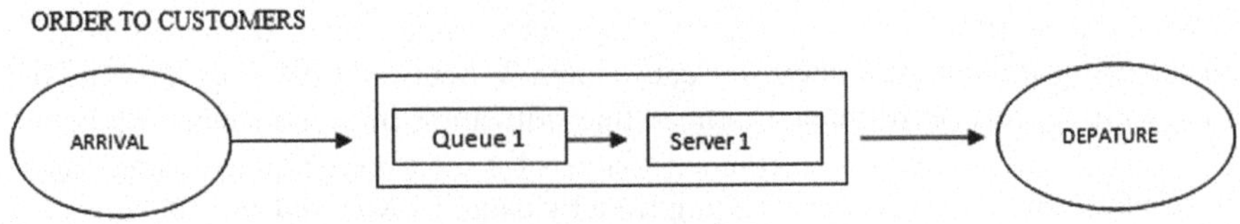


**Fig. 1** Queuing model for single queue with single server

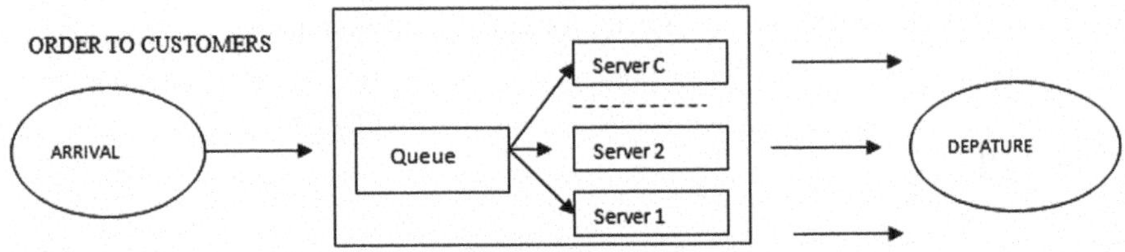


**Fig. 2** Queuing model for single queue with multiple parallel servers

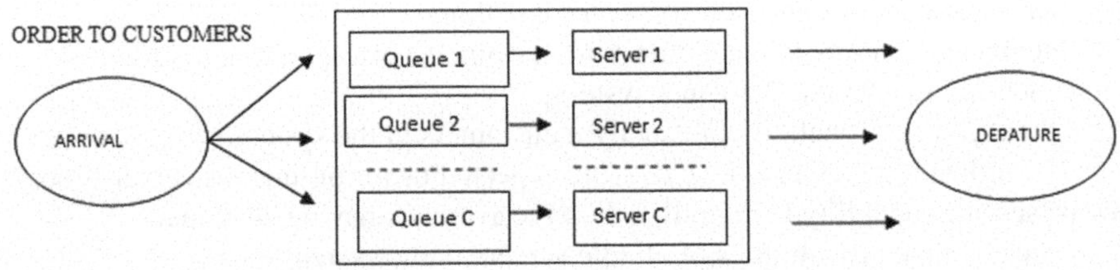


**Fig. 3** Queuing model for multiple queues with multiple parallel servers

## 4 Performance Measures

To construct various optimal paths to deliver the service in effective manner, performance measures have been used to identify the more appropriate optimal path to depict in Fig. 4.

We evaluate the different optimal paths in parallel fashion, which mentioned in Figs. 5 and 6.

### *4.1 Utilization Systems*

Applying M/M/C queueing model to obtain performance analysis as utilization, average queue length, average response time, and average waiting time with different stages (as store section, packing section, and transportation section) (Table 1).

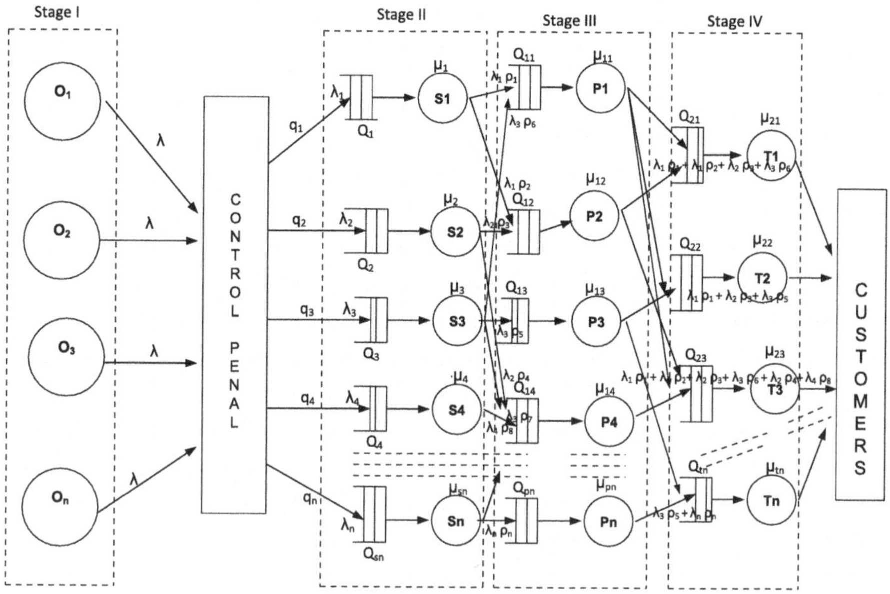


**Fig. 4** Structure origin to customer with different stages. **O** for order to customer, **S** for store things as (Digital, Clothing, Home and Kitchen, Health and Beauty, Footwear, Accessories, and others), **P** for section of Packing, and **T** for Transportation (ways) to order to customers

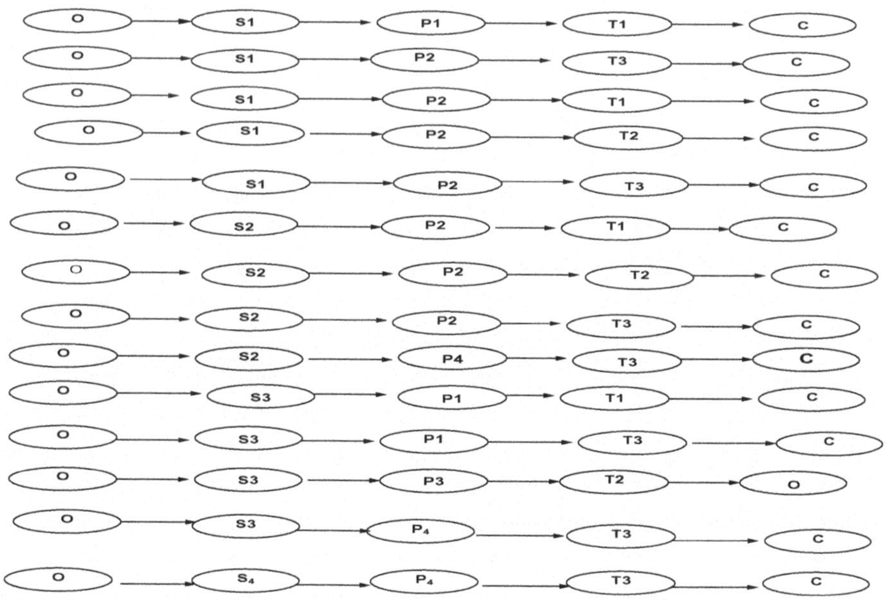


**Fig. 5** Different ways with single server

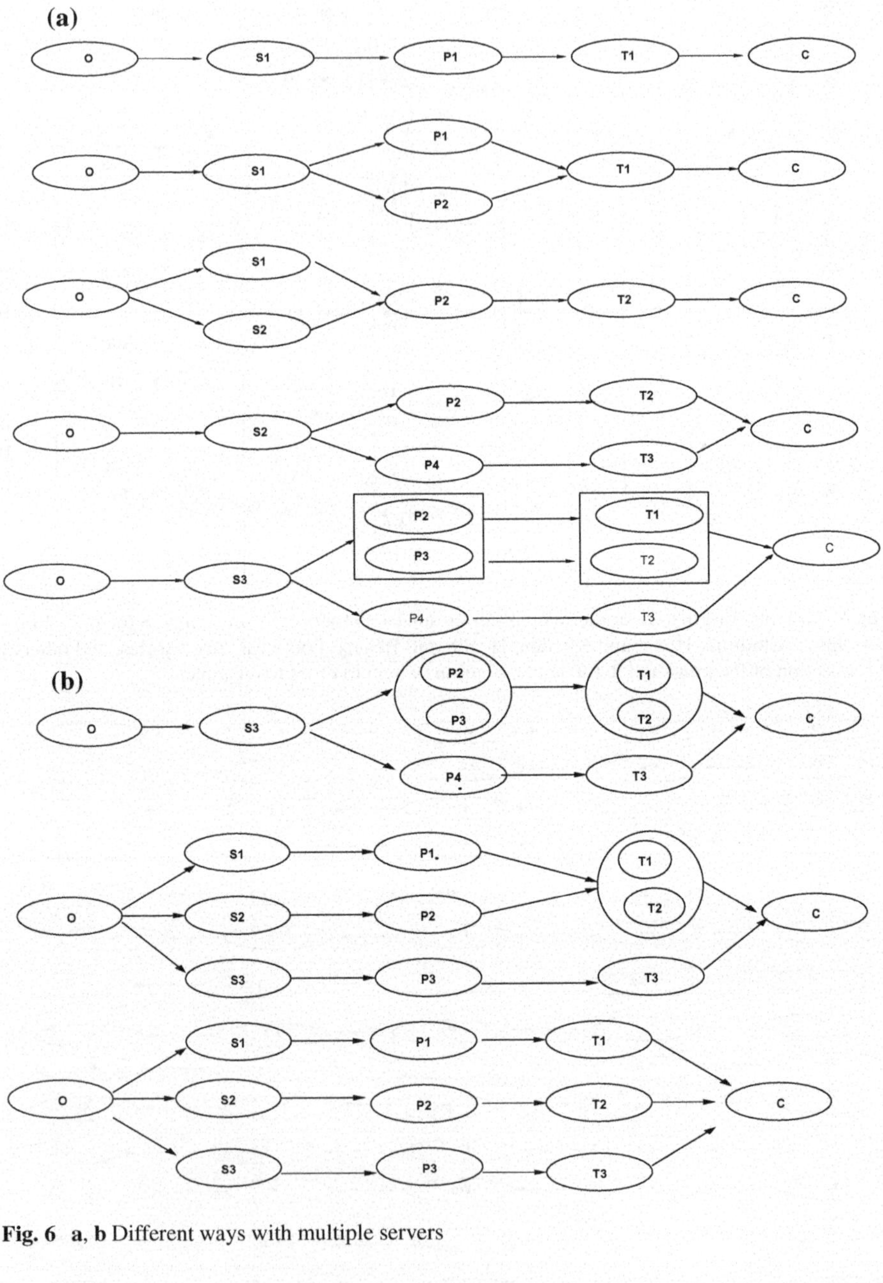


**Fig. 6** **a**, **b** Different ways with multiple servers

**Table 1** System utilization with different stages corresponding multi-server

| Stage II $(S_1, S_2, S_3, \ldots, S_n)$ | Stage III $(P_1, P_2, P_3, \ldots, P_n)$ | Stage IV $(T_1, T_2, \ldots, T_n)$ |
|---|---|---|
| $\rho_1^{(s_1)} = \frac{\lambda_1}{C\mu_1}$ where $\lambda_1 = \lambda.q_1$ | $\rho_1^{(P_1)} = \frac{\lambda_1\rho_1+\lambda_3\rho_6}{C\mu_{11}}$ | $\rho_1^{(T_1)} = \frac{\lambda_{T_1}}{C\mu_{21}}$ |
| $\rho_2^{(s_2)} = \frac{\lambda_2}{C\mu_2}$ where $\lambda_2 = \lambda.q_2$ | $\rho_2^{(P_2)} = \frac{\lambda_1\rho_2+\lambda_2\rho_3}{C\mu_{12}}$ | $\rho_2^{(T_2)} = \frac{\lambda_{T_2}}{C\mu_{22}}$ |
| $\rho_3^{(s_3)} = \frac{\lambda_3}{C\mu_3}$ where $\lambda_3 = \lambda.q_3$ | $\rho_3^{(P_3)} = \frac{\lambda_2\rho_4+\lambda_3\rho_5+\lambda_3\rho_9}{C\mu_{13}}$ | $\rho_3^{(T_3)} = \frac{\lambda_{T_3}}{C\mu_{23}}$ |
| $\rho_4^{(s_4)} = \frac{\lambda_4}{C\mu_4}$ where $\lambda_4 = \lambda.q_4$ | $\rho_4^{(P_4)} = \frac{\lambda_4\rho_8+\lambda_3\rho_7}{C\mu_{14}}$ | $\rho_4^{(T_4)} = \frac{\lambda_{P_4}}{C\mu_{24}}$ |
| $\rho_n^{(s_n)} = \frac{\lambda_n}{C\mu_n}$ where $\lambda_n = \lambda.q_n$ | $\rho_n^{(P_n)} = \frac{\lambda_{2n}\rho_{4n}+\lambda_{2n-1}\rho_{4n-1}}{C\mu_{1n}}$ | $\rho_n^{(T_n)} = \frac{\lambda_{T_n}}{C\mu_{2n}}$ |

## 4.2 *Average Queue Length of Ways in Stage II*

$$E\left[N_1^{(s_1)}\right] = \frac{\rho_1^{(s_1)}}{\left(1-\rho_1^{(s_1)}\right)} = \frac{\lambda_1}{(\mu_1-\lambda_1)} \tag{1}$$

$$E\left[N_2^{(s_2)}\right] = \frac{\rho_2^{(s_2)}}{\left(1-\rho_2^{(s_2)}\right)} = \frac{\lambda_2}{(\mu_2-\lambda_2)} \tag{2}$$

$$E\left[N_3^{(s_3)}\right] = \frac{\rho_3^{(s_3)}}{\left(1-\rho_3^{(s_3)}\right)} = \frac{\lambda_3}{(\mu_3-\lambda_3)} \tag{3}$$

$$E\left[N_4^{(s_4)}\right] = \frac{\rho_4^{(s_4)}}{\left(1-\rho_4^{(s_4)}\right)} = \frac{\lambda_4}{(\mu_4-\lambda_4)} \tag{4}$$

## 4.3 *Average Response Time of Ways in Stage II*

$$E\left[R_1^{(s_1)}\right] = \frac{1}{\lambda_1}E\left[N_1^{(s_1)}\right] = \frac{1}{(\mu_1-\lambda_1)} \tag{5}$$

$$E\left[R_2^{(s_2)}\right] = \frac{1}{\lambda_2}E\left[N_2^{(s_2)}\right] = \frac{1}{(\mu_2-\lambda_2)} \tag{6}$$

$$E\left[R_3^{(s_3)}\right] = \frac{1}{\lambda_3}E\left[N_3^{(s_3)}\right] = \frac{1}{(\mu_3-\lambda_3)} \tag{7}$$

$$E\left[R_4^{(s_4)}\right] = \frac{1}{\lambda_4}E\left[N_4^{(s_4)}\right] = \frac{1}{(\mu_4-\lambda_4)} \tag{8}$$

### 4.4 Average Waiting Time of Ways in Stage II

$$E\left[W_1^{(s_1)}\right] = E\left[R_1^{(s_1)}\right] - \frac{1}{\mu_1} = \frac{\lambda_1}{\mu_1(\mu_1 - \lambda_1)} \tag{9}$$

$$E\left[W_2^{(s_2)}\right] = E\left[R_2^{(s_2)}\right] - \frac{1}{\mu_2} = \frac{\lambda_2}{\mu_2(\mu_2 - \lambda_2)} \tag{10}$$

$$E\left[W_3^{(s_3)}\right] = E\left[R_3^{(s_3)}\right] - \frac{1}{\mu_3} = \frac{\lambda_3}{\mu_3(\mu_3 - \lambda_3)} \tag{11}$$

$$E\left[W_4^{(s_4)}\right] = E\left[R_4^{(s_4)}\right] - \frac{1}{\mu_4} = \frac{\lambda_4}{\mu_4(\mu_4 - \lambda_4)} \tag{12}$$

### 4.5 Average Queue Length of Ways in Stage III

$$E\left[N_1^{(P_1)}\right] = \frac{\rho_1^{(P_1)}}{\left(1 - \rho_1^{(P_1)}\right)} = \frac{\lambda_1\rho_1 + \lambda_3\rho_6}{[\mu_{11} - (\lambda_1\rho_1 + \lambda_3\rho_6)]} \tag{13}$$

$$E\left[N_2^{(P_2)}\right] = \frac{\rho_2^{(P_2)}}{\left(1 - \rho_2^{(P_2)}\right)} = \frac{\lambda_1\rho_2 + \lambda_2\rho_3}{[\mu_{12} - (\lambda_1\rho_2 + \lambda_2\rho_3)]} \tag{14}$$

$$E\left[N_3^{(P_3)}\right] = \frac{\rho_3^{(P_3)}}{\left(1 - \rho_3^{(P_3)}\right)} = \frac{\lambda_2\rho_4 + \lambda_3\rho_5 + \lambda_3\rho_9}{[\mu_{13} - (\lambda_2\rho_4 + \lambda_3\rho_5 + \lambda_3\rho_9)]} \tag{15}$$

$$E\left[N_4^{(P_4)}\right] = \frac{\rho_4^{(P_4)}}{\left(1 - \rho_4^{(P_4)}\right)} = \frac{\lambda_4\rho_8 + \lambda_3\rho_7}{[\mu_{14} - (\lambda_4\rho_8 + \lambda_3\rho_7)]} \tag{16}$$

### 4.6 Average Response Time of Ways in Stage III

$$E\left[R_1^{(P_1)}\right] = \frac{1}{\lambda_1\rho_1 + \lambda_3\rho_6} E\left[N_1^{(P_1)}\right] = \frac{1}{[\mu_{11} - (\lambda_1\rho_1 + \lambda_3\rho_6)]} \tag{17}$$

$$E\left[R_2^{(P_2)}\right] = \frac{1}{\lambda_1\rho_2 + \lambda_2\rho_3} E\left[N_2^{(P_2)}\right] = \frac{1}{[\mu_{12} - (\lambda_1\rho_2 + \lambda_2\rho_3)]} \tag{18}$$

$$E\left[R_3^{(P_3)}\right] = \frac{1}{\lambda_2\rho_4 + \lambda_3\rho_5 + \lambda_3\rho_9} E\left[N_3^{(P_3)}\right] = \frac{1}{[\mu_{13} - (\lambda_2\rho_4 + \lambda_3\rho_5 + \lambda_3\rho_9)]} \tag{19}$$

$$E\left[R_4^{(P_4)}\right] = \frac{1}{\lambda_4\rho_8 + \lambda_3\rho_7} E\left[N_4^{(P_4)}\right] = \frac{1}{[\mu_{14} - (\lambda_4\rho_8 + \lambda_3\rho_7)]} \tag{20}$$

## 4.7 Average Waiting Time of Ways in Stage III

$$E\left[W_1^{(P_1)}\right] = E\left[R_1^{(P_1)}\right] - \frac{1}{\mu_{11}} = \frac{\lambda_1\rho_1 + \lambda_3\rho_6}{\mu_{11}[\mu_{11} - (\lambda_1\rho_1 + \lambda_3\rho_6)]} \tag{21}$$

$$E\left[W_2^{(P_2)}\right] = E\left[R_2^{(P_2)}\right] - \frac{1}{\mu_{12}} = \frac{\lambda_1\rho_2 + \lambda_2\rho_3}{\mu_{12}[\mu_{12} - (\lambda_1\rho_2 + \lambda_2\rho_3)]} \tag{22}$$

$$E\left[W_3^{(P_3)}\right] = E\left[R_3^{(P_3)}\right] - \frac{1}{\mu_{13}} = \frac{\lambda_2\rho_4 + \lambda_3\rho_5 + \lambda_3\rho_9}{\mu_{13}[\mu_{13} - (\lambda_2\rho_4 + \lambda_3\rho_5 + \lambda_3\rho_9)]} \tag{23}$$

$$E\left[W_4^{(P_4)}\right] = E\left[R_4^{(P_4)}\right] - \frac{1}{\mu_{14}} = \frac{\lambda_4\rho_8 + \lambda_3\rho_7}{\mu_{14}[\mu_{14} - (\lambda_4\rho_8 + \lambda_3\rho_7)]} \tag{24}$$

## 4.8 Average Queue Length of Ways in Stage IV

$$E\left[N_1^{(T_1)}\right] = \frac{\rho_1^{(T_1)}}{\left(1 - \rho_1^{(T_1)}\right)} = \frac{\lambda_{T_1}}{\left(\mu_{21} - \lambda_{T_1}\right)} \tag{25}$$

$$E\left[N_2^{(T_2)}\right] = \frac{\rho_2^{(T_2)}}{\left(1 - \rho_2^{(T_2)}\right)} = \frac{\lambda_{T_2}}{\left(\mu_{22} - \lambda_{T_2}\right)} \tag{26}$$

$$E\left[N_3^{(T_3)}\right] = \frac{\rho_3^{(T_3)}}{\left(1 - \rho_3^{(T_3)}\right)} = \frac{\lambda_{T_3}}{\left(\mu_{23} - \lambda_{T_3}\right)} \tag{27}$$

### 4.9 Average Response Time of Ways in Stage IV

$$E\left[R_1^{(T_1)}\right] = \frac{1}{\lambda_{T_1}} E\left[N_1^{(T_1)}\right] = \frac{1}{(\mu_{21} - \lambda_{T_1})} \tag{28}$$

$$E\left[R_2^{(T_2)}\right] = \frac{1}{\lambda_{T_2}} E\left[N_2^{(T_2)}\right] = \frac{1}{(\mu_{22} - \lambda_{T_2})} \tag{29}$$

$$E\left[R_3^{(T_3)}\right] = \frac{1}{\lambda_{T_3}} E\left[N_3^{(T_3)}\right] = \frac{1}{(\mu_{23} - \lambda_{T_3})} \tag{30}$$

### 4.10 Average Waiting Time of Ways in Stage IV

$$E\left[W_1^{(T_1)}\right] = E\left[R_1^{(T_1)}\right] - \frac{1}{\mu_{21}} = \frac{\lambda_{T_1}}{\mu_{21}(\mu_{21} - \lambda_{T_1})} \tag{31}$$

$$E\left[W_2^{(T_2)}\right] = E\left[R_2^{(T_2)}\right] - \frac{1}{\mu_{22}} = \frac{\lambda_{T_2}}{\mu_{22}(\mu_{22} - \lambda_{T_2})} \tag{32}$$

$$E\left[\mathrm{W}_3^{(T_3)}\right] = E\left[R_3^{(T_3)}\right] - \frac{1}{\mu_{23}} = \frac{\lambda_{T_3}}{\mu_{23}(\mu_{23} - \lambda_{T_3})} \tag{33}$$

## 5 Evaluation of Performance with Single Server

To evaluate the various performance such as average queue length, average response time, and average waiting time corresponding to different stages which adopting the various ways by using queueing model with single server.

### 5.1 Average Number of Order to Customers in Way $\mathbf{X}_1$ ($\mathbf{S}_1$, $\mathbf{P}_1$, $\mathbf{T}_1$)

$$E[X_1] = E\left[N_1^{(S_1)}\right] + E\left[N_1^{(P_1)}\right] + E\left[N_1^{(T_1)}\right]$$

$$L_{\mathrm{q}} = \frac{\lambda_1}{(\mu_1 - \lambda_1)} + \frac{\lambda_1\rho_1 + \lambda_3\rho_6}{[\mu_{11} - (\lambda_1\rho_1 + \lambda_3\rho_6)]} + \frac{\lambda_{T_1}}{(\mu_{21} - \lambda_{T_1})} \tag{34}$$

$$R_t = \frac{1}{(\mu_1 - \lambda_1)} + \frac{1}{[\mu_{11} - (\lambda_1\rho_1 + \lambda_3\rho_6)]} + \frac{1}{(\mu_{21} - \lambda_{T_1})} \tag{35}$$

$$W_t = \frac{\lambda_1}{\mu_1(\mu_1 - \lambda_1)} + \frac{\lambda_1\rho_1 + \lambda_3\rho_6}{\mu_{11}[\mu_{11} - (\lambda_1\rho_1 + \lambda_3\rho_6)]} + \frac{\lambda_{T_1}}{\mu_{21}(\mu_{21} - \lambda_{T_1})} \tag{36}$$

## 5.2 *Average Number of Order to Customers in Way* X$_2$ *(*S$_1$*,* P$_1$*,* T$_3$*)*

$$E[X_2] = E\left[N_1^{(S_1)}\right] + E\left[N_1^{(P_1)}\right] + E\left[N_1^{(T_3)}\right]$$

$$L_q = \frac{\lambda_1}{(\mu_1 - \lambda_1)} + \frac{\lambda_1\rho_1 + \lambda_3\rho_6}{[\mu_{11} - (\lambda_1\rho_1 + \lambda_3\rho_6)]} + \frac{\lambda_{T_3}}{(\mu_{23} - \lambda_{T_3})} \tag{37}$$

$$R_t = \frac{1}{(\mu_1 - \lambda_1)} + \frac{1}{[\mu_{11} - (\lambda_1\rho_1 + \lambda_3\rho_6)]} + \frac{1}{(\mu_{23} - \lambda_{T_3})} \tag{38}$$

$$W_t = \frac{\lambda_1}{\mu_1(\mu_1 - \lambda_1)} + \frac{\lambda_1\rho_1 + \lambda_3\rho_6}{\mu_{11}[\mu_{11} - (\lambda_1\rho_1 + \lambda_3\rho_6)]} + \frac{\lambda_{T_3}}{\mu_{23}(\mu_{23} - \lambda_{T_3})} \tag{39}$$

## 5.3 *Average Number of Order to Customers in Way* X$_3$ *(*S$_1$*,* P$_2$*,* T$_1$*)*

$$E[X_3] = E\left[N_1^{(S_1)}\right] + E\left[N_1^{(P_2)}\right] + E\left[N_1^{(T_1)}\right]$$

$$L_q = \frac{\lambda_1}{(\mu_1 - \lambda_1)} + \frac{\lambda_1\rho_2 + \lambda_2\rho_3}{[\mu_{12} - (\lambda_1\rho_2 + \lambda_2\rho_3)]} + \frac{\lambda_{T_1}}{(\mu_{21} - \lambda_{T_1})} \tag{40}$$

$$R_t = \frac{1}{(\mu_1 - \lambda_1)} + \frac{1}{[\mu_{12} - (\lambda_1\rho_2 + \lambda_2\rho_3)]} + \frac{1}{(\mu_{21} - \lambda_{T_1})} \tag{41}$$

$$W_t = \frac{\lambda_1}{\mu_1(\mu_1 - \lambda_1)} + \frac{\lambda_1\rho_2 + \lambda_2\rho_3}{\mu_{12}[\mu_{12} - (\lambda_1\rho_2 + \lambda_2\rho_3)]} + \frac{\lambda_{T_1}}{\mu_{21}(\mu_{21} - \lambda_{T_1})} \tag{42}$$

### 5.4 *Average Number of Order to Customers in Way* $X_4$ *(*$S_1$*,* $P_2$*,* $T_2$*)*

$$E[X_4] = E\left[N_1^{(S_1)}\right] + E\left[N_1^{(P_2)}\right] + E\left[N_1^{(T_2)}\right]$$

$$L_q = \frac{\lambda_1}{(\mu_1 - \lambda_1)} + \frac{\lambda_1\rho_2 + \lambda_2\rho_3}{[\mu_{12} - (\lambda_1\rho_2 + \lambda_2\rho_3)]} + \frac{\lambda_{T_2}}{(\mu_{22} - \lambda_{T_2})} \quad (43)$$

$$R_t = \frac{1}{(\mu_1 - \lambda_1)} + \frac{1}{[\mu_{12} - (\lambda_1\rho_2 + \lambda_2\rho_3)]} + \frac{1}{(\mu_{22} - \lambda_{T_2})} \quad (44)$$

$$W_t = \frac{\lambda_1}{\mu_1(\mu_1 - \lambda_1)} + \frac{\lambda_1\rho_2 + \lambda_2\rho_3}{\mu_{12}[\mu_{12} - (\lambda_1\rho_2 + \lambda_2\rho_3)]} + \frac{\lambda_{T_2}}{\mu_{22}(\mu_{22} - \lambda_{T_2})} \quad (45)$$

### 5.5 *Average Number of Order to Customers in Way* $X_5$ *(*$S_1$*,* $P_2$*,* $T_3$*)*

$$E[X_5] = E\left[N_1^{(S_1)}\right] + E\left[N_1^{(P_2)}\right] + E\left[N_1^{(T_3)}\right]$$

$$L_q = \frac{\lambda_1}{(\mu_1 - \lambda_1)} + \frac{\lambda_1\rho_2 + \lambda_2\rho_3}{[\mu_{12} - (\lambda_1\rho_2 + \lambda_2\rho_3)]} + \frac{\lambda_{T_3}}{(\mu_{23} - \lambda_{T_3})} \quad (46)$$

$$R_t = \frac{1}{(\mu_1 - \lambda_1)} + \frac{1}{[\mu_{12} - (\lambda_1\rho_2 + \lambda_2\rho_3)]} + \frac{1}{(\mu_{23} - \lambda_{T_3})} \quad (47)$$

$$W_t = \frac{\lambda_1}{\mu_1(\mu_1 - \lambda_1)} + \frac{\lambda_1\rho_2 + \lambda_2\rho_3}{\mu_{12}[\mu_{12} - (\lambda_1\rho_2 + \lambda_2\rho_3)]} + \frac{\lambda_{T_3}}{\mu_{23}(\mu_{23} - \lambda_{T_3})} \quad (48)$$

### 5.6 *Average Number of Order to Customers in Way* $X_6$ *(*$S_2$*,* $P_2$*,* $T_1$*)*

$$E[X_6] = E\left[N_1^{(S_2)}\right] + E\left[N_1^{(P_2)}\right] + E\left[N_1^{(T_1)}\right]$$

$$L_q = \frac{\lambda_2}{(\mu_2 - \lambda_2)} + \frac{\lambda_1\rho_2 + \lambda_2\rho_3}{[\mu_{12} - (\lambda_1\rho_2 + \lambda_2\rho_3)]} + \frac{\lambda_{T_1}}{(\mu_{21} - \lambda_{T_1})} \quad (49)$$

$$R_t = \frac{1}{(\mu_2 - \lambda_2)} + \frac{1}{[\mu_{12} - (\lambda_1\rho_2 + \lambda_2\rho_3)]} + \frac{1}{\left(\mu_{21} - \lambda_{T_1}\right)} \quad (50)$$

$$W_t = \frac{\lambda_2}{\mu_2(\mu_2 - \lambda_2)} + \frac{\lambda_1\rho_2 + \lambda_2\rho_3}{\mu_{12}[\mu_{12} - (\lambda_1\rho_2 + \lambda_2\rho_3)]} + \frac{\lambda_{T_1}}{\mu_{21}\left(\mu_{21} - \lambda_{T_1}\right)} \quad (51)$$

## *5.7 Average Number of Order to Customers in Way* $X_7$ *(*$S_2$*,* $P_2$*,* $T_2$*)*

$$E[X_7] = E\left[N_1^{(S_2)}\right] + E\left[N_1^{(P_2)}\right] + E\left[N_1^{(T_2)}\right]$$

$$L_q = \frac{\lambda_2}{(\mu_2 - \lambda_2)} + \frac{\lambda_1\rho_2 + \lambda_2\rho_3}{[\mu_{12} - (\lambda_1\rho_2 + \lambda_2\rho_3)]} + \frac{\lambda_{T_2}}{\left(\mu_{22} - \lambda_{T_2}\right)} \quad (52)$$

$$R_t = \frac{1}{(\mu_2 - \lambda_2)} + \frac{1}{[\mu_{12} - (\lambda_1\rho_2 + \lambda_2\rho_3)]} + \frac{1}{\left(\mu_{22} - \lambda_{T_2}\right)} \quad (53)$$

$$W_t = \frac{\lambda_2}{\mu_2(\mu_2 - \lambda_2)} + \frac{\lambda_1\rho_2 + \lambda_2\rho_3}{\mu_{12}[\mu_{12} - (\lambda_1\rho_2 + \lambda_2\rho_3)]} + \frac{\lambda_{T_2}}{\left(\mu_{22}\left(\mu_{22} - \lambda_{T_2}\right)\right.} \quad (54)$$

## *5.8 Average Number of Order to Customers in Way* $X_8$ *(*$S_2$*,* $P_2$*,* $T_3$*)*

$$E[X_8] = E\left[N_1^{(S_2)}\right] + E\left[N_1^{(P_2)}\right] + E\left[N_1^{(T_3)}\right]$$

$$L_q = \frac{\lambda_2}{(\mu_2 - \lambda_2)} + \frac{\lambda_1\rho_2 + \lambda_2\rho_3}{[\mu_{12} - (\lambda_1\rho_2 + \lambda_2\rho_3)]} + \frac{\lambda_{T_3}}{\left(\mu_{23} - \lambda_{T_3}\right)} \quad (55)$$

$$R_t = \frac{1}{(\mu_2 - \lambda_2)} + \frac{1}{[\mu_{12} - (\lambda_1\rho_2 + \lambda_2\rho_3)]} + \frac{1}{\left(\mu_{23} - \lambda_{T_3}\right)} \quad (56)$$

$$W_t = \frac{\lambda_2}{\mu_2(\mu_2 - \lambda_2)} + \frac{\lambda_1\rho_2 + \lambda_2\rho_3}{\mu_{12}[\mu_{12} - (\lambda_1\rho_2 + \lambda_2\rho_3)]} + \frac{\lambda_{T_3}}{\left(\mu_{23}\left(\mu_{23} - \lambda_{T_3}\right)\right.} \quad (57)$$

## 5.9 Average Number of Order to Customers in Way X₉ (S₂, P₄, T₃)

$$E[X_9] = E\left[N_1^{(S_2)}\right] + E\left[N_1^{(P_4)}\right] + E\left[N_1^{(T_3)}\right]$$

$$L_q = \frac{\lambda_2}{(\mu_2 - \lambda_2)} + \frac{\lambda_4\rho_8 + \lambda_3\rho_7}{[\mu_{14} - (\lambda_4\rho_8 + \lambda_3\rho_7)]} + \frac{\lambda_{T_3}}{(\mu_{23} - \lambda_{T_3})} \quad (58)$$

$$R_t = \frac{1}{(\mu_2 - \lambda_2)} + \frac{1}{[\mu_{14} - (\lambda_4\rho_8 + \lambda_3\rho_7)]} + \frac{1}{(\mu_{23} - \lambda_{T_3})} \quad (59)$$

$$W_t = \frac{\lambda_2}{\mu_2(\mu_2 - \lambda_2)} + \frac{\lambda_4\rho_8 + \lambda_3\rho_7}{[\mu_{14} - (\lambda_4\rho_8 + \lambda_3\rho_7)]} + \frac{\lambda_{T_3}}{(\mu_{23}(\mu_{23} - \lambda_{T_3})} \quad (60)$$

## 5.10 Average Number of Order to Customers in Way X₁₀ (S₃, P₁, T₁)

$$E[X_{10}] = E\left[N_1^{(S_3)}\right] + E\left[N_1^{(P_1)}\right] + E\left[N_1^{(T_1)}\right]$$

$$L_q = \frac{\lambda_3}{(\mu_3 - \lambda_3)} + \frac{\lambda_1\rho_1 + \lambda_3\rho_6}{[\mu_{11} - (\lambda_1\rho_1 + \lambda_3\rho_6)]} + \frac{\lambda_{T_1}}{(\mu_{21} - \lambda_{T_1})} \quad (61)$$

$$R_t = \frac{1}{(\mu_3 - \lambda_3)} + \frac{1}{[\mu_{11} - (\lambda_1\rho_1 + \lambda_3\rho_6)]} + \frac{1}{(\mu_{21} - \lambda_{T_1})} \quad (62)$$

$$W_t = \frac{\lambda_3}{\mu_3(\mu_3 - \lambda_3)} + \frac{\lambda_1\rho_1 + \lambda_3\rho_6}{\mu_{11}[\mu_{11} - (\lambda_1\rho_1 + \lambda_3\rho_6)]} + \frac{\lambda_{T_1}}{\mu_{21}(\mu_{21} - \lambda_{T_1})} \quad (63)$$

## 5.11 Average Number of Order to Customers in Way X₁₁ (S₃, P₁, T₃)

$$E[X_{11}] = E\left[N_1^{(S_3)}\right] + E\left[N_1^{(P_1)}\right] + E\left[N_1^{(T_3)}\right]$$

$$L_q = \frac{\lambda_3}{(\mu_3 - \lambda_3)} + \frac{\lambda_1\rho_1 + \lambda_3\rho_6}{[\mu_{11} - (\lambda_1\rho_1 + \lambda_3\rho_6)]} + \frac{\lambda_{T_3}}{(\mu_{23} - \lambda_{T_3})} \quad (64)$$

$$R_t = \frac{1}{(\mu_3 - \lambda_3)} + \frac{1}{[\mu_{11} - (\lambda_1\rho_1 + \lambda_3\rho_6)]} + \frac{1}{(\mu_{23} - \lambda_{T_3})} \quad (65)$$

$$W_t = \frac{\lambda_3}{\mu_3(\mu_3 - \lambda_3)} + \frac{\lambda_1\rho_1 + \lambda_3\rho_6}{\mu_{11}[\mu_{11} - (\lambda_1\rho_1 + \lambda_3\rho_6)]} + \frac{\lambda_{T_3}}{\mu_{23}(\mu_{23} - \lambda_{T_3})} \quad (66)$$

## *5.12 Average Number of Order to Customers in Way* $\mathbf{X}_{12}$ *(*$\mathbf{S}_3$*,* $\mathbf{P}_3$*,* $\mathbf{T}_2$*)*

$$E[X_{12}] = E\left[N_1^{(S_3)}\right] + E\left[N_1^{(P_3)}\right] + E\left[N_1^{(T_2)}\right]$$

$$L_q = \frac{\lambda_3}{(\mu_3 - \lambda_3)} + \frac{\lambda_2\rho_4 + \lambda_3\rho_5 + \lambda_3\rho_9}{[\mu_{13} - (\lambda_2\rho_4 + \lambda_3\rho_5 + \lambda_3\rho_9)]} + \frac{\lambda_{T_2}}{(\mu_{22} - \lambda_{T_2})} \quad (67)$$

$$R_t = \frac{1}{(\mu_3 - \lambda_3)} + \frac{1}{[\mu_{13} - (\lambda_2\rho_4 + \lambda_3\rho_5 + \lambda_3\rho_9)]} + \frac{1}{(\mu_{22} - \lambda_{T_2})} \quad (68)$$

$$W_t = \frac{\lambda_3}{\mu_3(\mu_3 - \lambda_3)} + \frac{\lambda_2\rho_4 + \lambda_3\rho_5 + \lambda_3\rho_9}{\mu_{13}[\mu_{13} - (\lambda_2\rho_4 + \lambda_3\rho_5 + \lambda_3\rho_9)]} + \frac{\lambda_{T_2}}{\mu_{22}(\mu_{22} - \lambda_{T_2})} \quad (69)$$

## *5.13 Average Number of Order to Customers in Way* $\mathbf{X}_{13}$ *(*$\mathbf{S}_3$*,* $\mathbf{P}_4$*,* $\mathbf{T}_3$*)*

$$E[X_{13}] = E\left[N_1^{(S_3)}\right] + E\left[N_1^{(P_4)}\right] + E\left[N_1^{(T_3)}\right]$$

$$L_q = \frac{\lambda_3}{(\mu_3 - \lambda_3)} + \frac{\lambda_4\rho_8 + \lambda_3\rho_7}{[\mu_{14} - (\lambda_4\rho_8 + \lambda_3\rho_7)]} + \frac{\lambda_{T_3}}{(\mu_{23} - \lambda_{T_3})} \quad (70)$$

$$R_t = \frac{1}{(\mu_3 - \lambda_3)} + \frac{1}{[\mu_{14} - (\lambda_4\rho_8 + \lambda_3\rho_7)]} + \frac{1}{(\mu_{23} - \lambda_{T_3})} \quad (71)$$

$$W_t = \frac{\lambda_3}{\mu_3(\mu_3 - \lambda_3)} + \frac{\lambda_4\rho_8 + \lambda_3\rho_7}{\mu_{14}[\mu_{14} - (\lambda_4\rho_8 + \lambda_3\rho_7)]} + \frac{\lambda_{T_3}}{\mu_{23}(\mu_{23} - \lambda_{T_3})} \quad (72)$$

### 5.14 Average Number of Order to Customers in Way $X_{14}$ ($S_4$, $P_4$, $T_3$)

$$E[X_{14}] = E\left[N_1^{(S_4)}\right] + E\left[N_1^{(P_4)}\right] + E\left[N_1^{(T_3)}\right]$$

$$L_q = \frac{\lambda_4}{(\mu_4 - \lambda_4)} + \frac{\lambda_4\rho_8 + \lambda_3\rho_7}{[\mu_{14} - (\lambda_4\rho_8 + \lambda_3\rho_7)]} + \frac{\lambda_{T_3}}{(\mu_{23} - \lambda_{T_3})} \quad (73)$$

$$R_t = \frac{1}{(\mu_4 - \lambda_4)} + \frac{1}{[\mu_{14} - (\lambda_4\rho_8 + \lambda_3\rho_7)]} + \frac{1}{(\mu_{23} - \lambda_{T_3})} \quad (74)$$

$$W_t = \frac{\lambda_4}{(\mu_4 - \lambda_4)} + \frac{\lambda_4\rho_8 + \lambda_3\rho_7}{\mu_{14}[\mu_{14} - (\lambda_4\rho_8 + \lambda_3\rho_7)]} + \frac{\lambda_{T_3}}{\mu_{23}(\mu_{23} - \lambda_{T_3})} \quad (75)$$

## 6 Evaluation of Performance with Multi-server

To construct some nodes corresponding store, packing, and transportation with stages II, III, and IV as $(S_1, S_2)$, $(S_2, S_3, S_4)$, $(P_1, P_2)$, $(P_1, P_4)$, $(P_2, P_4)$, $(P_2, P_3)$, $(P_2, P_3, P_4)$, $(T_1, T_2)$, $(T_1, T_3)$, $(T_2, T_3)$ and $(T_1, T_2, T_3)$ and using M/M/C queueing model.

### 6.1 Node 1

For queue length, response time and waiting time in stage II $(S_1, S_2)$ with servers ($c = 2$) and arrival rate $\lambda = \lambda_1 + \lambda_2$ and service rate $\mu = \mu_1 + \mu_2$.

$$L_q = \frac{1}{(C-1)!}\left[\left(\frac{\lambda_1}{\mu_1}\right)^C \frac{\lambda_1\mu_1}{(C\mu_1 - \lambda_1)^2} + \left(\frac{\lambda_2}{\mu_2}\right)^C \frac{\lambda_2\mu_2}{(C\mu_2 - \lambda_2)^2}\right] \times P_0 \quad (76)$$

$$R_t = \left(\frac{1}{\mu_1} + \frac{1}{\mu_2}\right) + \frac{1}{(C)!}\left[\frac{\rho^{(S_1)}}{\lambda_1}\frac{(C\rho^{(S_1)})^2}{(1-\rho^{(S_1)})^2} + \frac{\rho^{(S_2)}}{\lambda_2}\frac{(C\rho^{(S_2)})^2}{(1-\rho^{(S_2)})^2}\right] \times P_0 \quad (77)$$

$$W_t = \frac{1}{\lambda}\left[\frac{1}{(C-1)!}\left[\left(\frac{\lambda_1}{\mu_1}\right)^C \frac{\lambda_1\mu_1}{(C\mu_1 - \lambda_1)^2} + \left(\frac{\lambda_2}{\mu_2}\right)^C \frac{\lambda_2\mu_2}{(C\mu_2 - \lambda_2)^2}\right] \times P_0\right] \quad (78)$$

where $P_0 = \left[\sum_{n=0}^{c-1}\frac{1}{n!}\left(\frac{\lambda}{\mu}\right)^n + \frac{1}{(C)!}\left(\frac{\lambda}{\mu}\right)^c\left(\frac{c\mu}{c\mu-1}\right)\right]^{-1}$.

## 6.2 Node 2

For queue length, response time and waiting time in stage II ($S_2, S_3, S_4$) with servers ($C = 3$) and arrival rate $\lambda = \lambda_2 + \lambda_3 + \lambda_4$ and service rate $\mu = \mu_2 + \mu_3 + \mu_4$.

$$L_q = \frac{1}{(C-1)!}\left[\left(\frac{\lambda_2}{\mu_2}\right)^C \frac{\lambda_2\mu_2}{(C\mu_2-\lambda_2)^2} + \left(\frac{\lambda_3}{\mu_3}\right)^C \frac{\lambda_3\mu_3}{(C\mu_3-\lambda_3)^2} + \left(\frac{\lambda_4}{\mu_4}\right)^C \frac{\lambda_4\mu_4}{(C\mu_4-\lambda_4)^2}\right] \times P_0 \tag{79}$$

$$R_t = \left(\frac{1}{\mu_2}+\frac{1}{\mu_3}+\frac{1}{\mu_4}\right) + \frac{1}{(C)!}\left[\frac{\rho^{(S_2)}}{\lambda_2}\frac{\left(C\rho^{(S_2)}\right)^2}{\left(1-\rho^{(S_2)}\right)^2} + \frac{\rho^{(S_3)}}{\lambda_3}\frac{\left(C\rho^{(S_3)}\right)^2}{\left(1-\rho^{(S_3)}\right)^2} + \frac{\rho^{(S_4)}}{\lambda_4}\frac{\left(C\rho^{(S_4)}\right)^2}{\left(1-\rho^{(S_4)}\right)^2}\right] \times P_0 \tag{80}$$

$$W_t = \frac{1}{\lambda}\left[\frac{1}{(C-1)!}\left[\left(\frac{\lambda_2}{\mu_2}\right)^C \frac{\lambda_2\mu_2}{(C\mu_2-\lambda_2)^2} + \left(\frac{\lambda_3}{\mu_3}\right)^C \frac{\lambda_3\mu_3}{(C\mu_3-\lambda_3)^2} + \left(\frac{\lambda_4}{\mu_4}\right)^C \frac{\lambda_4\mu_4}{(C\mu_4-\lambda_4)^2}\right] \times P_0\right] \tag{81}$$

where $P_0 = \left[\sum_{n=0}^{c-1}\frac{1}{n!}\left(\frac{\lambda}{\mu}\right)^n + \frac{1}{(C)!}\left(\frac{\lambda}{\mu}\right)^c\left(\frac{c\mu}{c\mu-1}\right)\right]^{-1}$.

## 6.3 Node 3

For queue length, response time and waiting time in stage II ($P_1, P_2$) with servers ($c = 2$) and arrival rate $\lambda_{P_1} = \lambda_1\rho_1 + \lambda_3\rho_6$ and $\lambda_{P_2} = \lambda_1\rho_2 + \lambda_2\rho_3$ and service rate $\mu_{11}$ and $\mu_{12}$ where $\mu = \mu_{11} + \mu_{12}$.

$$L_q = \frac{1}{(C-1)!}\left[\left(\frac{\lambda_{P_1}}{\mu_{11}}\right)^C \frac{\lambda_{P_1}\mu_{11}}{\left(C\mu_{11}-\lambda_{P_1}\right)^2} + \left(\frac{\lambda_{P_2}}{\mu_{12}}\right)^C \frac{\lambda_{P_2}\mu_{12}}{\left(C\mu_{12}-\lambda_{P_2}\right)^2}\right] \times P_0 \tag{82}$$

$$R_t = \left(\frac{1}{\mu_{11}}+\frac{1}{\mu_{12}}\right) + \frac{1}{(C)!}\left[\frac{\rho^{(P_1)}}{\lambda_{P_1}}\frac{\left(C\rho^{(P_1)}\right)^2}{\left(1-\rho^{(P_1)}\right)^2} + \frac{\rho^{(P_2)}}{\lambda_{P_2}}\frac{\left(C\rho^{(P_2)}\right)^2}{\left(1-\rho^{(P_2)}\right)^2}\right] \times P_0 \tag{83}$$

$$W_t = \frac{1}{\lambda}\left[L_q = \frac{1}{(C-1)!}\left[\left(\frac{\lambda_{P_1}}{\mu_{11}}\right)^C \frac{\lambda_{P_1}\mu_{11}}{\left(C\mu_{11}-\lambda_{P_1}\right)^2} + \left(\frac{\lambda_{P_2}}{\mu_{12}}\right)^C \frac{\lambda_{P_2}\mu_{12}}{\left(C\mu_{12}-\lambda_{P_2}\right)^2}\right] \times P_0\right] \tag{84}$$

where $P_0 = \left[\sum_{n=0}^{c-1}\frac{1}{n!}\left(\frac{\lambda}{\mu}\right)^n + \frac{1}{(C)!}\left(\frac{\lambda}{\mu}\right)^c\left(\frac{c\mu}{c\mu-1}\right)\right]^{-1}$ and $\lambda = \lambda_{P_1} + \lambda_{P_2}$.

## 6.4 Node 4

For queue length, response time and waiting time in stage II ($P_1, P_4$) with servers ($c = 2$) and arrival rate $\lambda_{P_1} = \lambda_1\rho_1 + \lambda_3\rho_6$ and $\lambda_{P_4} = \lambda_2\rho_4 + \lambda_3\rho_5 + \lambda_3\rho_9$ and service rate $\mu_{11}$ and $\mu_{14}$ where $\mu = \mu_{11} + \mu_{14}$.

$$L_q = \frac{1}{(C-1)!}\left[\left(\frac{\lambda_{P_1}}{\mu_{11}}\right)^C \frac{\lambda_{P_1}\mu_{11}}{(C\mu_{11}-\lambda_{P_1})^2} + \left(\frac{\lambda_{P_4}}{\mu_{14}}\right)^C \frac{\lambda_{P_4}\mu_{14}}{(C\mu_{14}-\lambda_{P_4})^2}\right] \times P_0 \quad (85)$$

$$R_t = \left(\frac{1}{\mu_{11}} + \frac{1}{\mu_{14}}\right) + \frac{1}{(C)!}\left[\frac{\rho^{(P_1)}}{\lambda_{P_1}} \frac{(C\rho^{(P_1)})^2}{(1-\rho^{(P_1)})^2} + \frac{\rho^{(P_4)}}{\lambda_{P_4}} \frac{(C\rho^{(P_4)})^2}{(1-\rho^{(P_4)})^2}\right] \times P_0 \quad (86)$$

$$W_t = \frac{1}{\lambda}\left[\frac{1}{(C-1)!}\left[\left(\frac{\lambda_{P_1}}{\mu_{11}}\right)^C \frac{\lambda_{P_1}\mu_{11}}{(C\mu_{11}-\lambda_{P_1})^2} + \left(\frac{\lambda_{P_4}}{\mu_{14}}\right)^C \frac{\lambda_{P_4}\mu_{14}}{(C\mu_{14}-\lambda_{P_4})^2}\right] \times P_0\right] \quad (87)$$

where $P_0 = \left[\sum_{n=0}^{c-1} \frac{1}{n!}\left(\frac{\lambda}{\mu}\right)^n + \frac{1}{(C)!}\left(\frac{\lambda}{\mu}\right)^c \left(\frac{c\mu}{c\mu-1}\right)\right]^{-1}$ and $\lambda = \lambda_{P_1} + \lambda_{P_4}$.

## 6.5 Node 5

For queue length, response time and waiting time in stage II ($P_2$, $P_4$) with servers ($c = 2$) and arrival rate $\lambda_{P_2} = \lambda_1\rho_2 + \lambda_2\rho_3$ and $\lambda_{P_4} = \lambda_2\rho_4 + \lambda_3\rho_5 + \lambda_3\rho_9$ and service rate $\mu_{12}$ and $\mu_{14}$ where $\mu = \mu_{12} + \mu_{14}$.

$$L_q = \frac{1}{(C-1)!}\left[\left(\frac{\lambda_{P_2}}{\mu_{12}}\right)^C \frac{\lambda_{P_2}\mu_{12}}{(C\mu_{12}-\lambda_{P_2})^2} + \left(\frac{\lambda_{P_4}}{\mu_{14}}\right)^C \frac{\lambda_{P_4}\mu_{14}}{(C\mu_{14}-\lambda_{P_4})^2}\right] \times P_0 \quad (88)$$

$$R_t = \left(\frac{1}{\mu_{12}} + \frac{1}{\mu_{14}}\right) + \frac{1}{(C)!}\left[\frac{\rho^{(P_2)}}{\lambda_{P_2}} \frac{(C\rho^{(P_2)})^2}{(1-\rho^{(P_2)})^2} + \frac{\rho^{(P_4)}}{\lambda_{P_4}} \frac{(C\rho^{(P_4)})^2}{(1-\rho^{(P_4)})^2}\right] \times P_0 \quad (89)$$

$$W_t = \frac{1}{\lambda}\left[\frac{1}{(C-1)!}\left[\left(\frac{\lambda_{P_2}}{\mu_{12}}\right)^C \frac{\lambda_{P_2}\mu_{12}}{(C\mu_{12}-\lambda_{P_2})^2} + \left(\frac{\lambda_{P_4}}{\mu_{14}}\right)^C \frac{\lambda_{P_4}\mu_{14}}{(C\mu_{14}-\lambda_{P_4})^2}\right] \times P_0\right] \quad (90)$$

where $P_0 = \left[\sum_{n=0}^{c-1} \frac{1}{n!}\left(\frac{\lambda}{\mu}\right)^n + \frac{1}{(C)!}\left(\frac{\lambda}{\mu}\right)^c \left(\frac{c\mu}{c\mu-1}\right)\right]^{-1}$ and $\lambda = \lambda_{P_2} + \lambda_{P_4}$.

## 6.6 Node 6

For queue length, response time and waiting time in stage II ($P_2$, $P_3$) with servers ($c = 2$) and arrival rate $\lambda_{P_2} = \lambda_1\rho_2 + \lambda_2\rho_3$ and $\lambda_{P_3} = \lambda_1\rho_1 + \lambda_3\rho_6$ and service rate $\mu_{12}$ and $\mu_{13}$ where $\mu = \mu_{12} + \mu_{13}$.

$$L_q = \frac{1}{(C-1)!}\left[\left(\frac{\lambda_{P_2}}{\mu_{12}}\right)^C \frac{\lambda_{P_2}\mu_{12}}{\left(C\mu_{12}-\lambda_{P_2}\right)^2} + \left(\frac{\lambda_{P_3}}{\mu_{14}}\right)^C \frac{\lambda_{P_3}\mu_{13}}{\left(C\mu_{13}-\lambda_{P_3}\right)^2}\right] \times P_0 \quad (91)$$

$$R_t = \left(\frac{1}{\mu_1}+\frac{1}{\mu_2}\right) + \frac{1}{(C)!}\left[\frac{\rho^{(P_2)}}{\lambda_{P_2}} \frac{\left(C\rho^{(P_2)}\right)^2}{\left(1-\rho^{(P_2)}\right)^2} + \frac{\rho^{(P_3)}}{\lambda_{P_3}} \frac{\left(C\rho^{(P_3)}\right)^2}{\left(1-\rho^{(P_3)}\right)^2}\right] \times P_0 \quad (92)$$

$$W_t = \frac{1}{\lambda}\left[\frac{1}{(C-1)!}\left[\left(\frac{\lambda_{P_2}}{\mu_{12}}\right)^C \frac{\lambda_{P_2}\mu_{12}}{\left(C\mu_{12}-\lambda_{P_2}\right)^2} + \left(\frac{\lambda_{P_3}}{\mu_{14}}\right)^C \frac{\lambda_{P_3}\mu_{13}}{\left(C\mu_{13}-\lambda_{P_3}\right)^2}\right] \times P_0\right] \quad (93)$$

where $P_0 = \left[\sum_{n=0}^{c-1} \frac{1}{n!}\left(\frac{\lambda}{\mu}\right)^n + \frac{1}{(C)!}\left(\frac{\lambda}{\mu}\right)^c\left(\frac{c\mu}{c\mu-1}\right)\right]^{-1}$ and $\lambda = \lambda_{P_2} + \lambda_{P_3}$.

## 6.7 Node 7

For queue length, response time and waiting time in stage II ($P_2$, $P_3$, $P_4$) with servers ($C = 3$) and arrival rate $\lambda_{P_2} = \lambda_1\rho_2 + \lambda_2\rho_3$, $\lambda_{P_3} = \lambda_1\rho_1 + \lambda_3\rho_6$ and $\lambda_{P_4} = \lambda_2\rho_4 + \lambda_3\rho_5 + \lambda_3\rho_9$ and service rate $\mu_{12}$, $\mu_{13}$, and $\mu_{14}$ where $\mu = \mu_{12} + \mu_{13} + \mu_{14}$.

$$L_q = \frac{1}{(C-1)!}\left[\left(\frac{\lambda_{P_2}}{\mu_{12}}\right)^C \frac{\lambda_{P_2}\mu_{12}}{\left(C\mu_{12}-\lambda_{P_2}\right)^2} + \left(\frac{\lambda_{P_3}}{\mu_{14}}\right)^C \frac{\lambda_{P_3}\mu_{13}}{\left(C\mu_{13}-\lambda_{P_3}\right)^2} + \left(\frac{\lambda_{P_4}}{\mu_{14}}\right)^C \frac{\lambda_{P_4}\mu_{14}}{\left(C\mu_{14}-\lambda_{P_4}\right)^2}\right] \times P_0 \quad (94)$$

$$R_t = \left(\frac{1}{\mu_{12}}+\frac{1}{\mu_{13}}+\frac{1}{\mu_{14}}\right) + \frac{1}{(C)!}\left[\frac{\rho^{(P_2)}}{\lambda_{P_2}} \frac{\left(C\rho^{(P_2)}\right)^2}{\left(1-\rho^{(P_2)}\right)^2} + \frac{\rho^{(P_3)}}{\lambda_{P_3}} \frac{\left(C\rho^{(P_3)}\right)^2}{\left(1-\rho^{(P_3)}\right)^2} + \frac{\rho^{(P_4)}}{\lambda_{P_4}} \frac{\left(C\rho^{(P_4)}\right)^2}{\left(1-\rho^{(P_4)}\right)^2}\right] \times P_0 \quad (95)$$

$$W_t = \frac{1}{\lambda}\left[\frac{1}{(C-1)!}\left[\left(\frac{\lambda_{P_2}}{\mu_{12}}\right)^C \frac{\lambda_{P_2}\mu_{12}}{\left(C\mu_{12}-\lambda_{P_2}\right)^2} + \left(\frac{\lambda_{P_3}}{\mu_{14}}\right)^C \frac{\lambda_{P_3}\mu_{13}}{\left(C\mu_{13}-\lambda_{P_3}\right)^2} + \left(\frac{\lambda_{P_4}}{\mu_{14}}\right)^C \frac{\lambda_{P_4}\mu_{14}}{\left(C\mu_{14}-\lambda_{P_4}\right)^2}\right] \times P_0\right] \quad (96)$$

where $P_0 = \left[\sum_{n=0}^{c-1} \frac{1}{n!}\left(\frac{\lambda}{\mu}\right)^n + \frac{1}{(C)!}\left(\frac{\lambda}{\mu}\right)^c\left(\frac{c\mu}{c\mu-1}\right)\right]^{-1}$ and $\lambda = \lambda_{P_2} + \lambda_{P_3} + \lambda_{P_4}$.

## 6.8 Node 8

For queue length, response time and waiting time in stage II ($T_1$, $T_2$) with servers ($c = 2$) and arrival rate $\lambda_{T_1} = \lambda_1\rho_1 + \lambda_1\rho_2 + \lambda_2\rho_3 + \lambda_3\rho_6$ and $\lambda_{T_2} = \lambda_1\rho_2 + \lambda_2\rho_3 + \lambda_3\rho_5$ and service rate $\mu_{21}$ and $\mu_{22}$..

$$L_q = \frac{1}{(C-1)!}\left[\left(\frac{\lambda_{T_1}}{\mu_{21}}\right)^C \frac{\lambda_{T_1}\mu_{21}}{(C\mu_{21}-\lambda_{T_1}^2} + \left(\frac{\lambda_{T_2}}{\mu_{22}}\right)^C \frac{\lambda_{T_2}\mu_{22}}{(C\mu_{22}-\lambda_2)^2}\right] \times P_0 \quad (97)$$

$$R_t = \left(\frac{1}{\mu_{21}} + \frac{1}{\mu_{22}}\right) + \frac{1}{(C)!}\left[\frac{\rho^{(T_1)}}{\lambda_{T_1}}\frac{(C\rho^{(T_1)})^2}{(1-\rho^{(T_1)})^2} + \frac{\rho^{(T_2)}}{\lambda_{T_2}}\frac{(C\rho^{(T_2)})^2}{(1-\rho^{(T_2)})^2}\right] \times P_0 \quad (98)$$

$$W_t = \frac{1}{\lambda}\left[\frac{1}{(C-1)!}\left[\left(\frac{\lambda_{T_1}}{\mu_{21}}\right)^C \frac{\lambda_{T_1}\mu_{21}}{(C\mu_{21}-\lambda_{T_1}^2} + \left(\frac{\lambda_{T_2}}{\mu_{22}}\right)^C \frac{\lambda_{T_2}\mu_{22}}{(C\mu_{22}-\lambda_2)^2}\right] \times P_0\right] \quad (99)$$

where $P_0 = \left[\sum_{n=0}^{c-1} \frac{1}{n!}\left(\frac{\lambda}{\mu}\right)^n + \frac{1}{(C)!}\left(\frac{\lambda}{\mu}\right)^c \left(\frac{c\mu}{c\mu-1}\right)\right]^{-1}$ where $\mu = \mu_{21} + \mu_{22}$ and $\lambda = \lambda_{T_1} + \lambda_{T_2}$.

## 6.9 *Node 9*

For queue length, response time and waiting time in stage II ($T_1$, $T_3$) with servers ($c$ = 2) and arrival rate $\lambda_{T_1} = \lambda_1\rho_1 + \lambda_1\rho_2 + \lambda_2\rho_3 + \lambda_3\rho_6$ and $\lambda_{T_3} = \lambda_1\rho_1 + \lambda_3\rho_7 + \lambda_2\rho_4 + \lambda_3\rho_6 + \lambda_4\rho_8$ and service rate $\mu_{21}$ and $\mu_{23}$.

$$L_q = \frac{1}{(C-1)!}\left[\left(\frac{\lambda_{T_1}}{\mu_{21}}\right)^C \frac{\lambda_{T_1}\mu_{21}}{(C\mu_{21}-\lambda_{T_1})^2} + \left(\frac{\lambda_{T_3}}{\mu_{23}}\right)^C \frac{\lambda_{T_3}\mu_{23}}{(C\mu_{23}-\lambda_{T_3})^2}\right] \times P_0 \quad (100)$$

$$R_t = \left(\frac{1}{\mu_{21}} + \frac{1}{\mu_{23}}\right) + \frac{1}{(C)!}\left[\frac{\rho^{(T_1)}}{\lambda_{T_1}}\frac{(C\rho^{(T_1)})^2}{(1-\rho^{(T_1)})^2} + \frac{\rho^{(T_2)}}{\lambda_{T_3}}\frac{(C\rho^{(T_2)})^2}{(1-\rho^{(T_2)})^2}\right] \times P_0 \quad (101)$$

$$W_t = \frac{1}{\lambda}\left[\frac{1}{(C-1)!}\left[\left(\frac{\lambda_{T_1}}{\mu_{21}}\right)^C \frac{\lambda_{T_1}\mu_{21}}{(C\mu_{21}-\lambda_{T_1})^2} + \left(\frac{\lambda_{T_3}}{\mu_{23}}\right)^C \frac{\lambda_{T_3}\mu_{23}}{(C\mu_{23}-\lambda_{T_3})^2}\right] \times P_0\right] \quad (102)$$

where $P_0 = \left[\sum_{n=0}^{c-1} \frac{1}{n!}\left(\frac{\lambda}{\mu}\right)^n + \frac{1}{(C)!}\left(\frac{\lambda}{\mu}\right)^c \left(\frac{c\mu}{c\mu-1}\right)\right]^{-1}$ where $\mu = \mu_{21} + \mu_{23}$ and $\lambda = \lambda_{T_1} + \lambda_{T_3}$.

### 6.10 Node 10

For queue length, response time and waiting time in stage II ($T_2$, $T_3$) with servers ($c$ = 2) and arrival rate $\lambda_{T_2} = \lambda_1\rho_2 + \lambda_2\rho_3 + \lambda_3\rho_5$ and $\lambda_{T_3} = \lambda_1\rho_1 + \lambda_3\rho_7 + \lambda_2\rho_4 + \lambda_3\rho_6 + \lambda_4\rho_8$ and service rate $\mu_{22}$ and $\mu_{23}$.

$$L_q = \frac{1}{(C-1)!}\left[\left(\frac{\lambda_{T_2}}{\mu_{22}}\right)^C \frac{\lambda_{T_2}\mu_{22}}{(C\mu_{22}-\lambda_2)^2} + \left(\frac{\lambda_{T_3}}{\mu_{23}}\right)^C \frac{\lambda_{T_3}\mu_{23}}{\left(C\mu_{23}-\lambda_{T_3}\right)^2}\right] \times P_0 \quad (103)$$

$$R_t = \left(\frac{1}{\mu_{22}} + \frac{1}{\mu_{23}}\right) + \frac{1}{(C)!}\left[\frac{\rho^{(T_2)}}{\lambda_{T_2}}\frac{\left(C\rho^{(T_2)}\right)^2}{\left(1-\rho^{(T_2)}\right)^2} + \frac{\rho^{(T_2)}}{\lambda_{T_3}}\frac{\left(C\rho^{(T_2)}\right)^2}{\left(1-\rho^{(T_2)}\right)^2}\right] \times P_0 \quad (104)$$

$$W_t = \frac{L_q}{\lambda} \quad (105)$$

where $P_0 = \left[\sum_{n=0}^{c-1}\frac{1}{n!}\left(\frac{\lambda}{\mu}\right)^n + \frac{1}{(C)!}\left(\frac{\lambda}{\mu}\right)^c\left(\frac{c\mu}{c\mu-1}\right)\right]^{-1}$ where $\mu = \mu_{22} + \mu_{23}$ and $\lambda = \lambda_{T_2} + \lambda_{T_3}$.

### 6.11 Node 11

For queue length, response time and waiting time in stage II ($T_1$, $T_2$, $T_3$) with servers ($C = 3$) and arrival rate $\lambda_{T_1} = \lambda_1\rho_1 + \lambda_1\rho_2 + \lambda_2\rho_3 + \lambda_3\rho_6$, $\lambda_{T_2} = \lambda_1\rho_2 + \lambda_2\rho_3 + \lambda_3\rho_5$ and $\lambda_{T_3} = \lambda_1\rho_1 + \lambda_3\rho_7 + \lambda_2\rho_4 + \lambda_3\rho_6 + \lambda_4\rho_8$ and service rate $\mu_{21}$, $\mu_{22}$, and $\mu_{23}$.

$$L_q = \frac{1}{(C-1)!}\left[\left(\frac{\lambda_{T_1}}{\mu_{21}}\right)^C \frac{\lambda_{T_1}\mu_{21}}{(C\mu_{21}-\lambda_{T_1}^2} + \left(\frac{\lambda_{T_2}}{\mu_{22}}\right)^C \frac{\lambda_{T_2}\mu_{22}}{(C\mu_{22}-\lambda_2)^2} + \left(\frac{\lambda_{T_3}}{\mu_{23}}\right)^C \frac{\lambda_{T_3}\mu_{23}}{\left(C\mu_{23}-\lambda_{T_3}\right)^2}\right] \times P_0 \quad (106)$$

$$R_t = \left(\frac{1}{\mu_{21}} + \frac{1}{\mu_{22}} + \frac{1}{\mu_{23}}\right) + \frac{1}{(C)!}\left[\frac{\rho^{(T_1)}}{\lambda_{T_1}}\frac{\left(C\rho^{(T_1)}\right)^2}{\left(1-\rho^{(T_1)}\right)^2} + \frac{\rho^{(T_2)}}{\lambda_{T_2}}\frac{\left(C\rho^{(T_2)}\right)^2}{\left(1-\rho^{(T_2)}\right)^2} + \frac{\rho^{(T_2)}}{\lambda_{T_3}}\frac{\left(C\rho^{(T_2)}\right)^2}{\left(1-\rho^{(T_2)}\right)^2}\right] \times P_0 \quad (107)$$

$$W_t = \frac{1}{\lambda}\left[\frac{1}{(C-1)!}\left[\left(\frac{\lambda_{T_1}}{\mu_{21}}\right)^C \frac{\lambda_{T_1}\mu_{21}}{(C\mu_{21}-\lambda_{T_1}^2} + \left(\frac{\lambda_{T_2}}{\mu_{22}}\right)^C \frac{\lambda_{T_2}\mu_{22}}{(C\mu_{22}-\lambda_2)^2} + \left(\frac{\lambda_{T_3}}{\mu_{23}}\right)^C \frac{\lambda_{T_3}\mu_{23}}{\left(C\mu_{23}-\lambda_{T_3}\right)^2}\right] \times P_0\right] \quad (108)$$

where $P_0 = \left[\sum_{n=0}^{c-1}\frac{1}{n!}\left(\frac{\lambda}{\mu}\right)^n + \frac{1}{(C)!}\left(\frac{\lambda}{\mu}\right)^c\left(\frac{c\mu}{c\mu-1}\right)\right]^{-1}$ where $\mu = \mu_{21} + \mu_{22} + \mu_{23}$ and $\lambda = \lambda_{T_1} + \lambda_{T_2} + \lambda_{T_3}$.

## 6.12 Special Node 12

For queue length, response time and waiting time in stage II $(P_2, P_3), P_4]$ with servers $(c = 3)$ and arrival rate $\lambda_{P_2}$, $\lambda_{P_3}$ and $\lambda_{P_4}$ and service rate $\mu_{12}$, $\mu_{13}$ and $\mu_{14}$.

$$L_q = \frac{1}{(C-1)!}\left[\left\{\left(\frac{\lambda_{P_2}}{\mu_{12}}\right)^C \frac{\lambda_{P_2}\mu_{12}}{\left(C\mu_{12}-\lambda_{P_2}\right)^2} + \left(\frac{\lambda_{P_3}}{\mu_{14}}\right)^C \frac{\lambda_{P_3}\mu_{13}}{\left(C\mu_{13}-\lambda_{P_3}\right)^2}\right\} + \left(\frac{\lambda_{P_4}}{\mu_{14}}\right)^C \frac{\lambda_{P_4}\mu_{14}}{\left(C\mu_{14}-\lambda_{P_4}\right)^2}\right] \times P_0 \tag{109}$$

$$R_t = \left(\frac{1}{\mu_{12}} + \frac{1}{\mu_{13}} + \frac{1}{\mu_{14}}\right) + \frac{1}{(C)!}\left[\left\{\frac{\rho^{(P_2)}}{\lambda_{P_2}} \frac{\left(C\rho^{(P_2)}\right)^2}{\left(1-\rho^{(P_2)}\right)^2} + \frac{\rho^{(P_3)}}{\lambda_{P_3}} \frac{\left(C\rho^{(P_3)}\right)^2}{\left(1-\rho^{(P_3)}\right)^2}\right\} + \frac{\rho^{(P_4)}}{\lambda_{P_4}} \frac{\left(C\rho^{(P_4)}\right)^2}{\left(1-\rho^{(P_4)}\right)^2}\right] \times P_0 \tag{110}$$

$$W_t = \frac{1}{\lambda}\left[\frac{1}{(C-1)!}\left[\left\{\left(\frac{\lambda_{P_2}}{\mu_{12}}\right)^C \frac{\lambda_{P_2}\mu_{12}}{\left(C\mu_{12}-\lambda_{P_2}\right)^2} + \left(\frac{\lambda_{P_3}}{\mu_{14}}\right)^C \frac{\lambda_{P_3}\mu_{13}}{\left(C\mu_{13}-\lambda_{P_3}\right)^2}\right\} + \left(\frac{\lambda_{P_4}}{\mu_{14}}\right)^C \frac{\lambda_{P_4}\mu_{14}}{\left(C\mu_{14}-\lambda_{P_4}\right)^2}\right] \times P_0\right] \tag{111}$$

where $P_0 = \left[\sum_{n=0}^{c-1} \frac{1}{n!}\left(\frac{\lambda}{\mu}\right)^n + \frac{1}{(C)!}\left(\frac{\lambda}{\mu}\right)^C \left(\frac{c\mu}{c\mu-1}\right)\right]^{-1}$ where $\mu = [(\mu_{12} + \mu_{13}) + \mu_{14}]$and $\lambda = \left[\left(\lambda_{P_2} + \lambda_{P_3}\right) + \lambda_{P_4}\right]$.

## 6.13 Special Node 13

For queue length, response time and waiting time in stage II $(T_1, T_2), T_3]$ with servers $(c = 3)$ and arrival rate $\lambda_{T_1}$, $\lambda_{T_2}$ and $\lambda_{T_3}$ and service rate $\mu_{21}$, $\mu_{22}$ and $\mu_{23}$ where $\mu = [(\mu_{21} + \mu_{22}) + \mu_{23}]$.

$$L_q = \frac{1}{(C-1)!}\left[\left\{\left(\frac{\lambda_{T_1}}{\mu_{21}}\right)^C \frac{\lambda_{T_1}\mu_{21}}{(C\mu_{21}-\lambda_{T_1}^2} + \left(\frac{\lambda_{T_2}}{\mu_{22}}\right)^C \frac{\lambda_{T_2}\mu_{22}}{(C\mu_{22}-\lambda_2)^2}\right\} + \left(\frac{\lambda_{T_3}}{\mu_{23}}\right)^C \frac{\lambda_{T_3}\mu_{23}}{\left(C\mu_{23}-\lambda_{T_3}\right)^2}\right] \times P_0 \tag{112}$$

$$R_t = \left(\frac{1}{\mu_{21}} + \frac{1}{\mu_{22}} + \frac{1}{\mu_{23}}\right) + \frac{1}{(C)!}\left[\left\{\frac{\rho^{(T_1)}}{\lambda_{T_1}} \frac{\left(C\rho^{(T_1)}\right)^2}{\left(1-\rho^{(T_1)}\right)^2} + \frac{\rho^{(T_2)}}{\lambda_{T_2}} \frac{\left(C\rho^{(T_2)}\right)^2}{\left(1-\rho^{(T_2)}\right)^2}\right\} + \frac{\rho^{(T_2)}}{\lambda_{T_3}} \frac{\left(C\rho^{(T_2)}\right)^2}{\left(1-\rho^{(T_2)}\right)^2}\right] \times P_0 \tag{113}$$

$$W_t = \frac{1}{\lambda}\left[\frac{1}{(C-1)!}\left[\left\{\left(\frac{\lambda_{T_1}}{\mu_{21}}\right)^C \frac{\lambda_{T_1}\mu_{21}}{(C\mu_{21}-\lambda_{T_1}^2} + \left(\frac{\lambda_{T_2}}{\mu_{22}}\right)^C \frac{\lambda_{T_2}\mu_{22}}{(C\mu_{22}-\lambda_2)^2}\right\} + \left(\frac{\lambda_{T_3}}{\mu_{23}}\right)^C \frac{\lambda_{T_3}\mu_{23}}{\left(C\mu_{23}-\lambda_{T_3}\right)^2}\right] \times P_0\right] \tag{114}$$

where $P_0 = \left[\sum_{n=0}^{c-1} \frac{1}{n!}\left(\frac{\lambda}{\mu}\right)^n + \frac{1}{(C)!}\left(\frac{\lambda}{\mu}\right)^c \left(\frac{c\mu}{c\mu-1}\right)\right]^{-1}$ where $\mu = [(\mu_{21} + \mu_{22}) + \mu_{23}]$and $\lambda = \left[(\lambda_{T_1} + \lambda_{T_2}) + \lambda_{T_3}\right]$.

# 7 Optimal Path Corresponding to Nodes and Ways

To obtain best optimal path by using nodes and different ways as described in pervious section. According to Fig. 4, to obtain performance measures as average queue length, average response time, and average waiting time in different stages with path and nodes

## 7.1 *I—Way* ($S_1$, $P_1$, $T_1$)

$$L_q = \frac{\lambda_1}{(\mu_1 - \lambda_1)} + \frac{\lambda_1\rho_1 + \lambda_3\rho_6}{[\mu_{11} - (\lambda_1\rho_1 + \lambda_3\rho_6)]} + \frac{\lambda_{T_1}}{(\mu_{21} - \lambda_{T_1})} \quad (115)$$

$$R_t = \frac{1}{(\mu_1 - \lambda_1)} + \frac{1}{[\mu_{11} - (\lambda_1\rho_1 + \lambda_3\rho_6)]} + \frac{1}{(\mu_{21} - \lambda_{T_1})} \quad (116)$$

$$W_t = \frac{\lambda_1}{\mu_1(\mu_1 - \lambda_1)} + \frac{\lambda_1\rho_1 + \lambda_3\rho_6}{\mu_{11}[\mu_{11} - (\lambda_1\rho_1 + \lambda_3\rho_6)]} + \frac{\lambda_{T_1}}{\mu_{21}(\mu_{21} - \lambda_{T_1})} \quad (117)$$

## 7.2 *II—Way* ($S_1$, ($\underline{P_1}$, $\underline{P_2}$), $T_1$)

$$L_q = \frac{\lambda_1}{(\mu_1 - \lambda_1)} + \left\{\frac{1}{(C-1)!}\left[\left(\frac{\lambda_{P_1}}{\mu_{11}}\right)^C \frac{\lambda_{P_1}\mu_{11}}{\left(C\mu_{11} - \lambda_{P_1}\right)^2} + \left(\frac{\lambda_{P_2}}{\mu_{12}}\right)^C \frac{\lambda_{P_2}\mu_{12}}{\left(C\mu_{12} - \lambda_{P_2}\right)^2}\right] \times P_0\right\} + \frac{\lambda_{T_1}}{\left(\mu_{21} - \lambda_{T_1}\right)} \quad (118)$$

$$R_t = \frac{1}{(\mu_1 - \lambda_1)} + \left\{\left(\frac{1}{\mu_{11}} + \frac{1}{\mu_{12}}\right) + \frac{1}{(C)!}\left[\frac{\rho^{(P_1)}}{\lambda_{P_1}} \frac{\left(C\rho^{(P_1)}\right)^2}{\left(1 - \rho^{(P_1)}\right)^2} + \frac{\rho^{(P_2)}}{\lambda_{P_2}} \frac{\left(C\rho^{(P_2)}\right)^2}{\left(1 - \rho^{(P_2)}\right)^2}\right] \times P_0\right\} + \frac{1}{\left(\mu_{21} - \lambda_{T_1}\right)} \quad (119)$$

$$W_t = \frac{1}{\lambda}\left\{\frac{\lambda_1}{(\mu_1 - \lambda_1)} + \frac{\lambda_1\rho_1 + \lambda_3\rho_6}{[\mu_{11} - (\lambda_1\rho_1 + \lambda_3\rho_6)]} + \frac{\lambda_{T_1}}{(\mu_{21} - \lambda_{T_1})}\right\}$$

where

$$\lambda = \lambda_1 + (\lambda_1\rho_1 + \lambda_3\rho_6) + \lambda_{T_1}. \tag{120}$$

## 7.3 III—Way ((S₁, S₁), P₂, T₂)

$$L_q = \left\{\frac{1}{(C-1)!}\left[\left(\frac{\lambda_1}{\mu_1}\right)^C \frac{\lambda_1\mu_1}{(C\mu_1-\lambda_1)^2} + \left(\frac{\lambda_2}{\mu_2}\right)^C \frac{\lambda_2\mu_2}{(C\mu_2-\lambda_2)^2}\right] \times P_0\right\} + \frac{\lambda_1\rho_2+\lambda_2\rho_3}{[\mu_{12}-(\lambda_1\rho_2+\lambda_2\rho_3)]} + \frac{\lambda_{T_2}}{(\mu_{22}-\lambda_{T_2})} \tag{121}$$

$$R_t = \left\{\left(\frac{1}{\mu_1}+\frac{1}{\mu_2}\right) + \frac{1}{(C)!}\left[\frac{\rho^{(S_1)}}{\lambda_1}\frac{\left(C\rho^{(S_1)}\right)^2}{\left(1-\rho^{(S_1)}\right)^2} + \frac{\rho^{(S_2)}}{\lambda_2}\frac{\left(C\rho^{(S_2)}\right)^2}{\left(1-\rho^{(S_2)}\right)^2}\right] \times P_0\right\} + \frac{1}{[\mu_{12}-(\lambda_1\rho_2+\lambda_2\rho_3)]} + \frac{1}{(\mu_{22}-\lambda_{T_2})} \tag{122}$$

$$W_t = \frac{1}{\lambda}\left\{\left\{\frac{1}{(C-1)!}\left[\left(\frac{\lambda_1}{\mu_1}\right)^C \frac{\lambda_1\mu_1}{(C\mu_1-\lambda_1)^2} + \left(\frac{\lambda_2}{\mu_2}\right)^C \frac{\lambda_2\mu_2}{(C\mu_2-\lambda_2)^2}\right] \times P_0\right\} + \frac{\lambda_1\rho_2+\lambda_2\rho_3}{[\mu_{12}-(\lambda_1\rho_2+\lambda_2\rho_3)]} + \frac{\lambda_{T_2}}{(\mu_{22}-\lambda_{T_2})}\right\} \tag{123}$$

where $\lambda = (\lambda_1 + \lambda_2) + (\lambda_1\rho_2 + \lambda_2\rho_3) + \lambda_{T_2}$.

## 7.4 IV—Way (S₂, (P₂, P₄), (T₂, T₃))

$$L_q = \left[\frac{\lambda_2}{(\mu_2-\lambda_2)} + \left\{\frac{1}{(C-1)!}\left[\left(\frac{\lambda_{P_2}}{\mu_{12}}\right)^C \frac{\lambda_{P_2}\mu_{12}}{\left(C\mu_{12}-\lambda_{P_2}\right)^2} + \left(\frac{\lambda_{P_4}}{\mu_{14}}\right)^C \frac{\lambda_{P_4}\mu_{14}}{\left(C\mu_{14}-\lambda_{P_4}\right)^2}\right] \times P_0\right\} + \left\{\frac{1}{(C-1)!}\left[\left(\frac{\lambda_{T_2}}{\mu_{22}}\right)^C \frac{\lambda_{T_2}\mu_{22}}{(C\mu_{22}-\lambda_2)^2} + \left(\frac{\lambda_{T_3}}{\mu_{23}}\right)^C \frac{\lambda_{T_3}\mu_{23}}{\left(C\mu_{23}-\lambda_{T_3}\right)^2}\right] \times P_0\right\}\right] \tag{124}$$

$$R_t = \frac{1}{(\mu_2-\lambda_2)} + \left\{\left(\frac{1}{\mu_{12}}+\frac{1}{\mu_{14}}\right) + \frac{1}{(C)!}\left[\frac{\rho^{(P_2)}}{\lambda_{P_2}}\frac{\left(C\rho^{(P_2)}\right)^2}{\left(1-\rho^{(P_2)}\right)^2} + \frac{\rho^{(P_4)}}{\lambda_{P_4}}\frac{\left(C\rho^{(P_4)}\right)^2}{\left(1-\rho^{(P_4)}\right)^2}\right] \times P_0\right\} + \left\{\left(\frac{1}{\mu_{22}}+\frac{1}{\mu_{23}}\right) + \frac{1}{(C)!}\left[\frac{\rho^{(T_2)}}{\lambda_{T_2}}\frac{\left(C\rho^{(T_2)}\right)^2}{\left(1-\rho^{(T_2)}\right)^2} + \frac{\rho^{(T_2)}}{\lambda_{T_3}}\frac{\left(C\rho^{(T_2)}\right)^2}{\left(1-\rho^{(T_2)}\right)^2}\right] \times P_0\right\} \tag{125}$$

$$W_t = \frac{1}{\lambda}\Bigg[\frac{\lambda_2}{(\mu_2-\lambda_2)} + \left\{\frac{1}{(C-1)!}\left[\left(\frac{\lambda_{P_2}}{\mu_{12}}\right)^C \frac{\lambda_{P_2}\mu_{12}}{\left(C\mu_{12}-\lambda_{P_2}\right)^2} + \left(\frac{\lambda_{P_4}}{\mu_{14}}\right)^C \frac{\lambda_{P_4}\mu_{14}}{\left(C\mu_{14}-\lambda_{P_4}\right)^2}\right]\times P_0\right\} + \left\{\frac{1}{(C-1)!}\left[\left(\frac{\lambda_{T_2}}{\mu_{22}}\right)^C \frac{\lambda_{T_2}\mu_{22}}{(C\mu_{22}-\lambda_2)^2} + \left(\frac{\lambda_{T_3}}{\mu_{23}}\right)^C \frac{\lambda_{T_3}\mu_{23}}{\left(C\mu_{23}-\lambda_{T_3}\right)^2}\right]\times P_0\right\}\Bigg] \tag{126}$$

where $\lambda = (\lambda_2) + \lambda_{T_3} + \lambda_{T_2}$.

## 7.5 V—Way ($S_3$, {($P_2$, $P_3$), $P_4$}, { ($T_1$, $T_2$), $T_3$})

$$L_q = \frac{\lambda_3}{(\mu_3-\lambda_3)} + \left[\frac{1}{(C-1)!}\left[\left\{\left(\frac{\lambda_{P_2}}{\mu_{12}}\right)^C \frac{\lambda_{P_2}\mu_{12}}{\left(C\mu_{12}-\lambda_{P_2}\right)^2} + \left(\frac{\lambda_{P_3}}{\mu_{14}}\right)^C \frac{\lambda_{P_3}\mu_{13}}{\left(C\mu_{13}-\lambda_{P_3}\right)^2}\right\} + \left(\frac{\lambda_{P_4}}{\mu_{14}}\right)^C \frac{\lambda_{P_4}\mu_{14}}{\left(C\mu_{14}-\lambda_{P_4}\right)^2}\right]\times P_0\right] + \left[\frac{1}{(C-1)!}\left\{\left(\frac{\lambda_{T_1}}{\mu_{21}}\right)^C \frac{\lambda_{T_1}\mu_{21}}{(C\mu_{21}-\lambda^2_{T_1}} + \left(\frac{\lambda_{T_2}}{\mu_{22}}\right)^C \frac{\lambda_{T_2}\mu_{22}}{(C\mu_{22}-\lambda_2)^2}\right\} + \left(\frac{\lambda_{T_3}}{\mu_{23}}\right)^C \frac{\lambda_{T_3}\mu_{23}}{\left(C\mu_{23}-\lambda_{T_3}\right)^2}\right]\times P_0\right] \tag{127}$$

$$R_t = \frac{1}{(\mu_3-\lambda_3)} + \left[\left(\frac{1}{\mu_2}+\frac{1}{\mu_3}+\frac{1}{\mu_4}\right) + \frac{1}{(C)!}\left[\left\{\frac{\rho^{(P_2)}}{\lambda_{P_2}}\frac{\left(C\rho^{(P_2)}\right)^2}{\left(1-\rho^{(P_2)}\right)^2} + \frac{\rho^{(P_3)}}{\lambda_{P_3}}\frac{\left(C\rho^{(P_3)}\right)^2}{\left(1-\rho^{(P_3)}\right)^2}\right\} + \frac{\rho^{(P_4)}}{\lambda_{P_4}}\frac{\left(C\rho^{(P_4)}\right)^2}{\left(1-\rho^{(P_4)}\right)^2}\right]\times P_0\right] + \left[\left(\frac{1}{\mu_{21}}+\frac{1}{\mu_{22}}+\frac{1}{\mu_{23}}\right) + \frac{1}{(C)!}\left[\left\{\frac{\rho^{(T_1)}}{\lambda_{T_1}}\frac{\left(C\rho^{(T_1)}\right)^2}{\left(1-\rho^{(T_1)}\right)^2} + \frac{\rho^{(T_2)}}{\lambda_{T_2}}\frac{\left(C\rho^{(T_2)}\right)^2}{\left(1-\rho^{(T_2)}\right)^2}\right\} + \frac{\rho^{(T_2)}}{\lambda_{T_3}}\frac{\left(C\rho^{(T_2)}\right)^2}{\left(1-\rho^{(T_2)}\right)^2}\right]\times P_0\right] \tag{128}$$

$$W_t = \frac{1}{\lambda}\Bigg[\frac{\lambda_3}{(\mu_3-\lambda_3)} + \left[\frac{1}{(C-1)!}\left[\left\{\left(\frac{\lambda_{P_2}}{\mu_{12}}\right)^C \frac{\lambda_{P_2}\mu_{12}}{\left(C\mu_{12}-\lambda_{P_2}\right)^2} + \left(\frac{\lambda_{P_3}}{\mu_{14}}\right)^C \frac{\lambda_{P_3}\mu_{13}}{\left(C\mu_{13}-\lambda_{P_3}\right)^2}\right\} + \left(\frac{\lambda_{P_4}}{\mu_{14}}\right)^C \frac{\lambda_{P_4}\mu_{14}}{\left(C\mu_{14}-\lambda_{P_4}\right)^2}\right]\times P_0\right] + \left[\frac{1}{(C-1)!}\left[\left\{\left(\frac{\lambda_{T_1}}{\mu_{21}}\right)^C \frac{\lambda_{T_1}\mu_{21}}{(C\mu_{21}-\lambda^2_{T_1}} + \left(\frac{\lambda_{T_2}}{\mu_{22}}\right)^C \frac{\lambda_{T_2}\mu_{22}}{(C\mu_{22}-\lambda_2)^2}\right\} + \left(\frac{\lambda_{T_3}}{\mu_{23}}\right)^C \frac{\lambda_{T_3}\mu_{23}}{\left(C\mu_{23}-\lambda_{T_3}\right)^2}\right]\times P_0\right]\Bigg] \tag{129}$$

where $\lambda = \lambda_3 + \lambda_{T_1} + \lambda_{T_3} + \lambda_{T_2}$.

### 7.6 VI—Way ({S₁, S₂, S₃} {P₁, P₂, P₃}, {(T₁, T₂), T₃})

$$
\begin{aligned}
L_q = & \left\{\frac{1}{(C-1)!}\left[\left(\frac{\lambda_1}{\mu_1}\right)^C \frac{\lambda_1\mu_1}{(C\mu_1-\lambda_1)^2} + \left(\frac{\lambda_2}{\mu_2}\right)^C \frac{\lambda_2\mu_2}{(C\mu_2-\lambda_2)^2} + \left(\frac{\lambda_3}{\mu_3}\right)^C \frac{\lambda_3\mu_3}{(C\mu_3-\lambda_3)^2} + \right] \times P_0\right\} \\
& + \left\{\frac{1}{(C-1)!}\left[\left(\frac{\lambda_{P_1}}{\mu_{11}}\right)^C \frac{\lambda_{P_1}\mu_{11}}{\left(C\mu_{11}-\lambda_{P_1}\right)^2} + \left(\frac{\lambda_{P_2}}{\mu_{12}}\right)^C \frac{\lambda_{P_2}\mu_{12}}{\left(C\mu_{12}-\lambda_{P_2}\right)^2} + \left(\frac{\lambda_{P_3}}{\mu_{14}}\right)^C \frac{\lambda_{P_3}\mu_{13}}{\left(C\mu_{13}-\lambda_{P_3}\right)^2} + \right] \times P_0\right\} \\
& + \left\{\frac{1}{(C-1)!}\left[\left\{\left(\frac{\lambda_{T_1}}{\mu_{21}}\right)^C \frac{\lambda_{T_1}\mu_{21}}{(C\mu_{21}-\lambda_{T_1}^2} + \left(\frac{\lambda_{T_2}}{\mu_{22}}\right)^C \frac{\lambda_{T_2}\mu_{22}}{(C\mu_{22}-\lambda_2)^2}\right\} + \left(\frac{\lambda_{T_3}}{\mu_{23}}\right)^C \frac{\lambda_{T_3}\mu_{23}}{\left(C\mu_{23}-\lambda_{T_3}\right)^2}\right] \times P_0\right\}
\end{aligned}
\tag{130}
$$

$$
\begin{aligned}
R_t = & \left\{\left(\frac{1}{\mu_1} + \frac{1}{\mu_2} + \frac{1}{\mu_3}\right)\right. \\
& + \frac{1}{(C)!}\left[\frac{\rho^{(S_1)}}{\lambda_1}\frac{\left(C\rho^{(S_1)}\right)^2}{\left(1-\rho^{(S_1)}\right)^2} + \frac{\rho^{(S_2)}}{\lambda_2}\frac{\left(C\rho^{(S_2)}\right)^2}{\left(1-\rho^{(S_2)}\right)^2} + \frac{\rho^{(S_3)}}{\lambda_3}\frac{\left(C\rho^{(S_3)}\right)^2}{\left(1-\rho^{(S_3)}\right)^2}\right] \times P_0\Bigg\} \\
& + \left\{\left(\frac{1}{\mu_{11}} + \frac{1}{\mu_{12}} + \frac{1}{\mu_{13}} + \right) + \frac{1}{(C)!}\left[\left[\left\{\frac{\rho^{(P_1)}}{\lambda_{P_1}}\frac{\left(C\rho^{(P_1)}\right)^2}{\left(1-\rho^{(P_1)}\right)^2} + \frac{\rho^{(P_2)}}{\lambda_{P_2}}\frac{\left(C\rho^{(P_2)}\right)^2}{\left(1-\rho^{(P_2)}\right)^2}\right.\right.\right. \\
& + \left.\left.\left.\frac{\rho^{(P_3)}}{\lambda_{P_3}}\frac{\left(C\rho^{(P_3)}\right)^2}{\left(1-\rho^{(P_3)}\right)^2}\right\}\right]\right] \times P_0\Bigg\} + \left\{\left(\frac{1}{\mu_{21}} + \frac{1}{\mu_{22}} + \frac{1}{\mu_{23}}\right)\right. \\
& + \frac{1}{(C)!}\left[\left[\left\{\frac{\rho^{(T_1)}}{\lambda_{T_1}}\frac{\left(C\rho^{(T_1)}\right)^2}{\left(1-\rho^{(T_1)}\right)^2} + \frac{\rho^{(T_2)}}{\lambda_{T_2}}\frac{\left(C\rho^{(T_2)}\right)^2}{\left(1-\rho^{(T_2)}\right)^2}\right\} + \frac{\rho^{(T_2)}}{\lambda_{T_3}}\frac{\left(C\rho^{(T_2)}\right)^2}{\left(1-\rho^{(T_2)}\right)^2}\right] \times P_0\right\}
\end{aligned}
\tag{131}
$$

$$
\begin{aligned}
W_t = & \frac{1}{\lambda}\left[\left[\left\{\frac{1}{(C-1)!}\left[\left(\frac{\lambda_1}{\mu_1}\right)^C \frac{\lambda_1\mu_1}{(C\mu_1-\lambda_1)^2} + \left(\frac{\lambda_2}{\mu_2}\right)^C \frac{\lambda_2\mu_2}{(C\mu_2-\lambda_2)^2} + \left(\frac{\lambda_3}{\mu_3}\right)^C \frac{\lambda_3\mu_3}{(C\mu_3-\lambda_3)^2} + \right] \times P_0\right\}\right.\right. \\
& + \left\{\frac{1}{(C-1)!}\left[\left(\frac{\lambda_{P_1}}{\mu_{11}}\right)^C \frac{\lambda_{P_1}\mu_{11}}{\left(C\mu_{11}-\lambda_{P_1}\right)^2} + \left(\frac{\lambda_{P_2}}{\mu_{12}}\right)^C \frac{\lambda_{P_2}\mu_{12}}{\left(C\mu_{12}-\lambda_{P_2}\right)^2} + \left(\frac{\lambda_{P_3}}{\mu_{14}}\right)^C \frac{\lambda_{P_3}\mu_{13}}{\left(C\mu_{13}-\lambda_{P_3}\right)^2} + \right] \times P_0\right\} \\
& + \left.\left.\left\{\frac{1}{(C-1)!}\left[\left\{\left(\frac{\lambda_{T_1}}{\mu_{21}}\right)^C \frac{\lambda_{T_1}\mu_{21}}{(C\mu_{21}-\lambda_{T_1}^2} + \left(\frac{\lambda_{T_2}}{\mu_{22}}\right)^C \frac{\lambda_{T_2}\mu_{22}}{(C\mu_{22}-\lambda_2)^2}\right\} + \left(\frac{\lambda_{T_3}}{\mu_{23}}\right)^C \frac{\lambda_{T_3}\mu_{23}}{\left(C\mu_{23}-\lambda_{T_3}\right)^2}\right] \times P_0\right\}\right]\right]
\end{aligned}
\tag{132}
$$

The utilization, average queue length, average response time and average waiting time in all the nodes of the queuing network are computed. The average queue length corresponding to different sections (as store, packing and transportation) with different paths from $X_1$ to $X_{14}$ (34–47), the average response time corresponding to different sections (as store, packing and transportation) with different paths from $X_1$ to $X_{14}$ (48–61), and the average waiting time corresponding to different sections (as Store, packing and transportation) with different paths from $X_1$ to $X_{14}$ (62–75), are computed and also obtained nodes (76–114) with different sections. Finally, to the obtain best optimal path corresponding to nodes and ways (115–132).

## 8 Numerical Illustration

An average queue length, average response time, and an average waiting time versus number of order to customer for any product are considered for searching optimal path through network. Let $\lambda$ be the arrival number of order to customers and $\mu$ is service rate corresponding different stages with different ways. Consider the arrival rate, $\lambda = 2, \ldots, 40$. The other parameters are assumed as follows:

- Probability of entering $\lambda_1$, $\lambda_2$, $\lambda_3$ and $\lambda_4$ networks from the original source to $q_1$, $q_2$, $q_3$, and $q_4$, respectively.
- Probability of arrival at queues $(Q_1, Q_2)$, $(Q_3, Q_4)$, $(Q_5, Q_6)$, $(Q_7, Q_8)$, $(Q_9, Q_{10})$ are $(q_1, q_2) = (0.3, 0.7)$, $(q_3, q_4) = (0.6, 0.4)$, $(q_4, q_5) = (0.5, 0.5)$, $(q_6, q_7) = (0.2, 0.8)$ and $(q_9, q_{10}) = (0.1, 0.9)$ respectively.
- Here, $c$ and $C$ is the number of servers/systems for $c = 2$ and $C = 3$.

The service rates of different servers with different ways in the network are $\mu_1 = 2.5$, $\mu_2 = 3.4$, $\mu_3 = 5.5$, $\mu_4 = 12.4$, $\mu_5 = 6.5$, $\mu_6 = 9.4$, $\mu_7 = 8.5$, $\mu_8 = 10.4$, $\mu_9 = 9.5$, $\mu_{10} = 15.4$, $\mu_{11} = 6.5$, $\mu_{12} = 4.5$, $\mu_{13} = 10.5$, $\mu_{14} = 3.6$, $\mu_{21} = 7.5$, $\mu_{22} = 4.2$ and $\mu_{23} = 8.2$.

## 9 Graphical Interpretation

See Figs. 7, 8, 9, 10, 11, 12, 13, and 14.

## 10 Conclusion

This paper is designed by queueing models, and supply chain system (SCS) is also incorporated with queueing network. The nodes in the optimal paths are $X_1$ to $X_{14}$. The identification of the optimal path depends on the specification used in numerical evaluation of the response time and waiting time of the queueing network system. The most optimal path constitutes the capacity of the network. Optimal routing is made easy at the last node in every stage of the network as to choose for the least response time. To obtain various performance measures such as mean number of item in queue length, mean response time, and mean waiting time along with numerical illustration and graph. The industrial system is modeled as an equivalent queue server system for which service rate is also computed. The model enhances the lower inventories, higher productivity, lower cost, shorter lead time, higher profit, customer satisfaction,

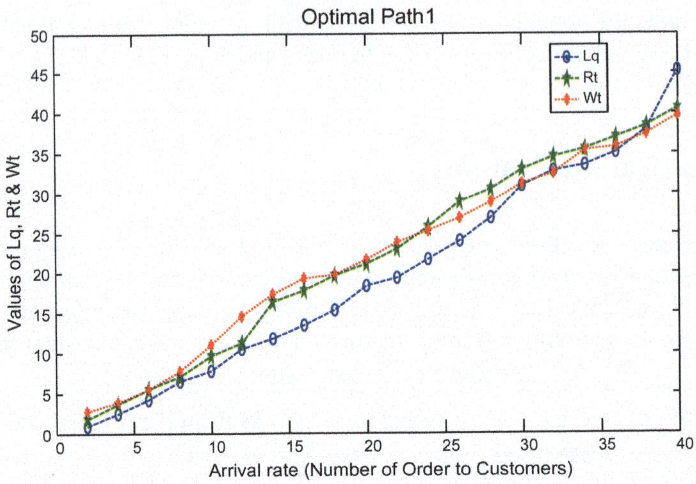


**Fig. 7** Optimal path 1

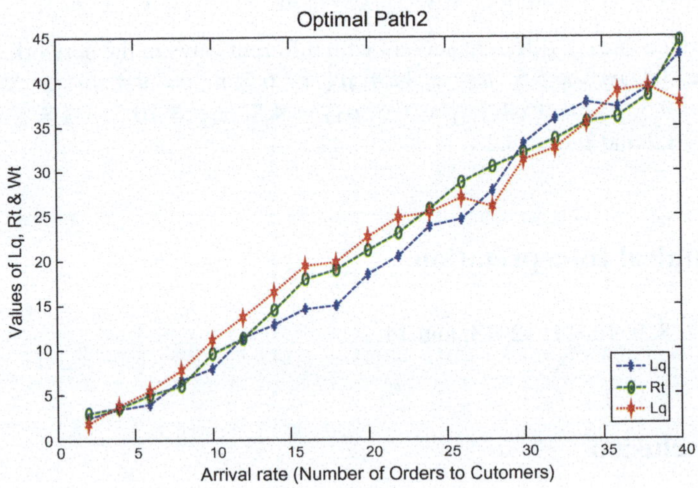


**Fig. 8** Optimal path 2

etc., by adopting supply chain system. The present investigation may helpful to create further pathways to explore substance research on other manufacturing industries based on local and global perspectives.

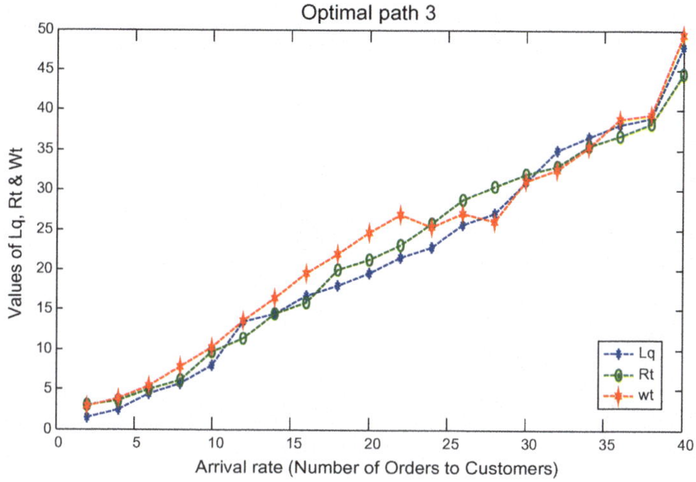


**Fig. 9** Optimal path 3

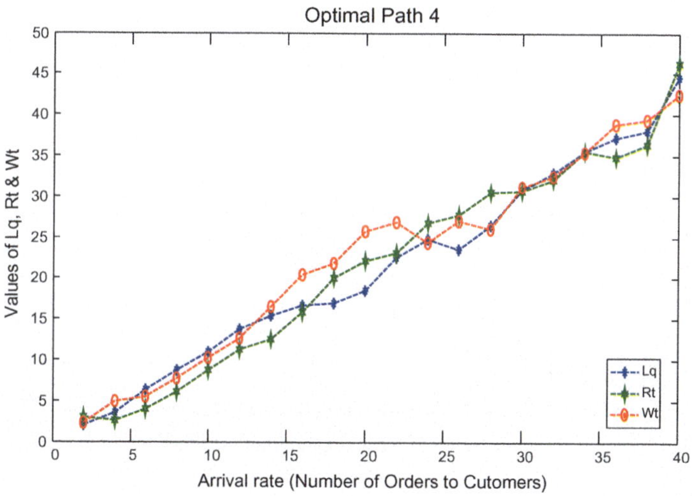


**Fig. 10** Optimal path 4

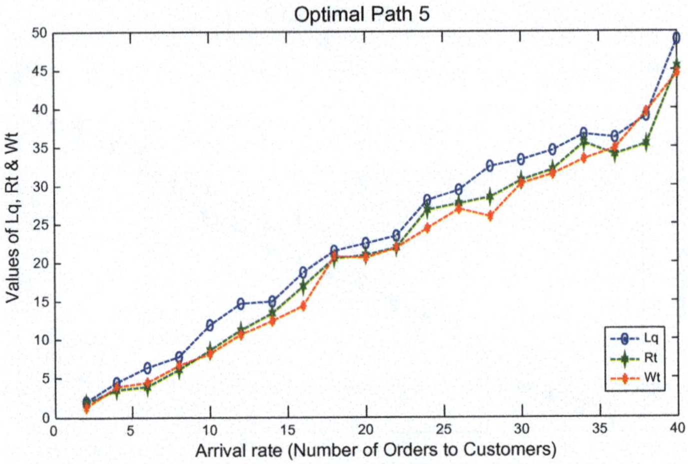


**Fig. 11** Optimal path 5

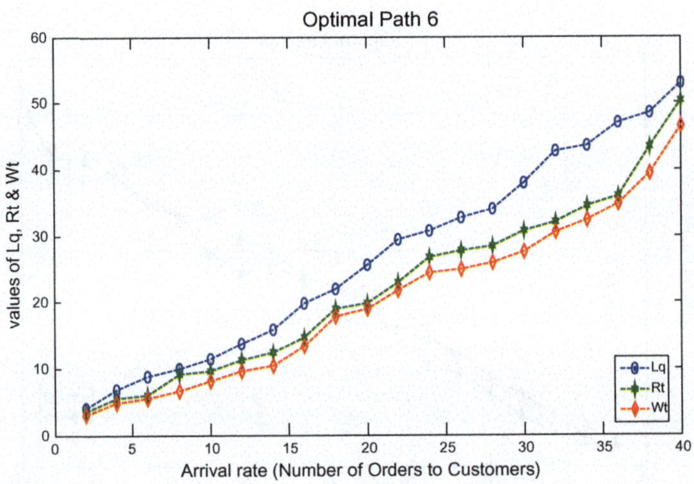


**Fig. 12** Optimal path 6

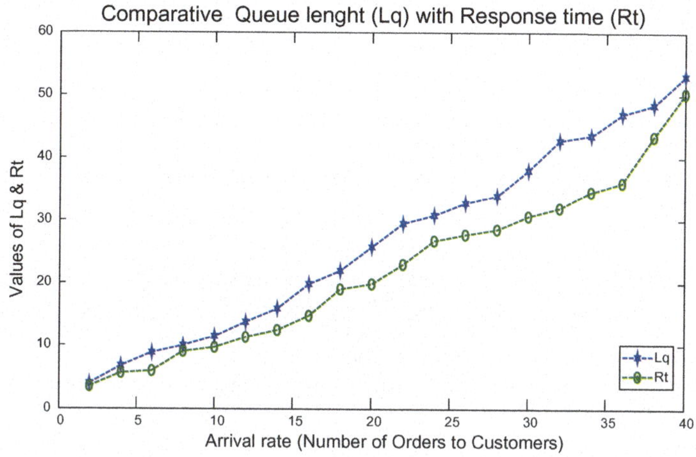


**Fig. 13** Response time versus queue length for path 6

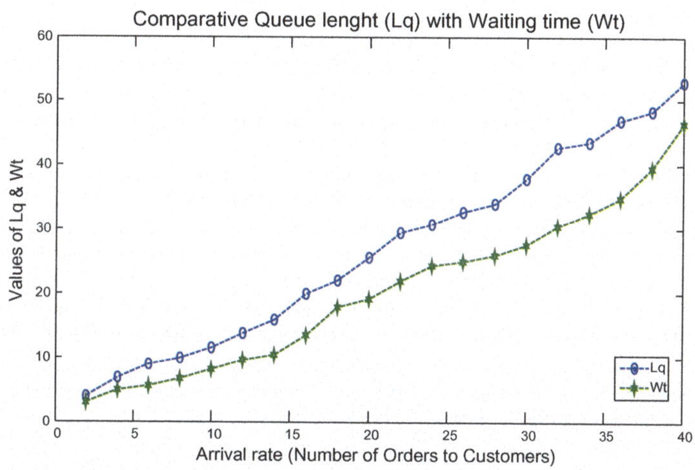


**Fig. 14** Waiting time versus queue length for path 6

## References

1. N. Viswanadhan, N.R.S. Raghavan, Performance modeling of supply chains using networks, in *Proceeding of the 2001 IEEE. International Conference on Robotics & Automation Seoul*, pp. 529-534, May 21–26, Korea (2001)
2. N. Agrawal, S.A. Smith, A.A. Tsay, Multi-vendor sourcing in retail supply chain. Prod. Oper. Manag. **11**(2), 157–182 (2002)
3. J. Scott, P. Mason, R. Mauricio, A.F. Jennifer, Integrating the warehousing and transportation functions of the supply chain. Transp. Res. Part E **39**, 141–159 (2003)
4. M. Bruce, L. Daly, N. Towers, Lean or agile: a solution for supply chain management for textile and clothing industry. Int. J. Oper. Prod. Manag. **24**(2), 151–170 (2004)
5. L. Kerbachea, Mac-Gregor S. James, Networks and the topological design of supply chain systems. Int. J. Prod. Econ. **91**, 251–272 (2004)
6. V. Bhaskar, P. Lallement, Modeling a supply chain using a network of queues. Appl. Math. Model. **34**, 2074–2088 (2010)
7. R. Sahraeian, M. Bashiri, M. Ramezani, A stochastic multi-product, multi-stage supply chain design considering products waiting time in the queue, in *Proceedings of the International Conference on Industrial Engineering and Operations Management* (2010)
8. G.S. Mokaddis, A. Ismail, M.K. Metry, A queueing model for solving three layer supply chain. J. Math. Comput. Sci. **2**, 226–240 (2012)
9. H. Taherdoost, S. Sahibuddin, S. Ibrahim, A. Kalantari, A review paper of e-services, technology concepts, in *8th International Conference Interdisciplinary in Engineering, INTER-ENG-2014, Romania* (2014)
10. W. Zhou, W. Huang, R. Zhang, A two-stage queuing network on form postponement supply chain with correlated demands. Appl. Math. Model. **38**, 2734–2743 (2014)
11. S. Jakhar, Performance evaluation and a flow allocation decision model for a sustainable supply chain of an apparel industry. J. Clean. Prod. **87**, 391–413 (2015)
12. J. Kumar, V. Shinde, *Study of Industrial Model for Five- input, Five-stage Network, Optimal Inventory Control and Management Techniques*. Published by IGI Global, USA, IBNS: 10.4018/978-1-4666-9888-8, Chap. 15, pp. 300–339 (2016)
13. T. Kvasnicova, I. Kremenova, J. Fabus, From an analysis of e-services definitions and classifications to the proposal of new e-service classification. Procedia Econ. Financ. **39**, 192–196 (2016)
14. X. Xu, C.L. Munson, S. Zeng, The impact of e-service offering on the demand of online customers. Int. J. Prod. Econ. **184**, 231–244 (2017)

# Secured Cluster-Based Distributed Dynamic Group Key Management for Wireless Sensor Networks

**R. Vijaya Saraswathi, L. Padma Sree and K. Anuradha**

**Abstract** Key management (KM) can be thought of as a process which assures security in various networking scenarios. It also supports establishment, revocation, and maintenance of keys among various interacting parties. Computing or generating a common secret value and distributing it among network sensor nodes is a significant goal. This key, which is called group key or conference key (CK), serves the purpose of encrypting/decrypting messages. Numerous applications are designed and recommended of wireless sensor networks to improve the security level through KM methods. A group key management (GKMP) is a process or a protocol where a shared group key is established for multiple sessions, between the cluster head and sensor nodes in a network clustering environment. The common use of this established group key (also termed as conference key) is to permit users to encrypt and decrypt particular broadcasted message that is meant for the total user group. So, without worrying, a group member can collaborate with other members about information disclosure. In this research work, existing group key management schemes have been investigated and the researcher proposes a cluster-based dynamic group key management protocol that is based on public key cryptography. A novel, dynamic, and practically applicable group key transfer protocol is proposed to offer secure communication in the network. Security analysis and computation complexity of the proposed work have also been investigated using a discrete event network simulator NS2. The experimental results demonstrate the efficiency of GKMP in resource-constrained WSNs.

**Keywords** Security · Cryptography · Key management · Group key management · Wireless sensor networks

---

R. Vijaya Saraswathi (✉) · L. Padma Sree
VNRVJ Institute of Engineering & Technology, Bachupally, India
e-mail: vijayasaraswathir@gmail.com

L. Padma Sree
e-mail: padmasree_l@vnrvjiet.in

K. Anuradha
Gokaraju Rangaraju Institute of Engineering and Technology, Hyderabad, India
e-mail: kodali.anuradha@yahoo.com


M. Pant et al. (eds.), *Computational Network Application Tools for Performance Management*, Asset Analytics,
https://doi.org/10.1007/978-981-32-9585-8_18

# 1 Introduction

Key management (KM) [1] can be thought of as a process which assures security in various networking scenarios along with that it supports establishment, revocation, and maintenance of keys among various interacting parties [2]. Computing or generating a common secret value [3] and distributing it among network sensor nodes is a significant goal. This key, which is called group key or conference key (CK), serves the purpose of encrypting/decrypting messages. Numerous amount of applications are designed and recommended for WSNs to improve their security level through KM methods.

WSNs are the flexible network arrangements that are thought of to strengthen the looming group applications. To provide the privacy and secrecy to these certain tasks, there arises a need to establish a general encryption key among cluster associates inside network. As WSNs normally stationed in some hostile situations, the selection of key management possessing dynamic property is remarkably significant. However, due to the following reasons, the issues of security are little complex:

- Change in topology
- Absence of a fixed infrastructure
- Merging and splitting of network clusters
- Frequent link failures.

Hence, in recent past years, various dynamic key management methods are proposed for WSNs [4, 5]. Depending on the various factors, these designs are categorized in two distinct categories: "Static key management design and Dynamic key management design." In former category, keys are fixed for longtime [6, 7]. While, in later category, the keys are refreshed in certain periods of time.

## *1.1 Secure Communication in Wireless Networks*

For secure communication between sensor nodes, pairwise and group key management protocols are used in WSN. In this subsection, we discuss four types of keys used in different key management schemes:

- "Certificate less Public/Private Key": At the base station (BS), the key generation center (KGC) generates private key and public key of the each node. The installation of these keys is done before deployment of node.
- "Individual Node Key": Each node decides on fixed key and shares this unique individual key with BS. Both use this key for encryption. To each node, the BS assigns individual key before node deployment.
- "Pairwise Key": For the secure communication and authentication processes, each node shares distinct pairwise key.
- "Cluster Key": All the nodes present in a cluster contribute a key named as "cluster key." The cluster head distributes this group key among their cluster nodes.

## 2 Related Work

This section overviews various protocols which evolved in past years. Researchers in [8] propose Chinese remainder theorem (CRT) along with Diffie–Hellman-based method for secure group communication. In [9], authors proposed two-round key agreement protocol. In [10], GKMPAN, a probabilistic approach is presented for group key management. [11] presents a distributed key management procedure, which is based on "threshold cryptography" [12, 13]. Topology-oriented group key authoritative methods are presented in [14–16]. In [17, 18], authors presented fault-tolerance ideas in ad hoc NETs. Li et al. [19] presents to divide the group into smaller chunked subgroups. GDH2 is generalization of two-party Diffie–Hellman key agreement protocol [20]. Tseng et al. [21] proposes secure group communication protocol. In [22], researchers propose a "cluster-based group key management protocol."

In [23], authors describe a group key management procedure for cluster chunks-based hierarchical groups. Amir et al. given first "robust contributory GKA protocol" [24]. Joux protocol [25] and the BS protocol, proposed by Boneh et al. [26], are one-round self-organized. Some recent schemes by [27, 28] are practically applicable asymmetric group key agreement protocols. Scheme, given by Zheng [29–31], is a CRT-oriented protocol.

Authors in [32] suggested a GKM framework which involves trust-based cryptographic methodology. Scheme presented in [33] has the ability to build a new group and establish a new group key when new member joins or existing node leaves. Using "linear secret sharing scheme (LSSS)" and "ElGamal cryptosystem," authors proposed a novel secure authenticated group key transfer protocol [34].

R. Bellazreg [35] given "DynTunKey (dynamic tunneling and group key management protocol)", which is considered as a novel group key management method. Guo and Chang [36] presented an authenticated group key distribution protocol utilizing secret sharing [37] based on CRT, which drastically reduces communication cost.

## 3 Motivation and Contribution

This section presents the discussion on motivation toward the problem of group key management and contribution of this paper.

In order to offer security and protection in any network, key management technique plays a vital role. In addition, computing or generating a common secret value and distributing it among sensor nodes in the network are a significant goal. Since the topology of a network frequently changes, creating and maintaining cluster is gaining more attention of researchers. The benefit of making clusters is that the process of rekeying can be performed in a quick manner.

This paper contributes a simple and efficient security scheme that focuses on group correspondence in WSNs. Computing or generating a common secret value and distributing it among network sensor nodes are a significant goal. This key is called group key or conference key (CK), which serves the purpose of encrypting/decrypting messages in the network. The following points have been discussed in the paper as part of the contribution.

- A novel dynamic and practically applicable group key transfer protocol is proposed to offer secure communication in the network.
- Security analysis and computation complexity of the proposed work have also been investigated using a discrete event network simulator NS2.

## 3.1 GKMP: System Model

Group key establishment protocols are generally modeled in two types:

1. Group key transfer (GKT) protocols
2. Group key agreement (GKA) protocols

The general system model for network cluster and group key establishment is presented as Fig. 1.

### 3.1.1 Group Key Transfer Protocols

This relies on single trusted entity, also thought of as KGC. The design is presented as below:

Suppose $n$ is the size of network, a group key is divided into $n$ chunks and is shared among $n$ nodes in such a manner that, with any $t$ or greater than $t$ number of share parts, it is possible to reconstruct the original secret; but, with lesser than $t$ number of shares, the original secret group key $K$ cannot be reconstructed.

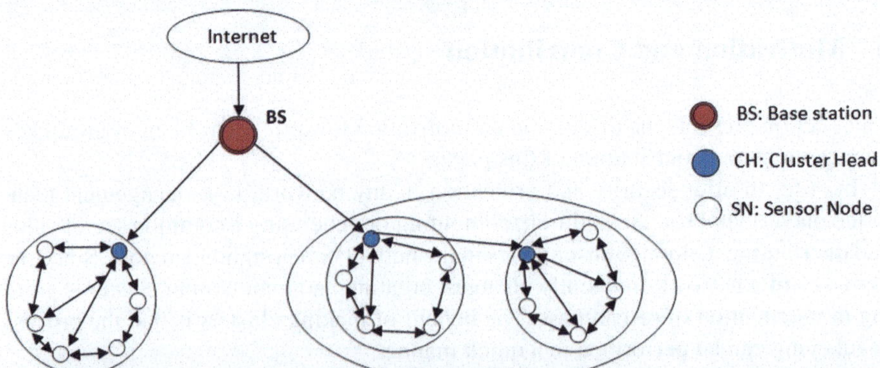


**Fig. 1** Clustered Network Model

- CH picks a polynomial $f(x) = a_0 + a_1(x) + a_2(x^2)+.......+ a_{t-1}(x^{t-1})$, which is a $(t - 1)$ degree polynomial. Here, group key $K = a_0 = f(0)$ and all coefficients $a_0$, $a_1 \ldots a_{t-1}-_1$ are in a finite field $F_p = \mathrm{GF}(p)$, having $p$ elements.
- CH computes $k_i = f(i) \bmod p$, for $i = 1\ldots n$.
- Then CH outputs list of $n$ shares $(k_1; k_2 \ldots k_n)$ to each $n_i$ privately.
- Now, each node can reconstruct the group key as following computation:

$$\mathbb{K} = f(0) = \sum_{i \in A} k_i \left( \prod_{j \in A-i} \left( \frac{x_j}{x_j - x_i} \right) \right) \bmod p.$$

where $A = \{i_1 \cdots i_t\} \subseteq \{1 \cdots n\}$ and $\left(\prod_{j \in A-i} \left(\frac{x_j}{x_j - x_i}\right)\right)$for $i \in A$ are Lagrange coefficients.

### 3.1.2 Group Key Agreement Protocols

In this, two or more parties agree on a common key in such a way that both influence the outcome. Diffie–Hellman proposed a key management algorithm. The general scenario is as below:

- Suppose two parties $P_1$ and $P_2$ are there, which will perform the common group key agreement. $P_1$ has the parameters $a$, $g$, $p$ and $P_2$ has the parameter $b$, where $a$ and $b$ are secret integers of $P_1$ and $P_2$, respectively, $g$ is generator and $p$ is prime. $P_1$ calculates $A = g^a \bmod p$ and sends to $P_2$. $P_2$ calculates $B = g^b \bmod p$ and sends to $P_1$. Then, $P_1$ calculates common group key as $K = B^a \bmod p$. Similarly, $P_2$ calculates common group key as $K = A^b \bmod p$. Both parties agree on common group key.

# 4 Proposed Group Key Management Scheme

In this section, we present our proposed group key management scheme. We introduce notations (Table 1) used in this protocol.

## *4.1 GKMP Algorithm Overview*

The entire network arrangement is segregated into clusters. Each cluster is possessing one cluster head (CH) and other participating sensor nodes. Group key establishment

**Table 1** Notations used in GKMP

| | |
|---|---|
| $G$ | Multiplication group |
| CH | Cluster head |
| $S_i$ | Sensor identity |
| $n$ | Total number of sensor nodes |
| $r_i$ | Random secret value of $S_i$ |
| $(x_i; y_i)$ | Random pairs chosen from $Z_p$ |
| $r_0$ | Initial seed value |
| $a; c$ | Parameters of CH |
| $N$ | Limit of the field for RSG, i.e., $N = \tilde{O}_{i=1}^{2} w_i$ |
| $H(I)$ | Hash value of information |
| $a_i$ | Secret key of $S_i$ |
| $K$ | Group key |

protocol will run inside a cluster in order to establish a common group key among cluster head and participating sensor nodes. The overview is presented below:

1. In GKMP protocol, first initialization step is performed inside a network cluster, where some initial parameters setup is performed.
2. Then, node registration step is performed, where each node sends a key generation request to the CH.
3. Further, cluster head (CH) is computing $r_i$ by employing RSG procedural steps and sends $r_i$ information to each of the sensor node independently.
4. Then, each $(S_i)$ calculates $g^{N=a}i$ and sends back to CH along with authentication.
5. Then, round 3 is performed by CH as already mentioned in GKMP procedure.
6. Further, the computation procedure of common group key and verification procedural steps are performed by sensor nodes.
7. The common use of this established group key (also called conference key) is to enable group of users to decrypt particular broadcasted message.

**Random Secret-value Generation(RSG)**

- Choose $n$, where $n$ : cluster size, $S_i$: Sensor node.
- Choose $(x_i, y_i)$ for each $S_i$, $1 \leq i \leq n$ such that g.c.d($x_i, y_i$)=1.
- CH calculate $w_1 = \prod_{i=1}^{n} x_i$ and $w_2 = \prod_{i=1}^{n} y_i$ .
- Compute $N = \prod_{i=1}^{2} w_i$.
- CH uses the following congruential equation to generate secret random values: $r_{j+1} = (a.r_j + c) \bmod N$.
  Here, $r_0$, $0 \leq r_0 < N$ is initial seed value.
- Choose $a$, $c$, $N$ as follows:-

  1. $N$ and $c$ must be co-prime.
  2. $(a-1)$ should be divisible by all prime factors of $N$.

**Proposed GKMP**

<u>GKMP for Cluster Environment</u>

1. Initialization :
    - Suppose $G$ be a multiplicative cyclic group of order $p$, where $p$ prime and $g$ is generator.
    - Select parameters $a, c$ and $N$ as mentioned in above mentioned RSG Algorithm.
    - Each $S_i$, choose own secret key $a_i \leftarrow^{R} \mathbb{Z}_p^*$ and g.c.d $(a_i, p) = 1$.
2. Node Registration
    - Each node sends a key generation request to the CH: $S_i \rightarrow CH : \{S_1, \cdots, S_n\}$
3. Round1: CH
    - Select $r_0$ and calculate $r_i$ for $i = 1, \cdots, n$ (use RSG algorithm)
    - Calculate $Auth_{1i} = H(r_i, S_i)$
    - Sends $CH \rightarrow (r_i, Auth_{1i})$
4. Round2: Node $U_i$
    - $(S_i)$ calculates $g^{N * a_i}$
    - Calculate $Auth_{2i} = H(r_i, CH_{ID})$
    - Sends $S_i \rightarrow (g^{N * a_i}, Auth_{2i})$
5. Round3: CH
    - Computes $(g^{N * a_i})^c$
    - Compute $U = g^c, V_i = K.(g^{N * a_i})^c$
    - Calculate $Auth_i = H(K, S_1, S_2, \cdots, S_n, r_i)$
    - Broadcost $CH \rightarrow (U, V_i, Auth_{3i})$
6. Group Key (K) Computation:
    - Each node $S_i$, Compute the common group key as follows:
        - Use public key, compute $(U)^{p-1-a_i} = U^{-a_i} = (g^c)^{-a_i} = g^{-c * a_i}$
        - Use $N$, Compute $(g^{-c * a_i})^N = g^{-c * N * a_i}$
        - Now, compute $K = V_i . g^{-c * N * a_i}$
7. Key Verification
    - Each node $S_i$, compute $Auth^1 = H(K, S_1, S_2, \cdots, S_n, r_i)$;
        - $flag \leftarrow 1$
        - For $i = 1, \ldots, n$
            - If $Auth = Auth^1$, $flag = flag * 1$, else $flag = flag * 0$
        - If $flag = 0$, return $\perp$
        - Else, Return K

# 5 Experiment Results

Below section presents and analyzes experimental results of proposed GKMP method on NS2 simulator.

## 5.1 Introduction to NS-2

It is an "open-source, event-driven" simulator, which is designed especially for research in modeling communication networks. It provides substantial support to simulate bunch of protocols like TCP, FTP, DSDV, UDP, HTTP, DSR, etc. NS-2 permits a user to contend with network traffic as it actually occurs on physical networks. The area of group key management gets benefit from a implementation on network simulator.

## 5.2 Network Topologies

In our experiment for simulation of key management (KM) in NS2 simulator, two distinct network topologies are been chosen. We simulate a cluster of 70 nodes in a topography having the routing protocol as AODV as well as the channel type is wireless. We use MAC protocol IEEE 802.11 for authentication and queue length was chosen as 50 packets. The nodes are chosen randomly in the network topology. The parameter selection and configuration are given in Table 2.

In the simulation, we analyze our GKM using several metrics such as bandwidth measure for throughput and network traffic. We collect the samples using our simulator in which it samples the traffic by adding the total amount of traffic on the entire network. This is done in different time intervals and collect the amount of traffic on the entire network.

**Table 2** Parameter selection and configuration

| S. No. | Parameter | Value |
|---|---|---|
| 1 | Channel type | Wireless |
| 2 | Routing protocol | AODV |
| 3 | Queue length | 50 packets |
| 4 | Number of nodes in topography | 70 |
| 5 | Topology | Star and Internet |
| 6 | Node placement | Random |
| 7 | Simulation end time | 50 s |
| 8 | MAC protocol | IEEE 802.11 |
| 9 | Packet size | 1024 bytes |
| 10 | Traffic type | CBR |
| 11 | Path loss model | Two-ray ground |
| 12 | Energy | 1000 J |
| 13 | Transmission power | 0.0075 |
| 14 | Receiving power | 0.0275 |
| 15 | Communication range | 550 m |

### 5.3 *Simulation Process Graphical Analysis*

In the entire simulation process, the graphs obtained are given as Fig. 2.

Figure 2a is total utilization of bandwidth for leaving operation in network cluster. In this graphical representation, *X*-axis represents our proposed GKMP method along with two other existing protocols, i.e., tree-based group key Diffie–Hellman (TGDH)

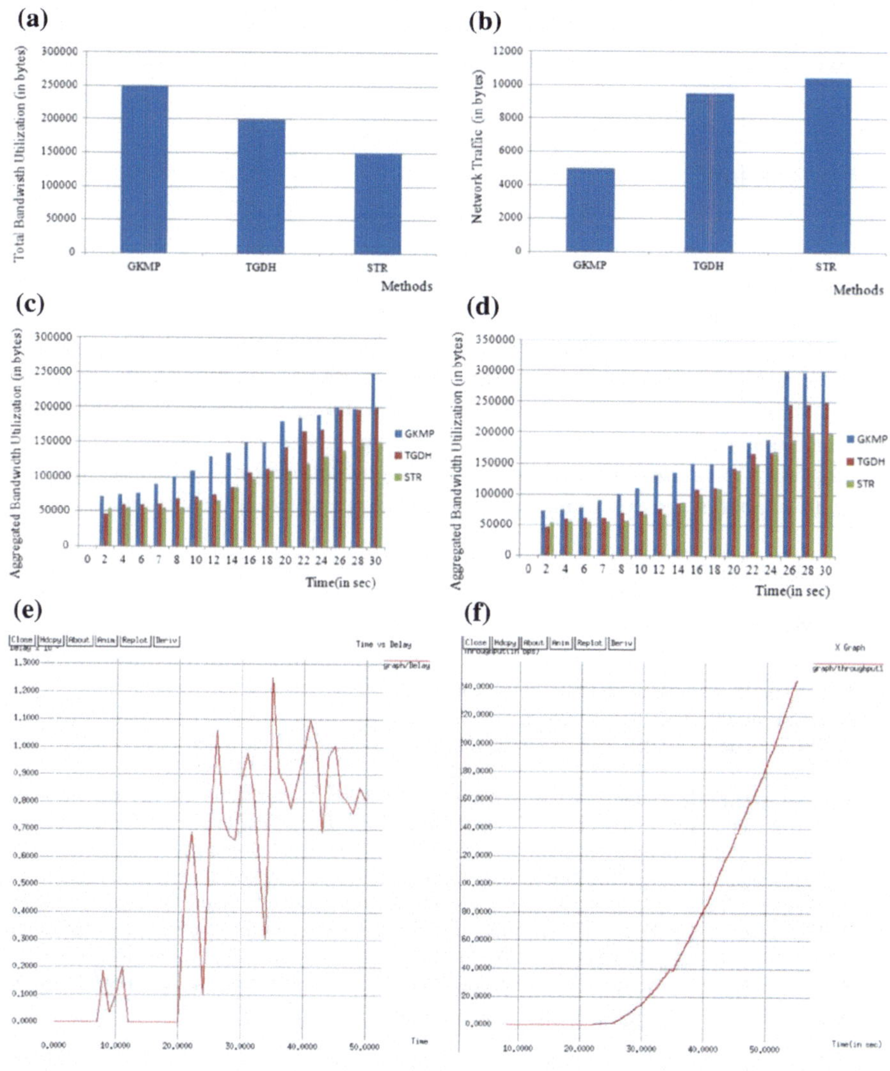


**Fig. 2** **a** Total utilization of bandwidth for leaving, **b** network traffic for joining, **c** join: bandwidth utilization, **d** leave: bandwidth utilization, **e** GKM: time versus delay, and **f** GKM: time versus throughput

and skinny tree-based group key management (STR), *Y*-axis represents the total bandwidth utilization in bytes while revocation.

Figure 2b is network traffic for joining in network cluster, here also in same manner GKMP protocol is compared graphically based on the *Y*-axis factor as network traffic.

Figure 2c is the representation of bandwidth utilization per sec while joining a node. Figure 2d is representing bandwidth utilization per sec while a node leaving from network.

Figure 2e is for time versus delay in group key management. Here, *X*-axis represents "time" (in seconds) and "delay" is represented in *Y*-axis.

Figure 2f is time (in seconds) versus throughput in group key management.

## 6 Conclusion

WSNs are the flexible network arrangements that are thought of to strengthen the looming group applications. To provide the privacy and secrecy to these certain tasks, there arises a need to establish a common encryption key among group members inside network. For providing security and protection in any network, key management is a significant element. Computing or generating a common secret value and distributing it among network sensor nodes are a significant goal. In this paper, some significant existing group key management schemes have been investigated and later we have proposed a novel group key distribution protocol along with authentication and security analysis. Experiment results are also presented at the end of this paper.

## References

1. T. Kavitha, D. Sridharan, Security vulnerabilities in wireless sensor networks: a survey. J. Inf. Assur. Secur. (JIAS) **5**, 31–44 (2010)
2. W. Hu, H. Tan, C. Corke, W.C. Shih, S. Jha, Toward trusted wireless sensor networks. ACM Trans. Sens. Netw. (TOSN) **7**(5), 1–5:25 (2010)
3. R.V. Saraswathi, L. Padma Sree, K. Anuradha, Dynamic and probabilistic key management for distributed wireless sensor networks. Published in: *IEEE Conference on Computational Intelligence and Computing Research (ICCIC)*, 15–17 Dec 2016, India
4. L. Eschenauer, V. Gligor, A key-management scheme for distributed sensor net-works, in *Proceedings of the 9th ACM Conference on Computer and Communications Security* (2002)
5. W. Du, J. Deng, Y.S. Han, P.K. Varshney, J. Katz, A. Khalili, A pairwise key pre-distribution scheme for wireless sensor networks. ACM Trans. Inf. Syst. Secur. **8**(2), 228–258 (2005)
6. B. Zhou, S. Li, Q. Li, X. Suna, X. Wang, An efficient and scalable pairwise key pre-distribution scheme for sensor networks using deployment knowledge. Comput. Commun. **32**, 124–133 (2009)
7. Y. Zhang, W. Yang, K. Kim, M. Park, An AVL tree-based dynamic key management in hierarchical wireless sensor network, in *International Conference on Intelligent Information Hiding and Multimedia Signal Processing* (2008)

8. R.K. Balachandran, B. Ramamurthy, Z. Xukai, N.V. Vinodchandran, CRTDH: an efficient key agreement scheme for secure group communications in wireless ad hoc networks, in *IEEE International Conference on Communications, (ICC 2005)*, vol. 2, May 2005, pp. 1123–1127
9. R. Bhaskar, D. Augot, V. Issarny, D. Sacchetti, An efficient group key agreement protocol for ad hoc networks, in *IEEE Workshop on Trust, Security and Privacy in Ubiquitous Computing*, Taormina, Italy, 12–16 June 2005
10. S. Zhu, S. Setia, S. Xu, S. Jajodia, GKMPAN, An efficient group rekeying scheme for secure multicast in ad-hoc networks, in *MobiQuitous* (IEEE Computer Society), pp. 42–51 (2004)
11. A. Mukherjee, A. Gupta, D.P. Agrawal, Distributed key management for dynamic groups in MANETs. Pervasive Mob. Comput. **4**(4), 562–578 (2008)
12. A. Shamir, How to share a secret. Commun. ACM **22** (1979)
13. M. Manulis, Contributory group key agreement protocols, revisited for mobile ad-hoc groups, in *Proceedings of the 2nd IEEE International Conference on Mobile Sensor Systems, MASS'05* (IEEE Computer Society), pp. 811–818 (2005)
14. Y. Kim, A. Perrig, G. Tsudik, Group key agreement efficient in communication. IEEE Trans. Comput. **53**(7), 905–921 (2004)
15. M. Steiner, G. Tsudik, M. Waidner, Key agreement in dynamic peer groups. IEEE Trans. Parallel Distrib. Syst. **11**(8), 769–779 (2000)
16. Y. Kim, A. Perrig, G. Tsudik, Tree-based group key agreement. ACM Trans. Inf. Syst. Secur. **7**(1), 60–96 (2004)
17. M. Striki, J.S. Baras, Fault-tolerance and efficiency considerations for key distribution protocols in MANETs, in *Proceeding of the 37th Conference on Information Sciences and Systems (CISS)*, Johns Hopkins University, Baltimore, MD, March 12–14, 2003
18. M. Striki, K. Manousakis, J.S. Baras, A robust distributed TGDH-based scheme for secure group communications in MANETs, in *Proceedings of ICC2006—IEEE International Conference on Communications*, Istanbul, Turkey, June 11–15, 2006, pp. 2249–2255
19. X. Li, Y. Wang, O. Frieder, Efficient hybrid key agreement protocol for wireless ad hoc networks. Comput. Commun. Netw. (2002)
20. W. Diffie, M.E. Hellman, New directions in cryptography. IEEE Trans. Inf. Theory (1976)
21. Y.-M. Tseng, C.-C. Yang, D.-R. Liao, A secure group communication protocol for ad hoc wireless networks, in *Advances in Wireless Ad Hoc and Sensor Networks*. Signals and Communication Technology Series (Springer, Berlin, 2007)
22. J.-H. Cho, I.-R. Chen, D.-C. Wang, Performance optimization of region-based group key management in mobile ad hoc networks, performance evaluation. Perform. Eval. **65**, 319–344 (2008)
23. J.H. Li, B. Bhattacharjee, M. Yu, R. Levy, A scalable key management and clustering scheme for wireless ad hoc and sensor networks. Future Gener. Comput. Syst. **24**, 860–869 (2008)
24. Y. Amir, Y. Kim, C. Nita-Rotaru, G. Tsudik, On the performance of group key agreement protocols, ACM Trans. Inf. Syst. Secur. **7**(3), 1–32 (2004)
25. A. Joux, A one round protocol for tripartite DiffieHellman. J. Cryptol. **17**, 263–276 (2004)
26. D. Boneh, A. Silverberg, Applications of multilinear forms to cryptography. Contemp. Math. **324**, 71–90 (2003)
27. Q. Wu, Y. Mu, W. Susilo, B. Qin, J. Domingo-Ferrer, Asymmetric group key agreement, in *EUROCRYPT 2009*, LNCS, vol. 5479, pp. 153–170 (2009)
28. L. Zhang, Q. Wu, B. Qin, J. Domingo-Ferrer, Identity-based authenticated asymmetric group key agreement protocol, in *COCOON 2010*, LNCS, vol. 6196, pp. 510–519 (2010)
29. X. Zheng, C.T. Huang, M. Matthews, Chinese remainder theorem based group key management, in *Proceedings of the 45th ACM Southeast Regional Conference* (2007)
30. G.-H. Chiou, W.-T. Chen, Secure broadcasting using the secure lock. IEEE Trans. Softw. Eng. **15**(8), 929–934 (1989)
31. X. Lv, H. Li, B. Wang, Group key agreement for secure group communication in dynamic peer systems. J. Parallel Distrib. Comput. **72**, 1195–1200 (2012)
32. K. Drira, H. Seba, H. Kheddouci, ECGK: An efficient clustering scheme for group key management in MANETs. Comput. Commun. **33**, 1094–1107 (2010)

33. Y. Yang, Y. Hu, C. Sun, C. Lv, L. Zhang, An efficient group key agreement scheme for mobile ad-hoc networks. Int. Arab J. Inf. Technol. **10**(1) (2013 Jan)
34. C. Hsu, B. Zeng, G. Cui, L. Chen, A new secure authenticated group key transfer protocol. Wirel. Pers. Commun. **74**, 457–467 (2014)
35. R. Bellazreg, N. Boudriga, DynTunKey: a dynamic distributed group key tunneling management protocol for heterogeneous wireless sensor net-works. EURASIP J. Wirel. Commun. Netw. **2014**, 9 (2014)
36. C. Guo, C.-C. Chang, An authenticated group key distribution protocol based on the generalized Chinese remainder theorem. Int. J. Commun. Syst. **27**, 126–134 (2014)
37. R.F. Olimid, On the security of an authenticated group key transfer protocol based on secret sharing, in *ICT-EurAsia 2013*, LNCS 7804, pp. 399–408

# Efficiency and Precision Enhancement of Code Clone Detection Using Hybrid Technique-Based Web Tool

**Ginika Mahajan**

**Abstract** With the advent and growth in the field of software reuse, the maintenance of code and respective repositories is becoming a great challenge. Code cloning is one of the major causes behind this. Code clone is a code portion which is identical or similar to other potions of code. Copy and paste of a code fragment is also considered as a form of code cloning which makes maintenance of software more complicated. Software maintenance (SM) is defined as the modification done to the existing software after development and implementation. Using SM process, the software companies provide add-ons and updates as per working environment and need to remove bugs and to correct any fault identified during it execution to improve the performance. This research work presents a large-scale study of existing tools which has been carried out for detection of code clones. These suggested tools employ different methodology for code clone detection. The work focus on pragmatic and detailed study on the detection of code clones. The research work further explores the various challenges in code clone detection in terms of bug propagation, irregularities in change propagation, design mistakes, increased challenge in refactoring, and increased code comprehension efforts. The study carried out suggests that more efficient algorithm and techniques are required to detect code cloning. The study also shows that a web-based tool to detect clones in code would be more beneficial. The authors propose a hybrid methodology for web-based code clone detection tool (WCCD) which can be used to detect code clones in any browser. The proposed tool implements a more powerful clone detector to identify clones in code in an efficient and precise manner. Repetition of code clones that seems to be vulnerable could be a malware whose detection using the existing tool is an issue. Hence, the proposed work has been further extended to detect malware to make the process of code clone detection more effective and efficient.

**Keywords** Code cloning · Software reuse · Software maintenance · Web clone detector

G. Mahajan (✉)
Department of IT, Manipal Univeristy, Jaipur, India
e-mail: ginika.5aug@gmail.com



M. Pant et al. (eds.), *Computational Network Application Tools for Performance Management*, Asset Analytics,
https://doi.org/10.1007/978-981-32-9585-8_19

## 1 Introduction

Code cloning is a similar type of code fragment used again and again in a program by software programmer. It is easy for software developers to reuse the code fragment by copying and pasting instead of starting the project from scratch. Though copying and pasting saves time and resources in developing software but raises the question on the quality of software.

The error in clone or copy-pasted code may propagate unceasingly and it becomes difficult to correct or modify the consistent error. Hence, it turns out to be more difficult to maintain the system and consequently software maintenance has become a major issue in IT industry. It is well known that software maintenance is very expensive part of software development.

As per various research studies, larger software development companies are spending a lot to maintain existing software. Maintenance defines the modification after development or during development phase to add other add-on and update to the environment and to remove bugs or correct the faults to improve the performance.

Clones are categorized as follows:

***Type-1 Clones***: These clones are the identical code segment without white spaces and comment.
***Type-2 Clones***: Clones having similar syntax but different identifier (variables, functions, class).
***Type-3 Clones***: Clones that have modifications like addition of a statement or deletion of a statement along with Type 1 and Type 2 clone.
***Type-4 Clones***: Two or more code fragments that are semantically or functionally same or perform the same computation but are implemented by different syntax for example for and while loop.

Following are basic techniques to detect code cloning [1–4]:

***STRING-BASED***: String-based or textual-based is a technique in which a program is first divided into line or string and then compared with another code and if the code fragment is similar, then it is considered as clone.
***TOKEN-BASED***: In this, we use lexical approach to detect clone. We convert source code into sequence token and then scanned for duplicate subsequence of token. As compared to string base, token base is more robust such as formatting and spacing.
***ABSTRACT SYNTAX TREE (AST)***: This method converts source code into parse tree or abstract syntax tree and the sub-tree having similar structure are detected as clone.
***PROGRAM DEPENDENCE GRAPH (PDG)***: Semantic approach generates program dependence graph (PDGs) from the source code. In PDG, the nodes represent the statement and condition while edges represent control and data dependencies. This technique looks in isomorphic subgraph to detect clone. Usually, the complexity of this approach is high.
***METRIC-BASED APPROACH***: Metric-based techniques are used to detect function clones. In this approach, we gather a number of metrices for code fragments and

compare metric vector which indicates their corresponding fragments which are detected as clone. This approach can also be applied to find out duplicate code in web pages and document.

***TRACKING CLIPBOARD OPERATION***: This technique depends on the programmer's activity of copy-paste code which is the primary reason for code clone. The technique tracks clipboard activities (inside IDE such as Eclipse) when programmer copies a code and reuse it by pasting it [5].

***HASH-BASED APPROACHES***: This technique is fast as well as scalable as it generates the hash value of the source code and processes it further to find the clones. This approach is used to detect near-miss clones [6].

***LOCALITY-SENSITIVE HASHING***: Locality-sensitive hashing (LSH) is to find the nearest neighbor vector of a given query vector. In spite of the fact that this procedure demonstrates some promising outcomes in distinguishing clone matches that are not precisely indistinguishable, its supposition on the uniform circulation of vectors may not hold as the quantity of components (i.e., measurements) increments, bringing about false negatives [7].

## 2 Challenges in Code Clone Detection

Following are some the challenges in code clone detection:

***Bug Propagation***: In the segment that a code piece contains a bug, reusing that code section in various parts of a framework with or without minor alteration expands the likelihood of bug proliferation [8].

***Irregularities in Change Propagation***: In the segment that a cloned part should be changed due to a bug settling or a component change, every single other piece like it perhaps requires a similar arrangement of changes, or to minimal should be analyzed to make sure about that. Neglecting to do as such may permit programming bugs to be lived in the code for quite a while. Along these lines, cloning builds exertion in change spread and prompts refresh peculiarities.

***Problems in System Reform***: Since code duplication builds code base size, support architects or designers require extra time and push to comprehend the framework. Along these lines, framework alterations require additional time and turn out to be all the more difficult. Additionally, changing a piece of a framework likewise requires identifying cases of duplication of that part in different spots of the framework since chances are high that they additionally require comparative arrangement of changes.

***Design Mistake***: Code duplication may present defective outline, absence of deliberation, or awful legacy structure. It additionally presents shrouded conditions among the copied parts and accordingly, reusing already created segments or parts of the arrangements wind up plainly troublesome later on extend.

***Increase Challenge in Refactoring***: One conceivable way to deal with handle code duplication issue is to refactor them. Various programmed refactoring or helping designers to physically refactor clones have been proposed. Be that as it may, Kim et al. [2] found that forceful refactoring is not a decent answer for oversee clones in light of the fact that countless in the framework are fleeting and refactoring those clones may not be advantageous in light of the fact that they are probably going to veer from each other in not so distant future modifications. Refactoring additionally presents the dangers and conditions. Along these lines, the nearness of clones makes refactoring a test.

***Increase Code Comprehension Effort***: THE bigger the measure of a codebase, the additional time it requires to comprehend where such comprehension is basic for effectively adjusting important changes. Since various occasions of a similar code pieces are situated in better places in the frameworks, they should be completely dissected to comprehend the distinctions among them. In this manner, cloning builds the push to comprehend the codebase. In addition, the reasons for replicating and gluing sections of code contrast and are not all around recorded, which additionally makes the code cognizance a troublesome undertaking.

## 3 Related Work

Roy and Cordy [8]: In their paper compared various clone detection techniques like textual, lexical or token, and semantic tree-based and metric-based approaches. Their work also did comparison of three clone detection tools—Duploc, Simian, and NICAD. Among these tools, NICAD provides more accurate results to detect clones.

Koschke et al. [9]: Uses metrics and textual-based technique to find the code clones in a software projects. They use a tool to implement the proposed work in JAVA. The technique easily deals with type-1 and type-2 clones.

Sharma et al. [1]: Present hybrid approach for detection of code clones. In this research, object-oriented metrics and text-based technique are used for the detection of exact clones. An automated tool for exact code clone detection was developed in VB.Net which calculates the metrics of the C/C++ projects and also performs the analysis of code clone detection, that is, which project function or the class had the code clone by using textual comparison. This approach has the limitation that it is only limited for C/C++ projects or software.

Kamiya et al. [10]: This paper proposed a tool CCFinder, a code clone detector software. This tool uses a token-based technique to detect clones in various programming languages. This paper also focuses on the clone identification process and various issues that are encountered while clone detection.

Koschke et al. [9]: This paper discussed abstract syntax tree approach, a technique that uses suffix trees to identify clones. Firstly, abstract syntax tree is generated which is serialized and then suffix trees are formulated. The technique detects type-1 and type-2 clones in an application.

Hotta et al. [5]: This paper provides a different approach on the impact of clones in software maintenance. They provide the notion that the existence of clones does not introduce extra difficulties in software maintenance phase. This paper measures the modification frequencies of duplicated and non-duplicated codes.

Kim et al. [2]: This paper proposed a model of clone genealogy on clone evolution. According to their study, refactoring of clones may not always improve software quality. They proved the fact based on the revisions of two medium-sized Java systems during their study.

Krinke [11]: In their work, it is found that type-1 clones can be changed consistently during maintenance as measured by clone detector tool Simian [12] and a comparison utility file tool Diff on Java, C, and C++ programs.

Bellon et al. [13]: They compared six clone detector tools in terms of recall, precision, and space-time requirements. They perform experiments on these detectors using eight large C and Java code.

Gayathri et al. [14]: This paper detects different types of clones using different approaches like textual analysis, metric-based distance algorithm, and mapping algorithm. The detected clones are categorized as extract clone, renamed clone, gapped cloned, and semantic clone. They used clone detection and metrics to evaluate the quality.

Rubala and Kodhai [15]: This paper worked on web application and used lightweight approach as textual and metrics value computation to detect clones. The proposed tool is compared with eMetrics tool and evaluated results in terms of precision and recall parameter.

## 4 Problem Identification

There are large-scale studies on detection of clones in codes. With detailed literature survey, we acknowledged various points where lot research is still required. type 3 and type 4 clones are very hard to detect. More efficient algorithm and techniques are required to detect them.

Detected clones can be removed manually, but is a time-consuming process if the code has thousands or millions of lines. A web-based tool to detect clones in code would be more beneficial. Repetition of code clones that seems to be vulnerable could be a malware (metamorphic or polymorphic).

Unfortunately, both researchers and code clone authors have demonstrated that the tools to identify clones in code are not completely efficient and precise. To address some of these shortcomings, we have implemented a more powerful clone detector. And we are extending it to detect malware.

## 5 Proposed Work

Having the capacity to distinguish all types of clones more efficiently will enhance its quality, increase its reuse, and furthermore diminish the general cost of software maintenance. In proposed work, we are implementing a hybrid technique to detect all types of clone. An automated web-based tool is created for detecting the clones.

Our work focuses specifically on detection of type 1, type 2, type 3, and type 4 clones, and to develop a tool which is easy to install and can work remotely on any operating system. That is why we created a web application which highlights the clones detected in two code samples.

The highlighted code can be manually inspected and modified to remove the flaws. The proposed work is shown in Fig. 1.

**Algorithm**

Step 1: Input two source code samples in.c or.java file.
Step 2: Normalize the code by removing extra spaces and header files. These codes after preprocessing will be input file for the tool.
Step 3: Tool will process the codes using hybrid technique where after normalization it will detect if it type 1 clone. If it is found, then the code will further be checked for type 2 clone. If a type 2 clone is detected, it will proceed to check for type 3 clone. If type 3 clone is detected, it will check for type 4 clone.
Step 4: Tool will show the different types detected clones in highlighted colors.

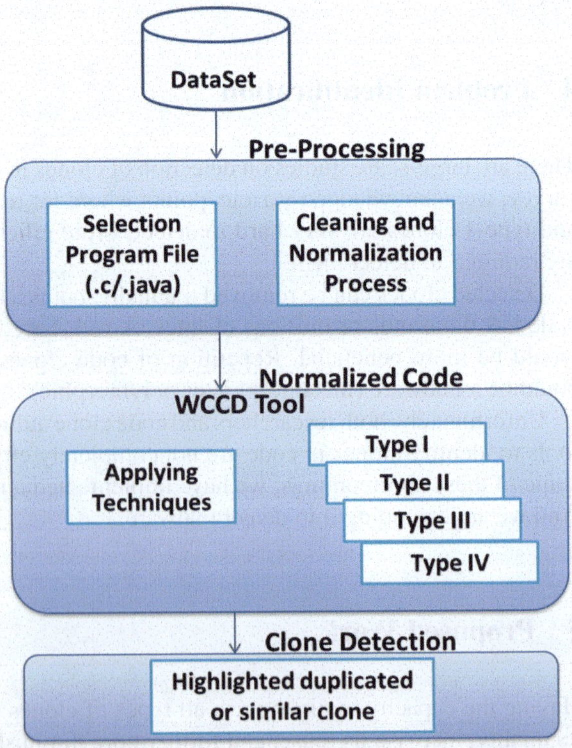


**Fig. 1** Block diagram of proposed solution using hybrid technique

We are extending our work to input other binary files and.apk file format. Also, we are working to check if cross-platform detection of clones could be done.

## 6 Experimentation and Analysis

In our process of clone detection, we have taken sample of 50 codes in c and java. To get results more accurately, firstly we have detected all types of clones manually and then we processed these code samples in WCCD tool. The tool takes two source files (c code or java code files) as input and output the clones detected in the source files by highlighting with specific colors. Yellow is for type-1, pink for type-II, green for type-III, and blue for type-IV clones.

Figure 2 shows the WCCD—web-based code clone detector tool that we have implemented. Although to enhance its functionality (to detect malware), we are working on this tool, The button "Compare Code" will pop-up a tool box which takes two input codes and detects the clones. Figure 3a and b shows the highlighted code segments.

**Fig. 2** WCCD tool (index page)

## 7 Conclusion and Future Work

Code clone detection is a dynamic research area. In this paper, a comprehensive literature survey on code clone detection research is done by emphasizing on types of clones detected, various types of techniques, their mechanism, and empirical evolution of different type of code clone detection tools.

This detailed survey will be beneficial for researchers who are new to this field of software cloning. We also proposed a web-based application for detecting clones which detects all type of clones and more efficiently detects type 1, type 2, and type 3 clones. It is hard to detect type 4 clones and still finding more ways to detect type 4 clones more accurately. We are extending our work to input other binary files and.apk

**(a)**

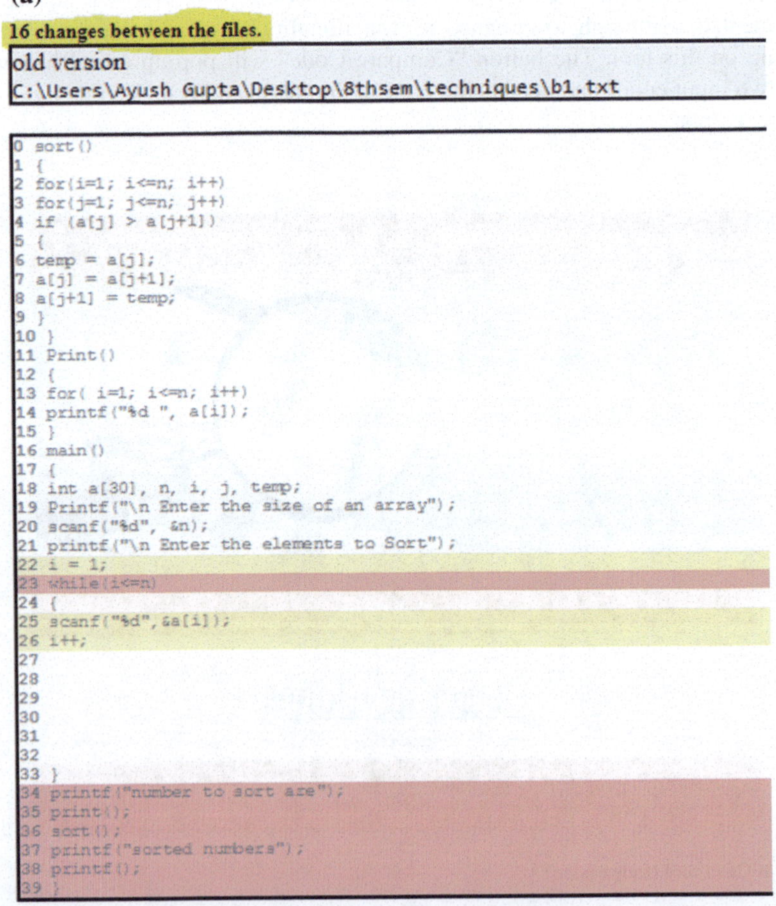


**Fig. 3** **a** Detected clones highlighted. **b** Detected clones highlighted

**(b)**

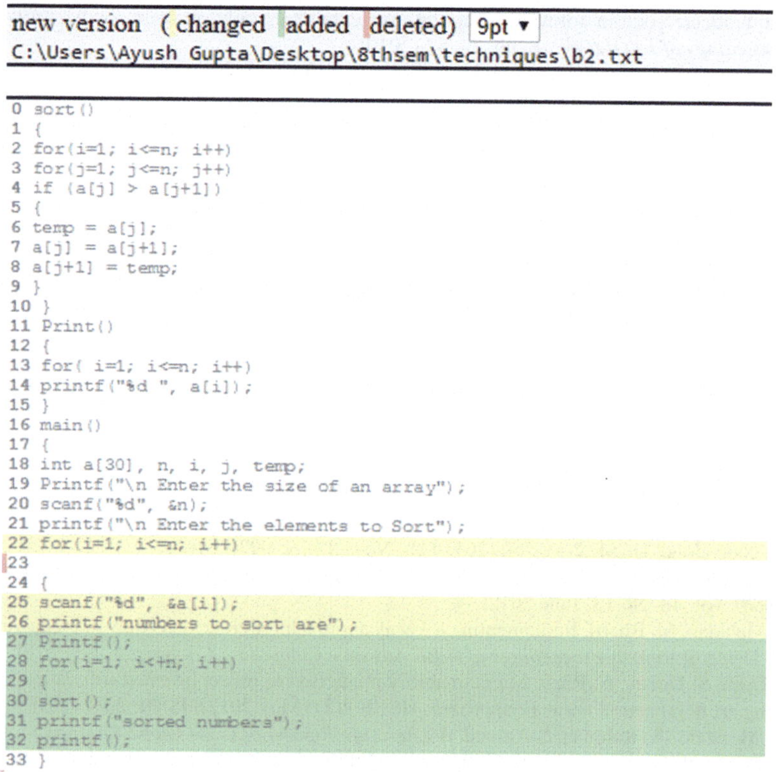
new version ( changed added deleted) 9pt ▾
C:\Users\Ayush Gupta\Desktop\8thsem\techniques\b2.txt

```
sort()
{
for(i=1; i<=n; i++)
for(j=1; j<=n; j++)
if (a[j] > a[j+1])
{
temp = a[j];
a[j] = a[j+1];
a[j+1] = temp;
}
}
Print()
{
for( i=1; i<=n; i++)
printf("%d ", a[i]);
}
main()
{
int a[30], n, i, j, temp;
Printf("\n Enter the size of an array");
scanf("%d", &n);
printf("\n Enter the elements to Sort");
for(i=1; i<=n; i++)

{
scanf("%d", &a[i]);
printf("numbers to sort are");
Printf();
for(i=1; i<+n; i++)
{
sort();
printf("sorted numbers");
printf();
}
```

**Fig. 3** (continued)

file format. Also, we are working to check if cross-platform detection of clones could be done.

Metamorphic malware are more likely to have cloning in their codes. The research can be forwarded toward malware detection by detecting clones in malware. And we are in process to detect malware using this proposed methodology [16–23].

## References


1. Y. Sharma, R. Bhatia, Hybrid technique for object oriented software clone detection, a thesis submitted in June 2011, Thapar University, Patiala
2. M. Kim, V. Sazawal, D. Notkin, G.C. Murphy, An empirical study of code clone genealogies, in Proceedings of ESEC-FSE, 2005, pp. 187–196
3. L. Jiang, Z. Su, Automatic mining of functionally equivalent code fragments via random testing, in *ISSTA'09* (2009)
4. M. Wit, A. Zaidman, A. Deursen, Managing code clones using dynamic change tracking and resolution, in *ICSM* (2009) pp. 169– 178.

5. K. Hotta, Y. Sano, Y. Higo, S. Kusumoto, Is duplicate code more frequently modified than non-duplicate code in software evolution? An empirical study on open source software, in *Proceedings of EVOL/IWPSE*, pp. 73–82 (2010)
6. M. Farhadi, B. Fung, P. Charland, M. Debbabi, BinClone: detecting code clones in malware. Softw. Secur. Reliab. IEEE (2014).
7. S. Ding, B. Fung, P. Charland, Kam1n0: MapReduce-based assembly clone search for reverse engineering, in *KDD '16 Proceedings of the 22nd ACM SIGKDD International Conference on Knowledge Discovery and Data Mining* (ACM, 2016)
8. C.K. Roy, J.R. Cordy, R. Koschke: Comparison and evaluation of clone detection techniques and tools: a qualitative approach. Sci. Comput. Program., 470–495 (2009)
9. R. Koschke, R. Falke, P. Frenzel, Clone detection using abstract syntax suffix trees. In *Proceedings of the 13th Working Conference on Reverse Engineering*, Washington, DC, USA. (IEEE Computer Society, 2006), pp. 253–262
10. T. Kamiya, S. Kusumoto, K. Inoune, CCFinder: a multilinguistic token-based code clone detection system for large scale source code. IEEE Trans. Softw. Eng., 654–670 (2002 July)
11. J. Krinke, A study of consistent and inconsistent changes to code clones, in *Proceedings of WCRE*, pp. 170–178 (2007)
12. Simian, Similarity analyser. http://www.redhillconsulting.com.au/products/simian
13. S. Bellon, R. Koschke, G. Antoniol, J. Krinke, E. Merlo, Comparison and evaluation of clone detection tools. Trans. Softw. Eng., 577–591 (2007)
14. D. Gayathri, M. Punithavalli, Comparison and evaluation on metrics based approach for detecting code clone. IJCSE **2**(5), 750 (2011 Oct–Nov). ISSN: 0976-5166
15. S. Rubala, E. Kodhai, Code clones detection in websites using hybrid approach, in *IJCA (0975 – 888)*, vol. 48–No.13, June 2012.
16. G. Mahajan, M. Bharti, Implementing a 3-way approach for clone detection and removal using PC Detector tool, in *Proceedings of IEEE Advance Computing Conference*, Feb 2014
17. Y. Dash, S. Dubey, A. Rana, Maintainability prediction of object oriented software system by using artificial neural network approach. IJSCE **2**(2) (May 2012). ISSN: 2231-2307
18. M. Morshed, A. Rahman, S Ahmed, *A Literature Review of Code Clone Analysis to Improve Software Maintenance Process*. (American International University-Bangladesh, Carleton University-Canada, SCICON & TigerHATS-Bangladesh, 2012)
19. C. Kapser, M. Godfrey, Aiding comprehension of cloning through categorization, in *Proceedings International Workshop on Principles of Software Evolution* (2004), pp. 85–94
20. S. Ducasse, M. Rieger, S. Demeyer, *A Language Independence Approach for Detecting Duplicate Code* (1999)
21. C. Fraser, E. Myers, A. Wendt, Analyzing and compressing assembly code, in *Proceedings of the ACM SIGPLAN'84 Symposium on Compiler Construction*, pp. 117–121.
22. R. Komondoor, S. Horwitz, Using slicing to identify duplication in source code, in *Proceedings of the 8th International Symposium on Static Analysis, SAS 2001* (2001), pp. 40–56.
23. S. Anju, P. Harmya, N. Jagadeesh, R. Darsana, Malware detection using assembly code and control flow graph optimization, in *Proceedings of the 1st Amrita ACM-W Celebration on Women in Computing in India* (ACM, 2010), p. 65.

# Performance Analysis of Ad Hoc on-Demand Distance Vector Routing Protocol for Mobile Ad Hoc Networks

**Swapnesh Taterh, Yogesh Meena and Girish Paliwal**

**Abstract** An ad hoc network is build up from the cooperative engagement of an accumulation of wireless mobile nodes and is capable of operating without the support of any fixed infrastructure. For a self-starting network having a dynamic nature, routing protocol has the ability to provide optimal communication capable of unicast, broadcast, and multicast routing protocol. An efficient dynamic routing is a challenge in such a network. To develop on-demand routing protocol, ad hoc networks have been widely utilized due to its effectiveness and efficiency in terms of performance factor. So far, a significant amount of research work has been done on routing in ad hoc networks. It is well-known that an Ad hoc network has no fixed routers that mean all nodes are capable to move dynamically be connected in an arbitrary manner. These nodes can act as end system and router at the same time. Transmission power of the nodes and location of MNs are two important factors on which the topology of the ad hoc network depends and may change with time. Since mobile ad hoc networks change their topology frequently, routing in such networks is a challenging task. This research work presents and highlights the significance of Ad hoc On-Demand Distance Vector (AODV) routing protocol, Load Balancing AODV, Modified AODV, and Adaptive Secure AODV. It also provides a comparative analysis of the mentioned protocols. To improve the performance of AODV protocol, a new multipath routing protocol (MAODV) has been used in the research work to discover path simultaneously for transmitting data, balancing load with energy efficiency and packet delivery ratio, and securing the routing in the wireless network.

**Keywords** AODVLB · VANET · AOMDV · TS-AOMDV · MAODV · MANET · GPSR-AODV

---

S. Taterh · G. Paliwal (✉)
Amity University Rajasthan, Jaipur, India
e-mail: gpaliwal@jpr.amity.edu

S. Taterh
e-mail: staterh@jpr.amity.edu

Y. Meena
MNIT, Jaipur, India



M. Pant et al. (eds.), *Computational Network Application Tools for Performance Management*, Asset Analytics,
https://doi.org/10.1007/978-981-32-9585-8_20

# 1 Introduction

In a mobile ad hoc Network (MANET), an assembly called the ad hoc routing protocol decides and controls the way in which wireless mobile nodes may route packets. The MANET is a self-organizing wireless network. It has got no definite infrastructure or central control station. In ad hoc networks, as nodes move randomly, the routing protocol should be able to respond quickly to the changes a network topology may encounter. Further, it should provide the various Quality of Services (QoS) such as guaranteed delivery, security, reduced overhead, etc. An efficient protocol is one which needs to have a mechanism which may maintain paths to other nodes. In addition to this, if the decided routes are affected, it should be able to use an existing alternate path to recover [1]. It is also shown in the history of any computer network development that intruders are finding new ways to attack and misbehave into the networks. So, therefore, it is important to apply the knowledge to develop a secure and protected MANET for fruitful feature activities [2].

It is well-known that an Ad hoc network has no fixed routers that mean all nodes are capable to move dynamically be connected in an arbitrary manner. To study the related issues and stimulated research in MANET, a working group namely "MANET" has been concoctive by the Internet Engineering Task Force (IETF). The primary function of any routing protocol should be the selection of an appropriate route and delivery of the packet to its correct destination. In MANET, routing protocols are based on the way in which the routing information is maintained by mobile nodes [3].

MANETs have several benefits over traditional networks, including lower infrastructure expenses, easy setup, and fault tolerance, as routing is done separately by nodes that use other intermediate network nodes to forward packets [4]. However, this multihopping reduced the chance of bottlenecks. Therefore, the key MANET attraction is greater mobility as compared with wired solutions. Since MANET is a collection of mobile nodes where each node is free to move about arbitrarily, one of the MANET's well-known and effective on-demand protocols is the Ad Hoc On-Demand Distance Vector (AODV) routing protocol.

In MANET, there are numbers of protocols in different classes. Each of the class proactive, reactive, and hybrid routing protocols are deeply analysis by the different researchers and find the conclusion that we cannot use one protocol for every circumstance so it is very difficult to say that only one protocol can handle all types of circumstances [6]. Here, we try to understand different AODV routing protocols and its comparison with GPSR–AODV.

# 2 Analysis of Different AODV Routing Protocols

## *2.1 Ad Hoc on-Demand Vector (AODV) Routing Protocol*

In MANETs, an ad hoc routing protocol is a convention that controls how nodes decide which way to route packets. The AODV routing protocol is a reactive protocol, i.e., paths are only developed when required and are intended to be used in mobile ad hoc networks. The AODV routing protocol uses one entry per location and sequence numbers in traditional routing tables to determine if routing data is up-to-date and to avoid routing loops (Perkins et al. 2004). Working group of IEFT community released the first version of AODV for routing purpose and it belongs to demand-oriented routing protocols. The AODV routing protocol is purely on-demand in nature and used to reduce the traffic overhead in which routes are established only whenever required. It also supports unicast, broadcast, and multicast without any further protocols. In AODV, sequence numbers and registration of the costs were used to solve the count-to-infinity and loop creation problem [5].

Patel et al. (2012) analyzed the performance of one of the popular routing protocols for MANET AODV with black hole AODV. The research work was aimed to simulate the AODV protocol with and without black hole attack on various performance metric parameters. It has been evaluated that AODV always performs better in absence of black hole attack. Many protocols have been reported in this field but it is difficult to decide which one is efficiently best. To avoid route breaking for the shortage of AODV protocol, a better protocol is needed which reduces message lose rate and decreases network delay [7]. B-AODV based on AODV was designed by assuming that the network link was bidirectional, as well as source node and the destination node could reach each other through one route. This protocol was based on the shortage of routing finding and routing repair of AODV. The working of B-AODV was initiated with a reverse request by sending by BRREQ to replace of RREP which can reduce the routing finding time. After that, two IP hops recorded in control messages and route table can improve the rate of routing repair and reduce the times of routing findings. This experiment was based on NS2 and compared the performance of AODV and B-AODV. It was observed that the B-AODV performed better than AODV protocol [8].

On-demand routing protocols AODV, DSR, and DYMO based on IEEE 802.11 were examined and their characteristic summary has been presented by Nand and Sharma [9]. The MAC and physical layer model were used to analyze their performance and compared on basis of measuring metrics throughput, jitter, packet delivery ratio, end-to-end delay. It was observed that AODV outshine both DSR and DYMO routing protocols. However, due to aggressive use of cache, the achievement of DSR was also ascribed to the lack of an adequate system for expiring the stale paths. Therefore, in comparison with AODV and DYMO, the jitter and average end-to-end delay were also very high. It was found that in the event of AODV with enhanced traffic load and mobility, the packet delivery was better.

Liwang et al. (2016) proposed Vehicular Ad Hoc Network (VANET) which deals an important and indispensable element in the Intelligent Transport System (ITS). The multiradio multichannel technology has been applied in VANET in order to provide a more efficient network performance. An enhanced Ad hoc On-Demand Multipath Distance Vector Routing has also been researched to make the multiradio network routing system fairer and more sensible [10]. The efficiency of the network is based on the Manhattan Grid Model so a true simulation scenario can be constructed. Indicators such as time limit, packet loss rate, network throughput, and overhead routing of the suggested technique were contrasted with other routing protocols that were frequently used. It was noted that the enhanced routing protocol for the multiradio VANET was clearly better adapted and could provide better data transmission efficiency.

An Ad hoc On-Demand Multipath Distance Vector (AOMDV) routing protocol, called Trust-based Secured Ad hoc On-Demand Multipath Distance Vector (TS-AOMDV) has been suggested to decrease MANET risks from such nodes and improve network security [11]. TS-AOMDV is based on the nodes' routing behavior and its aim to identify and isolate the attacks such as flooding, black hole, and gray hole attacks in MANET. It was concluded that the TS-AOMDV provided better routing performance and security in MANET. The NS2-based simulation model was used to compare Trust-based Secured AOMDV, TS-AOMDV with the existing AOMDV through. The suggested TS-AOMDV showed an enhanced throughput efficiency of 57.1 percent higher than that of an AOMDV in the opponent situation, and the TS-AOMDV also outperforms the AOMDV routing protocol.

Advantages of AODV Protocol

- AODV significantly decreased the amount of network routing emails.
- Because the bandwidth is effective, less battery energy is consumed.
- Its primary benefit is that only when one node raises a request to interact with another node are routes created.
- To overcome the problem of counting to infinity, as in other vector routing protocols, AODV uses sequence numbers to find a fresh route to the destination.

Disadvantages of AODV Protocol

- Bandwidth overhead, as RREQ & RREP packets need a lot of data to validate a path.
- If the intermediate node has not the recent destination sequence amount, stale entries may result.
- Multiple RREP packets can result in big overhead control in reaction to a single RREQ packet.
- Hello messages add substantial overhead to the protocol.

## 2.2 Modified AODV Protocols

Zonghua and Xiaojing (2011) compared and analyzed conventional AODV with a new modified AODV (MAODV) to evaluate the effectiveness of the MAODV. The conventional AODV and a new MAODV have been devised. It has route stability to establish a more stable pathway between the source and destination. They made some variation in Hello and RREQ message format to record the sending time and route stability factor, respectively. In the similar scenario, a network simulator-2.30 has been used to simulate both the AODV and MAODV protocols. According to observation, the MAODV shows a better performance in some ways [12].

The multipath routing protocol and modified reverse ad hoc on-demand vector (MRAODV) have been proposed by EffatParvar et al. (2010). Two methods were proposed to improve the performance of AODV protocol. A new multipath routing protocol has been used to discover path simultaneously for transmitting data. The data packets have been balanced over found routes, and energy consumption has been spread through the network across many nodes. A stability estimation method and applied that a certain modification to the RAODV algorithm was also proposed in an optimized version of the AODV routing algorithm. The MRAODV routing protocol is like as AODV that has not changed route request packet data. By using this connection stability in RAODV to reduce the overhead of routing detection and maintenance, and by increasing the packet shipping percentage in MANET [13].

Tang and Zhang (2004) proposed and analyzed the AODV routing protocol and a robust AODV protocol. These routes were built on demand and maintained by locally updating route information. The multiple backup routes were built around the active route and the highest priority backup route which switched to become the new active route when the currently active route breaks or is less preferred. Developed solid AODV protocol output has rapid topology variation to rapidly adapt paths and achieve local optimum. The findings indicate that the solid AODV protocol is more efficient than the initial AODV protocol [14].

## 2.3 Load Balancing AODV Protocols

There are a number of problems in MANET to provide energy efficiency and load balancing with quality of service routing. Load balancing problem of the routing protocols does not consider by most of routing protocols. An E2 AODV algorithm has been proposed for balancing the load using Ant Colony Optimization (ACO) technique in cluster-based mobile ad hoc networks. This system was provided in order to balance the load with energy efficiency considering both congestion and energy use of nodes for this purpose, an E2 AODV protocol selected for the optimum route with low energy use. This offered a better system for balancing the load with the ratio of energy efficiency and packet distribution. This algorithm was compared with AODV protocol and can be considered as a secure routing protocol for mobile ad hoc networks (Narmadha et al. 2014) [15].

AbdElmoniem et al. (2011) proposed two methods to enhance the performance of AODV protocol. The objective of the study was to design the protocol to reduce overhead routing, buffer overflow, end-to-end delay, and performance increase. A routing protocol based on AODV and Ant Colony Optimization (ACO) has been proposed for Multi-Route AODV Ant routing (MRAA). A load-balancing method was also proposed which used to discoverer all paths simultaneously for transmitting data. This Load Balanced Multi-Route AODV Ant routing algorithm (LBMRAA) method was used to balance the data packets over discovered paths, and energy consumption was distributed across many nodes through the network [16].

Some improvisations to the AODV protocol have been suggested to provide QoS and load balancing functionality by adding two extensions to the texts used during route discovery [17]. To study the performance of both the AODV and the QoS-AODV protocols, a detailed packet layer, average delay, packet delivery fraction, and normalized routing load were also compared. For these networks, 50 mobile nodes with distinct network loads, delay limitations, topological change rate, and simulations of mobility speeds were provided.

Soe and Khaing (2013) suggested a fresh system to improve the AODV routing protocol using Markov chain to prevent excessive load for reliable load balancing. In network communication, overloading is the major problem that decreases network performance and throughput. When the nodes that have overload, it will turn into link breakage and performance degradation. The scheme suggested and optimized the general life of the network as well as maximized part of the throughput and packet transmission. It also reduced the overhead and end-to-end delay routing and balanced the general network load [18].

Zhu et al. (2016)x proposed a load balance-based Ad hoc On-demand Distance Vector Routing Protocol (AODVLB) aimed at the jitter problem. In this context, tubules were discussed in the on-demand route protocol, delay forwarding technology was also introduced for route building control, and a load calculation function was developed. The simulated results using NS2 showed that the method decreases 20% in jitter time compared to AODV, significantly improving network performance [19].

## *2.4 Adaptive Secure AODV*

Secure communication in the mobile ad hoc wireless network (MANET) is a difficult task in the current situation owing to its basic features such as less infrastructure, wireless connection, distributed collaboration, vibrant topology, absence of connection, resource restricted, and physical node vulnerability. The protocols are analyzed by three standard techniques: simulation, security analysis, and real network testbed. AODV and Secure AODV (SAODV) routing protocols were selected for the study of securing the routing in the wireless network. Developed to add safety to the initial AODV, the SAODV routing protocol included cryptographic activities that significantly affect routing efficiency. An Adaptive SAODV (A-SAODV) was also developed to enhance performance, which based on the SAODV implementation. Following the introduction of SAODV and A-SAODV into the networks, the performance effect of safety application on the initial AODV was shown [20].

Cerri and Ghioni (2008) presented A-SAODV, a prototype implementation of the SAODV routing protocol. An adaptive mechanism for tuning SAODV's conduct was created due to its nature of cooperative and open systems and restricted resource accessibility. They consider a data link layer for Wi-Fi connectivity as a basis and concentrate on safety routing. An adaptive mechanism used that tunes SAODV behavior and analyzed its adaptive strategy and another technique that delays the verification of digital signatures to improve SAODV performance [21].

Sachan and Khilar (2001) proposed a method to secure AODV routing protocol. This technique offers safety for packet routing and can effectively stop attacks such as black hole, changing data about routing, and impersonation. The suggested technique was based on hashed message authentication code (HMAC), which offers quick verification and sending of messages as well as authentication of intermediate nodes. An original AODV and Secure AODV (SAODV) protocol have been simulated and compared with the proposed method by using network simulator tool (NS2). The findings acquired have minimized the time delay and network routing load engaged in computing and verifying safety areas during the route discovery process and have better performance than the initial AODV protocol in the presence of malicious nodes performing black hole attack [22].

Karp and Kung (2000) proposed a method to enhance the mobile routing protocols using Greedy Perimeter Stateless Routing (GPSR) algorithm and the Bird Flocking Algorithm (BFA) to create a new bioinspired routing algorithm that performs better than conventional routing algorithms [23]. The AODV routing algorithm and GPSR routing algorithm deployed are tested for various number of network nodes for a single topology and the performance of AODV, GPSR compared based on the throughput. The GPSR implemented in NS-3. The simulation work is done on the basis of the following network parameters; those are figure out in Table 1. Table 1 is used for the configuration of simulation in ns3 and Wireshark to analysis the capture data.

**Table 1** Simulation parameters

| Sr. No | Parameter | Values |
|---|---|---|
| 1 | Routing protocols | AODV, GPSR-AODV |
| 2 | Wireless channel | 802.11 |
| 3 | Topology | Grid topology |
| 4 | Distance between nodes | 100 |
| 6 | Mobility model | RandomDirection2d mobility model |
| 7 | Nodes | 2,4,8,20,40,80,100 |
| 8 | communication | Point to point |

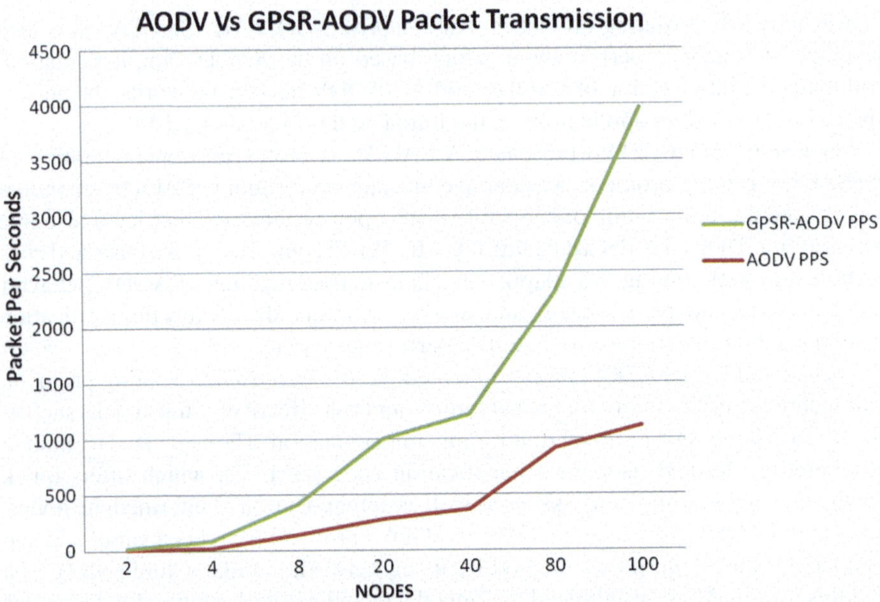


**Fig. 1** AODV and GPSR-AODV packet transmission

The simulation implemented into the network simulator—3 and the generated pcap file analysis by the Wireshark tool. After analysis of both the routing protocols, we observed that enhanced GPSR-AODV is working better than the AODV routing protocols. Figure 1 shows the comparison between AODV and GPSR-AODV packet transmission rate.

Next, Fig. 2 shows the comparison between both protocols on the basis of average packet size. That shows the GPSR-AODV is more efficient in the packet size transmission.

Finally, we have comparative analysis of AODV and GPSR-AODV throughput. Figure 3 shows that the throughput of GPSR-AODV has better than the AODV.

## 3 Conclusion

In this paper, the working of AODV protocols, modified AODV protocols, adaptive secure AODV, load balancing AODV protocols has been reviewed. The AODV routing protocol is a reactive protocol. To improve the performance of AODV protocol, a new multipath routing protocol (MAODV) has been used to discover path simultaneously for transmitting data. Also, load balancing problem of the routing protocols does not consider by most of the routing protocols to balance the load with energy efficiency and packet delivery ratio. AODV and Secure AODV (SAODV) routing protocols were selected for the study of securing the routing in the wireless network.

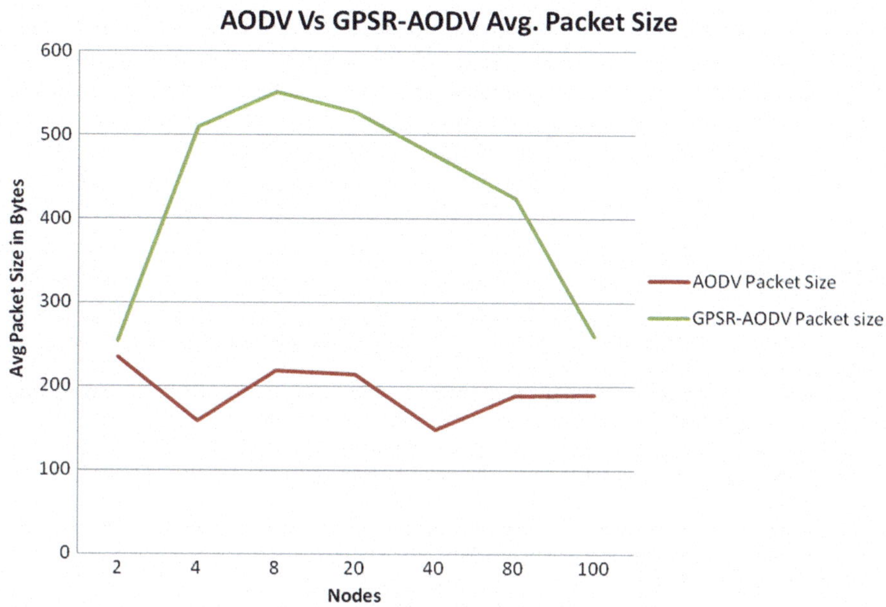


**Fig. 2** AODV and GPSR-AODV average packet size

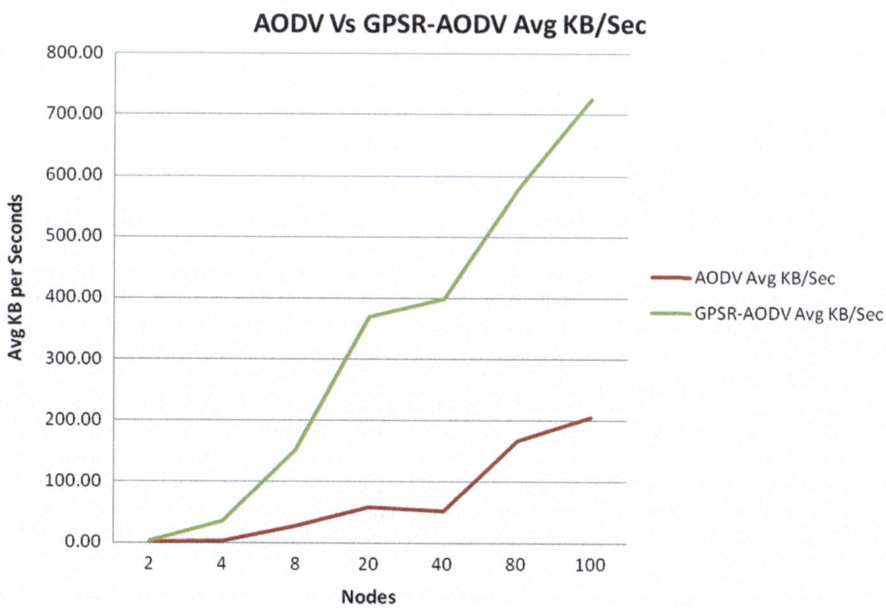


**Fig. 3** AODV and GPSR-AODV throughput

In the presence of malicious nodes performing black hole assault, a safe AODV minimized the time limit and network routing load engaged in computing and verifying safety areas during route discovery process and works better than the initial AODV protocol. The GPRS-AODV analysis with AODV and we find out the GPSR-AODV performed better than simple AODV routing protocols.

## References


1. A.M.A. Elmoniem, H.M. Ibrahim, M.H. Mohamed, A.-R. Hedar, Ant colony and load balancing optimizations for AODV routing protocol
2. G. Paliwal, A.P. Mudgal, S. Taterh (eds.), A study on various attacks of TCP/IP and security challenges in MANET layer architecture. (Springer, 2015)
3. S. Singh, S.R. Biradar, Comparative study of different routing protocols in MANET based on simulation using Ns-2. Int. J. Electron. Comput. Sci. Eng. (IJECSE, ISSN: 2277-1956), **1**(03), 984–991 (2012)
4. M. Zhang, P.H.J. Chong (eds.), Performance comparison of flat and cluster-based hierarchical ad hoc routing with entity and group mobility. (IEEE, 2009)
5. R. Baumann, *AODV presentation at ETH Zurich*: April
6. G. Paliwal, S. Taterh, A topology based routing protocols comparative analysis for *MANETs*
7. A. Patel, S. Patel, A. Verma, A review of performance evaluation of AODV protocol in Manet with and without black hole attack. Terrain **1**(2), 3 (2012)
8. S. Liu, Y. Yang, W. Wang, Research of AODV routing protocol for Ad Hoc networks1. **5**, 21–31 (2013)
9. P. Nand, S.C. Sharma, Performance study of broadcast based mobile adhoc routing protocols AODV, DSR and DYMO. Int. J. Secur Its Appl **5**(1), 53–64 (2011)
10. M. Liwang, L. Huang, Y. Tang, T. Hu (eds.), A routing protocol based on improved Ad-hoc on demand multi-path distance vector in multi-radio network. (IEEE, 2016)
11. A.O. Alkhamisi, S.M. Buhari (eds.), Trusted secure adhoc on-demand multipath distance vector routing in MANET. (IEEE, 2016)
12. M. Zonghua, M. Xiaojing, A modified AODV routing protocol based on route stability in MANET (2011)
13. M. EffatParvar, M. EffatParvar, A. Darehshoorzadeh, M. Zarei, N. Yazdani (eds.), Load balancing and route stability in mobile ad hoc networks base on AODV protocol. (IEEE, 2010)
14. S. Tang, B. Zhang (eds.), A robust AODV protocol with local update. (IEEE, 2004)
15. R.W. Banu, R.V. Kumar, E2AODV protocol for load balancing in ad-hoc networks. J. Comput. Sci. **8**(7), 1198–1204 (2012)
16. A.M.A. Elmoniem, H.M. Ibrahim, M.H. Mohamed, A.-R. Hedar, Ant colony and load balancing optimizations for AODV routing protocol. Int. J. Sens. Networkins Data Commun. **1**, 1–14 (2011)
17. B.S. Pradeep, S. Soumya, A new method for load balancing and QOS in on demand protocols—in the MANET's perspective. Int. J. Adv. Networking Appl. **1**(4), 275–281 (2010)
18. P.T. Soe, S.S. Khaing, A reliable load-balance RLB-AODV routing protocol. IJCCER **1**(4), 135–138 (2013)
19. Y.J. Zhu, Y.Q. Li, Q.G. Fan, Z. Wang (eds.), Ad hoc on-demand distance vector routing protocol based on load balance. (EDP Sciences, 2016)
20. M.A. Jaafar, Z.A. Zukarnain, Performance comparisons of AODV, secure AODV and adaptive secure AODV routing protocols in free attack simulation environment. Eur. J. Sci. Res. **32**(3), 430–443 (2009)
21. D. Cerri, A. Ghioni, Securing AODV: the A-SAODV secure routing prototype. Comm. Mag. **46**(2), 120–125 (2008). https://doi.org/10.1109/MCOM.2008.4473093

22. P. Sachan, P.M. Khilar, Securing AODV routing protocol in MANET based on cryptographic authentication mechanism. Int. J. Network Secur. Its Appl. **3**(5), 229 (2011)
23. B. Karp, H.-T. Kung (eds.), GPSR: Greedy perimeter stateless routing for wireless networks. (ACM, 2000)

# Precision Enhancement of Driver Assistant System Using EEG Based Driver Consciousness Analysis & Classification

**Prabha C. Nissimagoudar and Anilkumar V. Nandi**

**Abstract** The driver assistance systems are gaining lots of importance in automotives in recent years. Determination of driver's alertness being one among them and has a very important role to play as it is associated with the human life. Preventing accidents caused due to driver's lack of vigilance, drowsiness, tiredness or inability in perception, and recognition is one of the major applications in advanced driver assistance systems of automotives. Even though drivers' consciousness detection is one of the very essential features in today's automotives, most of the existing systems are based on image processing techniques used to determine eye blink or facial expressions. These methods being an indirect measure of consciousness lack in accurate determination of consciousness level. The presented research work discusses the direct measurement of driver's status of alertness by estimating the physiological signals like electroencephalogram (EEG) which reflects the brain activity. The alpha band of EEG signals ranging between 8 and 14 Hz is an indication of non-alert status of driver. The bio potentials like EEG are even though the direct indication of brain activity but are usually mixed with other signals like muscle movement and eye movement. Another important issue in the measurement of EEG is that the whole process needs to be carried out in moving vehicle and as such the vehicle vibration also gets mixed with EEG information. The extraction of EEG is a primary task, and which has been done by using independent component analysis (ICA) technique. ICA is used for extraction of EEG signals and also for overall reduction in data size. Further, the EEG analysis is carried out with power spectra analysis, and further support vector machine is used to train the system to classify between alert and drowsy conditions. This research work mainly focuses on EEG extraction and EEG analysis applied to non-alert state of driver. Alpha waves are a type of brain waves detected by EEG and reduce with open eyes, drowsiness, and sleep. Thus, in this project, the alpha band power frequencies and the attention values are used to analyze the consciousness level of the driver. The attention values and the alpha band

P. C. Nissimagoudar (✉) · A. V. Nandi
B.V. Bhoomaraddi College of Engineering and Technology, Hubli, India
e-mail: pcngoudar@gmail.com

A. V. Nandi
e-mail: anilnandy@bvb.edu



M. Pant et al. (eds.), *Computational Network Application Tools for Performance Management*, Asset Analytics,
https://doi.org/10.1007/978-981-32-9585-8_21

power frequencies are plotted against time through which the system can visualize the consciousness level of driver's mind, which may reduce the number of accidents reported worldwide.

**Keywords** Drowsiness detection · EEG analysis · EEGLAB · EEG electrodes · Independent component analysis · Alpha waves

## 1 Introduction

Advanced driver assistance systems have become an integrated part in all the recent vehicles. These systems will assist the driver to take better decisions and improve drivability, and are built with a smart integration of mechanical, electronic, and software-based systems. Driver alertness indication is one such system, which belongs to advanced driver assistance systems. This is commonly known as driver's drowsiness detection. According to the survey, there are around 30–40% of accidents happen because of driver's drowsy status. Recently, various methods have been proposed to distinguish between driver's alertness status and drowsiness using physiological signals. The physiological signals like electrooculogram (EOG) which measures basically the eye movement of driver, heart rate variability (HRV) were used as means of detecting driver's alertness level. These methods were considered as indirect methods for indicating driver's alertness. The EEG-based analysis is considered as a quantitative and accurate approach, which directly indicates the driver's consciousness level [1].

Electroencephalogram (EEG) the brain waves: The human brain consists of millions of brain cells called as neurons. These neurons communicate with each other using electrical signals. When millions of neurons communicate with each other, there would be a huge amount of electrical activity takes place inside the brain. These signals are measured using electroencephalogram (EEG). The activities correspond to different types of EEG signals which vary in frequency and amplitude. The gamma waves with the frequency ranging from 40 to 70 Hz represent the complete alert state of the human body. There is a direct correlation between high amounts of brain activity and to the increased brain functioning ability. The beta waves with frequency ranging from 13 to 30 Hz represent increased ability to focus on external reality. The alpha waves represent the relaxed status of brain with the frequency ranging from 8 to 13 Hz. The alpha activity in the brain increases with eye closure. These waves are the best indicators of drowsy condition. Theta waves with the frequency 4–10 Hz represent the early stage of sleep, and delta waves with the frequency 1–4 Hz represent deep sleep status. The study shows that the measurement of alpha waves gives the direct indication of drowsy status. The EEG spectrum is a combination of different type's brain waves, extracting alpha waves using the appropriate signal processing methods gives the status of the driver [2].

The paper discusses about performing EEG analysis using conventional electrodes and commercially available EEG electrode from Neurosky. The initial studies have been performed collecting information about various statuses of brain from different patients using conventional EEG electrodes. The electrode information is processed using EEGLAB toolbox along with the MATLAB. Various signal processing operations like ICA, filtering, and power spectra analysis are performed. Similar analysis is also performed for the data obtained from the Neurosky sensor. Neurosky uses a single dry electrode to collect the information about EEG. The information can be obtained in the form of an excel sheet. This data is further processed using EEGLAB and analyzed using various signal processing techniques [3].

This chapter is organized as: Sect. 2 discusses about sensors, Sect. 3 about analysis of EEG data using electrodes, Sect. 4 discusses about analysis using Neurosky electrodes, Sect. 4 discusses about result, and Sect. 5 about conclusion. Institute-Industry collaborative engagements.

## 2 Methodology

This section discusses about two methods being tested to analyze the driver's drowsy condition; the first method uses conventional EEG electrodes being used in clinical environment. The raw EEG data is obtained using these conventional electrodes. The data is further filtered to separate alpha waves. The decision-making about the drowsy condition is performed using machine learning technique support vector machine (SVM). The entire process is depicted in the following block diagram Fig. 1.

### *2.1 Data Acquisition Using EEG Electrodes*

The brain waves are sensed using the sensors which are EEG electrodes. These electrodes sense the brain waves from the scalp of the subject. The brain waves

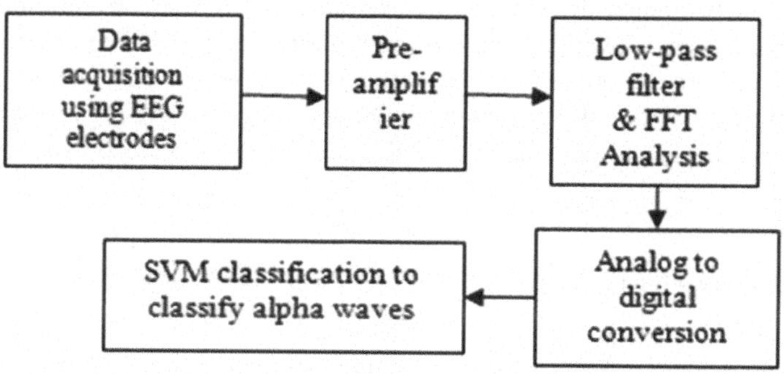


**Fig. 1** Block diagram

measured at the scalp are in the range of micro-volts. Accordingly, the sensors need to have low contact resistance with the scalp due to the low amplitude of the brain waves The pre-amplifier stage is located very near to the sensor stage. As brain waves are in the range of micro-volts and increasing the separation between the sensor and pre-amplifier adds noise to the signal. The pre-amplifier has the task of amplifying the signal (which is in micro-volt range) to the range of volts. An instrumentation amplifier with a high gain of 80d band a high CMRR of 100 dB is used in the pre-amplifier stage. The output of the pre-amplifier stage is coupled with the first stage. The filter needs to have two sub-stages: the low-pass filter and the notch filter. The low-pass filter is designed to have a cut-off frequency of 14 Hz. This is because, in healthy person, delta and theta waves are not emitted alpha waves occur below 13 Hz. The notch filter is used to remove the noise due to AC supply which occurs at 50 Hz. The filtered data is then digitized using analog to digital converter. Using SVM classification technique the filtered data is classified to separate alpha waves [4].

Method for detecting consciousness: Selection of filters plays a very important role in detecting alpha waves and consciousness. The filter used here is type 1 Chebyshev. This filter is used mainly to remove artifacts from the signals obtained from EEG electrodes. Type 1 Chebyshev band-pass filter with cut-off frequencies 0.5 and 50 Hz for removing artifacts. FFT analysis is performed on filtered data. The filtered data is converted to 256 points for applying 256 point FFT to estimate power spectra. The filtered data is stored and the SVM separation technique is applied to detect drowsiness.

### 2.2 SVM Separation Technique to Detect Drowsiness

Support vector machine (SVM) classification technique is used to distinguish EEG information into conscious and drowsy condition. The training technique used in SVM categorizes every new sample into one category. SVM uses hyperplane to distinguish the data into two classes SVM uses supervised learning technique, wherein the input data is labeled drowsy and awake states. Using which the model learns using different kernel functions [5]. Different models of SVMs were experimented, which included linear, quadratic, cubic, medium Gaussian, and Course Gaussian SVM techniques. Out of all these cubic SVM was found to give highest accuracy of 81.9%. The result of the same is discussed in results and discussion section.

### 2.3 Analysis Using Neurosky Mindwave Mobile Sensor

The alternate method of EEG analysis uses mindwave mobile sensor from Neurosky. The sensor basically consists of two-dry EEG sensors, one being the measuring electrode and other the reference electrode. Measuring electrode measures the signals

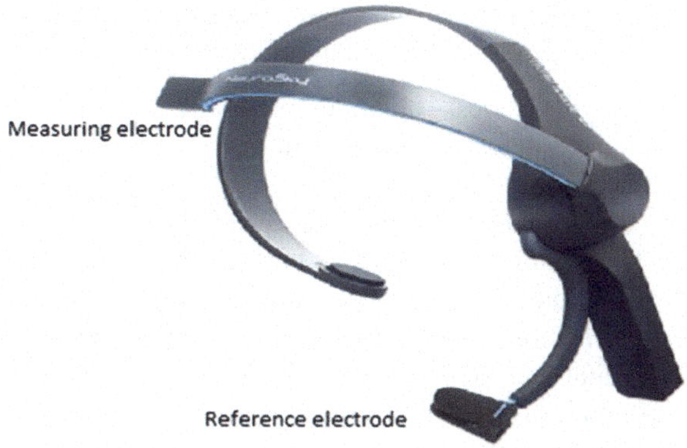


**Fig. 2** Neurosky mindwave electrode (Reference: Neurosky.com)

from the forehead. The signals, which are picked up from forehead include mainly EEG signals, and other signals related to eye movement, muscle movement, and some noise signals. The two ear clips act as reference electrodes, which are used to ground the noise. The Neurosky mindwave electrode is shown in Fig. 2. The sensor measures the information related to attention level, meditation level, eye blink, and also raw data containing different EEG signals such as alpha, beta, theta, delta, and gamma. These signals are obtained at the rate of 512 Hz. There are around more than 130 applications available to acquire the data.

The EEG signals are acquired using mindwave mobile sensor and the associated software EEGID. The sensor data is further processed in time and frequency domain. The entire process is divided into two categories, one the data acquisition and data; second, data import and analysis [6]. The next section gives details about the implementation methods and results.

## 3 Implementation

The implementation details of analyzing EEG signals to determine driver's drowsiness is discussed here. The first method includes using clinical EEG electrodes to acquire EEG signal, further the signals are separated and analyzed using suitable signal processing technique.

The characterization of brain waves during concentration is pivotal in designing the processing and decision block. This is because the knowledge of variation in brain waves (mainly beta and alpha) in amplitude and frequency is critical in setting the cut-off frequency and threshold levels for decision making. It was decided that EEG would be undertaken and the EEG results would be studied to adequately characterize the brainwaves. On the advice of the doctor, it is decided to take 10 EEG runs on different subjects (people). The parameters considered were—the characterization of brain waves, deciding the number, and location of leads (electrodes) on the brain. Placement of leads was important due to the fact that brain waves are highly localized and placing the matter right location is a critical issue. Following issues were considered for placement of electrodes:

1. Two electrodes—one main electrode and a reference electrode should be sufficient to detect the change in alpha and beta activity during concentration and drowsy states.
2. Choosing a bipolar montage system gives the best possible brain waves.
3. The locality of the sensors best suited for this application would be the occipital or the parietal lobe of the brain (backside of the head).
4. The occipital and/or parietal lobes are unaffected by the blink artifacts. Only the frontal lobe is affected.
5. In majority of the EEGs taken, the right hemisphere is found to have dominant alpha activity. Hence it is advisable to keep the main electrode on the right occipital lobe and the reference electrode on behind the left ear lobe where minimal brain wave activity is observed.

The following Fig. 3 shows the sample EEG recording.

EEG data separation: The EEG data obtained from electrodes is in raw form and is usually mixed with various artifacts. Suitable filtering techniques have to be applied to extract EEG signals. Here, type I Chebyshev band-pass filtering technique with the cut-off frequencies 0.5–14 Hz is applied to remove artifacts [7].

Chebyshev filters of type I with steeper roll-off and more pass-band ripple are used to separate EEG signals. The design procedure Chebyshev filter includes, selection of four parameters,

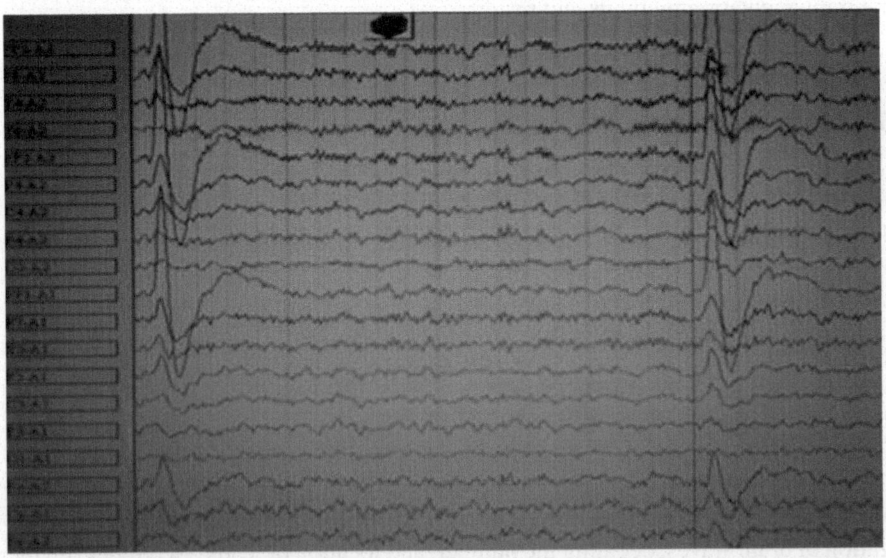

**Fig. 3** Sample EEG recording

1. A high-pass or low-pass response,
2. The cut-off frequency
3. The percent ripple in the pass band, and
4. The number of poles.

Power spectra analysis: The power spectra analysis is performed on the filtered data using 256 point FFT, which resulted in separating of alpha, beta, theta, and gamma waves. Training using support vector machine (SVM): SVM is a technique used for classification and regression analysis of data and patterns. It uses non probabilistic binary classifier technique, wherein for the given data sets, each sample are assigned to one of the two categories. An SVM model is a representation of the examples as points in space, mapped, so that the examples of the separate categories are divided by a clear gap that is as wide as possible. New examples are then mapped into that same space and predicted to belong to a category based on which side of the gap they fall on. SVM also can be used as a non-linear classification technique using kernel functions. A support vector machine constructs a set of hyper planes in an infinite-dimensional space, which can be used for classification, regression, or other tasks. A good separation is achieved by the hyper plane that has the largest distance to the nearest training-data point of any class called as functional margin. [8]

The following Table 1 shows the observations of the EEG taken on ten volunteers The following are the observations from the EEG taken:

- It could be inferred from the EEG that there was significant change in alpha activity when the subject closed and opened his eyes.
- Substantial change in beta activity could not be observed in the EEG records.
- It is concluded that after discussing with the doctor that considering alpha waves for decision-making would be advisable.

**Table 1** EEG recordings

| Sl No | Name | Age | Sex | Eye closed freq. | Eyes open without concentration | Eyes open with concentration |
|---|---|---|---|---|---|---|
| 1. | A | 21 | M | 10 | 13 | 18 |
| 2. | B | 21 | F | 10 | 14 | 16 |
| 3. | C | 21 | F | 13 | 17 | 19 |
| 4. | D | 21 | F | 11 | 15 | 18 |
| 5. | E | 40 | M | 9 | 14 | 16 |
| 6. | F | 29 | M | 10 | 19 | 17 |
| 7. | G | 37 | M | 10 | 20 | 16 |
| 8. | H | 30 | F | 10 | 16 | 17 |
| 9. | I | 32 | F | 11 | 15 | 18 |
| 10. | J | 27 | M | 9 | 15 | 17 |

### *3.1 Data Acquisition and Conversion*

In order to obtain the EEG signals from driver's brain, the mind-wave sensor has to be mounted on his head, such that the sensor tip lies on the forehead and ear loops are plugged at the ear lobe. Now, the mind-wave sensor must be turned on and paired to the device which has the EEGID application installed in it, through Bluetooth. This application receives the processed EEG data given by the mind-wave sensor. The application provides options to record the EEG data at desired time intervals. The data is recorded using the start and stop actions in the application. The values of recording interval and recording limit are set according to the users need. Once the data recording is complete, an excel sheet of the recorded data is formed which can be extracted via Gmail. The excel sheet generated is shared to the computer through mail, Bluetooth, drive, etc. The data is recorded in the form of an excel sheet, which is of the format.csv. This excel sheet is converted to the format.xlsx to make it compatible with MATLAB. The excel sheet has the recording of various parameters such as frequency of alpha signals, beta signals, gamma signals, delta signals, theta signals, attention, meditation, EEG raw voltage value, and blink strength. The separation of alpha and attention level is performed [9] (Figs. 4 and 5).

## 4 Results and Discussion

In this section, the result obtained in driver consciousness analysis is presented. Alpha waves are one type of brain waves detected by EEG, and they originate from the occipital lobe during wakeful relaxation with closed eyes. Alpha waves are reduced with open eyes, drowsiness, and sleep [10, 11]. Thus, in this project, the alpha band power frequencies and the attention values are used to analyze the consciousness level of the driver. The attention values and the alpha band power frequencies are plotted against time. The alpha frequencies are prominent when the driver is drowsy. Thus, high attention values correspond to low alpha values and vice versa. Figure 6 shows the alpha band power frequencies and attention values plotted versus time, through which we can visualize the consciousness level of drivers mind.

Further, these separated frequency bands are given to SVM for classification. The results of classification are shown in Fig. 7.

The frequency separated information, i.e., alpha frequency components which represent the drowsy state of the driver are used as the discriminating feature. Based on these features SVM will learn the driver state. The experimentation was done using MATLAB to realize different SVM kernels. The result shows that the classification accuracy is good for cubic SVM with the accuracy of 81.9%.

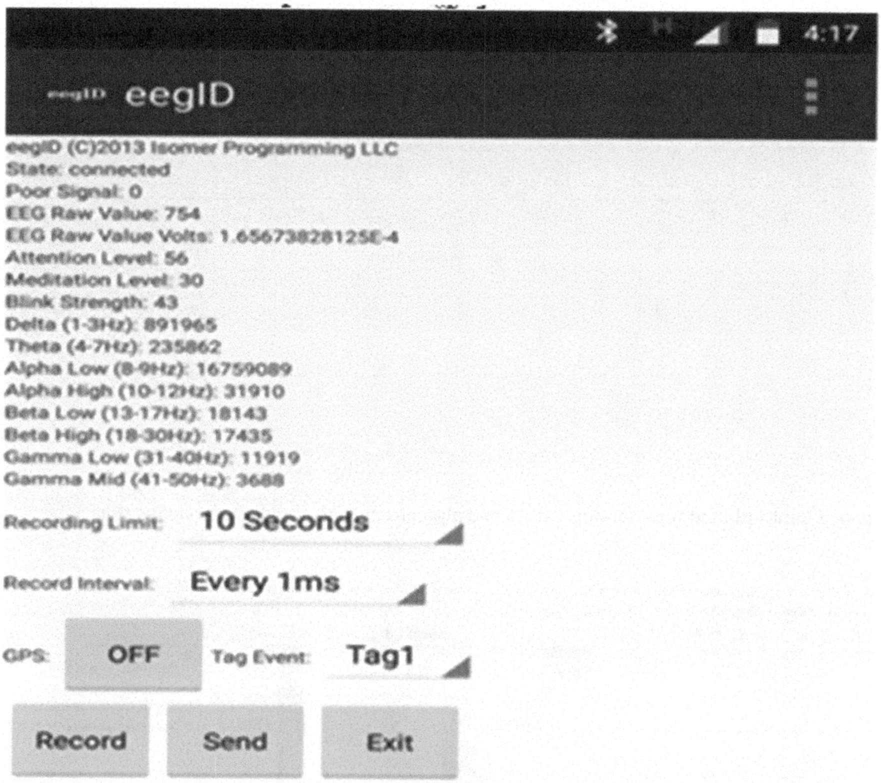


Fig. 4 EEGID

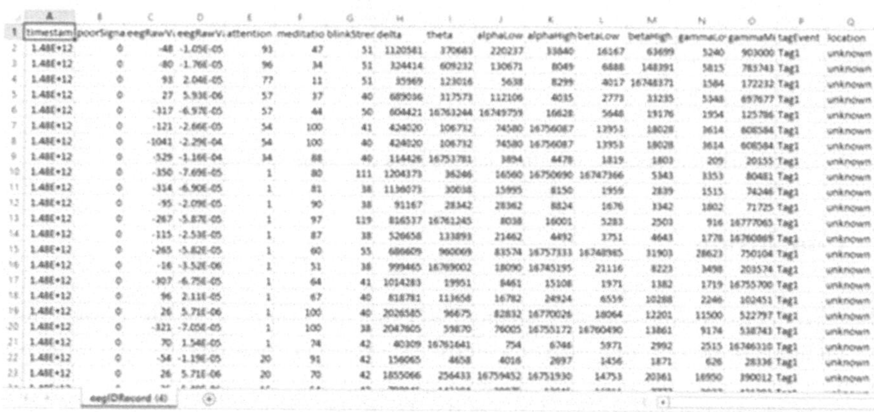

| | A | B | C | D | E | F | G | H | I | J | K | L | M | N | O | P | Q |
|---|---|---|---|---|---|---|---|---|---|---|---|---|---|---|---|---|---|
| 1 | timestam | poorSigna | eegRawVa | eegRawVa | attention | meditatio | blinkStrer | delta | theta | alphaLow | alphaHigh | betaLow | betaHigh | gammaLo | gammaMi | tagEvent | location |
| 2 | 1.48E+12 | 0 | -48 | -1.05E-05 | 93 | 47 | 51 | 1120581 | 370683 | 220237 | 33840 | 16167 | 63699 | 5240 | 903000 | Tag1 | unknown |
| 3 | 1.48E+12 | 0 | -80 | -1.76E-05 | 96 | 34 | 51 | 324414 | 609232 | 130671 | 8049 | 6888 | 148391 | 5815 | 783743 | Tag1 | unknown |
| 4 | 1.48E+12 | 0 | 93 | 2.04E-05 | 77 | 11 | 51 | 35969 | 123016 | 5638 | 8299 | 4017 | 16748371 | 1584 | 172232 | Tag1 | unknown |
| 5 | 1.48E+12 | 0 | 27 | 5.93E-06 | 57 | 37 | 40 | 689036 | 317573 | 112106 | 4035 | 2773 | 33235 | 5348 | 697677 | Tag1 | unknown |
| 6 | 1.48E+12 | 0 | -317 | -6.97E-05 | 57 | 44 | 50 | 604421 | 16763244 | 16749759 | 16628 | 5648 | 19176 | 1954 | 125786 | Tag1 | unknown |
| 7 | 1.48E+12 | 0 | -121 | -2.66E-05 | 54 | 100 | 41 | 424020 | 106732 | 74580 | 16756087 | 13953 | 18028 | 3614 | 608584 | Tag1 | unknown |
| 8 | 1.48E+12 | 0 | -1041 | -2.29E-04 | 54 | 100 | 40 | 424020 | 106732 | 74580 | 16756087 | 13953 | 18028 | 3614 | 608584 | Tag1 | unknown |
| 9 | 1.48E+12 | 0 | -529 | -1.16E-04 | 34 | 88 | 40 | 114426 | 16753781 | 3894 | 4478 | 1819 | 1803 | 209 | 20155 | Tag1 | unknown |
| 10 | 1.48E+12 | 0 | -350 | -7.69E-05 | 1 | 80 | 111 | 1204373 | 36246 | 16560 | 16750690 | 16747366 | 5343 | 3353 | 80481 | Tag1 | unknown |
| 11 | 1.48E+12 | 0 | -314 | -6.90E-05 | 1 | 81 | 38 | 1136073 | 30038 | 15995 | 8150 | 1959 | 2839 | 1515 | 74246 | Tag1 | unknown |
| 12 | 1.48E+12 | 0 | -95 | -2.09E-05 | 1 | 90 | 38 | 91167 | 28342 | 28362 | 8824 | 1676 | 3342 | 1802 | 71725 | Tag1 | unknown |
| 13 | 1.48E+12 | 0 | -267 | -5.87E-05 | 1 | 97 | 119 | 816537 | 16761245 | 8038 | 16001 | 5283 | 2503 | 916 | 16777063 | Tag1 | unknown |
| 14 | 1.48E+12 | 0 | -115 | -2.53E-05 | 1 | 87 | 38 | 526658 | 133893 | 21462 | 4492 | 3751 | 4643 | 1778 | 16760869 | Tag1 | unknown |
| 15 | 1.48E+12 | 0 | -265 | -5.82E-05 | 1 | 60 | 55 | 686609 | 960069 | 83574 | 16757333 | 16748985 | 31903 | 28623 | 750104 | Tag1 | unknown |
| 16 | 1.48E+12 | 0 | -16 | -3.52E-06 | 1 | 51 | 38 | 999465 | 16769002 | 18090 | 16745195 | 21116 | 8223 | 3498 | 203574 | Tag1 | unknown |
| 17 | 1.48E+12 | 0 | -307 | -6.75E-05 | 1 | 64 | 41 | 1014283 | 19951 | 8461 | 15108 | 1971 | 1382 | 1719 | 16755700 | Tag1 | unknown |
| 18 | 1.48E+12 | 0 | 96 | 2.11E-05 | 1 | 67 | 40 | 818781 | 113658 | 16782 | 24924 | 6559 | 10288 | 2246 | 102451 | Tag1 | unknown |
| 19 | 1.48E+12 | 0 | 26 | 5.71E-06 | 1 | 100 | 40 | 2026585 | 96675 | 82832 | 16770026 | 18064 | 12201 | 11500 | 522797 | Tag1 | unknown |
| 20 | 1.48E+12 | 0 | -321 | -7.05E-05 | 1 | 100 | 38 | 2047605 | 59870 | 76005 | 16755172 | 16760490 | 13861 | 9174 | 538743 | Tag1 | unknown |
| 21 | 1.48E+12 | 0 | 70 | 1.54E-05 | 1 | 74 | 42 | 40309 | 16761641 | 754 | 6746 | 5971 | 2992 | 2515 | 16746310 | Tag1 | unknown |
| 22 | 1.48E+12 | 0 | -54 | -1.19E-05 | 20 | 91 | 42 | 156065 | 4658 | 4016 | 2697 | 1456 | 1871 | 626 | 28336 | Tag1 | unknown |
| 23 | 1.48E+12 | 0 | 26 | 5.71E-06 | 20 | 70 | 42 | 1855066 | 256433 | 16759452 | 16751930 | 14753 | 20361 | 16950 | 390012 | Tag1 | unknown |

eegIDRecord (4)

Fig. 5 Excel sheet containing EEG signal values

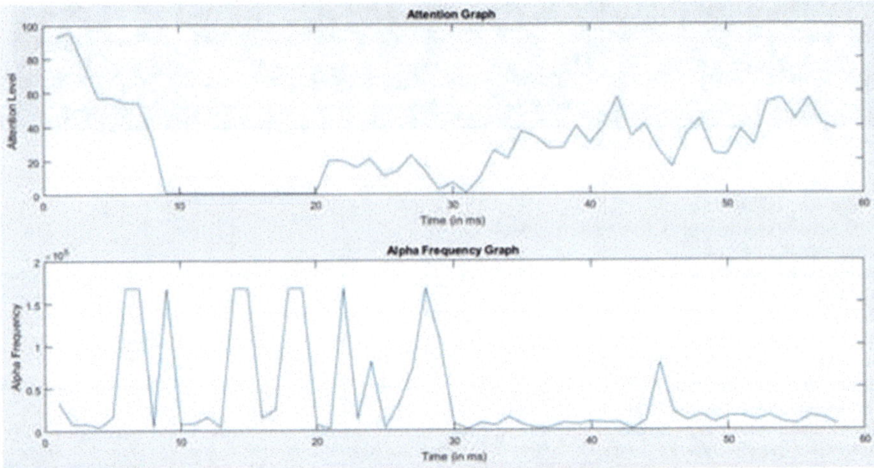


**Fig. 6** Graphs plotted for attention values and alpha frequency components versus time

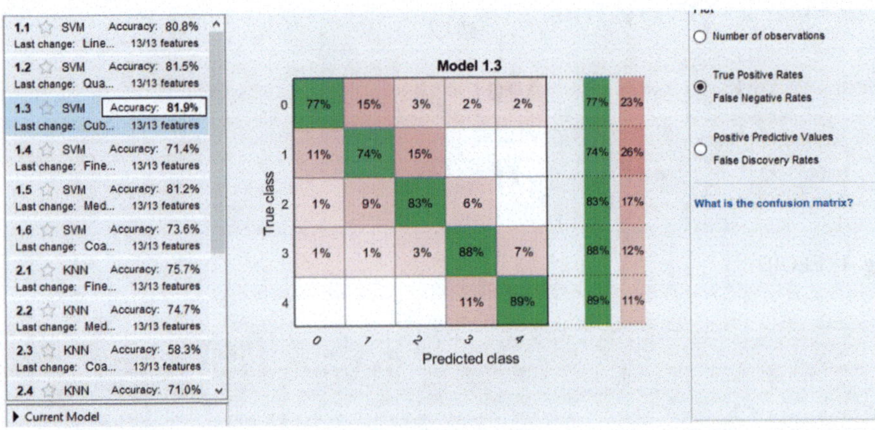


**Fig. 7** The confusion matrix showing the classification results using SVM

## 5 Conclusion

The driver consciousness analysis using EEG signals is found to be one of the effective methods of determining driver's alertness level. The methods discussed the use of direct measure of the brain signals are expected to give more accurate results. The results of clinical electrodes and wearable electrodes are presented. The EEG data obtained from clinical/mind-wave sensor helps to analyze the consciousness level of the driver by extracting the alpha band power frequencies and alertness.

## References

1. G. Li., Smartwatch-based wearable EEG system for driver drowsiness detection. Nanchang Hangkong University, Nanchang, IEEE Sens. J. **15**(12), Dec (2015)
2. Y. Su, B. Wu, W. Chen, J. Zhang, J. Jiang, Y. Zhuang, X. Zheng, P300-based brain computer interface: Prototype of a Chinese speller. J. Comput. Inf. Syst. **4**(4), 1515–1522 (2008)
3. Chin-Teng Lin, Fellow, IEEE, Ruei-Cheng Wu, Sheng-Fu Liang, Wen- Hung Chao, Yu-Jie Chen, and Tzyy-Ping Jung."EEG-Based Drowsiness Estimation for Safety Driving Using Independent Component Analysis." IEEE Transactions On Circuits And Systemsi: Regular Papers, Vol. 52, No. 12, December 2005
4. D. Kim, H. Han, S. Cho, Detection of Drowsiness with eyes open using EEGBased Power Spectrum Analysis.. in *Uipil Chong School of Electrical Engineering*. (University of Ulsan, Ulsan Korea)
5. R.V. Mathew, J. Basheer, An EEG based vehicle driving safety system using automotive CAN protocol. Int. J. Eng. Trends Technol. (IJETT). **26**, 4-Aug 2015
6. J. Park, L. Xu, V. Sridhar, M. Chi, G. Cauwenberghs, Wireless dry EEG for drowsiness detection. in *Proceedings Annual International Conference of the IEEE Engineering in Medicine and Biology Society*. (Boston, MA, USA, Aug./Sep. 2011), pp. 32983301
7. Rebsamen, C. Guan, H. Zhang, C. Wang, C. Teo, M.H. Ang Jr., E. Burdet, A brain controlled wheelchair tonavigate in familiar environments. IEEE Trans. Neural Syst. Rehabil. Eng. **18**(6), 590–598 (2010)
8. J. Williamson, R. Murray-Smith, B. Blankertz, M. Krauledat, K.-R. Muller, Designing for uncertain, asymmetriccontrol: Interaction design for brain–computer interfaces. Int. J. Human-Comput. Stud. **67**(10), 827–841 (2009)
9. J.D.R. Millán, R. Rupp, G.R. M¨uller-Putz, R. Murray-Smith, C. Giugliemma, M. Tangermann, C. Vidaurre, F. Cincotti, A. Kübler, R. Leeb, C. Neuper, K.-R. Müller, D. Mattia, Combining brain—computer interfaces and assistive technologies state-of-the-art and challenges. Frontiers Neurosci. **4**, 1–15 (2010)
10. V. Swarnkar, U. Abeyratne, C. Hukins, Objective measure of sleepiness and sleep latency via bispectrum analysis of EEG. Med. Biol. Eng. Comput. **48**(12), 12031213, Dec (2010)
11. B. Hong, F. Guo, T. Liu, X. Gao, S. Gao, N200-speller using motiononset visual response. Clin. Neurophysiol. **120**(9), 1658–1666 (2009)

# Financial Analysis of Solar Energy Development in India: Potential, Challenges and Policies

**Sandeep Gupta and Aamir Khan Nurkhani**

**Abstract** Presently, shortage of energy is an important, critical and debatable issue which is faced by the developing countries. Also, considering the environmental impact, we humans need to move from conventional source of energy towards non-conventional resources. These non-conventional resources have the potential to confer energy with negligible pollution. Among these non-conventional energy sources, the solar energy has appeared as the new face saving solution in the era of renewable energy sector. Solar energy is one of the most powerful renewable energy sources. Solar energy can be converted in the form of heat (thermal) and light energy. Due to the omnipresent sun, the solar resources may never exhaust. Hence, solar energy seems to be the best option to accelerate power sector expansion. In recent years, the Indian government has adopted and implemented appropriate policies to spreading the use of solar energy. Therefore, present scenario is better for the development of solar energy potential and the 100 GW energy target under National Solar Mission has started the new era of solar power in India. This research work showcases the evolution in the utilization of solar energy from different areas of India subcontinent. This research work also studies and reviews the development of various solar power plants operation in India with their benefits. Through this research work, the author(s) aims to provide a clear cut picture of the current scenario of the solar energy potential, challenges and policies with respect to India's energy plan and advocates for a steady and uniform approach to make the solar power project financially viable.

**Keywords** Solar energy · Solar plant · Solar project · India's energy plan · Solar plant policies

S. Gupta (✉) · A. K. Nurkhani
JECRC University, Jaipur, Rajasthan, India
e-mail: jecsandeep@gmail.com

A. K. Nurkhani
e-mail: amirnurkhani@gmail.com



M. Pant et al. (eds.), *Computational Network Application Tools for Performance Management*, Asset Analytics,
https://doi.org/10.1007/978-981-32-9585-8_22

## 1 Introduction

Solar energy is one of the most powerful renewable energy sources. There are two methods for convert solar energy, in the form of heat (thermal) and light energy [1]. Solar energy can be obtained by the solar cell [2, 3]. In photovoltaic system (SPV), the sun rays go through solar cells, where sunlight is directly converted into electricity using semiconductor(silicon (Si)) [4, 5]. Currently, the world use 10 TW energy, and by 2050, it is expected that it will be going to 30 TW. So, the world need 20 TW extra power without $CO_2$ [6].

Power consumption statistics shows that if the world does not move towards non-conventional energy resource, then the situation will become more complicated [7]. The increase in energy consumption in recent years has increased the fear of exhausting the reserves of petroleum and other conventional resources in future [8]. Solar energy is a significant resource for non-conventional energy [9]. Total reserve of renewable energy in India is 896,603 MW.

On 14 January 2016, India crossed its total solar energy capacity by 5000 MW with 1024 MW just under the region of Rajasthan [10]. The Government of India has set a target of achieving 100 GW solar power under its National Solar Mission by 2022 [8, 11]. This data very well shows that solar energy can change the traditional power system used earlier. For social as well as the economic development of a nation, power sector plays a significant role [12].

Not only India but also the world has accepted the potentials under solar energy [13]. Energy statistics shows that the percentage of solar energy in global energy supply could increase 10% by 2050 [14]. Solar energy satisfies almost all the conditions to become a good energy source [1, 15].

In this paper, past, present and future scenarios of the solar energy area in India are discussed. Benefits of solar energy are explained in Sect. 2. Solar power energy in India is explained in Sect. 3. This section also shows the progress in the solar power plants and statewide solar power utilization. Different government promotional policies are discussed in Sect. 4. Section 5 presents the recent scenario of solar energy in India with solar mission. Finally, Sect. 6 concludes this paper.

## 2 Benefits of Solar Energy

There are enough logic and reason to use solar energy. Even the whole paper proved it. Advantages of solar energy attracted not only India but also entire world to move towards solar energy as soon as possible. Some of them are listed here

(1) Not only its size, but solar energy has two different figures its support. Initially, not at all like petroleum products and atomic power, it is an earth clean wellspring of energy [16].
(2) It is cheap and available in most of the places in the world where the humans live [1].

(3) Scientist predicts that about 15% of the total power needs of the world will be met by the sun by 2025 [17].
(4) The rate of sunlight which come to the land of earth is 120 petawatts (1 petawatt = 1015 W) [18].
(5) On paper, a solitary quantum dot intermediate band can enhance productivity up to 63.2% of the normal cell and can enhance the conversion effectiveness up to 31% for single intersection gadget [19].
(6) The 100 GW energy through solar can reduce 1,704,820 lakhs tonne $CO_2$ [19].
(7) Solar energy is renewable energy, and this means that the world will never run out of it [1].
(8) It required less maintenance. Once the solar panels installed, perfectly there is barely a little amount of patronage necessary each year.
(9) The solar panel is a soundless energy maker due to the PV cells [10].
(10) Vitality security to the nation. No habituation on nation's assets for power.
(11) Sun-powered vitality can be allowed and introduced speedier than other conventional or inexhaustible power plants.
(12) Produces local and on-location sun-based energy, which decreases the necessity for broad high-voltage transmission lines or an unpredictable foundation.

## 3 Solar Energy in India

There is increasing knowledge in the scientific community and local peoples about the requirement of world energy future. Development of India increases the demand for energy. India is the fifth biggest power maker across the globe [20]. The target of the Jawahar Lal Nehru National Solar Mission (JNNSM) is from 20 to 100 GW by 2022 as shown in Table 1. This mission can change the energy scenario of India as well as also produce many job opportunities [18].

However, there are hurdles in between such as skilled or semiskilled workforce, electronic waste management [21, 22]. The sun-powered radiation episode over India is equivalent to 4–7 kWh per square metre every day. India's power needs can be met in an aggregate land zone of 3000 km$^2$ which is equivalent to 0.1% of aggregate land in the nation [23]. In India, there is 250–300 brilliant sunny days and 2300–3200 h daylight for every year [24]. Estimated renewable power in India is shown in Fig. 1

**Table 1** Solar power energy targets and actual installed capacity [21]

| Year | Target (MW) | Actual (MW) |
|---|---|---|
| 2010–11 | 200 | 27 |
| 2011–12 | 200 | 905 |
| 2012–13 | 1000 | 754 |
| 2013–14 | 1000 | 75 |
| 2014–15 | 2000 | 1117 |

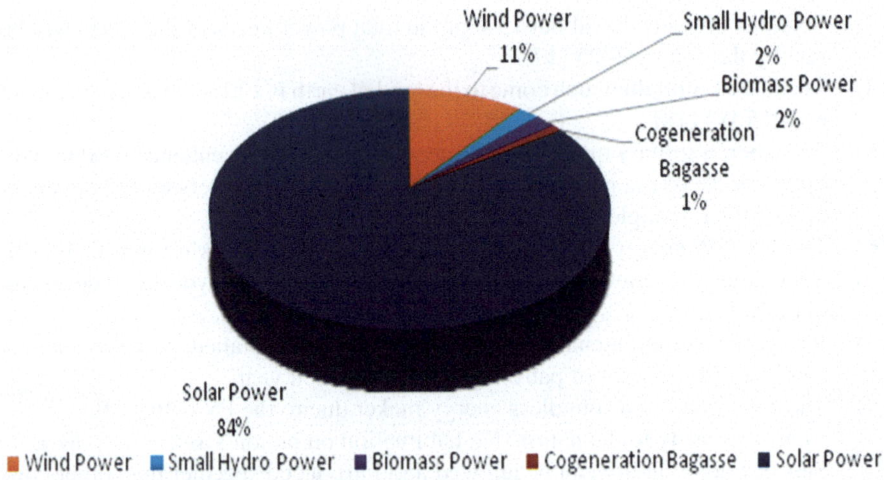


**Fig. 1** Roughly calculated renewable power in India

## *3.1 Solar Power Plants in India*

Solar thermal power plants (STE) generate energy in a practically similar route as ordinary power plants. To create mass power, STE is one of the innovations most appropriate to lessen environmental change in a practical manner. It likewise diminishes the utilization of non-renewable energy source. In this area, India has an STE established base of 4–5 GW by 2020. Some great STE exists in Delhi, Haryana, Punjab and Rajasthan [8]. Table 2 shows the main solar power plants in India. This data changes in every month because India moves towards solar energy rapidly day by day. Our solar power plants increase their capacity and new plants are also formed.

**Table 2** Main solar power plants in India

| S. No. | Name of solar power plant | Peak power (MW) | Commissioned year |
|---|---|---|---|
| 1 | Kamuthi Solar Power Project, Tamil Nadu | 648 | September 2016 |
| 2 | Charanka Solar Park, Charanka village, Patan, Gujarat. | 224 | April 2012 |
| 3 | Welspun Solar MP project, Neemuch, (M.P.) | 151 | March 2013 |
| 4 | Sakri Solar Plant, Maharashtra | 130 | March 2013 |
| 5 | Rajgarh Solar PV(NTPC), Rajghar (M.P.) | 50 | March 2014 |
| 6 | Welspun Energy Rajasthan Solar Project Phalodhi, Rajasthan | 50 | March 2013 |
| 7 | Dhirubhai Ambani Solar Park, Rajasthan | 60 | March 2012 |
| 8 | Unchahar Solar PV(NTPC), (U.P.) | 10 | March 2014 |

It is a big step to generate solar energy in huge amount. Radha Soami Satsang Beas in Amritsar 7.52 MW (Single Roof) is world's biggest rooftop solar power station [25].

## 3.2 Statewide Solar Power

After the success of JNNSM in 2010, many states have declared their state solar policies and programmes. Currently, India is witnessing an increase in solar energy application area [26–28]. 138,267 solar pumps have been sanctioned in India. Out of which 34,941 pumps have been installed till date. Rajasthan leads the list followed by Punjab, Madhya Pradesh and Uttar Pradesh. For drinking water, the government has sanctioned 15,330 solar pumps out of which only 200 pumps have been installed.

Gujarat was the main position to report its arrangement in 2009, and along with its sustaining condition for the financial specialists, the dominion is right now the pioneer in regard to introduced sun-powered limit [24]. Rajasthan has the highest potential of solar power. Jammu and Kashmir also have significant potential for solar energy. However, states have many challenges and barriers regarding solar energy as shown in Fig. 2 [29].

Thirteen states turned out with solar energy policy supporting grid-connected rooftop systems. These are Karnataka, Punjab, Kerala, Andhra Pradesh, Manipur, Rajasthan Chhattisgarh, West Bengal, Gujarat, Uttarakhand, Haryana, Tamil Nadu

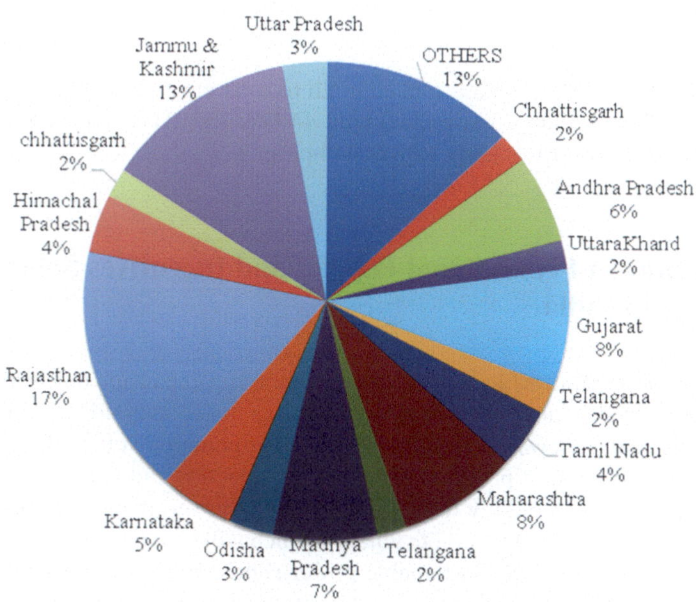


**Fig. 2** Statewide predictable renewable energy potential in India as on 31.03.15 [10]

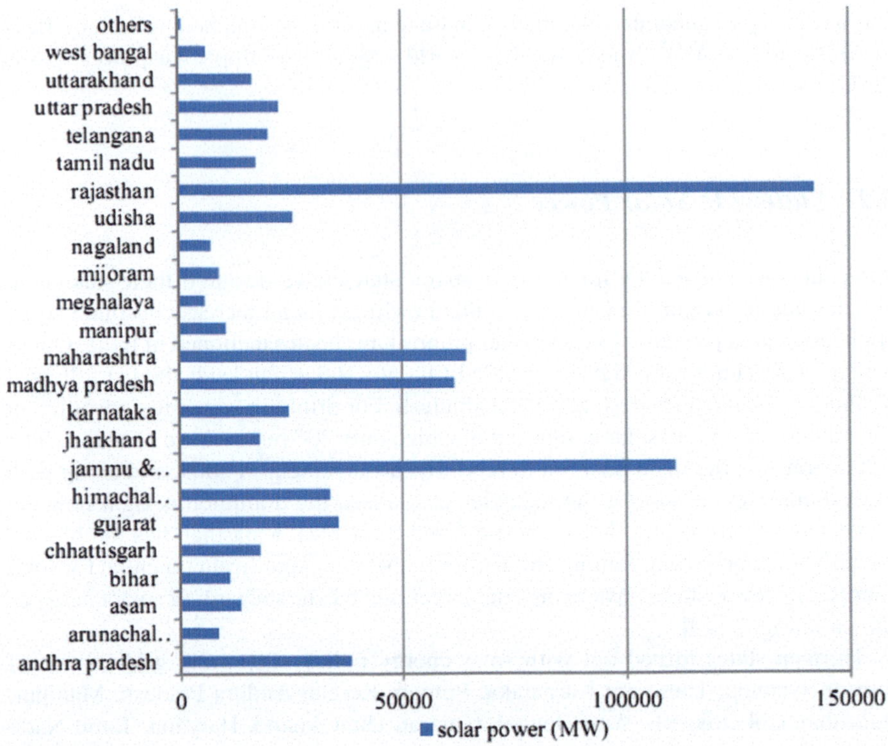


**Fig. 3** Statewide estimated potential of solar power in India (MW) [10]

and Uttar Pradesh [25]. India has ranked ninth in solar capacity with 5.2 GW in the world while China secured first ranked with 44 GW [30, 31]. Statewide estimated potential of solar power is clearly explained in Fig. 3.

## 4 Government Promotional Policies and Incentives Solar Energy in India

Solar energy cooperation of India (SECI) has planned on expansion on 6 lakh durable and well-organized solar lanterns for distribution in the countryside of India.

The ministry of renewable energy begins giving numerous of small grids under the off-grid electrification program amid the late nineties and early piece of 2000 cover villages that are unlikely to be covered by the government of India assessed that there were around 25,000 remote villages which will be hard to interface through grid supply frameworks. So, sustainable power source-based mini-grids or remain solitary frameworks were considered to electrify these remote villages.

Prime Minister Narendra Modi has reported that government needs to give power to entire family units by 2019. It is an assignment that is not effortlessly achievable. It is on the grounds that exclusive 55.3% rustic family units and 67.2% families in India approach power according to the 2011 statistics. 43.2% of rural families and 6.5% urban family units utilize lamp fuel for lighting and 30 crore Indians still have no grid power.

Another 30 crores have only very unreliable grid power. Agriculture sectors consume 20% of the total electricity produced in which irrigation pump sets consume 90%. The aim of 40 GW rooftop solar energy by 2022 took by government of India is the increasing installation of solar power systems rooftops all over the country including railway station and airports [32].

Since 2000, there are different strides taken by Government to increment sun-oriented energy in the nation. These following means help sun-based energy in India.

- NABARD is giving a sponsorship to sun-powered water pumps. The administration is advancing sun-oriented energy more than ever under national solar mission [21].
- 100% FDI is permitted under programmed course for activities of inexhaustible power production and appropriation subject to arrangements of the Electricity Act, 2003 [17].
- Under mission statement and guidelines for the advancement of smart cities in India, arrangement of rooftop sun-oriented and 10% sustainable power source is required [33].

## 5 Present Solar Energy Scenario in India

All India ranks sixth regarding renewable electrical energy global capacity. For the development of the solar segment, a number of great projects have been proposed in the region of Thar Desert, Rajasthan with an area of 35,000 $km^2$ set aside for it. If the reports are to be believed, the region has a capability of generating 700–2100 GW of solar power. A 157% increase in solar energy capacity addition 4132 MW during 2014–2016 [33]. India has the world's second biggest generation plant by solar energy with the capacity of 648 MW.

34 solar parks have been approved with the total 20,000 MW power. This data show the interest of Indian government and potential of solar energy. Many projects of 84 MW capacity have been tendered for Indian defence and paramilitary forces using solar cells and modules manufactured in India [33].

The government of India has set their target under Jawahar Lal Nehru National Solar Mission to increase their solar energy from 20 to 100 GW by 2022 and also providing two crores solar lighting system in place of kerosene lamps to rural communities [34–36]. MNRE set the goal to achieve 15 GW in 2017–18, 16 GW in 2018–19 and next two years 17.5–17.5 GW solar energy [19, 37].

## 6 Conclusion

In India, sustainable power sources are in substantial amount which can contribute fundamentally to the expanding interest for power. Without awful environment, sunlight-based renewable energy source is the better option. The spending assignment for Ministry of New and Renewable Energy (MNRE) must be expanded in perspective of the forceful limit expansion targets set up the states.

There are heaps of issues rising out of the talks in the present survey, some of them require quick consideration that can strengthen in relieving the potential obstructions and challenges and give stimulus to sunlight-based activities in India. A preparatory evaluation of the status of solar power improvement in conceivable conditions of India demonstrates that there ought to be a steady and uniform approach to make solar power projects financially alluring over the country.

Such endeavours may require returning to part and command of Jawahar Lal Nehru Solar Mission (JNNSM) and to position an establishment that can lead new activities in sunlight-based assets appraisal and innovation advancement. Thus, this paper shows that various government and private companies are trying to motivate the huge solar energy usage in different areas. Finally, from this paper, it can be say that in coming days, solar energy will be the most emerging renewable energy source.

## References


1. Z. Cao, F. O'Rourke, W. Lyons, Performance modelling of a small-scale wind and solar energy hybrid system. in *IEEE Irish Signals and Systems Conference* (ISSC), 28th July (2017)
2. R. Ramakrishna, A. Scaglione, V. Vittal, A stochastic model for solar photo-voltaic power for short-term probabilistic forecast. arXiv preprint arXiv:1706.05445 (2017)
3. B. Chandrasekar, T.C. Kandpal, Effect of financial and fiscal incentives on the effective capital cost of solar energy technologies to the user. Sol. Energy **78**(2), 147–156 (2005)
4. A.K.S. Tomar, K.K. Gautam, A review of solar energy—challenges, economics & policies in India. Int. J. Sci. Res. **6**(1), 2080–2083 (2017)
5. Nathan S. Lewis et al., Chemical challenges in solar energy utilization. Proc. Natl. Acad. Sci. **103**(43), 15729–15735 (2006)
6. T.M. Razykov et al., Solar photovoltaic electricity: current status and Future prospects. Sol. Energy **85**, 1580–1608 (2011)
7. S. Sharma et al., Solar cells. In research and applications—a review. Mater. Sci. Appl. **6**, 1145–1155 (2015)
8. N.K. Sharma et al., Solar energy in India: Strategies, policies, perspectives and future potential. Renew. Sustain. Energy Rev. **16**(1), 933–941 (2012)
9. F. Dinçer, M.E. Meral, Critical factors that affecting efficiency of solar cells. Smart Grid Renew. Energy **1**, 47–50 (2010)
10. Ministry of Statistics and Programme Implementation, Government of India: ENERGY—Statistical year book India 2016. Availability on http://mospi.nic.in/statistical-year-book-india/2016/185 (2016)
11. P. Raman et al., Opportunities and challenges in setting up solar photo voltaic based micro rids for electrification in rural areas of India. Renew. Sustain. Energy Rev. **6**(5), 3320–3325 (2012)

12. A.K. Ojha, G.K. Gaur et al., Solar energy and economic development in India: a review. Emerg. Technol. Adv. Eng. (1), 184–189 (2014). (ISSN 2250-2459)
13. V. Khare, S. Nema, P. Baredar, Status of solar wind renewable energy in ndia. Renew. Sustain. Energy Rev. **27**, 1–10 (2013)
14. G.R. Timilsina, L. Kurdgelashvili, P.A. Narbel, Solar energy: markets, economics and policies. Renew. Sustain. Energy Rev. **16**(1), 449–465 (2012)
15. S. Gupta, A. Sharma, Global scenario of solar photovoltaic (SPV) materials. in *International Conference on Advanced Computational and Communication Paradigms (ICACCP), Lecture Notes in Electrical Engineering (LNEE)*, vol. 475 (Springer, 2018), pp. 126–133
16. Y.J. Jeong, R. Kyung, Enhanced efficiency of solar cells using reflectors and metamaterials. Bull. Am. Physical Soc. **62.3** (2017)
17. V.M. Domkundwar, *Solar Energy and Non-conventional Energy Sources*. (Dhanpat Rai Publication, 2nd edition, 2006)
18. V. Devabhaktuni et al., Solar energy: trends and enabling technologies. Renew. Sustain. Energy Rev. **19**, 555–564 (2013)
19. E.P.W. Magazine, Yojna, Aug (2016)
20. I.R. Pillai, R. Banerjee, Renewable energy in India: Status and potential. Energy **34**(8), 970–980 (2009)
21. V. Kumar et al., Solar and wind power generation in India. Kurukshetra (A J. Rural Dev.) **64**, 07 may (2016)
22. A.A.M. Sayigh, *Solar Energy Engineering*. (Academic Press, Kindle Edition, 2012)
23. A. Kumar, K. Kumar, Renewable energy in India: current status & future potentials. Renew. Sustain. Energy Rev. **14**, 2434–2442 (2010)
24. K. Kapoor, K.K. Pandeya et al., Evolution of solar energy in India: A review. Renew. Sustain. Energy Rev. **40**, 475–487 (2014)
25. Report on "Grid connected solar rooftop system" by Ministry of New and Renewable Energy, (Government of India), March (2014)
26. E. Pérez-Denicia et al., Renewable energy sources in Mexico: A review. Ren. Sus. Energy Rev. **78**, 597–613 (2017)
27. E.P. Trindade et al., Sustainable development of smart cities: a systematic review. J. OITMC **3**(11), 2–14 (2017)
28. A. Ummadisingu, M.S. Soni, Concentrating solar power—technology, potential and olicy in India. Renew. Sustain. Energy Rev. Elsevier **15**, 5169–5175 (2011)
29. R.M. Swanson, A proposed thermo photovoltaic solar energy conversion system. Proc. IEEE **67**(3), 446–447 (1979)
30. S.S. Garud, *(Director, EETD Division): India's Solar Mission: Policies and Strategies*. (The energy and Resources Institute, New Delhi (MNRE), 2016)
31. K. Jethani, Renewable policy framework and wind energy programme in India. Ministry of New and Renewable Energy Government of India, 22 August (2016)
32. G. Mahapatro, *Renewable energy in India* (Sumy State University, Diss, 2016)
33. Department of Industrial Policy and Promotion, *New and Renewable Energy Sector Achievements Report*. Report by MNRE, January 18 (2017)
34. N.R. Prasad, A.S. Pidaparthia, India's first solar thermal parabolic trough pilot power plant. Energy Procedia **49**, 1840–1847 (2014)
35. S. Gupta, A.K. Sharma, STATCOM-Its control algorthim. I-Manager's J. Electr. Eng. **3**(4), 41–48 (2010)
36. A. Kumar, O. Prakash, A. Dube, A review on progress of concentrated solar power in India. RSER Elsevier J. **79**, 304–307 (2017)
37. Jawaharlal Nehru National Solar Mission (Revised), Press Information Bureau, Ministry of New and Renewable Energy, Government of India, 17 June (2015)

The manufacturer's authorised representative in the EU is Springer Nature Customer Service Centre GmbH, Europaplatz 3, 69115 Heidelberg, Germany. If you have any concerns regarding our products, please contact ProductSafety@springernature.com

Printed and bound by CPI Group (UK) Ltd, Croydon, CR0 4YY
25/09/2026
02222900-0011